OXFORD STUDIES
IN MODERN EUROPEAN HISTORY

General Editors

Simon Dixon, Mark Mazower,
and
James Retallack

D1475322

'his comparative urban histories are stimulating, especially in their approach to local, regional, and national problems, and their relations with each other'
Friedrich Lenger, *Bulletin of the German Historical Institute, London*

'Zimmer successfully demonstrates that the often overlooked characteristics of urban history clearly demonstrate the process of historical change and deserve the same type of careful study now accorded mainly to the great issues'
Eleanor L. Turk, *The Historian*

REMAKING
THE RHYTHMS
OF LIFE

GERMAN COMMUNITIES
IN THE AGE OF THE NATION-STATE

OLIVER ZIMMER

OXFORD
UNIVERSITY PRESS

OXFORD
UNIVERSITY PRESS

Great Clarendon Street, Oxford, OX2 6DP,
United Kingdom

Oxford University Press is a department of the University of Oxford.
It furthers the University's objective of excellence in research, scholarship,
and education by publishing worldwide. Oxford is a registered trade mark of
Oxford University Press in the UK and in certain other countries

First published 2013
First published in paperback 2015

Published in the United States of America by Oxford University Press
198 Madison Avenue, New York, NY 10016, United States of America

British Library Cataloguing in Publication Data
Data available

Library of Congress Cataloging in Publication Data
Data available

ISBN 978–0–19–957120–8 (Hbk.)
ISBN 978–0–19–876679–7 (Pbk.)

Preface

More than I could have predicted when the research for it began in 2003, this book took me in unexpected directions. Municipal archives are idiosyncratic places. It took me some time to establish fruitful connections between the rich past urban worlds that I tried to reconstruct through my labours. When I did, I began to regard the unevenness of the evidence as an opportunity to construct a different perspective from which to explore a much-researched period of German history. It centres on the tension between movement and place, and how this affected the relationship between both individuals and communities. I hope this perspective will prove useful to historians beyond the immediate field of modern German history.

My initial interest was in how nationalism was experienced by different religious communities in the Second German Empire. The primary areas of investigation were to be national and denominational associations, as well as patriotic and religious festivals and commemorations. My main aim then was to arrive at a better understanding of the under-researched experiential dimension of nationalism through applying the prism of comparative urban history. While these concerns retain an important place in the present book, the practice of research prompted me to shift its focus in a number of important respects. Among the substantive areas I began to stray into, in deviation of my original plan, were the files on local citizenship and on the economic life of the three towns. These excursions changed the way I think about the dynamics of communal life, and how they intersect with the larger entities, events, and structures. They also alerted me to the threads and sinews that connect its more implicit and mundane with its more symbolic and demonstrative aspects. They made me aware of the silent dialogues operating between, for example, the politics of economic reform and a Corpus Christi procession.

More importantly, these forays forced me to erect a different analytical framework, one that could channel the complexity I encountered into a meaningful narrative. Revealingly, many of the urban conflicts I observed appeared to derive from (real or imagined) alterations to the temporal and spatial parameters regulating people's lives. I realized that some urban residents perceived such alterations as a challenge to their sense of place. These could result, for instance, from an actual or announced transformation of a town's educational or economic landscape; or from disruptions to existing routines, as manifested, for instance, in an interruption of urban tramway traffic for half an hour. Many experienced such occurrences as deeply irritating, even unsettling. Yet movement and the threat of dislocation—rather than producing a transformation in spatial awareness, as has often been argued—prompted place-making activities of various kinds. It is this observation that led me to examine communal life in terms of struggles over the places and rhythms of life. It brought home to me that history is not only about visible change, but also about the creative defence of established patterns of life. For men and women could not (and cannot) do without these anchors, however fragile they may turn out to be. They had to construct new places with the aid of the resources they had at their disposal, just as they had to find new rhythms capable of sustaining their lives in meaningful ways. When it came to understanding these phenomena, the engagement with the practices of urban liberalism and nationalism proved pivotal. Yet, seen through the conceptual prisms of place and rhythm, they also appeared in a new light.

This book could not have been written without the support I received from a number of funding bodies and academic organizations. The Arts and Humanities Research Council (AHRC grant 16268/1) assisted the project with a grant that covered the expenses I incurred through my numerous extended visits to archives and research libraries in Augsburg, Ludwigsburg, Ludwigshafen am Rhein, Munich, Speyer, and Ulm. Other institutions provided me with fellowships and grants that allowed me to concentrate for sustained periods of time on this project. In this respect, I owe an enormous debt of gratitude to the German *Humboldt-Stiftung* in Bonn for twice electing me to a fellowship. I spent my first period as a Humboldt Fellow (which lasted from April 2004 to August 2005) in Tübingen, where I profited from the scholarly wisdom, liberality, and kindness of my then host, Professor Dieter Langewiesche. During the same period, I also paid a first extended visit to archives in Augsburg, where Professor Andreas Wirsching (now at the University of Munich) offered much appreciated advice and hospitality. My second stint as a Humboldt Fellow (January 2011–March 2011) took me to the Freiburg Institute for Advanced Study, whose directors, Professors Jörn Leonhard and Ulrich Herbert provided a congenial environment for working on the manuscript. Financial support for teaching cover was also forthcoming, on two occasions, from the John Fell Research Fund. University College and the History Faculty of the University of Oxford helped cover travel and other expenses that arose from the research on this project. I am deeply grateful to all these organizations for their support, as well as to the individuals I had the privilege to meet as one of their benefactors.

Historians who pay lengthy visits to municipal archives tell each other all sorts of stories about their experiences. Mine were invariably positive, for I was very fortunate in gaining the unstinting support of outstanding archivists. In Ulm I benefited from the exceptional generosity of Michael Wettengel, and his colleagues Matthias Grotz and Ulrich Seemüller. I also received great assistance from Stefan Mörz and his colleagues in the *Stadtarchiv Ludwigsahfen am Rhein*. I am equally grateful to Georg Feuerer, who was liberal with his time and advice while I was working in the *Stadtarchiv Augsburg*. The staff of the state archives located in Ludwigsburg and Augsburg, respectively, and of the diocesan archives of Augsburg, Rottenburg-Stuttgart and Speyer have also been helpful. I should also like to thank staff and librarians at the Bodleian Library in Oxford, the city libraries in Augsburg and Ulm, and the Staatsbibliothek in Munich.

Various parts of this project have been presented to seminar and conference audiences in Augsburg, Cambridge, Freiburg im Breisgau, Fribourg, Kentucky, Oxford, Paris (Sciences Po) Tübingen, Uppsala, Washington DC, and Zurich. In Oxford I have been privileged to have a colleague like Abigail Green, with whom I discussed this project from the moment I joined Oxford's History Faculty. Abigail was the first to suggest that I include a third city. Over the years, I further benefited from various conversations I've had with other members of Oxford's History Faculty, including Robert Gildea, Ruth Harris, Nick Stargardt, and William Whyte, while across the Atlantic, Celia Applegate, Geoff Eley, and Jim Retallack have offered much appreciated feedback and encouragement. Jean-François Chanet, now at Sciences Po, has become an intellectual inspiration and a friend. At University College, Oxford, I owe a great debt to my colleagues Catherine Holmes and Ben Jackson, each of them a model of tolerance and good humour, and to the college for providing such a humane and stimulating environment. I am also indebted to the readers for Oxford University Press, and to its History editor, Christopher Wheeler, for taking an early interest in this project, and for his patience when things took a little longer than expected. During the production process the cooperation with Emma Barber, Stephanie Ireland, Fiona Stables, and Cathryn Steele proved equally rewarding.

I feel extremely fortunate in having intellectual companions whose input over the years has mattered more to me than they may be aware of. With some friends and colleagues the debate about this book, as well as on questions of method and approach, began more or less when the project was first conceived in 2003–2004. Tobias Straumann, who read the entire first draft of the manuscript, has always been available for advice and feedback. The leading modern Swiss historian of his generation, Tobias was the first to suggest, after a few minutes reflection, that I pick Ludwigshafen am Rhein as my third city. Jim Brophy, who read and commented perceptively on several drafts, gave freely of his time and erudition, even as he was going through a time of great personal loss. Sharp, challenging and constructive in his observations, Jim is the reader and critic any historian could wish for. I was equally fortunate in being able to draw on the expertise of Holger Nehring, who followed this project from 2006, and of Julia Moses. Holger and Julia not only read the entire first draft of the manuscript, but also invited me to discuss it with them, chapter by chapter, in their house in Sheffield. They also commented on portions of the final draft, and on the Introduction and Conclusion. Their critical suggestions, as well as their unflinching encouragement, reached me at an important stage of the writing process. I also benefited from the comments of Henk te Velde, who offered detailed comments on the entire first draft. The same is true of David Rechter, who read the Introduction and the chapters of the first part. Paola von Wyss-Giacosa read the chapters of the final part and offered numerous important suggestions. My thanks are also due to Gemma Bowes, who read the entire manuscript with a view to clarity and style, while Joanna Lewis read and offered comments on the Introduction and Epilogue. Sonja Weinberg went through late drafts of the Introduction and various chapters, and encouraged me to make cuts. I also learned much from conversations with some of my graduate and doctoral students at Oxford, particularly Anna Geurts and Jean-Michel Johnston. Jean-Michel read a final draft of the manuscript and commented insightfully on various sections of the text, while Anna did the same for the Introduction and the Conclusion. The responsibility for the book's remaining omissions and errors of interpretation rests, of course, with me alone.

Finally, I would like to thank a group of close friends for having sustained me in a variety of ways over the years. They are Jan Baumann, Gemma Bowes, Eric Kaufmann, Joanna Lewis, Paola Pozzi, Tobias Straumann, Sonja Weinberg, Paola von Wyss-Giacosa, and Keiko Yokosawa. My brother Thomas and sister Selma and their families have offered me welcome distraction on my rare and usually all-too-brief visits back home, while my niece Noëmi continues to be a source of great joy. My parents continue to offer me a place on my regular journeys back home. Living in a world that is reassuringly different from the one I happened to join, they will probably always underestimate how much their presence has influenced my work as a historian. I dedicate this book to them, as well as to Thomas, Selma and Noëmi, and to my dear friends.

O.Z.
Oxford, April 2012

Contents

List of Illustrations

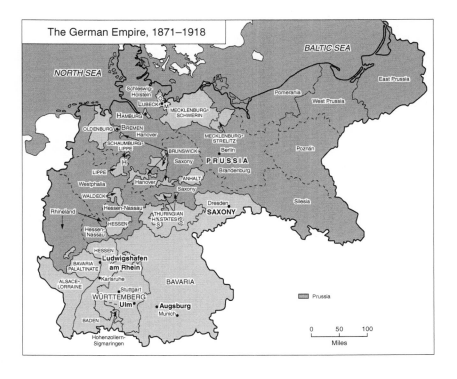

The German Empire, 1871–1918

BALTIC SEA

NORTH SEA

East Prussia

Schleswig-
Holstein

Pomerania

LÜBECK

West Prussia

HAMBURG

MECKLENBURG-
SCHWERIN

OLDENBURG

BREMEN

Hanover

MECKLENBURG-
STRELITZ

SCHAUMBURG-
LIPPE

Poznán

BRUNSWICK

Berlin

Saxony

PRUSSIA

LIPPE

Brandenburg

Westphalia

Hanover

ANHALT

Saxony

WALDECK

Silesia

Hessen-Nassau

Dresden

Rhineland

THURINGIAN
STATES

SAXONY

HESSEN

Hessen-
Nassau

HESSEN

Ludwigshafen
am Rhein

BAVARIA
PALALTINATE

ALSACE-
LORRAINE

Karlsruhe

BAVARIA

Stuttgart

WÜRTTEMBERG

Ulm

Augsburg

Munich

BADEN

Hohenzollern-
Sigmaringen

Prussia

0   50   100

Miles

Introduction

If something is to be 'delocalized', it means that it is being sent from one place to some other place, not from one place to no place.

Bruno Latour[1]

In the autumn of 1885, Ulm reverend Rudolf Pfleiderer inaugurated the *Herberge zur Heimat*. The new hostel for travelling journeymen and local apprentices was a testament to the founders' Protestant ethos in welcoming young men irrespective of their confessional allegiance.[2] The task they had set themselves was a challenging one. As Pfleiderer had reminded the local authorities just a few weeks before the *Herberge*'s inauguration: 200,000 journeymen roamed the streets of imperial Germany every day. Of these, between 50 and 100 set up camp in Ulm, amounting to several thousand accommodations per year. As well as a temporary home, Pfleiderer reminded his audience, these young people required moral guidance. The same was true, the clergyman explained, of many of the journeymen, factory workers, and apprentices who were resident in Ulm. Having arrived in the town only recently, most of them lacked local roots. They, too, longed for a place where they could go after work or on Sunday afternoons in search of 'physical and spiritual nourishment.' As Pfleiderer reminded the representatives of the council and local crafts associations, who attended the *Herberge*'s inauguration ceremony: what they needed was a 'quiet home.'[3]

The story of the *Herberge*'s inauguration offers a variation on the theme of this book: how men and women strove to regain a sense of place in a changing world. Its chronological focus is the second half of the nineteenth century, which marked a period of considerable transformation in the German lands.[4] What made these changes a cause for either excitement or concern was less their being the subject of newspaper reports or learned deliberation. What rendered them unnerving was the immediacy with which they manifested themselves. The labour migrants that long-established residents encountered as they made their way to the central railway station or the local inn; the new schools that catered for children's elementary and secondary education; the gradual shift in a town's confessional make-up; new opportunities at the level of cultural and material consumption, or the sight of a nationalist parade or religious procession in a town where such phenomena were unprecedented—these changes did not occur overnight, but they were often sufficiently perceptible for people to reconsider the places they thought they knew. These encounters with unfamiliar experiences induced a series of place-making activities at various levels. New social and cultural boundaries were drawn, existing patterns of work, trade, and cultural activity were reconfigured, and established practices of demonstrating collective loyalties were altered.[5]

People began to elaborate new rhythms and routines: less by resisting the novel than by reconfiguring their environments in ways that appealed to their sensibilities and aspirations; less by immersing themselves in learned representations of *Heimat* than by creating surroundings that could, once again, be accessible both physically and emotionally; less by lamenting the alleged decline of traditional civic virtues than by creating a multitude of new places that proved sufficiently meaningful to sustain lives. In a sentence, less by talking about the loss of established solidarities and routines (although such lamentations could at times become very conspicuous) than by attempting to foster new ones.[6] In their capacity as consumers or citizens, members of religious or economic associations, individuals, and groups embarked on a multitude of journeys whose final destination they could not know. As they did, larger phenomena such as religion, nationalism, and the state became intertwined with everyday affairs and concerns.

This book is about German townspeople who embarked on such journeys. By uncovering people's experiences as they lived through—to use some of the familiar abstractions—the spread of industry, urbanization, migration, religious conflict, nationalism, and political unification, individual chapters show how Germans responded to the consolidation of the imperial nation-state. The book thus raises a number of fundamental questions about the connections between urban and broader societal (including national) developments. It aims to re-establish a sense of the part that individuals played in reassembling the various communities which they inhabited, including that which we have come to refer to as Germany.[7]

More specifically, this book proceeds through an examination of three medium-sized towns. In terms of their size and importance, the three settings fell in the nineteenth century somewhere between town and city—*Stadt* and *Großstadt,* to use the German terms (with the latter designating municipalities of 100,000 inhabitants or larger). They therefore belong to the category of urban community that would remain predominant in Germany well beyond the First World War. They are the industrial town of Ludwigshafen am Rhein in the Bavarian Palatinate, and the imperial cities of Augsburg in Bavarian Swabia and of Ulm in the state of Württemberg. While all three were denominationally mixed, they diverged quite significantly with regard to their economic outlook and prospects. The predominantly Protestant town of Ulm remained mostly confined to crafts and various kinds of trade, while Augsburg, with a population that was two-thirds Catholic, developed a significant factory industry from the 1850s. In contrast to both Ulm and Augsburg, Ludwigshafen am Rhein, where Catholics and Protestants were evenly matched, was literally created by Germany's industrial take-off. With a population of little more than 3000 in 1860, it was by far the smallest of the three towns at the beginning of our period. By 1900, now a centre of the chemical industry, it had overtaken Ulm (45,000) and was about to catch up with Augsburg (89,000).[8]

Each town can be seen as the product of a particular combination of movement and stasis, aptly symbolized by the railway and the fortress that affected their respective fates. Thus, in 1846 Augsburg received its main train station, and by the mid-1850s railway lines were connecting it with Munich, Ulm, and Nuremberg. In 1866 the city's massive fortification ring, constructed after 1806 on Napoleon's request, was dismantled after the magistrate had agreed to pay the Bavarian state a sum of 200,000 gulden.[9] Ulm was not trailing far behind. Its first railway station opened in December 1850. When four years later the two-track railway bridge across the Danube entered into service, Munich could be reached within less than four hours, while Augsburg was only a two-hour train journey away. But since Ulm was also an important fortress town—completed in the early 1850s, the *Bundesfestung* hemmed in the city for half a century—the bridge could be locked up at both ends with large iron gates.[10] Fortress and the railway also shaped the history of Ludwigshafen am Rhein. There, however, the fortifications near the *Rheinschanze* were removed in 1843 on King Ludwig I's request, prompting the Palatinate Railway Company to set up its headquarters in Ludwigshafen in 1849. The company became the driving force behind the campaign to elevate Ludwigshafen to the status of an independent city, which it was granted in 1859.[11]

On the political front, liberal nationalists were influential in each of the three towns, at least until the turn of the century, when the democratic and socialist left, as well as political Catholicism, began to gain ground. While in Augsburg and Ludwigshafen National Liberals rose to predominance in the course of the 1860s, in Ulm their influence was checked from early on by an influential democrat faction. Of the three cities, Augsburg had evolved the most antagonistic political culture. Here, the city's ruling liberals faced strong opposition from conservative Catholics, whose leaders could rely on the backing of a numerically dominant Catholic population. Measured by the franchise restrictions in place in the last third of the nineteenth century, Ulm proved much more inclusive than both Augsburg and Ludwigshafen am Rhein.[12]

It is precisely this constellation of similarities and differences—socio-economic, denominational, political, cultural, and topographic—that renders the three towns illuminating for a study that seeks to explore how people living in different urban environments coped with very similar challenges. As more and more newcomers joined longer-established urban core populations, towns and cities grew more varied in terms of their socio-economic and cultural make-up. As existing rules and conventions determining local membership were redefined, more and more residents encountered each other as strangers in the public arena. Many responded by remaking existing and creating new places, both for themselves and for those who shared some of their concerns, expectations, and visions. In doing so, they remade not only the immediate worlds they inhabited as producers or consumers of meaning and material goods, but also the larger ones to which they were connected through a multitude of threads.

My aim is to recapture a sense of the creative energies people mobilized as they grappled with dislocation and change. In this way, I hope to show that the social orders constructed in the process often sit uncomfortably with one of the master narratives of German history, which assesses social, political, and cultural developments in terms of relative degrees of 'modernity' or 'modernization.'[13] There appear to be few other cases where a standard historiography concerned primarily with national developments and 'turning points' has been equally successful in shaping the research agendas and questions of historians working in many other areas, ranging from social to cultural and from regional to local history, even where they have challenged the assumption of a *Sonderweg*.[14] I have sought to resist this temptation, but I hope without losing sight of the ways in which local communities interacted with processes operating at different spatial and temporal levels.[15]

My decision to concentrate on towns does not spring from the belief that they can offer a privileged access to historical reality.[16] But nor do I wish to downplay the advantages they can offer for historians seeking to understand historical change through the lens of people's experience.[17] This owes much to what might be called their institutional density, which is greater than that of either regions or nations.[18] Towns provide stages from which to explore how small and large events and structures came together in a single location. They offer opportunities to tease out some of the motivations behind human agency, but without losing sight of the larger contexts outside of which people's actions cannot be understood. More so than villages or very small towns, middle-sized towns were exposed to a wide range of developments operating simultaneously at the regional, national and even global levels. Indeed, one of the more important recent findings in nineteenth-century European history is that many provincial towns acted as power brokers in the process of nation-state formation. One of the chief lessons here, it seems, is that Europe's nineteenth-century states were largely built from the margins and from the bottom up.[19]

Without downplaying the significance of the regional dimension for German history: the socio-economic and political spectrum opened up by the towns of Augsburg, Ludwigshafen, and Ulm thus points to the problems of projecting regional characteristics onto localities—whether villages, towns, or cities—that happen to be part of a particular region. Each had more in common with certain Prussian cities than with towns located within either Württemberg or Bavaria. There were towns in the North, such as Wetzlar, that could be described as Prussian Ulms. There were also industrial towns in the German South, such as Ludwigshafen am Rhein, which in terms of population growth and sheer economic dynamism were a match for the industrial cities in the Ruhr valley. To employ well-rehearsed stereotypes: there was a fair amount of southern corporatism to be found in certain Prussian towns (not only but especially in former imperial cities), just as there were southern towns that displayed the proverbial northern dynamism. As far as the second category is concerned, one thinks of Nuremberg or Fürth in Bavaria, or of Cannstadt, Reutlingen, and Esslingen in Württemberg.[20]

The towns examined in this volume can thus be seen as spaces in which people, material goods, institutions, events, cultural norms, and symbols interact in complex ways. While they should not be reduced to what Celia Applegate has termed 'social science servitude', they should not be regarded as *sui generis* either.[21] German townspeople were not simply pawns in a drama of modernization. But nor can we assume that the things they did, or how they did what they did, followed no logic whatsoever. Even if the patterns concealed behind their actions elude us in the end, the search for these patterns may turn out to be worthwhile. My contention is that, by reconstructing some of the social conventions in Germany in the latter part of the nineteenth century, we can come to understand how these patterns of human action fostered different kinds of communities.[22]

In concentrating on three very different cities whose geographical location happened to be south of the river Main, I therefore hope to gain an understanding of processes that point beyond the state or region to which they belong. The aim of such an approach is not to debunk yet more myths surrounding the largest German state, Prussia, or to emphasize the role of anti-modern (or, as is now more usual in historical accounts, eminently modern) features on the development of German culture and society. My aim, rather, is to shed light, for instance, on how each town engaged with economic liberalization, or when and why they used nationalist arguments to negotiate their place in the new social pecking order that was evolving. All this does not deny that some of the cultural frames that shaped these adaptations can be described as regional. What this book suggests, however, is that the provenance, as it were, of many of the most important mental maps were at once very local and very universal. Thus, while they derived from particular circumstances and manifested themselves locally, they point towards broader dispositions that cannot be ascribed to particular localities, regions or nations.[23]

A book of this kind requires a fresh analytical lens. The basic prism through which these processes are explored in the subsequent chapters is that of place and of place-making, conceived as both physical intervention and emotional attachment. People's emotional energies, it appears, fastened themselves onto specific places, whether old or new, whether established or in the making.[24] As human geographers have reminded us, meaningful places—whether a museum, a neighbourhood, the space demarcated by a religious procession, a village, a town, or the nation in its entirety—were not given, but had to be constructed. Human beings, in the words of William Sewell, are 'place-transforming animals.'[25] Yet while the particular focus of place-making is historically contingent, people's efforts to construct places that can speak to them are remarkably constant. Place hence seems to be a 'kind of necessary construction.'[26] According to J. E. Malpas, 'the structure of subjectivity is given in and through the structure of place.'[27]

Almost invariably, place has been discussed in relation to space. In one influential conceptualization of the relationship between these two categories of experience and of seeing the world, space is associated with modernization and the widening of cognitive horizons. In a suggestive work of cultural history, for example, Wolfgang Schivelbusch examined how the spread of railway transport in nineteenth-century Europe transformed people's spatial awareness. Such changes included, Schivelbusch tells us, the breakthrough of the panoramic vision as a result of frequent railway travel, or the evolution of the view that cities form part of a larger space of exchange and circulation as a result of the rapprochement of city and railway station.[28] One can easily sense the teleology that informs the arguments of Schivelbusch and others. Yet even if many German towns sometimes changed beyond recognition in the course of the nineteenth century, these changes were not necessarily accompanied by the grand epistemological shifts that modernization theory predicts.[29] Challenging such views, Michel de Certeau called the railway the 'perfect actualization of the rational utopia.' Yet dislocation, it seems, invariably called forth attempts at relocation.[30]

At times, the story of space colonizing place has focused less on anonymous forces than on the martinets of modernity working in the service of modern state administrations. For the exponents of ambitious national states, for example, the problem with historic communities was what the human geographer Robert D. Sack has termed territoriality, which refers to 'the human strategy to affect, influence and control things, social relations, and meanings by controlling areas.'[31] Towns are prime historic examples of this process of place-making through defending territoriality. By legally separating citizens from outsiders, or by defining rules for the functioning of urban markets and various kinds of public ritual, towns sought to constitute themselves as self-governing communities. This is what almost invariably irritated the proponents of modern state power. Inspired by the belief that the nation-state had the most legitimate claim to exercise authority over goods and people, national elites began to erect a scaffolding of new institutions designed to fortify the nation as a tangible community of praxis. This was part and parcel of an attempt to relegate any kind of corporation, including towns, from places to functional spaces. This is a story that tells us much about elite intentions and ambitions, but one that has often been told as if the intentions constituted the reality.[32]

Once we shift our gaze from state elites and bourgeois travellers to individuals embedded in their own localities, however, we are confronted less with large-scale cognitive transformations than with an intensification of the tension between different ideals of place. Here, as elsewhere, urban communities and their inhabitants proved much less predictable than such arguments would have us believe.[33] Above all, towns brought together individuals and groups entertaining different visions, intentions, and ambitions. Although it is not always possible to refrain from describing towns as actors, to do so represents an abstraction, and a bold one at that. The urban municipalities discussed in this book were not cohesive units. They resembled arenas in which various urban factions sought to manipulate existing spatial and normative arrangements, whether in the sphere of elementary education, public worship, local trade or public culture, to name just a few of the substantive areas that will figure prominently in this book. Individuals and groups within the same municipality conceived of space in a multitude of ways, and their practices of place-making diverged accordingly. When people endeavoured to put their ideals of place into practice—for example, by building a museum or a warehouse, or by taking part in a Corpus Christi procession or a Sedan Day pageant—they were thus constructing highly visible 'moral geographies.'[34]

One of the most illuminating reflections on urban place-making has been offered by Michel de Certeau. Building on the study by C. Linde and W. Lubov, which examined how New York residents constructed spatial stories, de Certeau elaborated his approach to space as social practice.[35] For the French scholar, this research revealed two 'symbolic and anthropological languages of space', which in turn demarcated 'two poles of experience.' The first, which concerns operations in space, he called the language of the 'itinerary.' A typical example here would be: 'You turn right and come into the kitchen.' The second spatial language, which relates to the definition of locations in space, de Certeau termed the language of the map. A characteristic phrase underpinned by its logic would be: 'The girl's room is next to the kitchen.' In the sample of the New York residents, the first type of spatial language was predominant.

The two languages reflect de Certeau's differentiation between space and place. Space is about 'vectors of direction, velocities and time variables', while place designates a 'configuration of positions.'[36] In practice, of course, most spatial narratives do not confine themselves to one of the two languages. Few, that is, are exclusively devoted to the designation of either direction of position. Most combine the aspects of space and place in particular ways. As de Certeau writes on the structure underpinning most New York stories: 'stories of journeys and actions are marked out by the "citation" of the places that result from or authorize them.'[37] To cite two typical examples: 'If you turn to the right, there is a butcher's shop.' Or: 'If you go straight ahead, you will see the new *Stadttheater.*'

Far from supplying us with a ready-made theory, de Certeau's conceptual metaphors can assist in framing this book's analytical narrative. One of the crucial tensions, I argue, arose because people subscribed to different conceptions of place. While some envisaged their town as the outcome of a journey, others imagined it as what de Certeau calls a 'well ordered place'. Whereas some residents conceived of their town as work in progress, others pictured it as a configuration of status positions. The differentiation highlights different ways of seeing, and hence of constructing, the world. It does not imply a contrast between 'backward' and 'modern' visions and realities (notwithstanding the fact that the self-appointed champions of reform often depicted others as not being up with the times). In practice, of course, the different spatial frameworks proved relatively flexible and subject to adaptation depending on circumstances. Most individuals and groups combined them as they saw fit. Nor were the journeys of the residents of Augsburg, Ludwigshafen, and Ulm demarcated by a visible endpoint. In practice if not necessarily in the imagination of the participants, their journeys were principally open-ended.

The third concept I employ—in addition to journey and place—is rhythm. If the concepts of place and journey evoke the spatial aspects of human agency, rhythms are constituted at the intersection of space and time.[38] Social life has a 'rhythmic structure.'[39] Men and women do not just do things in space. They do things according to certain temporal rhythms, resulting in recurrent activities being pursued at regular intervals. The rhythms that define people's 'temporal maps' are not natural but rely on (religious and other kinds of) convention. At various times and at different levels, nineteenth-century Germans took part in the often contentious construction of distinctive 'socio-temporal patterns.'[40] The rhythmicity of their lives manifested itself in various kinds of schedules—ranging from theatre programmes to schedules of work and public transport—and calendars—such as those guiding national or religious festivals. Rhythms provide a powerful window through which to explore a society's moral economy.[41] Some rhythmic structures—such as the seven-day week or certain national or religious calendars—are imbued with sacred or quasi-sacred meaning for those who adhere to them. Rhythms are most effective when they are out of view, but their emotional potency comes into evidence when challenges or disruptions occur.[42]

The book's three parts employ these concepts as analytical prisms. The two chapters that form part I—on local economies and elementary schools—examine the motif of the town as a journey and the conflicts this unleashed within an evolving shared urban space. The chapters that make up part II—which investigate citizenship from both a social, political, and consumption point of view—focus on the motif of place-making conceived as a struggle over civic exclusion and inclusion. Finally, the three chapters constituting part III—which are devoted, respectively, to the nationalist-inspired contests over urban progress, the Sedan Day parades, and the Corpus Christi processions—explore how men and women got engaged, in various capacities and roles, in public rituals through which alternative rhythms of communal life were constructed and performed in a competitive process.

This allocation of topics to motifs has not been inevitable, insofar as the motifs of journey, rhythm, and place-making are at play in all of the book's chapters. Rather, what guided me in the framing and organization of the book's narrative was the wish to offer sustained discussions of three central patterns undergirding urban life. Thus, although the chapters of part I place particular emphasis on how urban reformers used the vision of the journey to remake the local economy and urban landscape in particular ways, these examinations also offer a first taste of the centrality of rhythm, and of place as a configuration of positions, in the reconstruction of local communities. Likewise, the chapters of part II, which focus on citizenship broadly conceived, can help remind us that those who embarked on journeys were often obsessed with stability and status. The same holds true for the chapters of part III, where the overarching theme of the rhythms of life—embodied most literally in the Sedan parades and Corpus Christi processions—clearly builds on the discussions conducted in the previous parts. After all, what did those who conceived of their town above all as work in progress demand if not that a different rhythm be imposed on public life? Once again, all the three motifs are at play.

★★★

One aim of this book is to develop a sense for how its two substantive levels—the more social and everyday themes addressed in parts I and II (economies, citizenship, and schools), on the one hand, and the more symbolic processes that are the focus of part III (liberal nationalism, Sedan Day Parades, Corpus Christi processions), on the other—intersected in meaningful ways. When it comes to making sense of this dialogic relationship between the seemingly trivial and that which appears spectacular, the focus on life's rhythms can act as a bridge. While the socio-economic life of the three towns was marked by competing schedules and timetables (both real and imagined), the rhythmicity of life was the central theme of the parades and processions. Encounters and debates that affected life's temporal maps— particularly those imbued with sacred (i.e. the processions for pious Catholics or the Sedan parades for nationalists) or normative properties (e.g. the tramway timetables for liberal reformers)—turned into highly emotional affairs.

Another aim is to question the trust historians have often placed in established chronologies, whether reflecting political events (e.g. the dates of 1871 or 1890) or developmental assumptions ('rapid industrialization'). For although this book fastens itself onto a particular period, its central concern is not with chronology or presumed trajectories, let alone big 'turning points,' but rather with different temporalities and their interaction. The frequent claim that the late nineteenth century was a period of particular turbulence or transformative power in the history of modern Germany is unnecessary. What matters is that there were enough reasons for individuals and communities to take stock and, depending on their judgement of the situation, remake established routines.[43]

Exploring human place-making efforts in this way may help one regain a sense for the provinciality of both the national and the global; for how they converge and intersect in a single location, and for how the alleged provincials constructed not only the local but also the larger worlds they simultaneously inhabited.[44] The perspective can also make us aware that, while the self-referential German hometown had vanished as an institutional reality, it could still serve as a mental map in the struggle over urban reform. But the same old dance could rarely be resumed. As the century drew to a close, Germany's towns were more entangled than they had been at mid-century.[45] Men and women were busy learning to dance to new tunes.

PART
I

Journeys

Prologue

Anything Goes

Movements and displacements come first, places and shapes second.

Bruno Latour[1]

(Urban finances.) According to a survey detailing the budgets of the larger towns within our state in 1889/90, which was recently published in the Neckarzeitung, Heilbronn occupies second place, outperforming the town of Ulm by a considerable margin.

	Overall Revenues	Expenses	Deficit	Revenue from local tax
Stuttgart	3,035,247	5,637,282	2,602,035	1,945,000
Heilbronn	852,786	1,161,905	309,119	300,000
Ulm	609,142	783,563	174,421	165,000
Cannstatt	307,800	488,488	180,688	180,000
Esslingen	306,403	457,027	150,624	150,000

Ulmer Schnellpost[2]

People know who they are by comparing themselves with others. But then this form of self-assertion can be practised at various levels of intensity and explicitness. In the latter part of the nineteenth century, many German towns developed a veritable obsession with figures and statistics, and above all with rankings. On issues ranging from annual budgets to population growth, reformers, the editors of local newspapers, as well as growing sections of the public were keen to know how their municipality fared in relation to its closest rivals. In the thrall of this particular addiction, Ulm looked to the more industrialized Heilbronn and Reutlingen, while Augsburg peered to the more dynamic Nuremberg or Fürth. Only Ludwigshafen's folks kept arguing, with some plausibility, that their town had few equals in Germany, and none in the Palatinate. The causes behind these contests varied, as did their manifestations. What they had in common, however, was the conviction among sections of the public that modern towns represented work in progress. In the era of economic liberalization and free movement, many argued that change was not only inevitable but had to be instigated for the community's sake.

Such calls were invariably controversial. Indeed, one of the most frequent lamentations by German contemporaries was that economic liberalization had resulted in a society that lacked restraint; that it had fostered a mentality that valued quick profits over secure status, lofty *Bildung* over inherited skills, appearance over substance. These accusations were by no means confined to the middle-class protest movement that emerged in the late 1870s in defence of Germany's *Mittelstand*. Nor were they restricted to specific regions. Particularly among members of the local crafts and small trades, the view that an environment had been created in which 'anything goes,' often to the detriment of established solidarities and livelihoods, was widespread.[3] Yet these voices did not go unopposed. Calls for protectionist measures would almost invariably provoke opposition from other economic actors, many of whom had become influential players in the local political sphere.

Such conflicts over the merits of economic liberalization were rooted not in fantasy but in the reality of socio-economic life. Things did not change overnight, to be sure, but they changed within a very short space of time.[4] In the 1860s Germany's per capita level of industrialization was twenty-three per cent of that of the United Kingdom, which meant that it lagged significantly behind both Switzerland and Belgium, and still quite noticeably behind France. By 1900 Germany (now at 52 per cent of the United Kingdom's level of per capita industrialization) had overtaken France and moved closer to Belgium and Switzerland.[5] While in 1870 Germany was still not part of the 'industrial heartland of Europe' consisting of the United Kingdom, France, Belgium, and Switzerland, by 1913 it had become its locomotive.[6] Germany's annual rate of growth during these four-and-a-half decades was 4.1 per cent per annum on average, which was above the level of all the early industrializing countries, including the UK (2.1), France (2.1), Belgium (2.5) and Switzerland (3.2).[7] Her population rose from 33 to 40 million between 1850 and 1870, reaching 50 million in 1892 and about 68 million in June 1914. In

1920, John Maynard Keynes concluded that this exceptional demographic growth would have been impossible without Germany having transformed itself into 'a vast and complicated industrial machine,' one that needed to run at full capacity if it was to offer occupation to its increasing population.[8]

Coupled with this demographic transformation was the proliferation and growth of towns and cities: In 1870 Germany had only eight cities with a population of 100,000 or larger; in 1910, forty-eight cities were in this category, with almost half of the German population living outside their place of birth.[9] As late as 1914 nearly 40 per cent lived in small communities of less than 2000 people (in 1852 the figure had been 73.2 per cent). The proportion of people living in medium-sized towns (of 20,000–100,000 inhabitants) increased from 13 to almost 40 per cent. Finally, the percentage of those living in cities with more than 100,000 inhabitants rose from five per cent in 1871 to 25 per cent by the outbreak of the First World War. In other words, of all the different types of towns the medium-sized ones grew fastest.[10]

Yet contemporaries faced these changes not as free-floating individuals. They experienced them through the prism of the particular places they inhabited as citizens, consumers, employers, or members of particular economic professions or industries.[11] Remaining relatively straightforward, prevalent patterns of economic organization helped sustain a sense of place. For even though the very large corporation had become common in certain branches of industrial production—including mining, textile manufacturing, metallurgy, chemical, and machinery industries—small- and medium-sized firms continued to predominate, not only in the South. Thus, as late as 1907, firms with more than a thousand workers employed only 6.8 per cent of Germany's active workforce.[12] Yet while the mass factory remained the exception, there was a marked shift away from the miniscule that reflected a change in the structure of the urban *Handwerk*. The proportion of one-man and very small businesses fell from 60 per cent in 1871 to 32 per cent in 1907. In some branches, such as construction and foodstuffs, companies with more than a dozen employees became the norm. Those who continued to produce in very small workshops (such as shoemakers or tailors) tended to struggle, with few exceptions. In other branches of the crafts (such as furniture production, the traditional preserve of carpenters and cabinetmakers) trading activities became increasingly important, often as an add-on to traditional manufacturing.[13]

The populations of Württemberg and Bavaria grew more slowly than the imperial average. Between 1864 and 1871, Bavaria's rose by less than two per cent, while Württemberg's grew by approximately four per cent per annum. Between 1871 and 1900, moreover, the populations of Bavaria and Württemberg increased by more than 25 per cent, while the Empire's grew by nearly 40 per cent. The fact that both states combined above-average mortality rates with relatively low levels of factory industry goes some way to explaining these differences.[14] In terms of population density between 1841 and 1910, furthermore, Württemberg grew from 85 to 125 and Bavaria from 57 to 91 people per square kilometre. By comparison, during the same period Baden grew from 84 to 142, the Rhineland from 97 to 264, and Germany as a whole from 60 to 120. While 34.7 per cent of Germans lived in towns of between 20,000 and 100,000 residents by 1910, this was the case for only 21.1 per cent of Württemberg's population. Before the First World War, Stuttgart was Württemberg's only *Grossstadt*.[15]

The rate of small companies, and hence of self-employment, was relatively high: 24.5 per cent of Württemberg's population worked in companies with over five employees in 1875, at a point when the imperial average was 35.7.[16] Industrial sectors of considerable significance included salt production (mainly in Heilbronn), cotton and linen weaving (with centres in Urach, Münsingen, Heidenheim, and Reutlingen), machinery (particularly in Heilbronn, Stuttgart, Reutlingen, Cannstatt, Heidenheim, and Ulm), cement industry (Blaubeuren and Ulm), and foodstuffs (particularly in Heilbronn and Singen).[17] In Bavaria 85 per cent of the population lived in rural areas as late as 1882.[18] Yet, the share of the population living in cities of ten thousand or larger grew from less than ten to over twenty-five per cent in the three decades before the First World. By 1910, sixteen per cent of Bavaria's population lived in cities of over 100,000 inhabitants, at a time when the imperial figure was 21 per cent.[19] Bavaria's urban industrial centres included Augsburg (textile and machinery) and Nuremberg (machinery and electrical industry), cities with a strong tradition in the crafts and trades; while others, such as Ludwigshafen am Rhein (chemical industry) in the Palatinate, were modern creations that owed their expansion to a single industry.[20]

What characterized the socio-economic development of Bavaria and Württemberg was not backwardness per se, however. What gave it its distinctive flavour is that, more conspicuously than in other regions of Germany, economic liberalization occurred against the backdrop of marked corporatist structures and traditions. The pattern is commensurate with an argument the political economist Gary Herrigel formulated in an important revisionist account.[21] Instead of depicting German industrialization as a homogenous process in which advanced regions dragged along backward ones, Herrigel distinguished between two patterns of economic development. There was, on the one hand, the decentralized industrialization typical of the small and medium-sized towns of Württemberg, the Rhineland, Thüringen, Saxony, and (to some extent) Bavaria. Its driving forces were not the large factories but small- and medium-sized producers, many of them still firmly rooted in the traditional (family-based) crafts. In the historic *Gewerbelandschaft* of Württemberg, for example, the engine driving industrialization was the industrial middle class, which also dominated the culture and politics of many regional towns. This was in marked contrast to the industrial path commonly associated with Germany's northern and north-western regions. There it was the large, centralized iron- and steel-producing firms, many of whose owners entertained close links with the imperial administration, which played a central role.[22]

No doubt historians have good reasons to avoid the words 'advanced' and 'backward' when it comes to describing economic development with the benefit of hindsight. In the minds of many locals, however, these concepts occupied a central place, and hence mattered to the shaping of real communities. In Württemberg and Bavaria, perceptions of backwardness inspired local reform. These perceptions were created, sustained, and reinforced by the statistical data that nineteenth-century state bureaucracies, as well as various private associations specializing in the collection of statistical information, produced in great quantities. The *Kaiserliches Statistisches Amt* (founded in 1872) was pivotal in this respect, publishing statistical tables on population growth, agriculture, domestic and foreign trade, tax revenue, criminality, the educational standing of military recruits, insurance, mortality and health, to name but the most important areas. The information thus generated enabled the drawing up of comparisons not only between different German states but also between regions within the same state.[23] Figures and statistics drew considerable public interest well beyond the state officials that had this information to hand at all times.[24] Self-declared urban reformers were aware of the comparatively low rates of demographic and economic growth in Bavaria and Württemberg compared to, for instance, parts of the Rhineland or Saxony. What preoccupied them considerably more, however, was how their own town fared in relation to its nearest competitors. This awareness made them identify 'shortcomings' and 'anachronisms' closer to home. More consequentially, as well as more controversially, it made them prone to imagine their town as work in progress—as a place that had embarked on a journey.

I

Remaking Urban Economies

Everyone who promotes the telephone renders a service to public commerce and communication, which is why notably the guests of busy inns should demand a telephone connection.

Ulmer Tagblatt (1887)[1]

Where the vessels are steaming
And the chimneys are smoking
There lies Ludwigshafen a. Rhein
It is forcefully craning its neck
And gloriously stretching its spine
By its own strength, all on its own.

Inscription on postcard ('Ludwigshafen am Rhein'), 1890s[2]

Indeed, Augsburg seems to embody the comforting example of a transition from old manufacturing to modern factory production, aided by an environment blessed by both history and nature.

Wilhelm Heinrich Riehl, 1850s[3]

When in 1897 a state official reminisced about Ulm's recent past, the picture he painted of the previous half-century was one of loss, but also of hope in the salutary impact of impending reforms. The first signs that matters were about to get worse were visible as early as 1855, when the small circle of born-and-bred Ulmers, the so-called *Altbürger*, had to abandon an ancient cavalry exercise because they could no longer afford it. By the mid-1870s, economic liberalism and industrialization had altered the town's demographic composition: now only a third of those getting married had actually been born in Ulm, while the proportion of Catholics had significantly increased in a town that was among the first to embrace the Reformation. But none of this meant, the official was quick to add, that

Ulm's future might not be a happy one after all. With the aid of 'wise social legislation,' he concluded, Ulm might make the widely desired transition from a town of small craftsmen to one in which the 'small manufacturer' would serve as the main guarantor of a reasonable degree of growth and prosperity.[4]

What the state official tried to pinpoint on a map of progress was, in fact, a journey whose destiny remained open-ended. Urban economies played an important part in the construction of new worlds out of existing cultural and material resources. Promoting the exchange of goods, services, and information, they are place-transcending. In practice, however, such economies were constructed by locally embedded people who fashioned different road maps in the pursuit of their ambitions.[5] What some (e.g. merchants or liberal city councillors supporting supra-regional trade) regarded as initiatives to strengthen their city's development prospects, others (e.g. craftsman and small traders seeking to defend themselves against competition from outside) perceived as a threat to the territorial integrity of their town. For those who shared these concerns, what lay in store was the relegation of their city to a community whose internal contours were increasingly difficult to ascertain—a space in which unfamiliar economic projects and agendas began to challenge established norms and assumptions.[6]

Württemberg's *zweite Stadt*

A medium-sized town by German standards, Ulm's population grew from 12,000 in the 1840s to around 60,000 by the outbreak of the First World War. In economic terms, Ulm represents a *Gewerbe- und Handelsstadt*—a town dominated by independent artisans and small tradesmen, with merchants engaged in supra-regional trade and factory owners representing a small yet increasingly important minority. Small tradesmen (including many shopkeepers) and self-employed artisans (most of whom sold their products directly to the consumers) continued to dominate the local economy throughout the *Kaiserreich*. The size of the average business unit remained relatively small. Thus, in 1867, Ulm's handicraft businesses employed just 1.56 people on average. While the trade sector expanded markedly from the 1860s, what characterized this expansion was large numbers (there were 263 people classified as tradesmen in Ulm in 1860), rather than large firms.[7] With an average business size of 2.28 employees in 1882, Ulm ranked only 10th in Württemberg, behind Esslingen (4.09), Göppingen (3.52), Heilbronn (3.4), Schwäbisch Gmünd (3.25), Ludwigsburg (3.07), Stuttgart (2.87), Cannstatt (2.73), Ravensburg (2.68) and Reutlingen (2.68).[8]

Nor was Ulm able to keep pace with Württemberg's fastest growing towns. This had not always been so. During the boom years of the early 1870s, Ulm's population had grown by between three and four per cent per year, heightening expectations among the ambitious liberal public. Yet, as a glance at the annually published statistics on urban demography shows, these expectations would be disappointed thereafter. Between 1871 and 1885, Ulm's population had increased from 26,290 to 33,604, which was roughly in line with the imperial average; but between 1875 and 1880, the annual rate of population growth had fallen below one per cent; and during the first half of the 1880s the town's population grew by a mere 832 souls. Confronted with these figures, many began to express concern that Ulm's time as Württemberg's second largest city was about to expire. Indeed, the frequency with which Ulm was described as *die zweite Stadt Württembergs* ('Württemberg's second city') is indicative of these concerns. It was 'undeniable,' one newspaper noted in 1885, that Ulm did not experience the 'industrial boom affecting towns such as Heilbronn, Heidenheim, Göppingen, etc.' There was now a real danger that Ulm would 'not be able to pride itself of being *die zweite Stadt des Landes* ("the state's second city") for much longer.'[9] The narrative of the second city was employed, almost invariably, to express concerns about an impending loss of status.

From the 1870s onwards the voices lamenting that Ulm's demographic and economic expansion was lagging behind that of other Württemberg towns (including several up-and-coming industrial centres, such as Heilbronn) were becoming more frequent. Their ambition was to transform Ulm from an established *Gewerbestadt* into one of southern Germany's leading trade centres, an aim that was not unrealistic given the town's excellent position at the junction of several important railway lines. Some contemporaries were in no doubt that what prevented Ulm from experiencing the kind of expansion found elsewhere was the lack of factory industry. As an 1875 state report summed up the economic situation that characterized the *Donaukreis*, of which Ulm was the centre: 'Everywhere in this district...the city of Ulm included...factory production forms the exception rather than the rule.'[10]

In 1879, the *Ulmer Tagblatt* described the town's economic landscape as multi-faceted, with the boundaries between the various economic sectors being fluid rather than clear-cut: 'Our city comprises close to a thousand independent craftsmen, not counting the fifty or so gardeners, who, earning their living mostly by growing vegetables, plants, and seeds, in effect fall in the agricultural domain. Besides, it is hard to tell where the craftsman ends and the factory owner begins.'[11] But not everyone regarded this fluidity as a boon. Some associated it with a lack of dynamism, as evidenced, for instance, in the near-absence of the kind of commuter traffic that had become common in industrial towns such as Esslingen or Heilbronn. As the state of affairs was described in a district report in 1897:

> It is highly indicative of Ulm's situation with regard to industry and occupation that weekly train tickets for workers are rarely ever used. In 1894/95, such tickets were sold for journeys to Stuttgart: 83,268; Pforzheim: 43,454; Cannstadt; 28,390; Esslingen: 27,794; Heilbronn: 20,443; Ludwigsburg: 16,040. During the same period only 1,460 weekly tickets were purchased for journeys to Ulm, which means that it only comes 33rd among Württemberg's towns, reflecting the fact that the town is still in a position to draw its required workforce almost exclusively from the local population.[12]

Not that industry had failed to take hold in Ulm. The first steps towards mechanized production occurred in 1856, when Johann Krauss bought 60 looms and turned his traditional mill into a mechanical weaving mill. He was followed, just a decade later, by the hat maker Mayser and the brass manufacturer Wieland.[13] By 1860 there were around 1000 factory workers in Ulm (there were 2083 craftsmen at that time), most of them employed in the nine largest companies.[14] Yet most factories, even in the metal-working sector, remained relatively small. As the early years of the company of the Gebrüder Eberhardt (founded in 1863, the company would soon specialize in the production of agricultural machinery) was described in a Festschrift: 'When production began in the newly acquired premises in 1863 with three steam engines, the company comprised twelve journeymen, all of whom ate at the family table of Wilhelm Eberhardt.'[15]

By 1875, there were twenty-two factories employing a total of 1192 workers. The largest were the hat maker Mayser with 300–400 workers and an annual turnover of one million marks; two tobacco factories jointly employing 300 workers and producing a turnover of two million marks; two cement factories with a combined workforce of 130, whose main centres of production lay outside Ulm; a brass factory with 300 workers and using 300 horse powers; the machinery-producing factories of Gebr. Eberhardt and C. D. Magirus, each employing around 50 workers.[16] By 1895 the number of factory workers in Ulm had risen to 3204 (there were 2254 craftsmen in Ulm at that point in time). At the turn of the century, 35.8 per cent of Ulm's working population was employed in the industrial and crafts sectors. Yet while this was no doubt respectable, it was still markedly lower than in either Stuttgart (47.2 per cent) or Heilbronn (52.9), which Ulm's movers and doers regarded as the pertinent benchmarks.[17] Here, as elsewhere, progress lay in the eyes of the beholder.

The virtues of an urban economy dominated by small- and medium-sized businesses came at a prize for a town that ran a costly education system— Ulm's grammar schools enjoyed a high reputation across the region—and whose welfare provision was progressive by contemporary standards. As Mayor Wagner noted in his report on Ulm's economic development over the nineteenth century, at 84 marks Ulm's revenue from commercial tax per inhabitant was much lower than that of either Heilbronn (109) or Stuttgart (145). The same held true with regard to capital gains tax, where Heilbronn's income per head of the population was about thirty per cent above Ulm's, while Stuttgart's was more than twice that of Ulm.[18] What filled Wagner with hope was the incontestably high consumption of meat and beer—with annual consumption rates of 61.2 kilograms of meat and 421.3 litres of beer per resident, Ulm was in a league of its own. In this respect at least, the garrison undoubtedly worked in Ulm's favour. This was no small feat either: the tax on beer and meat was one of the most significant elements of municipal revenue. In 1880, income from beer tax (126,000 marks) amounted to almost a third of Ulm's total tax revenues, and in 1885 meat and beer tax combined made for over 40 per cent of the town's total expenses.[19]

Advancing more deeply into the practice of economic life, one of its outstanding features was a tension between craftsmen and small traders, on the one hand, and a number of ambitious local merchants on the other. Ever since the introduction of *Gewerbefreiheit* in 1862, Ulm's craftsmen, shopkeepers, and small traders saw themselves confronted with the presence of a small yet increasingly influential group of tradesmen and merchants. The former were organized in the local *Gewerbeverein*. Founded in 1847 (the year in which the guilds were officially dissolved in Württemberg) and with a membership of over 300 in 1875, it was the city's largest economic association. Many of the tradesmen and merchants, on the other hand, some of them recent arrivals, belonged to the local *Handelsverein*, which in the 1870s had a little over 100 members. In his detailed 1875 report to a state official, Ulm's mayor von Heim noted that the local community of traders and merchants, while of 'very recent vintage,' was promising and on the rise.[20] This was in contrast to the local *Kleingewerbe*, which, as the Free Conservative von Heim was keen to point out, was in need of reform.[21] Unlike the *Gewerbeverein*, Ulm's *Handelsverein* was widely known for its unreserved opposition to the protectionist economic policies that gained currency from the late 1870s.[22]

Von Heim was alluding to the fact that many crisis-ridden crafts had not been reduced in line with the shrinking demand for their produce. As late as 1885, for example, there were 85 master tailors and 159 master shoemakers running an independent business in the city.[23] Such a high concentration in one particular sector may have been appropriate in the early nineteenth century, before people were given easy access to cheap, factory-produced textiles. By the close of the century, however, this had become problematic. The widespread lamentations about the competition local craftsmen and small traders faced from travelling sales businesses, so-called *Wanderlager*, owed much to this structural problem.[24]

That Ulm's relatively small group of tradesmen and merchants soon made a significant contribution to the local tax revenue no doubt added to its weight and prestige. Yet, to many a member of Ulm's *Gewerbeverein* supra-local trade, as carried out by Ulm's small merchant community, represented an alien presence. For some local artisans in particular, people who traded in goods they had neither produced nor would necessarily sell locally were morally dubious. While local shopkeepers and craftsmen also engaged in trading activity, theirs remained fairly localized by comparison. Faced with such reservations, however, Ulm's merchants were increasingly unwilling to see their prospects dented by what they regarded as the protectionist activities of the *Gewerbeverein*. The resulting tension between these two sections of the local economy was one of the defining features of Ulm's economic life between the 1860s and the turn of the century. At the root of these tensions were conflicting visions for Ulm's future. While the merchants imagined Ulm as work in progress, many members of the *Gewerbeverein* defined it more in terms of a clearly defined configuration of positions.

A glance at attitudes towards the city's military fortifications provides us
with an entry into this phenomenon. Having been defortified during the
Napoleonic Wars, Ulm became the location for one the federal fortresses
build between 1815 and 1866 (along with Mainz, Landau, and Rastatt).
Between 1842 and 1859 the *Bundesfestung*, a large military fortress and fortification ring, was built around the town on the initiative of the German
Confederation. When on 11 August 1842 the German Diet gave its final
approval to the construction of the fortress, Ulm was destined to become
one of Württemberg's largest construction sites; and with its total building
cost of 16 million gulden, the fortress was just as expensive as the railway
line between Ulm and Cannstatt.[25] Unlike many German towns, including
Augsburg, whose fortresses were razed to the ground in 1866 or shortly
thereafter, Ulm's large fortress ring would not be pierced until the beginning of the twentieth century.[26]

The project proved a mixed blessing for Ulm's economic development,
in that the construction process itself (in which, on average, 3000 workers
were engaged, although that number nearly doubled during the summer
months) created a temporary boom for several of the local crafts, the construction trade, as well as in the foodstuff sector. Even after the boom had
subsided towards the end of the 1850s, Ulm's garrison still helped sustain a
respectable slice of the urban economy, particularly small- and medium-
sized businesses, and above all butchers, breweries and inns, as well as suppliers of wood and fuel. Thus, as late as 1895, a state report noted that the
garrison, with its more than 6000 military personnel, was the lifeblood of a
significant portion of Ulm's economy.[27]

Yet while the building of the *Bundesfestung* had encouraged certain
trades to expand, it also precipitated their rapid contraction once the works
had been completed. Ulm's bakers are a case in point. When the fortress
was completed in 1852 there were 72 master bakers in Ulm. As if this had
not hit the bakers hard enough, a garrison bakery was installed in 1857.
The protests of the baker guild, which sent petitions to both the King of
Württemberg and the town council, proved in vain.[28] Besides, the garrison,
with its fortifications and security requirements, imposed severe limitations
on Ulm's economic development. Building near the garrison walls was virtually impossible due to the legal restrictions imposed by the German
Confederation. In 1845, for example, the inventor and entrepreneur Johannes
Schwenk saw himself confronted with an expropriation order issued by the
German Bund.[29] Some sectors of industrial production required sites of a

Figure 1. Fortress walls, with Ulm's Cathedral in the background. © Stadtarchiv Ulm.

size that were unavailable in Ulm, while others were reluctant to move their production to a town that was hemmed in by fortification walls and towers, and in which military authorities possessed a virtual veto on many aspects of urban development.[30] As Ulm's mayor Heinrich Wagner concluded in an 1891 report: While the garrisoned military kept parts of the urban economy busy, they were 'merely' consumers, and only the officers (but not the soldiers) were subject to municipal tax.[31] It would take until 1906 for the fortress walls to be removed.[32]

Significantly, however, the faction that explicitly asked for the removal of the fortress, while no doubt influential, was also relatively small. It was composed of entrepreneurs organized in the local *Handelsverein*, who were seconded by liberal politicians who wanted Ulm to emulate some of the faster-growing and more industrial cities. Yet the fact that the fortress does not seem to have caused anything approaching widespread outrage is revealing. Reservations about economic liberalization and uncontrolled population growth appear to have played an important role here. Already in 1852, the then mayor Julius Schuster saw in the protection of 'domestic industry from foreign competition' a necessary precondition for Germany's prosperous development. His recommendation for Ulm was a gradual introduction of *Gewerbefreiheit*, one in which the municipalities would retain control over the inclusion of outsiders.[33] Furthermore, in a debate on the town's future economic prospects that was played out in the *Ulmer Tagblatt* in 1885, the newspaper's editors, after noting that Ulm's population had indeed grown more slowly than that of either Ravensburg, Göppingen, Esslingen, or Heilbronn, concluded that this was not all bad, since steep population growth came at a price:

> If the factory towns owe their population growth above all to the increase of workers employed in large factories and similar establishments, then the absence of such factories in our town, whose population grew only modestly, has spared Ulm of elements it can well do without for more than one reason.[34]

Among Ulm's small tradesmen and craftsmen, many of them organized in the local *Gewerbeverein*, the response to constant lamentations about the town's lack of factory industry—and, indeed, the inclination to view industrial progress purely in terms of large-scale production—was one of defiance. While other towns 'may excel in the field of factory industry,' Ulm, by 'investing in the generation of able journeymen and master craftsmen,' was 'taking steps to ensure that its small trade can be saved from irreversible decline.'[35] Their vision of urban development was a far cry away from that of a few local merchants. This explains their refusal to join the alliance demanding the removal of the fortress walls. For as the previous explorations suggest, for many craftsmen and small traders Ulm's *Bundesfestung* was as a source of reassurance, rather than anxiety; the incarnation of a vision in which Ulm appeared not as a journey but as a proper place.

Yet Ulm's merchant and business community continued to look for ways to widen the city's spatial horizons. Thus, in the mid-1880s the *Post- and Telegraphendirektion* had agreed to install a telephone exchange if at least 50 subscribers could be found. Yet when C. D. Magirus, the owner-manager of one of Ulm's few larger companies, tried to get local entrepreneurs to sign up for a telephone connection, the take-up was rather tardy. The subscription cost of 160 marks per annum, which to a patron of a small business was substantial, may have played its part. In June 1885, when Magirus started his lobbying campaign, 35 local businesses, as well as the municipal administration had expressed an interest in a subscription. In August, a committee—chaired by Magirus, its other members included the local chief of police and several businessmen—was given the task of finding the necessary number of subscribers.[36] In October of the same year, the *Ulmer Tagblatt* published a list of the 43 subscribers, including several private individuals, businesses, and public organizations. The latter category included several district courts, the city council, the police department, the administrations of gas and water works, as well as the city's main hospital.[37]

When by December the list of subscribers was still five short of the required fifty, the *Ulmer Tagblatt* expressed disappointment at the public's reluctance to embrace a technological innovation that had been adopted remarkably swiftly elsewhere.[38] Contemplating possible reasons for this reluctance, its editors identified the small size of Ulm's inner city, whose expansion had been prevented by the fortress walls. By and large, most businesses, as well as important public offices, were located in close proximity of each other. Many therefore regarded the telephone as a luxury, rather than a genuine need. Some businessmen had subscribed not out of necessity, but because they wished to 'prevent the town from staying behind' in this important area of modern communication.[39]

In spite of these efforts, however, it took the committee a full two years to fulfill its brief. On 1 June 1887 the *Fernsprechanstalt Ulm* was opened with 55 telephone connection points. In order to create an incentive for others to follow suit, the existing subscribers were once again listed by name in the local press, thus underlining the extraordinary nature of the event in the local perception.[40] The number of telephone connections would indeed increase over the next few years. By August 1890, the *Ulmer Telephonanstalt* had 140 subscribers, who could now benefit from the completion of new telephone lines to Stuttgart, Reutlingen, and Friedrichshafen. The enthusiastic news was accompanied by a warning to use the service with caution during a thunderstorm, as this increased the risk of hearing damage due to electric shocks.[41]

The debate surrounding Ulm's bid for a branch of the imperial central bank offers a further illustration of the contrasting developmental visions informing the town's main economic communities. After the Reichsbank had been set up as Germany's central bank in Berlin in 1875, the question arose as to which cities would be chosen as locations for one of its branches. Rumours about the imperial authorities' preferences had begun to circulate soon after the Reichsbank's executive had launched its round of bids. Some cities had clearly more grounds for optimism than others. In Württemberg, for instance, nobody really doubted that Stuttgart would be among the successful applicants. But speculation soon had it that more than one of Württemberg's towns might be chosen. Thus, there opened up a space for an increasingly nervous controversy, one that was invested with the status concerns of its most vocal participants. Some contended that a town such as Ulm could only expect to be granted a so-called *Nebenstelle*, a subsidiary branch, rather than, as part of Ulm's business community had hoped, a proper *Reichsbankfiliale*. As long as no official decision had been taken either way, however, rumours kept circulating and rival hopes continued to be expressed.[42]

Immediately after the imperial authorities had expressed their intention to establish a network of Reichsbank branches, the executive of the *Handelsverein* set up a committee whose task was to prepare Ulm's bid. It included 17 of Ulm's leading entrepreneurs, several members of commercial organizations, as well as representatives from the district towns of Biberach, Blaubeuren, Ehingen, Geislingen, Giengen, Isny, Leutkirch, Ravensburg, Riedlingen, Gaulgau, Tettnang, and Waldsee. One of the committee's first actions was to draft a document in which the legitimacy of Ulm's claim was spelled out in considerable detail. The document was then sent to Württemberg's Ministry of the Interior. Its author was the Jewish merchant Gustav Maier, the leading intellectual light of Ulm's *Handelsverein*.[43] At the end of the 40-page report, completed within a matter of weeks, Maier expressed the *Handelsverein*'s hope that, 'contrary to the original intention, Ulm may be awarded not only an agency but an independent banking branch (*Bankstelle*).'[44]

Maier set out on his task with a rich portrait of Ulm's economic history, highlighting its glorious past as a trading town during the medieval and early-modern periods. Ulm had been the 'most influential among the Swabian free cities.' This position had been lost in the decades and centuries following the Thirty Years War, due above all to political feuds and recurrent warfare. One of the chief reasons for the slowness of Ulm's economic recovery during the nineteenth century, Maier contended, was the building of a large garrison and fortress in the 1850s on the orders of the German Confederation. If industrialists had tended to avoid Ulm in the recent past, this had in large part been due to the restrictions the fortress had imposed on industrial expansion. At the same time, however, Maier argued that 'an independent bank branch' was of particular importance to a town of Ulm's military significance. He even insisted that the German Empire owed Ulm something, given that its fortress had so adversely affected his hometown's development prospects.[45]

At the same time, however, Maier emphasized that these drawbacks and obstacles had in no way dispirited Ulm's entrepreneurs. They had certainly not prevented Ulm from regaining its former status as one of southern Germany's foremost trading centres. The town was noted for its trade in wood, cheese, metal, leather goods, as well as for its commerce in tobacco, beer, hats, and textiles.[46] What had enabled Ulm's economic regeneration was its location at the intersection of five major railway lines. Thanks to these favourable transport links, the town was not only connected with the economic centres of its more immediate hinterland, but also with Switzerland via Friedrichshafen (important because of the soon-to-be-completed railway tunnel through the Gotthard), with Austria via Augsburg and Munich, and with northern Germany via Stuttgart and Heidenheim. In the main part of the report, Maier offered a painstaking compilation of the various business activities taking place both in Ulm and within the wider district of which it was the capital. Drawing on both established figures and estimates, he concluded that the district's annual turnover was 382,547,000 marks. This sum, he pointed out, was a sign of the 'enormous economic activity' that characterized upper Swabia. It would therefore be no more than just, he concluded, if Württemberg would be given not one but two Reichsbank branches. Ulm was to cover the southernmost parts of Germany for which Stuttgart was simply too distant.[47]

When in June 1875 Ulm and Reutlingen each submitted their separate bids, the debate, now fought out mainly in the editorials of local newspapers, was getting more heated.[48] It centred on two inter-related arguments. One was chiefly concerned with the concrete economic advantages Ulm would gain from hosting a major financial institution. The other couched the question more in terms of Ulm's present status within Württemberg. Some argued that, surely, Württemberg's second city was entitled to be awarded its own branch, while others insisted that the success of Ulm's bid was a precondition for its ability to retain its status as *Württemberg's zweite Stadt* (the latter expression was again used with great frequency). Overall, the latter argument prevailed. Its chief proponent was the liberal *Ulmer Schnellpost*, the voice of the local *Deutsche Partei*. Its editors demanded that Ulm, rather than the more industrialized Heilbronn, be chosen to become Württemberg's second seat of the Reichsbank. One reader may have spoken for many when he argued that the establishment of a Reichsbank branch was of existential importance for Ulm's economic future. With a bank of this importance, Ulm would be in possession of financial instruments similar to larger towns such as Berlin or Frankfurt, which would make it the financial centre of upper Swabia. Without it, however, it would be 'on a par with every small provincial town.'[49]

Not everyone agreed, however. One reader, possibly acting as the voice of the *Gewerbeverein*, maintained that the jury was still out on Ulm's real significance as a trading town. As far as he and many others were concerned, Ulm's *Handelsstand* had still a lot to prove.[50] His intervention caused considerable consternation among merchants and manufacturers. Responding to what he saw as a lamentable manifestation of self-doubt and small-mindedness, one representative of the *Handelsverein* retaliated thus:

> It reflects unfavourably on us Ulmers when we openly express our doubts about Ulm's importance as a trading town. One should be able to expect of each citizen that they strongly support efforts to elevate our town's eminence in the present times; and that they are willing to recognize the significance of these efforts, instead of diminishing them by describing them as being of secondary importance.[51]

In terms of its potential as a trading centre, the reader insisted, Ulm would not have to fear comparison with cities such as Karlsruhe, Darmstadt, Mainz or Heilbronn. He concluded by asking fellow Ulmers to give up their 'narrow-minded viewpoint': 'Respect yourself, and you will be treated with respect. Think lowly of yourself and you will be met with contempt.'[52]

A fortnight after the publication of the said reader's letter, the supporters of the Reichsbank project discussed their strategy at a special meeting attended by local entrepreneurs, merchants, industrialists, as well as several municipal councillors. A committee was set up and charged with presenting Ulm's case to the Ministry of the Interior in Stuttgart.[53] The resolution expressed dissatisfaction at what many perceived as Ulm's long-standing subordination to Stuttgart.[54] Yet in spite of the concerted exertions by the local *Handelsverein*, the special committee and the district's chamber of commerce and trade, in the end Ulm and Heilbronn were each only awarded an agency rather than a full branch. This decision was greeted with a marked sense of relief by those who had long resented the ambitious stance displayed by Ulm's merchants and industrialists. Many felt vindicated in their objections to what they regarded as the excessively high-minded attitude adopted by the *Handelsverein* and the lobbying committee. This strategy, the

Figure 2. Panoramic view of Ulm, circa 1880. © Stadtarchiv Ulm.

sceptics were keen to point out, supported as it had been by elements within Ulm's local press, had not gone down well with the authorities in Berlin and Stuttgart. Several representatives of the *Gewerbeverein* accused the *Handelsverein* of arrogance and self-delusion, claiming that its intense lobbying campaign had made Ulm appear immodest.[55] Thus, only if Ulm knew its place, the opponents of the project seemed to suggest, could it have a prosperous future.

This did not prevent Ulm's merchants from continuing to imagine their town as a journey whose engine was trade; this came out most clearly over the proposed construction of transit and storage warehouses. From the 1870s, members of the *Handelsverein* tried to persuade the municipal council of the economic benefits these would bring to Ulm's trade. Such warehouses, thus their persistent credo, were to turn Ulm into a centre of the South-German grain trade, outstripping larger cities such as Munich, Nuremberg, Stuttgart, and Augsburg. The champions of the warehouse project doubtless had the economic logic behind them. The expansion of the railway network in southern Germany since the 1840s had reinforced competition in the grain trade. As a result, Ulm had gradually lost out as a market place for grain to more favourably located centres such as

Mannheim, to the point where it was in danger of becoming redundant. The only way to prevent this, Gustav Maier and other members of the *Handelsverein* were convinced, was to create a market capable of attracting grain merchants from all over Germany. As the *Handelsverein* justified its project in a statement to the municipal authorities in 1874:

> Ulm's exceptionally favourable location at the junction of six railway lines...is bound to attract the attention of the agile trader. Situated between two of the main producers and consumers of trade—namely, Austria-Hungary and Galicia on the one hand, and France, Italy and Switzerland on the other—Ulm...would be ideally placed to act as broker for the significant export trade carried out each year between these countries and Germany.[56]

When, four months later, the municipal council had still not responded, the *Handelsverein* insisted that the matter was urgent, all the more so as Stuttgart had recently decided to build a number of transit storehouses to revitalize its grain trade. If Ulm failed to act now, it would miss the boat. For a while, things seemed to proceed in the way the merchants had hoped for. Thus, in 1875, Ulm's mayor expressed his strong support for the warehouse project in a report to a state official. Given the obvious lack of large-scale industry in Ulm, and in view of the difficulties in which the local *Gewerbe* presently found itself, the flourishing of Ulm's nascent merchant community was all the more important. Mayor von Heim thus reassured the state official that the city council was keen to pursue the warehouse project. In fact, he noted, the construction of the 'warehouses and trading areas will begin shortly.'[57] When, in 1875, the authorities took a first step towards the project's realization by purchasing a piece of real estate near the railway line to Heidenheim, Ulm's '*Handelsstand* was delighted.'[58]

But the municipal council, supported by the local small-trade lobby, proved more reluctant than the supporters of the warehouse project had envisaged, delaying the building of the first warehouses for more than a decade. When by the summer of 1877 no progress had been made, the association launched a more concerted campaign, using both the local press and public meetings to argue its case. Against those who insisted that the storage houses should be paid for by its greatest benefactors, some merchants and building contractors retorted that the projected buildings would benefit the local economy as a whole.[59]

In a new bid submitted to the town council in August 1877, the *Handelsverein* pointed out that the 'Suez Canal and the railway through the Gotthard' were only 'two of a series of transport innovations' that were about to 'transform world trade.' Those towns that were 'quickest to grasp the significance of these profound transformations and make the necessary adaptations are bound to assume great significance.' Provided Ulm's political leaders acted quickly and decisively, the town would be ideally placed to benefit from these momentous developments.[60] In September 1877, the national-liberal *Ulmer Schnellpost* reprinted an article from the *Frankfurter Zeitung*. Its author claimed that 'in all of Germany's larger towns that do not yet possess their own warehouses, the question of creating ones has been put on the agenda.'[61] The seemingly self-evident conclusion from this assessment was drawn in an editorial three days later: If Ulm continued to hesitate, it was bound to lose out even more to Stuttgart and Heilbronn, where the relevant circles had taken a much more proactive stance on this question.[62]

The opponents of the warehouse project only entered the frame after the *Handelsverein* had renewed its campaign in the summer of 1877. Some of their arguments were straightforward, including the charge that an investment that mostly benefited a particular section of Ulm's economy—namely merchants engaged in supra-local trade—should not be paid for by the public purse. Here the 'Manchester men' of the *Handelsverein*, whose usual instinct was to shout 'help yourself' whenever the local *Gewerbe* called for municipal assistance, were accused of inconsistency. Another argument Ulm's small traders marshalled against the warehouse project reveals their thorough familiarity with international markets. Hungarian grain, so they insisted, tended to be more expensive than that imported from the United States, for which Mannheim and Heilbronn had established themselves as the main trading centres.[63] This charge was designed to question the community-mindedness of Ulm's merchants, who kept insisting that the warehouses would benefit the interest of the local consumer.[64]

What added insult to injury was that the members of formerly marginal communities—the sons of workers, people without local citizenship rights, or Jews, whose economic activities had for centuries been subject to legal restrictions—appeared to be doing rather well. Whether these perceptions were real or imagined (and they were usually a bit of both), it is against this background that the attitudes and political initiatives of the *Gewerbeverein* must be judged. Thus, in a remarkable statement published in the *Ulmer Tagblatt* in 1877, one of the association's members did not so much oppose the warehouse project than argue that Ulm's native merchant community was not really as dynamic and vibrant as it liked to portray itself.[65] 'Warehouses of this kind,' the said member contended, 'presuppose a commercial and speculative ingenuity' that Ulm's native tradesmen did on the whole not possess. They were not even imbued, so he argued in continuation of his assertion, with the 'entrepreneurial alertness of those whose ancestors were not Ulmers and who used to earn their livelihood not as traders, but ped-dlers.' Thanks to their 'tireless activity,' the 'descendants' of these peddlers had already begun to make significant inroads into 'the terrain traditionally occupied by Ulm's merchant community.' It was therefore a question not of if, but of when, they would become the 'sole representatives of Ulm's *Handelsstand.*'[66]

The author of the article was referring to the less than a handful of Jewish merchants, such as Gustav Maier or Max Dreyfuss, who played an important role in the *Handelsverein*. For quite a few members of Ulm's small-trade community, it seems, the important role of Jews in Ulm's eco-nomic life symbolized the decline of a world in which both status and movement could be controlled. In promoting more complex and dynamic modes of economic interaction and exchange, Jews were instrumental in making Ulm feel not like a well-ordered place, but as work in progress.

It was once again Gustav Maier who, at a meeting of Ulm's *Deutsche Partei* in January 1880, insisted that Ulm should have both a storehouse for grain and a transit warehouse for the storage and onward transport of other kinds of goods and merchandise. Yet the meeting's final resolution, which took account of reservations raised by the local *Gewerbe*, was more modest, merely inviting the municipal council to 'revisit the warehouse question and reach a final decision on it.'[67] In the course of the same year, the *Ulmer Schnellpost* published a series of articles in which the economic benefits of warehouses were once again emphasized, while existing fears and reservations—for instance, that such warehouses would damage the established local grain trade and thus further exacerbate economic hardship—were revealed as unfounded.[68] The envisaged warehouses, its proponents insisted, did not constitute 'a revolutionary invention,' but merely the modern adaptation of an age-old institution.[69] The warehouses were described as timely instru-ments, to be used to promote and enliven Ulm's trade to the point where it could regain its place as one of southern Germany's major trading towns.[70] But the municipal authorities would not lend their financial support to the project, let alone take the lead in its realization. It was only in 1888 that things began to move, after the grain merchants Nathan and Steiner had rented an estate near the main station to build warehouses for the storage of 300 wag-ons of grain.[71] By that time, however, Gustav Maier, the driving force behind both the Reichsbank and the warehouse bids, had left Ulm to become the head of the Frankfurt branch of the Reichsbank.[72]

Rather than leave their familiar habitat, the members of Ulm's *Gewerbeverein* continued to foster a different vision of economic development. It was a vision in which Ulm was defined not in terms of a journey, with people moving in and out of town, but in terms of a configuration of status. Its embodiment became the museum for the local crafts, the so-called *Gewerbemuseum*. For the first time in 1878, leading members of the association proposed to found a local museum for trade and industry. The project was a response to the crisis of the local crafts, of the German *Handwerk*, which received so much public attention from the late 1870s. According to the chairman of the *Gewerbeverein*, the furniture manufacturer Foerstler, the museum was to become a forum for exhibiting the products of the local and regional crafts. Its main purpose was 'to raise and cultivate the handicrafts, whose economic basis has been undermined by big industry.' The museum, Foerstler contended, would not only serve the revival of 'German crafts' but also make 'a contribution to the resolution of the social question.'[73]

The idea of a *Gewerbemuseum* quickly attracted the interest from other parties, too. *Dombaumeister* Scheu, acting spokesperson for the bourgeois *Kunst- und Altertumsverein*, asked that the envisaged museum not be restricted to the crafts. Scheu stressed the need for cultural education, or *Bildung*. According to him and fellow lovers of local history and culture, both producers and consumers were lacking in taste and skill. It was thus only through a deeper engagement with the 'works of our forebears' that the contemporary crafts could hope to regain some of the sophistication and artistic skill they had once possessed.[74] Not included in the negotiations over the future use of the museum was the *Handelsverein*. Gustav Maier's suggestion to involve merchants and industrialists in the relevant committee would remain unheeded.[75]

When the renovation of the building for the new museum had been completed in January 1879, the main parties were still at loggerheads over its future mission; and when by the summer the museum had still not opened its doors to the public, several critics of the *Gewerbeverein* began to vent their anger in the form of newspaper articles and readers' letters. Confronted with this unsatisfactory situation, the municipal council, in conjunction with the *Kunst- und Altertumsverein*, decided to stage an exhibition of historic arts-and-crafts objects. The exhibition also featured a section on foreign industrial

products, including American cast-iron stoves, which the local press immediately praised for their 'elegance and practicality.'[76] Most members of the
Gewerbeverein stayed aloof in protest.[77] At a meeting held shortly after the
exhibition's closure, several members complained that it had 'attracted competitors from Stuttgart.' At that point the association's chairman, furniture
manufacturer Foerstler, intervened, reprimanding members that, unless competition was deemed acceptable, then 'neither provincial, nor regional or
world exhibitions could ever take place.'[78] Foerstler's intervention came after
the *Gewerbeverein's* virtual boycott of the museum's opening exhibition had
cast a negative shadow over his association, with many local newspapers publishing critical reports on the stance of individual members. Speaking for
many, one editorial asked 'why the local *Gewerbeverein*, whose members stand
to benefit most from the exhibition,' had adopted such a 'hostile attitude
towards it.'[79]

When the museum officially opened its doors in December 1882 under
the auspices of the *Gewerbeverein*, its popularity with the public was modest
at best. The museum's membership in the 1880s never exceeded much
beyond 200.[80] The number of annual visitors during the 1880s ranged
between 2500 and 4000, which the association's executive considered disappointing. Exhibitions of works from the locality or region, whether historic
or contemporary, rarely attracted large crowds. The only exception to the
otherwise modest success was an exhibition of Japanese works of art drawn
from a private collection and from the *Zentralstelle für Industrie und Gewerbe*
in Stuttgart. The first exhibition of its kind in Germany, it attracted up to
600 visitors on a single day.[81] The wider public, it seems, were more than
willing to broaden their horizons beyond the confines of their city. On one
occasion the entire staff of the local machine works of Gebrüder Eberhardt
(which numbered more than two-hundred men) attended the exhibition
and stayed on for almost two hours.[82] The vocational school of Geislingen,
led by its art teacher, also seized the opportunity, as did several elementary
schools from Ulm and the wider district.[83]

When the exhibition closed its doors after six weeks and several extensions, 12,000 visitors, half of them from outside Ulm, had attended it, and
a profit of 1000 marks had resulted.[84] Roughly a week before the exhibition closed its doors to the public, the *Ulmer Zeitung* noted that the event,
having brought numerous 'strangers' into town, had proved a boon for
'tourism': 'Not a day passes without a person of distinction viewing the
collection.'[85] Several members of the public described the exhibits on

display in terms of undisguised excitement. The Japanese interior in particular attracted strong interest, with several commentators emphasizing the 'transparency' of a Japanese living room: 'The Japanese don't have to keep secrets from each other.'[86] In Japan, 'artistic taste' was not the 'exclusive preserve of the rich and well-to-do,' but belonged 'to everyone.'[87] But the momentum could not be maintained: by 1890 the average number of visitors was back to normal, and the number of members of the recently created *Museumsverein* had dropped to 162.[88] The museum remained a bastion of Ulm's *Kleingewerbe*, who jealously guarded it from what they perceived as acts of illegitimate interference from those whose economic vision was place-transcending.

A 'German Chicago'

Of the three towns examined here, Ludwigshafen may have been the most difficult to imagine as a well-ordered place, even for its long-term residents. Here, the combination of newness and extraordinary economic dynamism had created an atmosphere of the provisional that was embodied in the urban landscape. As late as 1872, when Ludwigshafen had around 8000 residents, the total length of its roads was only little more than three kilometres. This was not because of the small size of the urban territory. It was because a settlement plan for Ludwigshafen's northern district, home of the *Badische Anylin- und Sodafabrik* (BASF)—the chemical factory that was to become a world leader in the production of dyestuffs, and which by that point employed 800 of the city's 1700 factory workers—was only just coming into being.[89] Much more visibly so than either Ulm or Augsburg, Ludwigshafen constituted work in progress.

Having been established by the Bavarian state as an economic counterweight to prospering Mannheim on the opposite bank of the Rhine,[90] from the 1870s Ludwigshafen had more in common with the heavy-industry towns of the Ruhr valley than with any other city of the German South.[91] Initially, however, regional and supra-regional trade had dominated the local economy. Thus, in 1853, the year of its founding as an independent municipality, a state official noted its significant potential as a trading town: 'Where we used to see a dinghy go ashore perhaps once in a fortnight, we are now receiving... 1,500 ships every year.'[92] Yet while trade remained important, two decades later the science-driven chemical factories took over from the merchants, shipping companies and hauliers as the engine of Ludwigshafen's economy (although the former continued to thrive under these conditions).

In 1853, Ludwigshafen had little more than 1500 inhabitants. When in 1859 it was awarded the status of a municipality or *Stadt*, that figure had risen to almost 3000, with an economy still centred on crafts and various kinds of trade. Of 299 heads of household in 1852, 142 were craftsmen, 40 were engaged in trade of some kind, 36 were day labourers and office clerks, 58 railway employees, seven academics and directors, 14 peasants, and two were without profession.[93] Yet by the time of its fiftieth anniversary, in 1903, Ludwigshafen's population had reached 71,500, reflecting a staggering annual average increase of five per cent. Admittedly, the town's exceptional expansion owed much to the incorporation of the two neighbouring towns of Friesenheim and Mundenheim in 1892 and 1897, respectively. Yet these incorporations did not occur by chance. They were part of the economic conquests of a sprawling industrial city. The result was not lost on its inhabitants or on those who had been among its regular visitors. Within the space of half a century, Ludwigshafen had been transformed from a small town, a true *Kleinstadt*, into Bavaria's fifth largest city behind Munich, Nuremberg, Augsburg, and Würzburg. Thanks to its large industrial sector, it had also become one of the most significant contributors to the state's revenue from communal taxation.[94]

The at times antagonistic rhetoric notwithstanding, the proximity to Mannheim appears overall to have acted as a stimulus rather than a hindrance. Not only did it serve as a foil for comparing Ludwigshafen's accomplishments and status as a regional economic centre. There were also important synergies. Ludwigshafen's two large roller mills and grain refineries (the *Ludwigshafener Walzmühle* and *Kaufmann, Strauss & Co.*), for example, would not have been established had it not been for the proximity of Mannheim's grain market. The same holds true for its numerous large beer breweries.[95] While leading steam and ship engine producers such as the Swiss company Sulzer sold their products worldwide, they nevertheless benefited from the considerable demand in machinery and spare parts generated by Mannheim's metal-working companies.

If Ludwigshafen grew faster than almost any other German town during the second Empire (outpaced only by a few mining communities in the Ruhr), this was because it developed into one of the centres of Germany's chemical industry.[96] In 1900, the large chemical corporations, along with companies specializing in metal manufacturing and machinery, accounted for close to 40 per cent of the town's working population. These dominant branches were followed by trade and communications (20 per cent), building and construction (roughly ten per cent), textile and cleaning (seven to eight per cent); with four per cent each, foodstuffs, public administration and the wood trades were other economic sectors of some importance. In 1893 the proportion of factory workers, self-employed and employed/civil servants was respectively 33, 32, and 16 per cent in the more established, southern district, and 71, 7, and 10 per cent in the *Hemshof*, the town's heavily industrial northern part. The soon-to-be incorporated towns of Friesenheim to the North and Mundenheim to the South of Ludwigshafen were also (certainly at the point of their *Eingemeindung*) overwhelmingly working-class.[97]

In spite of the quantitative predominance of chemical companies such as the BASF, the Swiss engineering firm Gebrüder Sulzer, the service works for the regional railway company, or the building and construction company Josef Hoffmann & Söhne, however, trade remained important, particularly in foodstuffs, iron, coal, and wood. Nor could an industrial town of Ludwigshafen's size have functioned without a sizeable small trade and crafts sector. Thus, in 1900, the city featured 380 restaurants, wine and beer halls; 141 shoemakers; 119 seamstresses; 110 bakers; 102 tailors; 87 butchers, and 67 cabinetmakers.[98] But in terms of financial turnover and tax revenue, the small-business sector was dwarfed by the big factories, large building firms and significant trading establishments.

When it comes to understanding Ludwigshafen's evolving identity as an urban community, three things prove crucial: the merchants arrived first on the scene; they were soon accompanied by exponents of big industry; both saw Ludwigshafen above all as an economic project. The committee that from the 1850s began to lobby for Ludwigshafen's establishment as an independent municipality was dominated by merchants, hauliers, and building entrepreneurs. While the committee itself comprised a state-civil-servant-turned-entrepreneur (Oekonomierat Hoech), a merchant (Handelsmann Lichtenberger), a farmer (Landwirt Frank), a haulier (Spediteur Huss), and a brewer (Bierbrauer Deutsch), the list of local businesses it submitted as part of its bid to the Bavarian state included 20 trading companies. Of the 55 other businesses on the list, 13 belonged to the building trade, and five each were either tailors or shoemakers; there were also two bakers, two butchers, a brewer, and a bookbinder. And when in 1853 the first city council was elected, its 18 members included eight traders and six artisans, two lottery agents, and one innkeeper. The merchant Lichtenberger became the city's first mayor.[99]

At the very root of Ludwigshafen's expansion was its ideal location at the intersection of the Rhine and the Palatinate railway lines. While there were other towns on the left bank of the Rhine that benefited from these conditions, in the second half of the nineteenth century none assumed greater importance as a storage and distribution centre (especially for coal from the Ruhr valley and from the Saar, and for grain from Germany and abroad) than Ludwigshafen. In 1867, when the rail- and road-bridge to Mannheim was finally completed, Ludwigshafen had the largest Rhine port in the German West next to Cologne and Mannheim. In 1870, when four private railway lines joined forces, the newly established *Pfälzische Eisenbahnen* established its headquarters in Ludwigshafen, which further improved the links between the urban economy and the evolving system of transportation.[100] The latter company also invested heavily in the expansion of Ludwigshafen's harbour, and the marshalling yard it built close to Mundenheim comprised more than 48 kilometres of track.[101]

Postal and financial services were evolving at a similar pace. In 1853 Ludwigshafen received its first postal office, in 1854 its first telegraph, and by 1866 it had become the centre of telegraphic exchange in the Palatinate. Bavaria's first telephone system was installed in Ludwigshafen on the initiative of its leading entrepreneurs. It took up its service on 1 December 1882 with 13 subscribers, mainly companies with several hundred employees, and by 1902 the number of telephone connections had risen to 780.[102] Ludwigshafen's financial sector took off in 1852 with the establishment of a branch of the *Königlich Bayerische Bank Nürnberg*, which until 1876 would remain the town's major financial institute, reaching an annual turnover of close to 100 million marks. In 1883 the *Pfälzische Bank* (founded in 1867) was transformed into a joint-stock company. A universal bank, it would soon become one of the more important financial institutes in the German South, reaching an annual turnover of 7 billion marks by 1899. Finally, from the 1870s several important regional banks set up branches in Ludwigshafen, including the *Süddeutsche Bodenkreditbank* (1872), the *Bayerische Notenbank* (1875), and the *Pfälzische Hypothekenbank* (1886). A subsidiary of the *Reichsbank* was established in Ludwigshafen in 1876, to be upgraded to a *Reichsbankstelle* in 1905. Ludwigshafen also featured 23 insurance companies of various size and importance in 1871, rising to 73 by 1913.[103]

Even more consequential for people's sense of place was the creation of the BASF. The company was founded on 6 April 1865 in Mannheim by Friedrich Engelhorn. Engelhorn's gasworks, which he had been running for the city of Mannheim since 1861, produced tar as a byproduct, which the entrepreneur began to use to produce dyes. Soon thereafter, he decided to establish a factory specializing in the production of soda and acids needed for the production of dyestuffs, including indigo. On the afternoon of 12 April, just hours after Mannheim's town council (out of concerns that the planned factory might cause an unacceptable degree of air pollution) had rejected his plan to create his factory on the soil of his native city, Engelhart crossed the Rhine to enter into negotiations with local farmers. After he had reached an agreement, on 21 April Ludwigshafen's council endorsed his plan, and in June 1867 the production could begin. As the town history published on the occasion of Ludwigshafen's 50th anniversary proudly stated: 'Even though the company was founded in Mannheim and thus carries the word *Badische* in its name, its entire production takes place on Bavarian soil, in the town of Ludwigshafen, which is also the seat of its headquarters.'[104]

The BASF transformed Ludwigshafen's fate forever. In 1870, when its population was still well under 10,000, roughly half of its 1670 factory workers were employed by the town's largest corporation; by 1903 its workforce was made up of 7300 skilled and unskilled workers, 190 chemists, 90 engineers and technicians, and 502 office and administrative staff.[105] While its impact on the town's economic and demographic makeup can hardly be overestimated, the BASF affected urban life in much more encompassing a sense. Directly or indirectly, its presence shaped Ludwigshafen's cultural life, urban politics and social-welfare institutions almost as much as it affected the quality of its air and water, or its total tax revenue. Whether as a source of pride or as an abhorrent example: the BASF served as a point of reference, a source of self-definition even, for thousands of urban inhabitants. It became Ludwigshafen's economic dynamo, most powerful organization, and main provider of housing for the factory workers and their families. The town's largest construction company, Josef Hoffmann & Söhne, for example, which at the height of the boom around 1900 employed more than 1000 workers, owed its expansion to the BASF. Its chimneys and factory buildings, along with the dozens of ships that frequented its docks on a daily basis, left an indelible imprint on the city's visual landscape, just as the sounds and smells they released defined its atmosphere.[106]

Figure 3. BASF production plant, with adjacent workers' housing estates, circa 1900. © Stadtarchiv Ludwigshafen am Rhein.

Industries of this size generate a constant flow of people. Ludwigshafen's demographic fluctuation, measured by the percentage of those settling in and leaving within a single year, was among the highest in the German Empire. Consistently over 40 per cent during the entire imperial period, it reached 60 per cent during boom years.[107] To some extent, this high fluctuation was the result of seasonal migration from the rural parts of the Palatinate, as well as from neighbouring Baden, Hessen, and Württemberg. Workers from rural areas tended to leave Ludwigshafen in the spring and summer months, when those employed in the building trade returned there and stayed on until late in the autumn.[108] Much more important, however, was the extraordinarily high turnover typical of the chemical industry. Thus, in 1900, only about one out of ten employees hired by the BASF during the year would still work for the company by the end of the year.[109] Only five per cent of working migrants that found a living in the city between 1890 to 1894 chose Ludwigshafen as their permanent place of residence; and, as late as 1910, only a quarter of those getting married in the city were also born there, while nearly 60 per cent hailed from other municipalities of the Palatinate.[110]

The chemical industry discriminated in favour of young males: in 1900, the under-30-year-olds made up around 68 per cent of the town's male population. Most of these young, working-class men lived in the *Hemshof*, the town's northern suburb in close proximity to the production plants of the BASF.[111] This bias in favour of the young resulted in an extraordinary employment rate of close to forty per cent.[112] Women (who in the machinery industries and the construction trade constituted a tiny minority) and people over 60 played a less prominent part in Ludwigshafen's urban landscape than they did in either Ulm or Augsburg. As the writer Adam Ritzhaupt tried to capture this atmosphere of youthful restlessness in his characteristically evocative style (his implicit point of comparison, one has to assume, was the kind of bourgeois culture on display in some of the older towns nearby, including Speyer or Mannheim):

> There were hardly any old people living here. But there were more children born here per thousand than in other towns per three thousand. The contrast with one of the slow-paced cities inhabited by pensioners could not have been more stark. Where are all the quiet alleys inhabited by old spinsters, retired *Landräte* and majors? The town of youth makes no allowances for the pleasantries of old age. There are no facilities and promenades for old folks here. No *Kaffeekränzchen* are being held here, and there are no quiet corners and gardens where one could repose after a day's work. Everything is new. Everything is young—the houses, the families.[113]

This image of the tentative—of the always-in-the-making—was reflected in Ludwigshafen's townscape. It took until 1885, for example, for the city council to name the town's 59 streets and sideways, replacing the Napoleonic quadrature system that was common in parts of the Palatinate and Baden. Of those, 29 were defined by stating their location in relation to existing streets and buildings, while more than ten street names were issued in advance, to be used when needed.[114] The leading entrepreneurs and their supporters on the town council, too, liked to locate Ludwigshafen's virtues in its capacity for change and expansion. Many saw it as the embodiment of Germany's dynamic potentials, as an entity that pointed beyond the confines of the present and towards an even more powerful future. As this vision was formulated, in a special report on the town's working-class district at the city's northern periphery, that appeared in the liberal *Pfälzischer Kurier* in 1889: 'The Hemshof, this factory town par excellence, is the seat of Ludwigshafen's big industry, a piece of America as is hardly to be found anywhere else on German soil, one of the capitals of modern paint industry.

The Hemshof is Germany's Chromopolis.'[115] In the same report, the BASF was described as the 'brightest star within the galaxy of Ludwigshafen's big industry,' 'the queen of the industrial towns of the Palatinate,' 'the dyeing capital of Germany.'[116]

How did this powerful self-description affect those who, in more than one sense, did not belong to this world? Was there a place for the *Kleingewerbe* in a town of this kind, for the crafts and small trade whose members played such an important role in Ulm? Could a city founded on movement and competition accommodate those who defined themselves in terms of position and place? Did they have a voice and, in case they did, how did they fare in the contest over the city's self-definition? What about the place of the crafts in the city's pecking order?

If the recollections of the artisan Georg Kuhn are anything to go by, there was little of that to be found in early Ludwigshafen.[117] There was, he tells us, no crafts sector to speak of in 1853. Kuhn even doubted whether a *Handwerkerstand* (which is the term Kuhn uses in his memoirs, a term that evokes a corporatist identity) existed when Ludwigshafen was officially

Figure 4. Workers posing for a photo shoot at the BASF's main gate. 1895.
© Stadtarchiv Ludwigshafen am Rhein.

declared a town in 1859, at which point its economy consisted mainly of companies engaged in the Rhine trade. A collective spirit—*Gemeinschaftsgedanke* is the word Kuhn employs—among Ludwigshafen's crafts had only emerged in the course of the 1870s, when the chemical factories and machine works began to dominate the urban landscape. Its first manifestation was the establishment of the *Gewerbeverein Ludwigshafen* in 1872. Yet this association was unusual for its kind. Its pillars were not the established craftsmen, small traders, and innkeepers, as was the case in towns such as Ulm. According to Kuhn, the early membership of Ludwigshafen's small-trade association had included 'artisans, tradesmen, factory owners, civil servants, etc.' Its activities had been 'neutral,' rather than geared 'towards representing the interests of its members.' A library had been established from the outset; 'visits to industrial plants and other objects of interest' formed an integral part of the association's menu of activities. This was complemented by discussions surrounding proposed legislative reforms and other 'measures and projects relating to town and state.' Not until the late 1880s had this standard programme been complemented by debates focusing 'on questions of specific concern to the crafts.'[118]

Even though he downplays the size of the crafts sector in early Ludwigshafen, Kuhn offers an intriguing explanation of why a corporatist identity took so long to germinate among the members of Ludwigshafen's local crafts and small trade. The chief reason, he asserted, was that they could not rely on a shared sense of place. The absence of local roots among those who worked in this sector proved a serious obstacle to their ability to define themselves as a professional estate, or *Stand*. Unlike in older towns, where the local population served as the recruiting ground for the *Kleingewerbe* including the *Handwerk*, Ludwigshafen's artisans and craftsmen in particular had been comprised of 'young elements' who originated 'from all over the world.'[119] Of course, the latter assertion represents a massive exaggeration, as the bulk of Ludwigshafen's population consisted of short-distant migrants; the majority hailed from the Palatinate, followed by Bavaria, Baden, and Württemberg, with a small minority originating from Prussia, and an even smaller contingent consisting of non-Germans. But this does not really invalidate the core of Kuhn's interpretation. As a former *Handwerker* himself, Kuhn knew a thing or two about the culture of the crafts, so his insistence on the centrality of a sense of place for the emergence of a corporatist identity should be taken seriously.

Kuhn does not mention another, perhaps even more important, reason: the bulk of Ludwigshafen's artisans and craftsmen, certainly from the 1870s, were not self-employed entrepreneurs working individually or heading a small workshop, as was common in more established towns. They were part of that industrial workforce that gave the local economy its distinctive flavour. In the late 1880s, for example, the BASF alone employed more than 900 workers with a background in the building trade. This workforce consisted of dozens of bricklayers, locksmiths, blacksmiths, turners, carpenters, electricians, and coopers, to name just the most important professions.[120] The majority of them had been socialized not during the era when the guilds were still operating in many towns, but under a more recent regime, one that was geared towards exchangeable skills in a fast-changing economic environment. The majority of Ludwigshafen's craftsmen were employees; only a few were master craftsmen.

The pre-eminence of factory industry notwithstanding, Ludwigshafen did possess an independent crafts sector; and the same holds true for small trade.[121] Particularly in the town's southern district, about a third of the working population were self-employed, and even if slightly less than half of these belonged to the *Kleingewerbe*, this was still a respectable figure. Even if the number of those running small- and medium-sized businesses was comparatively small compared with other cities, that does not mean that they had been reluctant to make their voices heard. The decisive question, however, is how much resonance they found. An examination of the debate over license restrictions for inns—flaring up in 1885 and 1886, it featured as its protagonists the city council, the association of inn keepers, the district government and the government of the Palatinate—throws some light on this question. It demonstrates that initiatives to prevent the proliferation of inns through protectionist measures stood little chance in a town where the ambitions of influential groups translated into a continual reconfiguration of existing spatial arrangements.

At a meeting on 20 April 1885, the city council decided to abolish the charter regulating the licensing of inns, the so-called *Ortsstatut über den Wirtschaftsbetrieb*, which had been in place since 1881.[122] This charter had made the issuing of new licenses for inns subject to a means test, to be administered by a committee composed of the city's existing innkeepers.[123] Yet, as the town council was keen to point out, this particular mechanism had served the interests of Ludwigshafen's innkeepers much better than those of its wider population. The council's decision triggered fierce protests from the association of local innkeepers, whose stance found the support, at least initially, of the district authorities in Speyer. Just a week after the town council had announced its unwillingness to shield any section of the urban economy from the icy wind of competition, the district government declared its ruling invalid. Its justification was that decisions of this kind required the consent of a municipal assembly, a so-called *Gemeindeversammlung*. The council was asked to consult with the local innkeepers to settle the remaining disagreements. It took the mayoral office four weeks to comply with this directive, a clear indication of the dismay it must have felt at the district authorities' annulment of a municipal decision.[124]

Encouraged by this seemingly favourable turn of events, the *Wirteverein* replied to the mayor's invitation within a matter of days. In their letter, the innkeepers defended the *Orsstatut* by invoking a time when many local inns had been 'in the hands of scoundrels and deadbeats,' people who had sometimes been 'unable to pay their gas bills, let alone their taxes.' Innkeepers of this sort had been 'so dependent on their guests that they were unable to take action when the latter conducted themselves in a reprehensible and immoral way.' As the licensed innkeepers were keen to stress, however, what had prompted them to oppose the abolition of the existing charter was by no means fear of increased competition, as some council members had implied. Mixing the language of corporatism with expressions of local civic pride, they reassured the council that what had really swung them into action was the damage the envisaged reforms were bound to cause to 'the honour' of both their trade and the municipality at large.[125]

Yet the innkeepers' plea had no effect on the outcome of the ballot taking place on 18 October. At the beginning of the specially called *Gemeindeversammlung*, which was chaired by Mayor Kutterer, the 161 citizens in attendance (amounting to about a third of Ludwigshafen's then 509 citizens with full voting rights) agreed to carry out an oral vote. Of the 161 citizens taking part in the ballot, 156 voted in favour and five against ditching the existing charter on the licensing of inns.[126]

While we do not know who voted for and who voted against the abolition, the records offer detailed information on the professions that were represented at the meeting preceding the ballot. The list includes ten factory overseers; 13 innkeepers/brewers; four grocers; two pensioners; 15 teachers; one boat owner; 58 artisans; four members of the food trade; ten civil servants; one office clerk; 38 tradesmen; six railway or factory workers; and two factory owners. What appears to have prompted the near-unanimous vote in favour of reform was the belief that *Gewerbefreiheit* was indivisible. Many of those who voted may well have harboured reservations about the virtues

of economic liberalism. Yet this did not, it seems, change their view that it
would constitute a gross injustice if certain sections of the urban economy
were to be exempt from its effects. This at least is how Mayor Kutterer, in
his response to the district government, summed up the deliberations that
preceded the vote. Several citizens had argued that the *Ortsstatut* had created
'a monopoly for one local trade'; and since this went 'against the intentions
of the freedom of trade,' it needed to be abolished in the interest of having
a level-playing field for all members of Ludwigshafen's economy.[127]

The mayor also stressed the negative repercussions of protectionism for
house prices. Restrictions on granting licenses for inns had led to 'a rapid
rise in the value of commercial buildings,' which he described as an 'outra-
geous injustice.' Furthermore, in a letter he sent to the district government
on 25 October, Kutterer maintained that the licensing restrictions for inns
had been used by 'external breweries' that owned 'a large number of
Ludwigshafen's inns.' What was even more important was that these restrictions had prohibited the increase of the number of inns in line with the
growth of the population. There were now 21 inns in a town of 21,000
inhabitants, roughly the number that had been in operation before the
Ortsstatut had been introduced in 1881. Particularly in and around the
Hemshof, the town's working-class district on the city's northern edge
(whose population, Kutterer noted, had 'increased by 4000' since the introduction of the restriction), 'not a single new inn had been approved.'[128]

The question of adequate provision for a fast-growing population again
moved to the centre of the debate when, on 13 November 1885, the district
government in Speyer refused to accept the municipal assembly's verdict on
the existing *Orsstatut*.[129] In its appeal a fortnight later, now directed to the
government of the Palatinate, Ludwigshafen's council insisted that the decision of how to regulate the local economy should be left up to the local
authorities concerned: 'For it is the local authorities alone that are in a position to judge whether economic restrictions of this kind are commensurate
with all the relevant conditions at the local level.'[130] Nor did the state government doubt that Ludwigshafen's mayor and council had judged the local
innkeepers' true motives correctly: 'That the concerns expressed by the innkeepers' association spring from sectional material interests cannot be seriously doubted.' The government of the Palatinate thus unreservedly endorsed
the council's decision. It even censured the district government for its
obstructive behaviour: 'When the municipal council, which along with the
municipal assembly is closest to the situation on the ground,... decides

to abolish the existing *Ortsstatut*, then the superior authority has no reason to deny its approval, thereby maintaining a situation which those most affected experience as outmoded and even burdensome.'[131] In 1896, the innkeepers' association made another attempt at subjecting the issuing of licenses to a means test, but to no avail.[132]

Another area of open disagreement between city authorities and local *Gewerbe* concerns the provision of vocational education. At the beginning of the 1880s, Ludwigshafen's council for the first time expressed its intention to establish a secondary school, a so-called *Realschule*. With its broad curriculum, ranging from more specific vocational courses to ones covering broader subjects, it represented the kind of school that the city council thought best suited to meeting the educational needs of upwardly mobile middle classes who played an increasingly central role in the life of the city; of people, that is, who started out as office clerks in the large companies, or as lower civil servants in the municipal and state administrations. Yet, as a secondary school that combined a focus on technical and commercial subjects with a broad focus in the tradition of German *Bildung*, the *Realschule* was not to the taste of the local crafts. In the summer of 1884 the local *Gewerbeverein* approached the city council with a proposal demanding the creation of a different type of school: a *Gewerbeschule*, a vocational school geared to the needs of apprentices in the local crafts and trades.[133]

The *Gewerbeverein* used a series of arguments to justify its request. Above all, the new school had to meet a number of urgent needs: it had to offer a comprehensive 'theoretical and practical education' for members of the crafts, many of whom, the association frankly conceded, displayed serious deficits in this respect; it had to be an instrument against the 'indifference' and 'lethargy' that had become widespread among the *Gewerbe*; it had to fight the decline of moral standards, a problem the petitioners deemed particularly evident in a town dominated by a working class population attracted to socialist ideas; and, lastly, it had to enable the local crafts to catch up with 'other towns, even small ones, both within and without the Palatinate,' some of which had already established similar schools. The last remark was a reference to Mannheim's vocational school, which at the time was attended by 43 apprentices from Ludwigshafen. The costs of the school had to be borne by 'the entire municipality, which stands to benefit most from a *Gewerbeschule*.' For all these reasons, the establishment of a *Gewerbeschule* was not just in the municipal authorities' interest according to the *Gewerbeverein*. It was also to be regarded as both an 'honour' and a 'duty.'[134]

After the municipal council had given no urgency to the matter, the *Gewerbeverein* organized a meeting at which a resolution was agreed and sent to the town council. Its text conveys a sense of the frustration many local craftsmen felt at what they perceived as the persistent neglect of the crafts and small-trade sector by the municipal authorities. While Ludwigshafen's founders had been quick to set up a *Lateinschule* and a *höhere Töchterschule*—higher schools geared mostly towards the better-off segments of urban society, these institutions opened their doors in 1873 and 1875, respectively, the latter on a private basis—they had shown little interest in schools that catered to the needs of the *Gewerbestand*. What the members of the crafts needed, the petitioners maintained, was a school that would deepen the knowledge children had acquired at elementary school. Their preferred option was a vocational institute that pupils would enter at age 13, and which would offer a specific curriculum that could be absorbed within 'a relatively short space of time.' The alternative currently favoured 'in certain circles' (the *Realschule*) was judged as largely irrelevant to apprentices entering the crafts sector. As the petitioners elaborated their thoughts on this matter: 'Even though the knowledge of French or English does not cause anybody any harm, it will be of very limited use to most members of the crafts and small trades.' The same was true of lessons in singing and swimming. Ultimately, they concluded, the *Realschule* represented a 'higher school for the bourgeois classes' (*höhere bürgeriche Schule*). Its graduates were frequently noted for being 'vain and pompous,' with many regarding the learning of a craft as being below their station.[135]

Drawing on an independent report, the town council concluded that the vocational school championed by the *Gewerbeverein* would merely satisfy the needs and interests of a small minority of Ludwigshafen's population. Besides, the *Gewerbeschule* would be just as expensive to run as the proposed *Realschule*, even thought it had little to offer to the 'municipality in its entirety.' The opposite was said to be true of the *Realschule*. Not only did it offer better value for money, but it was also more in tune with the needs of the time: A highly industrialized town such as Ludwigshafen, a city 'where trade and communications' were constantly gaining in importance, had much to benefit from a school that offered a higher education, yet one flexible enough to cater for various tastes and professional paths. 'The still flourishing young town of Ludwigshafen am *Rhein*,' one councillor argued, was 'the commercial hub of the entire Palatinate.' There was no doubt, the council concluded, that a *Realschule* (which in its Bavarian form would include a sub-section designed for vocational training) was preferable to a vocational school with a rather narrow curriculum. The city's representatives later endorsed this position in a unanimous vote, and the new school would open its doors in 1886.[136] Once again, an institution had won out that appeared commensurate with the predominant self-image of a city as work in progress, as a project rather than a place.

A petition by the local *Bäcker-Innung* (founded in 1879) offers an apt example to round off this section on Ludwigshafen. The *Innungen* that proliferated all over Germany in the last third of the nineteenth century were an attempt to revive guild-style corporatism in the context of economic liberalism. From the late 1870s onwards, these organizations gained in both influence and public recognition in many parts of Germany.[137] In its original statutes (deemed invalid on formal grounds by the district authorities), the *Bäcker-Innung* restricted membership to 'master craftsmen who had passed through a regular apprenticeship'; members also had to be resident in Ludwigshafen or its immediate vicinity. These restrictive regulations were in clear violation of imperial trade legislation, as the *Reichsgewerbeordnung* determined that any crafts association had to take new members irrespective of whether they were masters.[138]

While imperial law forced the bakers association to become less exclusive, this was not to the taste of its leading members. In 1887, they sent a petition to the district government in Speyer. The petitioners demanded that the permission to train apprentices be delimited to masters who were also members of the association, as this was 'in the interest of both the apprentices and the trade as a whole.' Since not all master bakers were members of the association, the right to train young would-be-bakers had to be restricted; and, as far as Ludwigshafen's *Bäcker-Innung* was concerned, the only way to do so was by introducing guild-like regulations.[139]

The mayoral office turned down the bakers' request at once. They did so in spite of the fact that only five of the town's master bakers (most of them recent arrivals who had brought their own apprentices) did not belong to the association. The mayor justified the council's unanimous decision by pointing to the city's exceptional needs. Few things were more vital, the mayor asserted, than the population's daily provision with decent and affordable bread. The high demographic fluctuation Ludwigshafen was experiencing meant that introducing the restrictions the bakers were demanding would be 'both harsh and unjust.' Why should a master baker who had recently set up his business in Ludwigshafen be forced to join the *Innung?*

Why should he be prohibited from training apprentices if he did not wish to become a member of a professional corporation?[140]

This time the district government endorsed the municipal authorities' position without further ado. In its letter to the state government, the official in charge noted that Ludwigshafen's *Bäcker-Innung* was a very recent creation. Having adopted statutes in accordance with existing imperial law only in 1885, the *Innung* had still a lot to prove when it came to training apprentices.[141] The district authorities' final comment caught the special attention of the government of the Palatinate, who decided to commission a detailed report on the association's previous performance in training future bakers. The report was to include the number of apprentices supervised by the association's master bakers; and it was to provide information on whether the apprentices in question would 'regularly and assiduously attend the classes of the *Realschule*.'[142]

The final report must have made humbling reading to the bakers' association. For a start, it concluded that only three of its master bakers (including the association's chairman) were in the business of training apprentices; and that each of them was merely responsible for a single apprentice. Of the three apprentices Ludwigshafen's *Bäcker-Innung* had recently taken under its wings, two (including the one supervised by the chairman) did not attend the vocational school at all; the third attended it 'without much enthusiasm,' and his knowledge was deemed 'very modest at best.'[143] In its response to the report, the government of the Palatinate noted bluntly, that an association that played such a marginal role in the recruitment and training of its professional offspring, and whose members did not even urge their apprentices to attend the recently established *Realschule*, ought to refrain from making demands in the first place.[144] The 1887 petition by Ludwigshafen's *Bäcker-Innung* represented something of a last stand by those who envisioned their town as a well-ordered place.

A 'comforting example' of a modern factory town

To an even greater extent than Ludwigshafen, whose contours were hammered out in the maelstrom of industrial production, Augsburg's urban landscape was physically divided: into an industrial belt that had developed since the 1830s, on the one hand, and a central-city area inhabited mostly by artisans, small traders and representatives of the service sector, on the other. Thus, the fortress walls that had been removed during the 1860s were replaced by a socio-economic boundary separating the bourgeoisie and established middle classes from the growing industrial working class. Substantial working-class areas had developed on Augsburg's northwestern periphery. Large contingents of workers lived in the surrounding municipalities, particularly Lechhausen, Oberhausen, Pfersee, Göggingen, Kriegshaber, Hochzoll, Friedberg, etc. Between 1855 and 1905, the populations of Lechhausen, Oberhausen, and Pfersee increased by 389.9, 327.7, and 823.7 per cent respectively, levels of demographic growth that would have been inconceivable without their proximity to Augsburg's industrial periphery. In 1910, Oberhausen, Siebenbrunn, and Pfersee were incorporated into Augsburg.[145]

Insofar as Augsburg's economy constituted work in progress, then, the visible construction work took place mostly outside the city's traditional core. In 1880, roughly 50 per cent of Augsburg's factory workers lived outside the former fortress walls, a figure that further increased in the decades preceding the First World War. At the same time, the last third of the nineteenth century saw an expansion of the traditional city centre into new, fashionable districts in the West and South. The bourgeois strata—entrepreneurs, privateers, and well-to-do pensioners, civil servants, and members of the free professions, the few remaining affluent craftsmen, tradesmen, and merchants, as well as skilled members of the town's industrial workforce—lived in the four districts B, C, and D. With its representative buildings and streets, moreover, the West End emerged as the preferred choice of Augsburg's industrial bourgeoisie. To simplify a complex process: While in Ludwigshafen industry prevailed vis-à-vis the crafts and in Ulm the *Gewerbe* managed to keep the merchants and industrialists in check (at least until the turn of the century), in Augsburg industrial workers and the city's middle and bourgeois strata were physically segregated without any sustained attempt at fusing them into a common civic community.

Yet if Augsburg's urban landscape was segregated geographically along lines of class and professional status, its population was relatively homogenous in terms of its regional origins (though less so with regard to denomination, where industrialization worked to accentuate Catholic predominance from 60 per cent in the 1840s to 70 per cent in 1905). The large majority of its migrants hailed from Bavaria, with over 30 per cent originating from the district of *Schwaben & Neuburg*, of which Augsburg was the administrative and economic centre.[146] Most of the long-distance migrants—amounting to approximately 18 per cent in 1871, 20.5 per cent in 1885, and 19.1 per cent in 1900—originated from neighbouring Württemberg and northern Bavaria, while migrants from Germany's middle and northern regions formed a small minority; foreign nationals were even rarer.[147] In spite of this, however, the combination of low fertility and high mortality rates meant that the native population was relatively small in Augsburg, ranging between 35 and 40 per cent between 1871 and 1907. Furthermore, a relatively large proportion of the native-born population left Augsburg in search for employment elsewhere. The low-wage-paying textile sector in particular was not attractive to those who had to support large families.[148]

Not unusual for a city with a dominant textile industry, women dominated Augsburg's population, particularly among the relatively large group of domestic servants, which in 1900 included over 3000 people. The preponderance of women was particularly marked among short-distance-migrants, as well as among the still very respectable contingent of migrants from Württemberg. Between 1885 and 1907 the percentage of women in selected branches of the urban economy developed as follows: from 29.9 to 27.4 in industry and crafts; from 25.6 to 35.6 in trade and communications; from 42.5 to 84.5 in the domestic service and related areas; and from nine to twenty in the public service and free professions. In 1885, most women worked in industry and crafts (namely 69.8 per cent of all women employed), 16.8 in trade and communications, 7.5 in the public service and the free professions, and 5.3 in the domestic services. By 1907 the figures for these branches would be 56.9, 26.0, 9.2, and 6.3 per cent, respectively. Women made for more than a quarter of Augsburg's total working population in 1885, and by 1907 their share would increase to around 30 per cent, which was more than ten per cent higher than the average for the German Empire.[149]

Augsburg's economy combined the tendencies present in Ulm and Ludwigshafen. Like Ulm, it retained a significant crafts and small-trade sector throughout the nineteenth century. Thus, in 1861, when it possessed a population of about 45,000, Augsburg featured just over 1000 independent master craftsmen and about 2200 journeymen, which at that point amounted to roughly 20 per cent of its working population.[150] At the same time—and here it was much more akin to Ludwigshafen than to Ulm—a large part of its residents worked in factories, particularly in the textile and machine-works companies located along the town's northern and eastern peripheries. In the mid-1880s, roughly a quarter of Augsburg's working population was employed in either metalworking (3.9 per cent), machinery (5.7 per cent), or textile manufacturing (15.1 per cent). Other important economic sectors included trade, insurance and communications (15.4 per cent), the civil service and free professions (13.8 per cent), clothing and cleaning (9.6 per cent), foodstuffs (5.2 per cent), and building and construction (15.4 per cent). In terms of the population growth rates it achieved during the second half of the nineteenth century, Augsburg is more comparable to Ulm than to Ludwigshafen. If we take the period between 1861 and 1895 as our benchmark, for example, Augsburg's population grew by less than 100 per cent (while Ludwigshafen's grew more than ten-fold): from 45,389 to 81,896.[151]

Augsburg was particularly successful during the early phase of industrialization, when textile was the leading sector. Its largest factories, situated along the rivers *Lech* and *Wertach*, were almost exclusively engaged in cotton weaving for the domestic market. The *Spinnerei am Stadtbach* (founded in 1853) was the largest weaving factory within the German Zollverein.[152] The first machine works were founded in the 1840s and 1850s. Producing mostly turbines and steam engines, they played a significant role as suppliers of Augsburg's textile industry. Of particular importance was the *Maschinenfabrik Augsburg*, which employed more than half of all workers occupied in machine manufacturing. In 1873 the MA—in 1898, when it fused with a company from Nuremberg, the acronym was changed to MAN, which stands for *Maschinenfabrik Augsburg-Nürnberg*—produced Germany's first rotation printing press. The company would later play a leading role in the manufacturing of ice machines and diesel motors.[153] Another large machine works, *L.A. Riedinger*, specialized in the manufacturing of gas appliances, cast-bronze parts, as well as appliances for refrigeration and for breweries.[154]

In some sectors of Augsburg's economy, large companies with a minimal workforce of 50 were the norm. In 1895 this applied to the overwhelming majority of employees of the town's textile industry. In the mid-1870s the list of Bavaria's 30 largest companies (firms with over 500 employees) included five of Augsburg's spinning and weaving mills.[155] Of Augsburg's total working population in 1895, 28.1 per cent were employed in small (10 employees or fewer), 23.3 in medium (fewer than 50 employees) and 48.6 in large companies. The trend towards large companies was aided by the proliferation of joint-stock-companies, of which there were three in 1850, eight in 1860, 12 in 1873, 34 in 1890, and 38 in 1900.[156] This also accounts for the comparatively low level of self-employment so typical of more traditional urban

economies based on crafts and various forms of small trade. In 1871, 27.3 per
cent of those working in the industry or crafts sectors were self-employed,
which was higher than in Ludwigshafen but considerably lower than in Ulm.
With 59.9 per cent, the rate of self-employment was even higher in trade and
communications, where smaller companies were the norm.[157]

Augsburg's overall industrial and demographic development was steady,
rather than spectacular. Thus, if we compare the growth of Augsburg's industry and crafts sector with that of Munich, Nuremberg, Würzburg and Fürth
for the period from 1882 to 1907, we note that only Würzburg's grew more
slowly. While in Augsburg the number of people occupied in these sectors
doubled during this period, it tripled in both Munich and Fürth and almost
quadrupled in Nuremberg.[158] The increase in the five towns' populations
between 1852 and 1890 reveals a similar trend: the respective figures are 92
per cent for Augsburg, 104 per cent for Würzburg, 158 per cent for Fürth,
219 per cent for Munich, and 266 per cent for Nuremberg.[159] To be sure,
by 1890 Augsburg was still one of Bavaria's largest and most industrialized
towns. For some of Augsburg's liberal reformers, however, their city's
demographic and economic development left much to be desired.
Nuremberg in particular emerged as a source of considerable envy. While
its population grew by over 600 per cent between 1840 and 1910, Augsburg's
increased by a 'mere' 178 per cent. In part, this was because Augsburg's
leading and most labour-intensive industrial sector, textile manufacturing,
was not growing as fast as some of the new industrial sectors (machinery,
as well as electrical and chemical manufacturing) that had become predominant elsewhere.[160]

Yet while many urban liberals saw much room for improvement, some
were clearly intrigued by what they saw as Augsburg's journey through
the industrial era. The pattern of modernization it appeared to exemplify
certainly fascinated Wilhelm H. Riehl, who had spent part of his life
in Augsburg. For what Riehl had observed approvingly in the early
1850s—namely, the spatial separation between industrial and historic city,
between an order whose dominating feature was movement and one that
was defined more in terms of position and status—still held true in important ways at the century's end:

> There is something peculiar about Augsburg, the modern factory town, in
> that it is for the most part not located in the city but at its gates. This explains
> why [the factories] have so far not affected the town's physiognomy in any
> negative fashion. Outside the town's gates we have seen the emergence of

mammoth factory plants, while within it hardly more than a handful of new buildings have been raised. This explains why only a small portion of the army of factory workers has their domicile in the town... Indeed, Augsburg seems to embody the comforting example of a transition from old manufacturing to modern factory production, aided by an environment blessed by both history and nature.[161]

No doubt Riehl liked what he saw. A shrewd observer with an unabashedly romantic bent, he took solace from the fact that here at last seemed to exist an old city that had managed to keep the ugly face of industrialization at bay. Here was, Riehl seemed to say, an ideal fusion of old and new. Here at last was proof that the modern hometown was more than just a dream.

Yet the picture that Riehl was painting was the product of a good amount of wishful thinking. For in Augsburg, too, the tensions became marked, from the 1860s onwards, between liberals who wished to reconfigure urban space under the banner of modern reform, and those who opposed their endeavours. However, what remains remarkable is that this conflict did not manifest itself primarily in the economic field. Instead, in Augsburg the struggle over urban space was much more visible in other areas. These included public culture (exemplified, for instance, in the controversy over the *Stadttheater*), elementary education (with non-denominational schools becoming a bone of contention), as well as public hygiene (where the city's high mortality rates threatened liberal expectations). So Riehl may have had a point after all, insofar as the division of the city's economic space appears to have alleviated some of the inevitable tension between the champions of functional space and those who defended the city as a place that, while by no means static, was to change in a more controlled fashion.

On closer inspection, however, a similar conflict can be detected in Augsburg too. For, while the quasi-segregation of the city into separate socio-economic communities may have alleviated some of the tensions arising elsewhere, it created problems of a different kind. Above all, the fact that the districts on the city's outskirts were not included in the urban community proved a source of protracted acrimony and friction. When the inhabitants of the industrial districts looked to historic Augsburg, they experienced a contrast that reinforced their feelings of being second-class residents. The provisional state that characterized the infrastructure in the industrial periphery confirmed this perception on a daily basis. Many of the streets connecting the districts both internally and within the rest of the city did not carry proper names, but merely numbers or basic descriptors such as *erste Querstrasse* or *zweite Querstrasse*. Whereas in Ludwigshafen the provisional appearance of the urban landscape could serve as a cause for positive self-descriptions, this was much less the case in an established city like Augsburg. Here the tentative and unfinished was more likely to be read as a sign of exclusion.

As late as 1880, the suburbs left and right of the river *Wertach* did not have a single doctor among its residents, with mortality rates, particularly among children, being particularly high there.[162] Other items appearing on residents' lists of complaints included the unpaved roads, which during periods of bad weather metamorphosed into a virtually uninhabitable wasteland, a state which some residents saw as symbolic of the 'discrimination of the inhabitants of the *Wertach-Vorstädte*.'[163] As one member summed up his frustration: 'they have better roads in Turkey than we do here!'[164] Another source of grievances consisted in the worn-out desks that furnished the classrooms of their schools, shipped over from the city-centre schools as soon as their guardians deemed them unfit for purpose.[165] In the early 1880s, furthermore, the *Bürgerverein der Wertach-Vorstädte* urged the city council to build a telegraph station in the district, pointing out that such devices were now 'even installed in the countryside.'[166] These and similar lamentations grew out of the frustration of people who wanted to make their neighbourhood into something that could be called a *Heimat*; a familiar environment that could inspire a sense of pride. As things stood, however, the inhabitants of the *Wertach* districts felt they were left to their own devices; that they were treated not as members of an urban community but merely as inhabitants of an urban space whose function was to help sustain industrialist ambitions.

The realization of this ambition required a reconfiguration of the urban landscape, one that did not meet with the support of the two economic strata who occupied the city's historic centre: the industrialists on the one hand, and the established crafts and small traders on the other. Although their interests to some extent divided them, both came to endorse a language of space that was less about movement than about established configurations of status.

For the city's crafts, this conception was hardly new. The master artisans in particular, who before the introduction of *Gewerbefreiheit* in 1868 had supplied the core of the urban citizenry, had traditionally enjoyed a high degree of recognition. Thus, Augsburg's master craftsmen had been actively involved in the surveillance of journeymen on behalf of the police authorities. They were obliged to inform Augsburg's authorities whenever they appointed a new journeyman or apprentice, or if one of their employees had unexpectedly left them. Throughout the imperial period, moreover, self-employed craftsmen and small traders often continued to occupy important functions within the urban social-welfare system, mainly as voluntary helpers charged with assessing benefit claims from applicants living in the same urban neighbourhood. In occupying such roles, many continued to act as gatekeepers for their towns, controlling access to communal resources and seeking to defend the exclusivity of local citizenship as best they could.[167]

Initially at least, however, Augsburg craftsmen in particular, who had sometimes suffered from the corporatism of the guilds, became champions of reforms. Many supported the radical liberal movement of the *Fortschritt*. In 1860, for example, the *Augsburger Anzeigeblatt* published a poem by an Augsburg locksmith praising the movement for economic reform and even associating it with a broader liberation of mankind: 'Mechanization conquers the world peacefully, through machines and steam... Let us unite, let us be brave and take a new path! Only progress, not police, can protect us. May science and work be free!... Fill up the glasses and join in: Long live the free crafts association!'[168] In the same year, the mouthpiece of the *Fortschritt* movement contended that 'the majority of our craftsmen and traders' had come to the conclusion that the economic restrictions still in place in Bavaria were out of touch with the 'reforms currently taking place in a number of neighbouring states.'[169]

However, in the 1870s Augsburg saw a revival of the corporatist spirit that even affected the formerly liberal section of the crafts trades, masters and non-masters alike. During the same period, the *Fortschritt*, Bavaria's liberal movement with a strong following in Augsburg, switched from a pro-free-trade to a pro-protectionism stance; and in 1878, Augsburg's liberals around their leaders Joseph Völk and Mayor Ludwig Fischer explicitly endorsed economic tariffs, distancing themselves from left-liberal opposition to Bismarck's protectionist agenda.[170] Although Augsburg's self-employed craftsmen, most of whom worked on their own or in small workshops for the local market, had little to gain economically from measures designed to protect Germany's agricultural producers and industrialists, the majority endorsed protectionist measures. During the crisis of the 1870s, for instance, many supported restrictions to *Gewerbefreiheit*; not a few joined one of the various *Innungen*, corporatist interest groups that were proliferating and often coalescing into national organizations. In 1880 Augsburg's magistrate reported the existence of close to 20 voluntary *Innungen* representing various local trades, describing their activities—such as the issuing of regulations for apprentices, the 'solemn registration of both new and leaving apprentices,' or the provision of support for travelling journeymen—as 'salutary' and worthy of unreserved support.[171]

What undoubtedly strengthened this tendency in Augsburg was that, compared to Ulm and particularly to Ludwigshafen, unreconstructed free marketers were relatively thin on the ground. The leading sector of Augsburg's economy throughout the nineteenth century, and which to an important degree shaped its political culture too—textile manufacturing—was at the very least ambivalent about *Gewerbefreiheit*. Many of the town's leading textile manufacturers had turned protectionist well before the oft-cited nation-wide conservative shift of the late 1870s. Thus they would oppose, almost in unison, the 1862 free-trade agreement between Prussia and France, using arguments that were reminiscent of Friedrich List's *Das nationale System der politischen Ökonomie* (1841).[172] It was in this spirit, at any rate, that an Augsburg industrialist like Georg Heinzelmann could insist that the relative superiority of the textile industries of France and above all of England meant that Germany was not yet ready for an agreement of this kind. In 1861 these convictions led Heinzelmann to found the protectionist *Verein für deutsche Industrie*. Several southern-German industrialists joined the association.[173] In the 1870s, moreover, some of Augsburg's foremost industrialists (such as Theodor Hassler or Albert Frommel) played a leading role in the *Centralverband deutscher Industrieller* (founded in 1876). Spearheaded by Rhenish heavy industrialists and southern textile manufacturers, this association was to exert a key influence on Bismarck's protectionist turn at the end of the 1870s.[174] Augsburg's industrialists of the second half of the nineteenth century needed no Bismarck to be convinced of the benefits of tariffs.[175]

Their attitude was at least in part a reflection of their position in the economic marketplace. Germany's textile industry was growing relatively slowly, certainly in comparison with other sectors such as machinery or the chemical and electrical industries. More importantly, like the textile sector as a whole, Augsburg's cotton-weaving and cotton-spinning factories produced overwhelmingly for the German mass market.[176] By contrast, Ludwigshafen's chemical industry was overwhelmingly export-orientated. Given that Germany was fast becoming the world's leading producer of chemical products, the largest companies in this sector had to fear competition from German, rather than foreign competition, a problem which after 1900 they would try to solve through the creation of cartels. By 1880 German firms' share of the world market in dyeing products was 50 per cent, rising to 90 per cent after 1900. The major player in this sector, the BASF, displayed an even stronger export-orientation than its competitors.[177]

That Augsburg's manufacturers were more protectionist than their Ludwigshafen counterparts in part explains why, from the late 1870s, a degree of common ground emerged between them and Augsburg's crafts-men and small traders. The shared reservations about economic liberalism that to some degree united Augsburg's crafts and industrial sectors came out during several meetings of the liberal *Bürgerverein*, the town's most important liberal association. At an 1875 meeting, for example, the associa-tion conducted a 'lengthy debate' on the issue of travelling salesmen, some of whom sold their merchandise locally via so-called *Wanderlager*. In the subsequent discussion, banker Rosenbusch, after conceding that these trav-elling sales units were causing 'great damage' to local businesses, expressed his support for the imposition of a 'high commercial tax' on those who engaged in such commercial activity.[178]

At a 1878 meeting of the *Bürgerverein*, in which the future of *Gewerbefreiheit* was discussed, factory owner and magistrate Pfeil, after insisting that free-dom of trade was 'here to stay,' nevertheless noted that the German people were 'in their majority not yet ready for the enjoyment of full liberties.' Specifically, Pfeil contended that 'both apprentices and workers' still required 'strong supervision if they are to achieve anything.'[179] Speaking on the same theme in 1880, master builder Gollwitzer lamented that the liberalization of trade had tempted many young craftsmen into setting up their own business before they had 'acquired the necessary training.' The results were 'overpro-duction and tastelessness.' Master tinsmith Zimmermann located the main problem in the 'pride of many parents,' who were eager for their offspring 'to enter the state civil service,' rather than 'learn the father's craft.'[180] Part of the problem, they appeared to suggest, was that the ambition to rise above one's station had become part of the *zeitgeist*.

The question of guild-like organization continued to preoccupy the local crafts and small-trade sectors; particularly after an 1881 imperial law offered encouragement, as well as new opportunities, for corporatist-style organization. Yet on the important question of what kind of *Innung* was best for the future of the local *Gewerbe*, the association remained divided.

When it was first discussed in the summer of 1879, two small minorities were forming among those present. The first supported the setting up of compulsory *Innungen*, a step that would have amounted to a return of the former guilds in all but name. The second group advocated free trade without any interference from corporatist organizations. The discussions that ensued showed that most supported the setting up of voluntary professional associations (so-called *freie Innungen*) whose rules would be binding for members only.[181]

The imperial law on voluntary *Innungen* was the subject of a special meeting held in March 1883. Organized by Augsburg's *Gewerbehalle* (the town's most important crafts association, which, as its name indicates, also ran a trading hall), the meeting was attended by 200 people.[182] The event started with a talk by master tailor Brach on whether the existing *Gewerbeordnung* was in need of reform, and, if so, which reforms were most pressing. That the crafts needed help was beyond debate as far as Brach was concerned. But the question was whether this task could best be achieved through the introduction of voluntary *Innungen*, as the imperial law seemed to suggest. In drawing up rules guiding the registration, employment, and examination of apprentices, as well as in staging exhibitions and awarding prices, Augsburg's *Gewerbehalle* had, in Brach's view, begun to move in the right direction. But if these efforts were to bear fruit in the long run, a larger proportion of the local crafts would have to participate. Brach expressed his preference for encouragement over compulsion. Compulsory examinations for master craftsmen he described as counter-productive, as they were likely to lead to 'all sorts of chicanery,' for reasons that were only too obvious. After putting on record his opposition to peddling and to the placing of contracts by tender, Brach invited those present to accept the following three-point resolution: that compulsory professional corporations were unsuitable to improve the lot of the crafts; that the imperial law of 18 July 1881 (which encouraged the setting up of voluntary professional corporations) was to be exploited to the full; and that the abolition of the freedom of trade would 'bring disadvantages for the entire German people, as well as for each craftsman who is qualified, intelligent, eager, and industrious.'[183]

Just before the final vote on the resolution was to be taken, two further speakers asked to address the audience. Seconding his colleague Brach, chairman Goebel insisted that compulsory *Innungen* would be 'a national misfortune for the entire German people.' For while they would cause great damage to able craftsmen, they would be of no help to those who lacked the required skills to compete in the marketplace. Upon hearing this, printing shop owner Racke shot up from his chair, insisting that compulsory corporations—in effect a version of the former guilds—were the only way to 'improve the lot of the *Handwerkerstand*.' The majority was with Racke, and the final ballot resulted in a resounding defeat of the proposed resolution.[184]

One possible way to judge this final episode would be to adopt the position of those free-market liberals who fought people like Racke because they viewed them as remnants of a bygone age. Such a perspective would not throw much new light on the development of urban communities in this period. Nor would it be illuminating to portray the conflict between Racke and his critics as a local version of the socio-economic divisions that came to the fore after what some historians call the Bismarckian turn. German towns were not merely local stages in a national drama. What Racke and like-minded individuals had done was not to deny that change was necessary for a town of Augsburg's significance. But they had begun to distance themselves from the spirit of competitive comparison that many local reformers had come to endorse under the banner of an allegedly superior morality of progress. In doing so, they challenged the vision of towns as the product of a journey. Rather than imagining Augsburg as work in progress, they continued to envisage their city as a place based on a configuration of positions. In Ulm, meanwhile, the proponents of these two competing motifs were even more visibly at loggerheads with each other. The two visions had been promoted, respectively, by the *Gewerbeverein* and the *Handelsverein*. In 1880 Gustav Maier, the Jewish merchant and leading light of the merchants' association, left Ulm to become the head of the Frankfurt branch of the *Reichsbank*. Although none of the two factions gained a clear cut victory, Maier's decision to move on, after years of loyalty to his native town, is none the less symbolic. Ludwigshafen offers a sharp contrast to both Augsburg and Ulm, in that its economic landscape epitomized the city as a socio-economic and cultural building site. As the writer Adam Ritzhaupt characterized the town of his youth:

> No part of our fatherland is as rich in historic relics as the cities and counties along the Rhine. But it is here that we know of a town on which we have to conclude: She's got no past. She has come into existence as the product of most recent times. She is so young that her first children might still be alive today.[185]

A place without history or venerable traditions, the city of industry offered little that could have pleased the genteel traveller. Yet for people like Ritzhaupt, that lack of a historical legacy was also Ludwigshafen's capital. It allowed it to be free. Better still, it enabled it to travel faster than many of its more venerable counterparts.

2

Schools on the Move

Of course, one needs interconfessional schools because the newspapers no longer suffice to spread the lies about progress, and because the Catholic youth is to be impregnated with old and new lies about Catholicism from a very early age.

Neue Augsburg Zeitung (1865)[1]

We should like to point out that the conscripts who have done abysmally in the Rekrutenprüfungen *belong to a generation that was drilled in the learning-by-heart of religious songs, bible verses, issues relating to catechism and bible history.*

Extract from a petition by the Mayor and council of Ludwigshafen am Rhein to the Bavarian Ministry of the Interior (1872).[2]

The number of schools has multiplied since the last inspection. Even more than the increase of the population, what has caused this is the decision of the fathers to have their children educated in the best possible way.

Ulm's Mayor v. Heim to district inspector (1875)[3]

Refitting schools for the journey

The school question left few German townspeople cold. In its 1871 administrative report, Augsburg's magistrate noted that 'local affairs' were being pushed to the background as a result of the 'world-historical events' that had recently excited the town's population. The only exception, the magistrate observed, was the debate over local schools, where the public was in favour of reforms even at the price of 'large sacrifices.'[4] To this the liberal-dominated magistrate added a long list of desiderata: additional schools had to be built to cater for the needs of new urban districts; existing class sizes had to be reduced, with pupils being divided more rigorously according to their age and gender; close to 30 new teachers had to be appointed to cope with the rapid increase in the number of school-aged children; teachers' salaries had to be raised in line with rising living costs if Augsburg was to attract the best primary-school teachers, rather than only those wishing to teach at the more prestigious grammar schools. The report concluded that Augsburg's future as a prosperous town would depend, to a significant degree, on its ability to realize at least some of these objectives.[5] As the city's secular school inspector defined his educational mission in his 1872 inaugural address: 'I intend to make advancement of the local primary school in the service of the citizens of Augsburg... the source of my pride. I regard the development of the *Volksschule* as the best guarantor of a healthy national life.'[6]

Similar ambitions were reported from Ulm, although there the language of educational progress focused more on the city's advanced secondary schools. In an 1875 report to a district inspector, Mayor von Heim attributed the 'proliferation' of the town's secondary schools over the previous 15 years above all to a conspicuous shift in parental preferences. 'The fathers' in particular had been 'keen to get the best possible education for their children.'[7] Grammar schools of various kinds, not only the traditional *Gymnasium*, were thriving in Ulm, which in the 1870s also saw an expansion of vocational secondary education for girls.[8] Pondering the town's efforts to accommodate the growing number of pupils, a liberal editorial concluded that Ulm was witnessing a *Zeit der Schulenwanderung*, a period that saw pupils moving out of their original and into new, larger buildings.[9] The school that opened in the Olgastrasse in 1878 is a case in point. Built at the cost of nearly one million marks and uniting Ulm's three advanced secondary schools under one roof, it embodied the city's educational ideal. Numerous guests of honour attended the school's inauguration ceremony, including the director of Württemberg's ministry of culture and several high-ranking state civil servants based in Ulm. The city was represented by the members of the council, hundreds of teachers and pupils, and by the leaders of Ulm's Protestant, Catholic, and Jewish communities. Teachers and pupils first assembled in front of their old school buildings, from which they then set off before joining the main procession to the new school.[10] Shortly before 11 a.m., the pupils and teachers were welcomed there by Ulm's master builder, who then handed over the keys to Mayor von Heim. After a brief tour of the building, during which the public had the opportunity to view the various classrooms, the festive act continued in the richly decorated main hall.[11]

In Ludwigshafen am Rhein, meanwhile, the bulk of resources were poured into the town's rapidly expanding elementary schools. At the turn of the century, just a little less than 6000 children attended the local *Communalschule*, as the city's interdenominational school was called. This was more than 20 times the figure of 1856. Throughout the imperial period, close to one-quarter of the municipal budget was spent on educating primary school children.[12] According to the town's inspection report for 1888/89, the main challenge was to reduce average class sizes. In his detailed report, school inspector Dr Geistbeck noted an 'overcrowding of numerous classes.' But Geistbeck saw nevertheless grounds for optimism, provided the present levels of investment were maintained. As he explained to the assembled members of the city council: the reduction of the average class size, to 74 in the town centre, and to 87 in the northern district, had been accomplished thanks to the appointment of eleven additional full-time teaching staff. Through the appointment of five additional teachers the average class size might be brought down even further, to a very respectable 63. If Ludwigshafen was to attain this target, it would 'come very close' to cities such as Mannheim (where the average class size was 51) or Munich (where it was 59). Thus, Geistbeck proposed further reforms in view of what he termed the 'abnormal movement in our school population,' particularly in the 'working-class district of the Hemshof.'[13] By 1897 the average class size had fallen to a very respectable 61.28. When a member of the local school commission accused the inspector of being obsessed with numbers, Ludwigshafen's school inspector retorted that any increase in class sizes would go 'at the expense of performance.'[14]

Taken together, the three vignettes tell a story of diverging educational landscapes. What they share, however, is a concern for being up with the times, expressed in the language of competitive comparison we also encountered in the previous chapter on the local economies. Nineteenth-century schools were no mere tools for lubricating the wheels of industrialization, least of all, perhaps, in Germany.[15] For the urban reformers we have just encountered, schools constituted transformative agents in an evolving shared space.[16] But before they could fulfill their allotted task, the schools themselves had to undergo a renewal. As far as the reformers were concerned, they had to be refitted for the journey that lay ahead.[17]

When it comes to assessing what this process of refitting entailed, the heated debate over interdenominational schools proves particularly instructive. What most opponents of confessional schools attacked was not religion per se, let alone existing social hierarchies, both of which they regarded as legitimate, even reassuring.

Christianity, too, remained a central referent of the German *Volksschule*. Thus, when the *Communalschule* was inaugurated in Ludwigshafen in 1869, the school's only Jewish teacher had to consent, in writing, to teaching his classes even when they fell on a Sabbath or Jewish religious holiday.[18] Six years previously, when the local synagogue commission enquired about the arrangements for a new school, the magistrate let it be known that there was no separate classroom for the Jewish children. They were simply asked to assemble at the school yard on its opening day, where they would be allocated, 'according to their age and ability, to the different classes of the Protestant school.'[19] When Augsburg's magistrate asked the *israelitische Cultusverwaltung* to provide a report on the education of the city's Jewish children, its reply was that there had never been a 'Jewish-German school' in Augsburg, and that in practice most Jewish children joined one of the town's Protestant elementary schools.[20] In Ulm, too, where interdenominational schools were unknown, most Jewish children attended the Protestant elementary school for a few years, before joining one of the local preparatory or secondary schools.

Yet if liberals and those further to the left did not question that Germany's elementary schools should adhere to an essentially Christian morality and calendar, they still wished to strengthen the status of secular subjects, particularly reading, writing, arithmetic, drawing, history, and geography. They also worked for the reduction of large class sizes, supported the removal of ineffective teachers, and demanded greater accountability. They further requested that classes be composed of children of roughly the same age and ability, which in the 1860s was by no means common. Throughout the late nineteenth century, the absence of children due to participation in religious services as sacristans or members of church choirs was a cause of considerable agitation among liberals in particular. Responding to such complaints, in 1878 Augsburg's bishopric instructed the city's parish priests to schedule services that involved children's participation outside normal school hours.[21] The schedule of the German *Volksschule* was to prevail over that which structured the rhythm of the various churches. Schools thus occupied a central role in the project of preparing children for the temporal schedules of modern life.[22]

These ambitions proved difficult to accomplish where confessional schools were predominant. But things changed on a number of fronts: the

average class-size decreased from close to 80 to less than 60 within the
Empire between 1871 and 1911;[23] and the multi-grade school, which comprised six grades ranging from age 6 to 13, became increasingly common.[24]
There also occurred a change in the school physical infrastructure used for
elementary education: the large houses municipalities had often acquired in
order to accommodate the increasing number of school-aged children were
replaced, from the 1860s onwards, by specially designed and furnished school
buildings. This move from the domestic house to the purpose-built school
can be observed in each of the three towns.

Then as now, however, educational reforms proved highly contentious.
Many wished to maintain religion as the pillar of educational organization,
insisting that what schools had to provide was above all a sense of place and
moral guidance. As a teacher from Augsburg put it: what elementary schools
had to provide was first and foremost 'moral and disciplinary instruction.'[25]
For clerics and parents defending confessional schools, the liberal premise
that a child's or a teacher's religious background was irrelevant to the aims
and ambitions of a modern educational institution made no sense at all.
Some opponents of inter-confessional instruction maintained that religion
mattered even when it came to the teaching of secular subjects such as
arithmetic, geography, or history. Seen from this angle, the notion of a purely
secular subject was a liberal invention designed to mask sectional political
interests.[26]

Of all the reforms that Germany's education system underwent in the
latter half of the nineteenth century, none therefore generated greater emotional waves than the one concerning interdenominational schools: what
contemporaries described as *Simultanschulen* or *Communalschulen*.[27] The
replacement of such schools through a *Volksschule* that was blind to confessional bonds became a central ambition. How, the champions of the interdenominational school asked, could Germans come to endorse their larger
fatherland if municipal schools continued to separate children according to
the religious creed to which they belonged by accident of birth? Conversely,
conservative Protestants and Catholics, drawing on a mixture of religious
and secular arguments, staunchly defended confessional schools.

The emotional heat these schools generated was inversely proportional
to their significance within Germany's educational landscape. Thus, by
1896, 88 per cent of the schools in Prussia's towns were still organized
according to denominational criteria, rising to 91 per cent by 1911.[28] Even
in left-liberal-dominated Berlin only 36 out of 249 schools were inter-

confessional in 1901.[29] The percentage of Protestant and Catholic children receiving instruction in schools of their own confession was over 90 per cent within the Empire (but only around 30 per cent for Jewish children, most of whom joined either Protestant or interdenominational schools).[30] The *Simultanschule* was even less popular in predominantly Catholic Bavaria, where by the middle of the 1880s less than two per cent of primary schools were interdenominational. However, like in other German states, the share of such schools could be considerably higher in urban areas. In some Bavarian cities, the rate of inter-confessional education was 20 per cent or more.[31] Meanwhile, in Württemberg (as well as in Saxony, Mecklenburg, Braunschweig, and Oldenbourg) the hegemony of confessional schools had never been called into question (extending even to the so-called *Mittelschulen*, the secondary schools preparing for careers in trade and the lower civil service).[32] It was only in some western parts of Germany, especially in the Palatinate and in Baden, that the *Simultanschulen* made deep and lasting inroads.[33]

Viewed in comparative perspective, however, the story of interdenominational schooling is less one of failure than of considerable variety. Here, too, investigating the dynamics of local conflict and dialogue can teach us much about the bigger picture, more perhaps than we are able to extrapolate from national aggregates on the state of the German *Volksschule*. For the advocates of confessional schools, elementary schools in particular had to strengthen, or at the very least protect, the religious identity of the children. For a few hours each day, the *Schulhaus* (the child's school) substituted for *das elterliche Haus* (the parental home). In contrast, interdenominational schools had been established not to consolidate existing solidarities but to foster new ones.

A new kind of community

Ludwigshafen was one of the comparatively few German towns where the interdenominational school emerged triumphant. A little more than a decade after its foundation, a movement in support of such a school sprang up and quickly gathered pace. On 17 June 1869, a so-called *Bürgerkomitee* handed over a petition to Ludwigshafen's then mayor, the building contractor Joseph Hoffmann. Signed by 290 male residents, which at that point in time amounted to roughly 60 per cent of all citizens, the petition asked for the town's existing denominational schools to be replaced by a secular elementary school, a so-called *Communalschule*.[34]

What the petitioners demanded was not a secular school, if by that we mean a school in which either religion or denomination had no place. Not only would religion continue to be taught in the *Communalschule* they envisaged, but the authorities would even try to ensure that its teaching staff would reflect the town's confessional demography. Nor was the fundamentally Christian character of the *Volksschule* called into question.[35] What they demanded, rather, was a school in which children from different denominational and religious backgrounds would be taught in the same classroom, by teachers whose religious allegiance might (and often did) differ from that of the majority of pupils they were charged to instruct in a series of secular subjects.

For their opponents, confessional schools were a costly form of exclusion, and hence an affront to the meritocratic society they claimed to represent. As they put it in their pamphlet that preceded the 1869 ballot: 'Our public life no longer recognizes religious differences in the way this used to be the case. One does not ask, "What is your background?", but rather, "What do you do?" One no longer asks, "What is your faith?" but rather, "What are your abilities?"'[36] *Communalschulen*, to cite the text of the petition, were schools where children would 'grow together from their first lesson, without hatred towards the Catholic or resentment against their Protestant *Christenkind*, and without unkindness towards the son or daughter of Jewish parents.'[37] There was, they insisted, 'only the one father upstairs.'[38] As the petitioners sought to defend themselves against the charge that the interdenominational schools were inspired by hostility towards all things religious:

> And if someone were to ask you if religion will be taught at the *Communalschule*, then you need to tell them as follows: Yes, religion will and, indeed, must be taught; since it is our innermost conviction that religion is the first and indispensable condition of human morality. Tell them that the communal or interdenominational schools are by no means irreligious.' '*An die Bewohner Ludwigshafens!*'[39]

As the petitioners stressed throughout their campaign, the state had already recognized the superiority of educational institutions that disregarded denomination. How else was it conceivable, they asked, that most secondary schools, as well as universities and even training seminaries for clerics, appointed their pedagogues on the basis of their ability rather than their confession. There was no reason why the German *Volksschule*, the school entrusted with the education of all Germans irrespective of their class and religious background, should deviate from this principle.

Just a few days after the petition had been submitted, close to 500 inhabitants congregated for a meeting in the *Drei Mohren*, a popular local inn. Among those who had the courage to express their views openly during the event were people of education and standing, including a local notary, or the young philosopher Robert Goldschmidt. But the group of those who rose from their seats to get their views across was not confined to local notables. It also included two primary-school teachers as well as leading representatives of the *Arbeiterbildungsverein*, an association devoted to workers' education. When the convenor of the meeting invited the known as well as the suspected opponents of the *Communalschule* to speak to the matter, nobody raised their hand. For the commentator writing in the *Pfälzischer Kurier*, the lack of diverging voices had turned the occasion into a 'celebration' of the idea of the interdenominational school.[40]

Once the authenticity of the signatures on the petition had been confirmed, the mayoral office announced the procedures for a ballot to be conducted on the question of the *Communalschule*. Only 'adult and independent males' were entitled to vote, and for the ballot to be valid, at least two thirds of the town's 680 Catholics, 605 Protestants, 16 Mennonites, and 31 Jews had to take part. Within these cohorts, the decision would be taken by absolute majority vote. The voting proceeded in four separate ballots: Protestants were instructed to hold their ballot at 9 a.m. in the hall of the *Gasthof Drei Mohren*, while Catholics were asked to hold theirs at the same venue at 3 p.m. The much smaller contingents of Jews and Mennonites were invited to deliver their vote, on the following day, in the hall of the municipal council at 9 and 10 a.m., respectively.[41] None of the four communities failed to achieve the required participation rate of two-thirds; yet with 156 of its members abstaining, the turnout was lowest among Ludwigshafen's Catholic community. Of the 605 Protestants entitled to take part, 577 made their way to the allocated polling station, with only 28 abstentions. And of the 31 Jews entitled to vote, not a single one abstained. The outcome could not have been clearer. While not a single of the Protestant and Jewish voters opposed the proposal, 16 Catholics voted against it.[42]

The next day the police commissioner reported that the four ballots had been conducted in a 'peaceful and orderly fashion.'[43] Not only 'Ludwigshafen's citizens but also its working-class population' had demonstrated a commendable appreciation for 'temperance and legality.' Some inhabitants, upon learning the outcome of the ballot on Friday around noon, had begun to decorate their houses with flags; and the choral society *Frohsinn* had gathered in one of the local inns to celebrate the event by performing a number of songs. The commissioner was eager to stress, however, that 'no public procession' or other kinds of public celebration had taken place. Rumours about cacophonies 'in front of the houses of local priests' who were known opponents of the interdenominational school had likewise proved entirely unfounded. Yet the absence of open conflict during and after the ballot cannot be ascribed solely to the prevalence of harmonious social relations in the town. As the records reveal, the local police had taken measures to prevent large-scale disturbances. Considerable efforts had been undertaken, for example, to curb the enthusiasm of the winning side (a planned torchlight procession by the local gymnast society was prohibited), and generally to control the situation (the fire brigade had been put on alert for several days after the outcome of the ballot became public knowledge).[44]

Whatever tensions needed containing in the immediate aftermath of the ballot, however, the basic fact remains: henceforth, and throughout the impe-rial period, Ludwigshafen would be known as a town whose 6- to 12-year-old children would be taught in denominationally-mixed classes. Only when in the course of the 1890s the city government decided to incorporate the towns of *Friesenheim* (which was predominantly Protestant) and *Mundenheim* (which was overwhelmingly Catholic) did the authorities deviate from this principle. Not because they had changed their view on elementary educa-tion, but because the two incorporated communities had made their consent contingent on the preservation of their existing confessional schools. However, even after their incorporation the proportion of children attending confessional elementary schools never rose above 40 per cent, which was low by German standards.[45] The new school soon left a conspicuous imprint on local educational practice and culture. Children were divided into various grades, while of the six weekly hours of religious instruction prescribed by Bavarian law, four were taught by the class teacher, and two by a cleric cater-ing for children of his own confession.[46] Thus, when in 1869 the petition was launched, there were 640 elementary school children taught by six teachers, with the largest class comprising 140 children.[47] By the mid-1880s the aver-age class-size was in the high 60s; and by 1904 it had fallen to an average of 58, and hence to Prussian levels.[48]

In spite of this successful outcome, the realization of the *Communalschule* had never been a foregone conclusion. In 1856 the town's 246 school-aged children were taught in two classrooms. When the district government asked the municipal council to appoint an additional teacher to take on a class of first-year pupils, the Catholic school inspectorate objected. Instead of creating one class composed of children from different religious backgrounds, the inspectors demanded that two additional classes, one Catholic and one Protestant, be established. The district government rejected the request on financial grounds, and because there was only one additional classroom available. At the same time, in an apparent attempt to mollify the situation, it decreed that the teaching of first-year children would henceforth alternate between a Protestant and a Catholic teacher, with the first post-holder being of Protestant confession.[49] In this way, the average class size was brought down from 123 to 82 children.[50] Yet when, in 1859, the increase in the population of school-aged children necessitated the appointment of a fourth teacher, the first-year class was again split into a Protestant and a Catholic class on the request of the clerical school inspectors.[51] The founding of a Jewish school in 1861, whose 19 children had previously attended the Protestant school, further reinforced the move in favour of confessional education.[52]

The outcome of the 1869 ballot strengthened, rather than weakened the opposition to inter-confessional schools.[53] In the months following the successful referendum, the opponents of the *Communalschule* advanced several objections against the new school.[54] To begin with, the Catholic school inspectors protested against the 'allocation of a class with children of Christian confession' to the town's only Jewish teacher, Lazarus Mai.[55] On one occasion they even drew on a law of 1817 to prove their point that the inclusion of a Jewish teacher in a school mostly attended by Christian children was illegal, unless the local Jewish community was 'too small or lacking the financial' means to set up its own school.[56] The logic of their argument is revealing: Faced with a communal *Volksschule* that failed to recognize confession as its organizing principle, the Catholic inspectors clung to religion as a next line of defence, insisting that the local schools had to retain their Christian character. It is out of such concerns, it seems, that they demanded the retention of the Christian prayer, to be said at the beginning and end of each class; and it is out of such concerns, too, that they began to challenge the legitimacy of the only Jewish teacher in what they saw as a Christian school for Christian children. How could a Jewish teacher, one of

Figure 5. Goethe School in Ludwigshafen am Rhein. Boys' class no. 3. 1900–1901. © Stadtarchiv Ludwigshafen am Rhein.

the Catholic inspectors asked, say a Christian prayer 'without it being bereft of any Christian consciousness'?[57]

The delays resulting from these interventions caused resentment not only among urban liberals but also among middle-class parents. Fearing that over-crowded classrooms would dent the prospects of their children; on 19 April 1870 several family fathers (including the brick manufacturer Carl Friedrich Ludowici) threatened to stop sending their offspring to the local school unless the municipal authorities would establish the envisaged *Communalschule*. They even cited scientific studies whose authors identified over-crowded classrooms as a major health hazard for young children.[58] Just a year after German unification, in a letter to the Bavarian Ministry of the Interior, the municipal assembly made a vigorous plea for a radical reduction of clerical influence on the local *Volksschule*. As the councillors wrote in justification of their opposition to the current system of clerical schools:

[Primary] schools are communal institutions, paid for by the municipal purse. The teachers are elected by the municipal council, and in their professional capacity they are accountable to the municipal authorities. Pedagogy is an independent science, not an appendage of theology. An able theologian is not necessarily also an able pedagogue. In fact, in our experience, clergymen who are capable teachers are few and far between.[59]

In stressing that a town such as Ludwigshafen could ill-afford the luxury of running denominational schools, the authorities appear to have struck a chord with large sections of the population.[60] Yet the opposition to the *Communalschule* would not go away, with the confession of the teachers remaining a major bone of contention. Thus, when in 1872 several classes had grown to a level that made effective teaching impossible, necessitating the appointment of two additional assistant teachers, parish priest Hofherr, the Catholic representative on the municipal school committee, demanded that the first of the two new posts be filled with a Catholic teacher. This was necessary, Hofherr explained, because the existing teaching staff comprised four Protestants, but only three Catholics.[61] Seconded by two other members on the committee, Mayor Kutterer disagreed. Even though the municipal authorities had always 'endeavored to achieve or maintain parity,' they nevertheless insisted that the chief consideration had to be the candidates' qualifications.[62] Should the two most qualified candidates turn out to be Catholics, the mayor reassured Hofherr, the committee would appoint them without the slightest hesitation. This reassurance did not satisfy the Catholic parish priest, however. In a letter to the district government in Speyer, he claimed that parity did not presently exist among Ludwigshafen's *Volksschule* teachers, neither in terms of numbers nor in relation to wage levels. According to Hofherr, the city's Catholic teachers earned about 60 gulden less per annum than their Protestant colleagues.[63] But the district authorities rejected Hofherr's point of view, emphasizing that what mattered for a *Communalschule* was first and foremost a teacher's qualification.[64]

As long as clerics continued to act as local school inspectors, however, limiting their influence proved difficult. One way by which the authorities hoped to subvert the impact of confessional interests was by establishing a new, secular regime of inspection. The first calls for a secular school inspector were expressed soon after the 1869 ballot. In May 1872, the mayor informed the district government that the size of existing classes (which at that point was around 100 pupils per class) rendered vital the appointment of a full-time secular school inspector. It was simply not possible in these circumstances, the mayor summed up the city council's position, to achieve educational standards in line with the needs of 'modern times.' As if to demonstrate that what was at stake was more than a local issue, the mayor drew attention to the results of a recent inspection of the Bavarian army. These had revealed an 'unusually high percentage of conscripts from the Palatinate with poor basic education.'[65] The mayor's letter was followed up, a mere week later, by a petition that was sent to the district government. It requested that all elementary schools in the Palatinate, but 'especially the Kommunalschulen,' be given permission to appoint a secular school inspector with overall authority.[66]

But the district authorities proved reluctant to take a decisive stance on the matter, in part, it seems, because a municipal inspectorate could be construed as an implicit challenge to the state's authority in the field of elementary education. After no response had been forthcoming by early August, Ludwigshafen's council took the unusual step of applying directly to the state authorities in Munich. Its proposal rested on three key assertions: that the regulation dating from 1817, which placed school inspection in the hands of the Christian confessions, was out of date; that, because elementary schools were now mainly funded by revenues from municipal tax, with teachers being elected and appointed under the auspices of municipal councils, the communal authorities should be given greater powers in the area of school inspection; and, lastly, that the secular school inspector should be superior, in terms of his education and expertise, not only to the members of the teaching profession but also to the clerics sitting on the local school board. As Ludwigshafen's government summed up their stance on the future of local school inspection:

> Our experience in the Palatinate is that the clerical school inspectors tend to prioritise, some might say over-prioritise, religious instruction, the subject matter that is dearest to them, and in which they feel most at home. This, we hardly need to add, goes at the expense of other subjects. We should like to point out, in this context, that the conscripts who did so badly in the *Rekrutenprüfungen* belong to a generation that was drilled in the learning-by-heart of religious songs, bible verses, and in various questions relating to the catechism and the history of the bible.[67]

In the course of the 15 years it took to fill the post of secular school inspector, the town authorities missed no opportunity to highlight the inadequacy of the existing inspection regime. In 1876, for instance, the council informed the district government that the two parish priests acting as school inspectors had proved incapable of coping with the demands of a rapidly expanding urban school. Not even the threat of disciplinary action had prompted them to change their ways.[68] A few years later a series of unannounced state inspections confirmed these allegations. The list of detected shortcomings included teachers who had failed to keep an account of unexcused absences;[69] and, on one occasion, several teachers had even gone on holiday without informing the municipal school committee of their absence from school duties. What to the city authorities was most alarming, however, was that the local inspectorate had not kept a record of any of these transgressions.[70] The implicit charge advanced through their petition was thus that clerical inspectors were biased; that their immediate instinct was to protect their own teachers, who they treated like family members, even where the latter had evidently failed to serve the public interest.

The 1880s appeared to offer further confirmation of an inept inspectorate having lost control of the situation. This time the proof resided in numbers. As far as the city council was concerned, the clerical school inspectors had shown themselves unable to run an urban school whose population had grown more than tenfold since its foundation. There were 870 primary-school pupils in Ludwigshafen in 1872, a number that would rise to 3682 by 1887. What worried the authorities was not only that the average class-size was still around 70 in the mid-1880s. What had prompted their disapproval was the absence of a strategy to deal with the influx of new children into Ludwigshafen's schools year on year.[71] And what positively alarmed them was that the registers detailing the composition and size of new classes, or which teacher was responsible for which class, were for the most part either incomplete or missing.[72] Many local educators of liberal conviction joined in these concerns. In July 1876, for example, numerous elementary-school teachers expressed their dissatisfaction with the state of the urban primary school, insisting that a secular inspector was the only way to overcome existing problems.[73]

But it was not until 1884 that the district government openly acknowledged the 'unedifying state' of elementary education in Ludwigshafen, urging the mayoral office to appoint a secular school inspector.[74] Two weeks later, the local school board would act upon the district government's advice. 'After lengthy debate' its members decided to issue a recommendation for the attention of the municipal council in support of the appointment of an 'academically and pedagogically trained layperson as school inspector, at a starting salary of 4000 marks (the equivalent of four times the average salary of an elementary-school teacher) and with effect of 1 October 1884.'[75] Out of the 62 candidates that had applied for the position, the appointment panel drew up a shortlist of six candidates, with the two secondary school teachers, Dr Alois Geistbeck from Munich and Georg Möller from Neu-Ulm, emerging as the front runners. 'After extended debate' the municipal council decided, with a majority of 14 against 9 votes, that Geistbeck be offered the post.[76] After the state authorities had expressed no objections to his appointment, on 29 December 1885 Geistbeck took the following oath in the presence of a district official:

> I swear allegiance to the King and obedience to the laws of the state and its constitution. I swear that I wish to fulfil my duties as local school inspector of the town of Ludwigshafen faithfully and conscientiously and that I shall carefully obey the school regulations that are currently in place as well as those that shall be enforced in future years.
>
> I also confirm, by virtue of this oath of office, that I do not belong to any association whose existence is unknown to the state, or that I shall ever belong to such an association; nor will I retain membership of an association whose prohibition has been ordained by the relevant police office or authority, or whose meetings I have been prohibited from attending on the basis of existing disciplinary regulations.[77]

The inspection regime that Geistbeck installed in Ludwigshafen not only restricted clerical influence. It also did away with a series of informal arrangements held dear by sections of the teaching profession. According to one such arrangement, the teachers of the Hemshof were entitled to move, after a few years of service, to one of the schools in the centre of town. Transfers of this kind had in fact become quite common since 1879, when the new school opened its doors to the sons and daughters of factory workers and other employees of the BASF. Within a few weeks of taking up his post Geistbeck abolished this custom.[78] What infuriated some of the Hemshof teachers was that several novices had been appointed to city-centre schools without first having to serve a stint at a school near the big chemical plants, a kind of teachers' *corvée*, bearable only because of the certain prospect of an imminent transfer.[79] They also believed, quite rightly, that their job was more demanding than their colleagues in the city centre schools cared to imagine. Their school buildings were situated near chemical factories that 'filled the classrooms with such insalubrious air, particularly when the wind blows from the North or North-East,' making normal instruction difficult and at times even impossible. Few teachers, the petitioners noted, would even have accepted a post at Ludwigshafen's *Communalschule* had they not assumed that their stint at the Hemshof 'would be only temporary.'[80]

What also rendered a post at one of the Hemshof schools unattractive for many teachers was that 'the overwhelming majority of the children belonged to the lowest social classes of the population.'[81] As well as making instruction more arduous, this also minimized opportunities for gaining additional income from private tuition. This was only partly because of the money. Income from tuition conferred status, as did the ability to acquire private teaching from middle-class families. Hemshof teachers were concerned that their teaching working-class children near the factories might be construed as a sign of their inferior ability as teachers. The teachers repeated their demand in a petition to the district authorities in 1890.[82] As in 1887, Geistbeck emphasized that the Hemshof teachers were confusing an outdated habit with a legal entitlement. The town would appoint its teachers according to its needs, not according to criteria of seniority among existing teachers. As far as the mayor was concerned, clinging to this request was all the more objectionable in light of the evident progress the Hemshof schools had made in recent years.

In the same vein, the mayor criticized the teachers' preoccupation with private tuition, given that Ludwigshafen was widely known for the competitive salaries it offered to its teaching staff. Furthermore, the average class-size at the schools had gone down to about 60 children, and the new schools had been built in line with modern pedagogical prerogatives. As a result, several teachers had taken up permanent residence in the town's northern district. Much had been undertaken, in the mayor's view, to improve the situation of the Hemshof teachers.[83] What Ludwigshafen's reformers wished to defend against the teachers' wishes was not a two-class system among the city's elementary school teachers. What they wanted to prevent, rather, was that their vision of educational progress was undermined by the teachers' status concerns. There was to be no place for corporate interests in schools that were to act as transformative agents in the creation of a new shared urban space.

'Each religion has to be confession'

Of the three towns examined in this book, Augsburg not only featured the largest contingent of school-aged children but also allocated the biggest sum to the running of its elementary schools. There were 5324 elementary-school children in 1865, rising to 8372 by 1896; the total expenditure per annum rose from close to 300,000 in 1886 to over 450,000 marks in 1897, amounting to between 15 and 17 per cent of the town's total expenditure.[84] Only Ludwigshafen contributed a somewhat larger slice of its annual budget to its *Volksschule*.[85] Confessional schools had long been the exclusive norm in Augsburg, even if the interdenominational schools began to make some inroads from the 1860s. As late as 1892, only 1426 of 8011 elementary-school pupils—of whom 5447 were Catholic, 2456 Protestant, and 108 Jewish—attended the inter-confessional schools that had been established in the city's south-western and northern peripheries. Catholic children were slightly over-represented in these schools: Of the approximately 1426 children who attended such schools in 1892, 998 were Catholic.[86]

Like its counterpart in Ludwigshafen, Augsburg's reform-minded public believed that confessional solidarities were a hindrance to progress. Many feared that they would prevent people from unlocking their potential, and hence from making a fruitful contribution to the life of both town and nation. Conversely, for the proponents of confessional religion, a loose faction spearheaded by ultramontane Catholics and conservative Protestants, the chief purpose of elementary schools was moral education. Denouncing the universal claims of liberals as hypocritical and self-serving, they insisted on the legitimacy of protecting confessional interests and sensibilities. As Adolf Hass, editor-in-chief of the *Augsburger Postzeitung* and one of the more moderate representatives of Augsburgs's ultramontane Catholicism, challenged the concept of the interdenominational school: 'Each religion, if it is to constitute positive religion rather than merely a philosophical position, has to be confession.'[87] The predominant attitude towards religion, which Haas described as a mere 'drawing on Christianity's heritage,' would result in a depletion of the Christian faith. Ten years later, at a meeting of the Catholic Casino, Haas asserted that the real purpose of the inter-confessional schools was 'to suppress the Catholic faith.'[88] For people like Haas and the many who shared his views, elementary schools had to be an extension of the home; a place capable of reinforcing an established community in a time of crisis; not an engine in the forging of a new one.

As far as the liberals were concerned, however, the confessional schools were the problem, rather than the solution. The city's schools had long been hampered by a lack of space and a shortage of adequate school buildings. In 1858, for example, the average space allocated to every first-year pupil in the

Catholic girls' school at St. Ursula was 8½ square feet in a class numbering 75 girls.[89] In 1865 its headmistress, sister Acquinata Lauterbach, complained to the magistrate that the school building was not only too small, but also too noisy, with the result that both children and teachers would get tired very quickly.[90] An even more serious situation seems to have developed at the Catholic *Dompfarrschule*, where, on top of the noise, children were taught in damp classrooms.[91] An examination of the city's school policy during the 1850s and 1860s reveals a fair degree of short-term thinking. It was only once a school class had outgrown its allocated classroom, or when a teacher had evidently lost control over his or her pupils, that the city's political representatives would step in. The Protestant school at St. Ulrich offers a case in point. When the school's expansion threatened to undermine its effective functioning, the council's initial reaction was to propose the purchase of two nearby properties to accommodate additional classes. Only after a lengthy debate did the council adopt the school commission's proposal to build a new school, a proposal the magistrate had endorsed without hesitation.[92] Large class sizes remained a cause of much agitation, however. In 1867, a Protestant school inspector explained why class-sizes had to be reduced as a matter of urgency:

> In cases where the class size is between seventy and eighty children, the teacher usually has to pour all his energy into maintaining discipline. Besides, where the number of pupils is unusually large, so is the proportion of those who are lazy and lacking in both talent and manners. It is nearly impossible, in these circumstances, to ask each pupil at least one question per lesson, which means that the teacher cannot accomplish what may well be regarded as a minimal requirement.[93]

The inspector was not engaging in scare-mongering. In 1862, one class in the girls' school at the cloister school of Maria-Stern comprised close to 100 children.[94] The situation was equally serious in the Catholic parish district of St. Georg, where class sizes had grown rapidly due to the influx of families working in the nearby textile factories. When a new teacher was appointed to head the school's first grade, the council justified his appointment with the predominance of 'children of a less well-off population,' which, as experience had demonstrated, made the task of the teacher more arduous. Like in Ludwigshafen, however, with time liberal efforts to reduce class sizes bore fruit. If the average school class at Augsburgs's *Volksschule* until the 1860s had been well over 70, it came down markedly in the course of subsequent decades: to 56 children per class in 1885, and to 53 by 1896.[95] What prompted just as much trepidation as their often large size was the existence of classes composed of children of varying age. To rectify this problem, many liberals demanded that the so-called *Einkurssystem* be made compulsory. In Augsburg the one-course system was introduced relatively early, in 1866, but initially only in the Protestant schools. Their Catholic counterparts would not adopt it until 1874.[96]

From the point of view of Mayor Ludwig Fischer and his allies, the school commission and the teaching staff, such reforms were needed if Augsburg was to compete with German towns renowned for their educational achievements. One of the main tasks of the city's chief school inspector Carl Ludwig Bauer—appointed in 1872, Bauer was a liberal and a Catholic—was thus to identify Augsburg's performance within the wider educational landscape that characterized post-unification Germany. With the creation of the imperial state, educational authorities everywhere gained access to an unprecedented wealth of information. The newly created Ministry of the Interior housed a massive administrative section, the *Statistisches Amt*, which compiled data on a near-endless range of parameters.[97]

But local school inspectors did not merely rely on statistics. They also sought to gain first-hand-experience through paying visits to schools in other states. Thus, when in 1875 school inspector Bauer returned from an inspection tour in Thuringia and Saxony, he concluded that Augsburg was on a par with these cities in relation to infrastructure (particularly buildings and school books, the latter with the exception of the natural sciences); but that it was lagging behind with regard to examination results. The history behind Bauer's visit is instructive. He had initially planned it as a private tour, to be conducted during his sabbatical. But when the magistrate heard of his intentions it decided to offer him a fee in return for the production of a detailed report. Bauer was in no doubt concerning the reasons for the relative superiority of the Thuringian and Saxon schools. What he regarded as decisive was the eight years of compulsory elementary education common in these states, compared to the six years known in Augsburg and much of Bavaria. Bauer also pointed to the better training of the Thuringian and Saxon teachers. As he summed up his recommendations:

> We will, and we must, succeed in our task of getting our advanced grades up to the standards achieved by the better among the Saxon schools. This we shall

achieve if all our classes are sealed at a maximum of 50 children, and if the teaching of natural sciences is finally allocated the amount of time and effort that is commensurate with its importance. This will only be possible if our teachers are given the opportunity to acquire the basic knowledge and the skills required to handle physical instruments in specially established courses.[98]

As far as the liberals on the town council were concerned, furthermore, the *Einkurssystem* was the only way forward. This became evident in the discussions surrounding the necessary establishment of a new school in the Hettenbach district in 1872. After the magistrate had proposed the building of a new school there at the cost of close to 50,000 marks, the liberal-dominated council endorsed the proposal on condition that the children attending the new school would be divided into classes according to their age and ability, rather than on the basis of their religious creed.[99] The district government endorsed the decision against the protests of the bishop and the Protestant consistory, adding that Augsburg's parents were free to send their children to confessional schools if they so wished.[100]

Deep-seated reservations about confessional schools, reinforced by doubts in the educational ability of teachers from religious orders, provided the impetus behind the liberal campaign in favour of the municipal *Simultanschule*. Although this campaign had got under way in the mid-1860s, it only gained momentum in the wake of German unification. Thus, when in 1873 a new girls' school opened its doors, this triggered a controversy over the use of teachers belonging to the religious order of the *englische Fräulein*. During a meeting of the magistrate, school inspector Bauer recommended that three classes at two Catholic schools, which were taught by nuns belonging to the order, be handed over to the secular teachers. The school inspector justified his proposal by pointing to the presumed Jesuit leanings of the female teachers in question. The magistrate endorsed his recommendation, noting that the said teachers held a subscription to the *Sendbote d. göttlichen Herzen Jesu*, a Jesuit organ. There was therefore no doubt in the magistrate's mind that Augsburg's *englische Fräulein* were in the thralls of the Jesuits. The magistrate also criticized the three teachers' insufficient 'level of education,' with the school inspector claiming that the order as a whole included 'only three or four talented teachers.' In the discussion that ensued, Mayor Fischer even suggested that the order of the *englische Fräulein* might fall under the Jesuit law and hence be prohibited.[101]

Fischer's recommendation, although it may have struck a chord with many magistrates and councillors, was not acted upon. The prohibition of an established religious order like the *englische Fräulein*, one that enjoyed a good and longstanding reputation for charitable work, would have prompted outrage in Catholic quarters.[102] Ever since the liberals had begun to promote the case of the interdenominational schools, they faced vigorous opposition from the city's powerful Catholic conservatives. As early as 1865, Augsburg's most influential Catholic daily claimed to know the deeper cause behind the liberals' championing of inter-confessional schools. As its editors proclaimed in a diatribe against Augsburg's Progress Party: 'This is what the party wants which hides behind the phrase: through light to truth and justice. If it didn't have absolute confidence that it could fill those schools with teachers and books of its own taste, then it would everywhere fight the inter-confessional schools with every available means at its disposal.'[103] Commenting on the magistrate's 1873 meeting concerning the role of the *englische Fräulein*, the Catholic *Augsburger Postzeitung* stressed that only one of the female teachers had held a subscription to a Jesuit newspaper. Its editors also denied that the teachers from the order were lacking in pedagogic prowess, as only two had been given 'less than satisfactory marks' by the local inspectors. For the *Postzeitung*, the incident offered 'yet another proof that all caution and co-operation on the part of convents and religious orders will not suffice to satisfy our liberals.' All of them, 'even those who think they have come to a workable arrangement with them,' would be placed on the 'liberals' list of proscription.[104]

A glance at the evolution of Augsburg's school inspection regime can help bring the most pressing issues into sharper relief. Prior to the liberals' rise to power in the 1860s, the tone of the reports was remarkably conciliatory even where an inspection might have given cause for concern, suggesting a rather close rapport between the state and municipal authorities at the time. The inspections carried out between 1855 and 1860 in both the Catholic and Protestant *Volksschule* are instructive in this regard. In each case the district government's report identified a host of shortcomings. At the Catholic schools, these included the poor performance by an elderly teacher suffering from signs of dementia, or the sub-standard quality of the drawing lessons provided at the boys school at the parish St. Moritz. Meanwhile, in the third grade of the Protestant boys' school of St. Anna the 'insufficient progress' in orthography was attributed to 'teacher Eichleitner's notorious laziness.'[105] But the most serious failing, which affected Catholic and Protestant schools in equal measure, was an extraordinarily large number of unexcused absences. As the district authorities pointed out, such absences were in violation of the 1856 ministerial decree concerning compulsory school attendance. In spite of these failings, however, the report concluded on an emphatically positive note, even praising the then chair of the local school commission, the Catholic Mayor Forndran, as well as the district school inspector, parish priest Büschl, for their 'untiring and successful efforts' on behalf of Augsburg's elementary schools.[106]

All this changed, as a result of the liberal ascendancy, from the mid-1860s. Not only did the inspection reports grow in length, but they also became more critical, pointing out palpable shortcomings and suggesting ways to rectify them. Gone was the assuaging tone of the 1850s. In 1861 and 1875, for example, the girls' school taught by the order of the *Englische Fräulein* came in for special scrutiny after many of the pupils had shown problems with orthography.[107] The 1875 report mentioned that in the second grade of a Catholic centre-city school, several children had been unable to count to 21. But this newfound scrutiny was by no means confined to Catholic schools. In the same report, the children of the second class of the Protestant girls' school were singled out for their reading difficulties: while most pupils had read 'in too low a voice' to camouflage their deficiencies, many had evidently struggled with clear pronunciation. The sixth grade of the Protestant school at St. Jakob prompted an even harsher verdict. Not only had its children shown 'insufficient skill in their oral and written expression;' just as worrying was the fact that they were 'not sufficiently familiar with the new currency symbols, krone and mark.' What the inspector deemed equally serious (he called it a 'disgrace') was that children in their sixth grade had 'not yet received any history teaching.'[108] Meanwhile, the lessons of the Catholic school at St. Georg, although they had contained some basic history, had been insufficiently focused 'on the recent and most recent times.'[109]

Teachers, too, came in for considerable criticism. According to the 1875 school report, several teachers had shown themselves incapable of maintaining discipline in class. A German language lesson had attracted the attention of the inspector because the teacher's approach had been too theoretical and 'lacking in vividness.'[110] One teacher was castigated for having instructed the children in Swabian dialect rather than in high-German; another was assailed for 'having constantly moved from one place to another' during his lesson, a style of instruction the inspector deemed distracting and, hence, highly ineffective.[111]

Teachers remained under close scrutiny for decades to come. Thus, in 1894 *Schulrat* Bauer released a report on pedagogic performance. Based on 147 individual reports (one for each class), the report offered a mixed picture. The city's elementary-school teachers received the sort of praise that any champion of school reform would read as an indication that there was still considerable room for improvement. Thus according to the district inspector, the *Volksschule*'s overall achievement was 'quite satisfactory;' of the 147 acting class teachers, 54 got awarded the highest grade ('Note I'), 85 achieved a good or very good grade ('Note I-II oder II-I'), with the performance of only six teachers being deemed unsatisfactory ('II. Qualifikationsnote'). The three *Oberlehrer* Fesenmayr, Schiele and Schubert—teachers who on top of their normal teaching duties had supported the district inspector in carrying out the regular inspections—received special praise. Thanks in no small part to their 'great assiduousness and touching sense of duty,' Augsburg's schools were said to be in very good shape.[112]

In the liberal reading of the story, then, the satisfactory results of the 1890s were the fruit of the more rigorous inspection regime they had created since the late 1860s. Like their counterparts in *Ludwigshafen am Rhein*, what Augsburg's educational authorities had in mind was a shift of the centre of power and responsibility from the parish priests to the town's secular authorities. This ambition was realized in 1872 through the appointment of Carl Ludwig Bauer as urban *Schulrat*, who replaced the Protestant and Catholic priests who had hitherto chaired the town's Catholic and Protestant school commissions. Towards the end of the inauguration ceremony following Bauer's appointment, Mayor Fischer addressed the new school inspector with the following words: 'I ask the school inspector to embark on his new duties with courage and perseverance, and that he does not allow himself to get distracted by the difficulties he is bound to encounter. Whenever these difficulties threaten to embitter him, he ought to take comfort in the fact that he works for a good cause, and that he can be certain of the gratitude of all our well-meaning citizens.'[113]

There was a background story to Fischer's emphasis on the need for Bauer to remain unflinching in his dedication to his chosen task. For just a few days before Bauer's inauguration, a meeting of the Protestant school inspectorate had queried the legality of his appointment. According to the Protestant members of the local school board, the appointment of a Catholic as secular school inspector represented a violation of the Bavarian constitution. And it was only after a two-hour debate that those present at the said meeting decided, by nine votes to three, that Bauer's appointment was in accordance with existing regulations. As one of the initial opponents of

Bauer's appointment explained, what had caused resentment among portions of Augsburg's Protestant establishment was that the magistrate had
failed to consult the municipal school commission in a 'matter of the foremost importance.' The magistrate responded by expressing its disdain at the
actions of the three Protestant parish priests who led the charge against
Bauer's appointment. In fact, the magistrate went so far as to judge their
behaviour as a threat to Augsburg's 'confessional peace.' In his own comment on the three rebellious clergymen, Mayor Fischer reminded the
Protestant school inspectors that the days had gone when parish priests
were effectively running the local school board.[114]

Bauer and his numerous allies knew that they could not expect an easy
ride; but they may not have foreseen the uphill struggle that they would soon
find themselves fighting. The opposition against the liberal school policy, and
particularly against the interdenominational schools, gathered pace from the
late 1870s. Although these schools were never attended by more than 20 per
cent of the town's primary-school pupils, this was enough to engage liberals
and religious conservatives in a protracted conflict over its future. What constituted the divide was thus not in the first instance confession, but moral
conviction. Catholics and Protestants could be found on both sides of the
battle lines. The *Neuer Bürgerverein*, for instance, a heterogeneous political
association founded in protest against the dominant liberals, put the school
issue at the centre of its campaign in the 1878 communal elections, which led
to tensions within the association.[115] The most spirited opposition admittedly
came from ultramontane associations such as the *Casino* and the *Christlicher
Arbeiterverein*. In 1879, a member of the former society noted that the
Simultanschule was of 'great interest to many a Catholic heart.'[116]

Overall, however, efforts to bolster interdenominational schools in the city
appear to have strengthened their opponents. In 1879, for instance, 1040
inhabitants of the *Wertach* district signed a petition against inter-confessional
education.[117] The Bavarian government's confessional turn of the 1880s
added further weight to the movement. Augsburg's Centre Party quickly
capitalized on this. Thus, when the founding of a new school was discussed
in the town council in 1889, Centre Councillor Schweiger justified his
opposition to the project by pointing to the Bavarian government's recent
recognition of denominational school as 'the norm.' It was now widely
agreed, Schweiger noted, that interdenominational schools bred 'indifference
towards all things religious.' This was all the more problematic, he opined, in
a district 'inhabited mostly by workers.' Schweiger's observations were refuted

by Councillor Mayer from the *Wertach* district, who claimed that only 'a small minority' among its inhabitants were opposed to the *Simultanschule*. Councillor Forster, a member of the local school board, seconded Mayer's claim, insisting that parents who wished to send their children to confessional schools were free to do so. His view was challenged by councillor Schweiger, however, who pointed out that the *Wertach* district's interdenominational school was in effect compulsory, as the only Catholic school to which parents could send their children (which was in the parish of St. Georg) was already heavily over-subscribed.[118] Nothing suggests that by the turn of the century Catholic parents had lost interest in the debate surrounding confessional schools. Thus, an 1895 meeting in a local inn devoted to the issue attracted more than 100 'Catholic heads of family'.[119]

By the 1890s the state authorities had ceased to defend the *Simultanschule* against its numerous critics. In fact, from that point onwards some state inspectors began to pick on the alleged weaknesses of interdenominational schools. Thus in an 1897 report, the district inspector responsible for Augsburg, while he praised the commitment of the teachers working for the mixed schools, noted that the 'cooperation between teachers and clergy (especially the Catholic clergy) could be much more heartfelt and collegial.'[120] A subsequent inspection report on the situation at the *Wertach* schools pointed out several areas of concern. These included the number of unexcused absences; the lack of parental guidance and encouragement, as well as the poor overall grasp of religious knowledge that made the work of the religious teachers more difficult.[121] Another major problem concerned the exceptionally high number of pupils having to repeat a school year. As the district inspectorate noted with astonishment in its report on the schools in the *Wertach* district: in some classes the rate of pupils failing promotion was above 30 per cent, which the local school board attributed to the high number of working-class children having migrated to Augsburg from rural areas.[122] The liberal *Verein der Wertach-Vorstädte* begged to disagree. The children of the district had shown that their knowledge of religion was 'just as sound as that of the children attending the confessional schools in the city centre.' But the charge that the interdenominational schools provided 'inferior religious instruction' was also rejected on grounds of first principle: 'Not the school, but the parents, are responsible for [religious education].'[123] In this reading at least, the school, rather than an extension of the family, was a public space; and because it was public, it had to be secular.

Even so, it seems that, by the 1890s at the latest, commentators from various political and confessional backgrounds (with the notable exception of liberals and those further to the left) had begun to associate inter-denominational schools not only with a lack of moral standards, but also with poor performance. The Catholic Casino in particular attacked the schools in its lecture series throughout the 1890s. In a talk entitled 'The Simultanschule and its tendency,' dome preacher Steigenberger gave a damning verdict of the school's moral impact on the children and on society at large. He began by noting that, although the 'former excitement' (*Weissglühhitze*) about this type of school was on the wane, there were still 'regions in the Reich' where such schools were held 'in high esteem' (Steigenberger referred to Baden, the Palatinate, and parts of Hessen in particular). Referring to the liberal position on inter-confessional schools, Steigenberger noted that there were people who thought these schools 'conducive to confessional peace,' as well as to the welfare of the German Reich more widely. The opposite was true according to Steigenberger: Interdenominational schools had resulted in a deepening of the 'rift between the different religions.' The *Simultanschulen*, instead of serving as 'places engendering harmony and religious peace,' were in fact 'godless places' (*Orte der Religionslosigkeit*), which many liberals supported because they saw them as a 'bulwark against the Catholic Church.' Steigenberger concluded with the assertion that those Catholics who 'endeavoured to defend religion' were the 'most German of all Germans,' since religion was 'the most German of all works.' He buttressed his point by citing Wilhelm I: 'The people's religion must be retained.'[124] Just a few years later, an even more radical invective against the institution of the *Simultanschule* was let loose by a Catholic teacher from Pfersee. It culminated in the view that Catholic teachers supporting interdenominational schools acted in violation of the 'dogma of godly truth' (*Dogma von der göttlichen Wahrheit*).[125] For the liberal reformers, the hope in the capacity of elementary schools to act as engines of socio-cultural change, both in the town and beyond, had been dashed.

Aiming higher

In more than one respect, Ulm's elementary schools faced similar challenges to those of Augsburg and Ludwigshafen. Over-crowding was one.

Up until 1867, for example, its Catholic primary school consisted of a single class of more than 150 children of widely varying age and ability. In 1868, a three-grade system was introduced that divided the then 190 Catholic elementary-school children into age cohorts. By that point the average class size had fallen to about 65 pupils, which satisfied both experts and the general public.[126] The situation did not differ fundamentally at the Protestant *Volksschule*, which in 1837 consisted of ten school classes of, on average, 90 children; as late as 1895, the largest of the Protestant elementary-school classes comprised 89 pupils.[127]

The average classroom was small, with 60 children being taught in a room of about 50 square metres being on the comfortable side. Complaints about over-crowded classrooms thus resurfaced throughout the imperial period. Liberals in particular asserted that Ulm could ill-afford to fall behind the most successful providers of elementary-school education in the state. Thus, in 1872, one reader of a liberal daily opined that as a *Gewerbestadt* Ulm needed good schools to be able to 'take on the fight with factory industry.'[128] A few months later, another reader warned that the 'shortage of teachers' threatened to undermine 'the people's education, and hence the nation's education and invigoration. In one word: our entire *Volksschulwesen* is in need of reform!'[129] The problems readers identified cannot really be attributed to a lack of commitment to the *Volksschule*. Thus in 1874, liberal commentators noted that Ulm was 'currently sparing no effort to establish new, well equipped schools and classrooms;' a fact which they attributed to the 'lively contest' in which 'towns both in and outside Württemberg' were currently engaged.[130] Nor did Ulm shy away from committing large sums to its schools. By 1880, Ulm was spending 111,854 marks on its primary and secondary schools, which accounted for just under a fifth of total municipal expenditure.[131]

Yet in a number of significant respects, Ulm differed from both Augsburg and Ludwigshafen. Above all, Ulm did not appoint a secular school inspector, and its schools continued to be organized according to denominational criteria. The city's school boards were chaired by clerics, who were responsible for the inspection of schools representing their own confession. More importantly, Ulm only had confessional schools at the elementary level. No doubt, many National Liberals would have welcomed inter-confessional schools. In the immediate aftermath of the victory over France—for a period of about two years during which the formerly dominant democrats carried the stigma of particularism—many claimed that in the past Württemberg's *Volksschule* had been 'too particularistic.' Many attributed this deficiency to a less regulated, less uniform approach to education than had been practised in Prussia since the 1850s. Ulm's supporters of the *Deutsche Partei*, while conceding that a 'mechanistic approach' might not be right for Württemberg, still maintained that the Prussian *Volksschule* had 'taught its people how to be victorious.' But there was hope, many argued, that Württemberg would be able to make up for lost opportunities. There was hope, that is, that national unification might inject 'a spirit of national enthusiasm into our schools.'[132]

But at no point did these ambitions threaten the confessional organization of the city's elementary schools. Ulm's city council, composed as it was of both *Deutsche Partei* liberals and *Volkspartei* democrats, knew how divisive the school question had proved in other states and regions of the Empire. The fact that Ulm's *Oberbürgermeister* during this period were moderate reformers whose support cut across political and confessional boundaries (von Heim was a Free Conservative, while his successor Wagner sympathized with a moderate brand of National Liberalism) seems to have enabled a more conciliatory climate. Relations between the confessions were relatively good, at least at the level of elites.

The opening of the new Catholic *Volksschule* at the *Sedelhofgasse* in 1886, built to house the steadily rising number of Catholic primary-school children under one roof, offers a case in point. In the same year the Catholic teaching staff had increased from 7 to 11 full-time members, who between themselves were responsible for four boys' and five girls' classes. The so-called *Frauenschule*, a school designed to prepare girls who had completed the compulsory period of elementary schooling for work, was housed in the same building.[133] The inauguration of the new school building was performed in a public act in which the mayor, the council, Catholic clergy, and teachers, as well as a large crowd of other guests, participated.[134] After the ceremony, parish priest Berger, who also acted as chair of the town's Catholic school commission, thanked the authorities 'in the name of the Catholic community' for the 'trust' they had shown towards him and his parishioners. He also expressed his gratitude at the financial sacrifices the municipality had made, and for providing his community 'with a beautiful building.' Berger ended by reassuring the mayor of his intention to 'watch over the progress of both children and teachers.'[135]

Yet what renders Ulm illuminating is not that it was 'exceptional,' which it was not, but the fact that it offers an alternative story of educational reform.[136] The long-standing controversy surrounding the appointment of new elementary school teachers offers particularly rich material in this respect. The absence of a secular inspection regime, as existed in both Augsburg and Ludwigshafen, did not mean that Ulm's authorities lacked ways of influencing appointment decisions; only that they had to be more inventive on this plane. Württemberg law did not entitle secular representatives of the municipality to occupy a seat on the appointment committee for teaching positions. Their involvement depended entirely on the willingness of the respective committee (which was usually chaired by a local cleric acting in accordance with his superior clerical authority) to grant them representation. What proved significant, however, was that Ulm's Protestant school committee was more willing to accommodate secular demands than its Catholic counterpart: While the city's Protestants had since 1848 offered the municipality a say in the appointment of new teachers, the Catholic school committee steadfastly refused to do likewise.

It was this divergence that the city authorities would exploit to promote their own educational agenda within the given legal parameters. This they did by offering different wages to Catholic and Protestant teachers. The logic by which the council justified its decision to pay Catholic primary-school teachers' salaries that were, on average, about ten per cent below those of their Protestant colleagues was as follows: In withholding a right which the Protestant school committee had afforded the municipality, the Catholic committee had forfeited an entitlement it would otherwise be able to enjoy. Ulm's authorities were on safe ground in legal terms, since Catholic teachers received a salary that was in accordance with the state's wage scale for elementary school teachers. All they did was to pay Protestant teachers an extra allowance in recognition of the role the municipality was allowed to play in their appointment. At the same time, the door for equal pay remained wide open. Thus, whenever the Catholic Consistory in Stuttgart requested equal pay for Ulm's Catholic teachers, the council offered to comply in exchange for being given a seat on the Catholic appointment committee, a request that the Catholic authorities refused to grant.[137] Ulm's request was exceptional by Württemberg standards, for no other municipality consistently demanded a say in the appointment of Catholic elementary-school teachers.[138]

Those who paid the price for the Catholic Consistory's rejection of any secular involvement were the Catholic teachers. Some of them expressed serious misgivings about their financial discrimination. Just a few weeks after the battle at Sedan, for instance, the chair of Ulm's Catholic school committee, the 45-year-old elementary teacher Anton Häussler, wrote to the city authorities to demand a pay rise for himself and his Catholic colleagues.[139] The council rejected Häussler's request out of hand, encouraging him to double his efforts to convince the Catholic authorities in Stuttgart to reconsider their stance.[140] After receiving a negative answer from the Catholic Consistory, Häussler put the ball back in the municipality's court, insisting that he had done all he could to make the Consistory fall in line on this matter. It was now up to the town council, he protested, to treat him fairly by meeting his demand for a wage increase. But the council remained undeterred. While expressing their regrets, its members recommended that Häussler and his colleagues be encouraged to continue putting pressure on their superiors in Stuttgart.[141] In April 1872, in offering Catholic teachers an annual pay rise of 50fl (which still placed them well below their Protestant colleagues), Ulm's council created a further incentive for Catholic teachers to lobby the Catholic Consistory in support of increased secular involvement.[142]

It took another two decades until the Catholic Consistory began to alter its position on this question. In 1891, it offered Ulm's authorities the right to participate in the election of teachers at Catholic schools with effect from December.[143] But the fact that this right was restricted to a period of ten years shows the degree of scepticism that accompanied this apparent change of heart. In 1900, shortly before the trial period came to an end, the Catholic Consistory announced that it would not extend the arrangement.[144] It gave two reasons for its decision. The first was that Ulm was the only municipality in Württemberg to enjoy representation on a Catholic school board.[145] It further criticized the town authorities for not having done enough to prevent the over-crowding at Catholic schools, unlike their counterparts in Stuttgart, Heilbronn or Esslingen. Ulm's mayor Wagner chose not to engage with these two points, the first of which was a fact and the second an accusation. Instead, he merely informed the town's Catholic school board that, should the Catholic Consistory deliver on its promise, Ulm would have no choice but to lower the wages of Catholic teachers to the state's prescribed minimum.[146] At a subsequent meeting, the council once again asked the *Katholischer Kirchenrat* to reverse its decision in the interest of Ulm's Catholic teachers.[147]

But the Catholic authorities remained firm, arguing that Stuttgart, Heilbronn, Esslingen, and Cannstatt all paid salaries above the legal minimum despite having no say in the appointment of Catholic teachers. They also surmised that, in contrast to their Protestant colleagues, most Catholic candidates were from outside Ulm, which made it difficult for the secular authorities to judge their ability as teachers.[148] Refusing to accept this argument, Ulm's council resorted to another strategy to retain the pressure on the Catholic Consistory. It confirms that its basic aim was to create a rift between the teachers and their superiors in Stuttgart. Thus, whereas Catholic teachers appointed before the expiration of the agreement in 1901 continued to receive a salary equal to their Protestant colleagues, those appointed thereafter would be paid the legal minimum.[149] The strategy apparently bore some fruit, since on 29 March 1904, the Catholic authorities returned to the previous agreement, allowing secular representation in return for higher wages.[150]

Yet agreements of this kind did not put an end to existing tensions, however subdued, between the council and the Catholic authorities overseeing elementary education. In 1904, the council's representative on the Catholic school board, Kasimir Mangold (a Catholic teacher and member of the liberal-leaning *Katholischer Lehrerverein*) accused the clerical majority of holding prejudices against liberal teachers. According to Mangold, all four of the candidates the panel had selected from a field of 68 applicants were members of the *Katholischer Schulverein*, an association he accused of opposing school reforms. Within days of the decision, Mangold informed two municipal councillors—the liberal Dr Schefold and the left-liberal Mayer—about what had happened during the short-listing meeting. His version of events quickly entered the pages of the democratic *Ulmer Zeitung* (founded in 1890) and two regional newspapers of liberal orientation, the *Beobachter* and the *Schwäbische Kronik*. Infuriated by what it described as anti-Catholic reports, the *Kirchenrat* in Stuttgart responded by instituting legal proceedings against Mangold for his alleged breach of confidentiality. Mangold was further accused of having acted out of frustration, because 'none of the short-listed teachers was a member of the liberal *Katholischer Lehrerverein* that he himself represents.' The Consistory denied that Ulm's Catholic school committee had selected the four teachers for any reason other than their proven pedagogic ability.[151]

It is at this point that we need to contemplate another reason why Ulm's council refrained from adopting a more hardline approach towards the Catholic authorities in the school question. It will bring us back to the point made at the outset, namely, that the reform-minded public, and liberals in particular, viewed schools as transformative agencies; as places from which a shared urban space, and hence a new community, could, with time, evolve. What proved decisive here was the place elementary schools occupied in the considerations of the city's reform-minded population. A significant portion of Ulm's public projected their aspirations more onto the secondary schools than on the local *Volksschule*. Thus, while for many middle-class parents the established elementary schools were not really an attractive proposition, the more advanced schools—for which the town's newspapers and other exponents of reform used terms such as *bessere Schulanstalten* (better educational institutes), *höheres Schulwesen* (higher schools), or *gelehrtes Schulwesen* (learned schools)—were thriving.

These included the *Mittelschule*, a school that offered an advanced curriculum for 9- to-14-year olds. It also entailed the *Gymnasium*, the traditional grammar school providing a humanistic education centred on the learning of Latin and Greek. Also gaining in prestige was the *Realschule*, a secondary school with a strong vocational bent; and the same applies to the *Oberrealschule*, a modern-type grammar school based on a more science-based curriculum. The 1870s also saw an expansion of secondary education for girls: the vocationally orientated *Mädchenschule* reformed its traditional curriculum in the course of the 1870s, while the formerly private *höhere Töchterschule*, a school that offered a classical education for girls, was taken over by the municipality in 1878.[152] In response to the public's craving for higher forms of education, in the early 1870s the *Oberrealschule* was renamed *Oberrealgymnasium* on parental request.[153]

A glance at the figures suggests that this was more than a game of words. Of Ulm's 3800 school-aged children in 1878, only a third attended the local elementary schools.[154] Within the region, Ulm was known for the quality and range of its secondary schools, and particularly for its *höheres Schulwesen*.[155] The class background of the parents who sent their children to the two higher secondary schools was by no means uniform. Among the children attending the *Realgymnasium*, where science and maths subjects were prominent, the sons of traders and merchants (44 per cent) were predominant. What is at least as instructive, however, is the fact that lower civil servants (23 per cent) and artisans (18 per cent) also figured prominently among

Figure 6. Gymnasium Ulm, Olgastrasse, 1870. © Stadtarchiv Ulm.

those who sent their children to this type of grammar school. Of the pupils attending the more traditional humanistic *Gymnasium*, the sons of traders and merchants (31 per cent), those with parents who had attended a similar school (27 per cent), as well as higher civil servants and the military (15 per cent) supplied the largest contingents. Yet, in Ulm at least, this prestigious secondary school also appealed to lower civil servants (17 per cent) and artisans (eight per cent).[156]

In an 1875 report to a district inspector, Ulm's mayor von Heim ascribed the increasing popularity of the town's secondary schools to the city's educational ethos. As he proudly stated on the occasion of a swearing-in ceremony for new councillors: 'Every able boy, whether rich or poor, is here given the opportunity to attend the best educational institutes, and to acquire knowledge that he can apply in his later life.'[157] The mayor was by no means alone in attributing the costly expansion of Ulm's higher schools to the ambition of a broad cross-section of the population; their wish to see their sons, and increasingly their daughters, too, receive an advanced education, if necessary with the help a scholarship provided by one of the city's well-endowed charities. That Ulm's population displayed a remarkable degree of educational aspiration was not lost on other observers, including those who lamented the trend. To quote from a reader's letter to a local daily:

Every small tradesman or inn-keeper, subaltern civil servant, railway worker, or postman, everyone it seems, even the most penniless artisan, regards it as his duty to send his sons to the *Gymnasium* or the *Realanstalt* and—which is just as deplorable—to have his daughters educated at the *höhere Mädchenschule*, irrespective of whether he can afford it, and regardless of whether the children possess the talent which alone entitles someone to pursue higher education. What is to become of a grammar school boy of fifteen, sixteen or eighteen years of age? Is he to become an artisan? He will be much too old and too educated for that. He who has immersed himself into foreign languages will regard a manual profession as being below his station.... It is time to change course. It is time to warn of the addiction to 'higher education,' and above all of making children 'highly educated.'[158]

According to several critics, this hunger for education favoured a series of despicable habits. In 1878, for example, a reader lamented the behaviour of many ambitious parents, who were in the habit of taking their children along to public lectures on highbrow subjects. These lectures, the reader opined, went over the head of school-attending teenagers.[159]

And while some in Ulm condemned the middling sort of people for using advanced schools to rise above their station, others expressed regret at the persistent predominance of confessional schools. Thus in 1892, an article in the *Ulmer Tagblatt* decried the state's retreat in the question of interdenominational schools. What, less half a century ago, 'Germany's educated classes, and even the pious and observant men among them' would have found 'difficult to comprehend,' had come to be regarded as normal: namely, that the state would object to 'Protestant and Catholic children gathering in the same classroom in order to receive instruction in matters of a human and secular nature.'[160] What is noteworthy, however, is that the article in question appeared as a reprint from an editorial published in the Bremen-based liberal *Weser-Zeitung*. Its author criticized the new *Volksschulgesetz* then debated in Prussia's *Abgeordnetenhaus*, in which Conservatives and the Centre predominated. Originating from the Ministry of Culture headed by Robert von Zedlitz, the law proposed a series of far-reaching concessions towards confessional education at elementary-school level, including a wholesale handover of school inspection to clerical authorities (the law would provoke a degree of public outrage that in 1892 led to von Zedlitz's resignation as Minister of Culture). That a liberal newspaper like the *Ulmer Tagblatt* would cover an important school law proposed in Germany's largest state is hardly surprising. What is revealing, however, is that its editors did not exploit this incident to challenge Ulm's educational status quo.

Why did they refrain from doing so? Resorting to Württemberg's alleged exceptionalism would mean to substitute a convenient shortcut for an explanation. The fact that many liberals felt more ambivalent about interdenominational schools than they were willing to admit in public may have played its part here. What the comparison of the three towns suggests, however, is that what proved even more crucial is the degree to which liberals, and the reform-minded public that supported them, could integrate the local schools into a communal narrative from which their town emerged as a place that was engaged in a journey towards progress. This powerful narrative, in which local progress enhanced the status of the nation, was difficult to reconcile with a situation in which the confessional schools reigned supreme. As far as the reform-minded public was concerned, schools had to be refitted for the journey.

Yet few things are perfect. The tensions that arose between expectation and reality produced different educational dynamics and scenarios. In Ludwigshafen, the liberals exploited their own predominance, facilitated by the lack of long-standing confessional structures, to make the interdenominational schools the educational norm even before unification. In Augsburg, where liberal nationalists had ruled since the 1860s over a city numerically dominated by Catholics, the *Simultanschulen* remained confined to the young working-class districts. The result was a particularly marked divergence between reality and expectations. Following this logic, one would expect the tensions to be even more marked in Ulm. Yet here, the urban public developed a conspicuous taste for the advanced secondary schools. Many began to push for their expansion and diversification. By becoming accessible to wider strata that benefited from the city's private funding opportunities, the secondary schools provided the transformative agents that were commensurate with the narrative of the town as work in progress— a narrative that rhymed with the aspirations of many parents. This applies despite the fact that, as the century drew to a close, not everyone felt as confident as the author of the history that had been commissioned for Ludwigshafen's 50th-year anniversary:

[W]e can conclude that our *Volksschule* is well suited to imparting in our youth the cultural achievements of the present, thereby equipping it for the fierce competition that is modern life. Yet just as human life never reaches the end of its development, the organization of our school must never come to an end.[161]

PART II

Place-Makers

Prologue
Coming and Staying

The stranger will thus not be considered here in the usual sense of the term, as the wanderer who comes today and goes tomorrow, but rather as the man who comes today and stays tomorrow—the potential wanderer, so to speak, who, although he has gone no further, has not quite got over the freedom of coming and going.

Georg Simmel, 1908[1]

If we consider the experiences of millions of Germans in the latter part of the nineteenth century, coming and staying was at least as salient as coming and going. Numerous people were on the move. Yet while many moved overseas, the bulk of German migration in this period was short-distance: most migrants either remained within their home state or migrated to a neighbouring one.[2] By the century's end about one-sixth of Germany's urban population had resided in their city for less than one year.[3]

But if moving was a widespread reality, staying was a pervasive ambition. The late nineteenth century was therefore also a period of strangers trying to create a place for themselves in their new municipalities of residence. Like so much else, of course, strangeness lay in the eyes of the beholder. In a society where small and medium-sized communities remained fairly common, strangers could be those living in a nearby municipality. Individuals hailing from another state were almost certainly labelled strangers. Well into the 1870s, German municipal authorities habitually referred to close-distance migrants (who in their large majority were citizens of other German states) as *Ausländer*, or foreigners.

Indeed, few phenomena more preoccupied German municipal governments than the civic status of their resident populations. Whereas economic liberalization in practice meant displacement, municipal citizenship appeared to offer a means to control the dynamics that the liberal economy had unleashed. Many regarded it as a bulwark of urban territoriality as they understood it; as a promise that the town in which they earned their liveli-hood would continue to exist as a meaningful place, grounded in a set of rules and conventions, rather than as a functional space shaped, for the main part, by the effects of markets and imperial laws. Even urban liberals, who habitually envisaged their communities as having embarked on a journey, often imagined the civic life of their towns in terms of a relatively fixed cosmos—as a place whose basic parameters were set.

The profound economic transformation that Germany experienced in the latter half of the nineteenth century would have been inconceivable had people been unable to move freely without fear of discrimination at the hands of local communities. The first steps towards a more liberal regime of internal migration were taken in Prussia during the 1840s and 1850s, when the right of settlement was effectively decoupled from the possession of municipal citizenship. From that point onwards, one year of official or two years of confirmed settlement entitled Prussian citizens to receive welfare benefits and at the same time protected them from expulsion.[4] This princi-ple, called *Unterstützungswohnsitz*, became the basis of the constitution of the North German Confederation (1867), and subsequently of the German Empire (1870). The imperial Relief Residence Law of 6 June 1870 (*Reichsgesetz über den Unterstützungswohnsitz*) decreed that the community of residence would be responsible for providing poor relief after a two-year period of residence, irrespective of whether someone possessed full citizen-ship rights in the municipality in which they had come to reside.[5]

The southern states adopted the imperial law with a slight delay. In both Baden and Württemberg it entered into force on 1 January 1873, while Bavaria nominally retained its *Heimatrecht* until 1 January 1916. While the imperial Relief Residence Law was unpopular among municipalities across the German lands (the bulk of the liberal-dominated ones included), there is no doubt that the challenge was greatest where the *Heimatrecht* had until recently supplied the undisputed norm. In the South, for instance, poverty relief entitlements based on residence disappeared with Napoleon's defeat at Leipzig in 1813. Indeed, both the Bavarian *Gemeindeedikt* of 1818 and the Württemberg Constitution of 1819 rested on the principle of *Heimat*. As §62 of the Württemberg Constitution of 1819 stated: 'The *Gemeinden* are the pillars of the state.' And a little further down: 'Each member of the state must belong to a *Gemeinde*.'[6] In Württemberg the *Heimat*-based conception of citizenship was barely altered until the 1870s, while in Bavaria it would remain in place until the First World War.

Whatever the benefits of *Gewerbefreiheit* and of freedom of movement, these reforms left a number of thorny practical problems unresolved. For in reality, people's freedom of movement was bound to remain restricted so long as they could not expect to receive basic poor relief in the case where they fell ill, or suffered an accident or another blow of fate that would endanger their material existence (such as the loss of the main bread winner). The imperial social insurance scheme of the 1880s would no doubt improve matters, but not without a time lag of several decades.[7] It was one thing to create the legal conditions for people to be able to circulate freely within a national economic space; and quite another to ensure that they could realize this ambition in a society where much of the real power remained concentrated in the hands of local communities.[8]

Many liberals, particularly in the South, continued to regard municipalities 'as independent corporations.' In the debates that took place in the Frankfurt parliament in 1848, for instance, representatives of the southern states were particularly adamant in their defence of local autonomy, while calls to make sacrifices in the name of national unity came usually from delegates who represented constituencies from north of the River Main. Carl Mittermaier, professor of criminal law and delegate for Baden, offers a good example. In a heated exchange over free movement Mittermaier argued that, were the new residence law to be introduced as some of his colleagues from Prussia had requested, his folks back home would batter him to death. Other liberals and democrats also demanded that the distinction between state and municipal citizenship be retained in the interest of the social and economic cohesion of the *Gemeinde*.[9]

Even delegates who supported economic liberalization spoke out in defence of the municipalities' right to grant or deny communal citizenship to newcomers as they saw fit. Only a small minority on the far Left condemned municipal citizenship as a 'device in the hands of the privileged classes.' For left-wing republicans in particular, a system in which not someone's place of residence (*Wohnsitz*) but his or her place of origin (*Heimat*) provided the basis for entitlement to poor relief was unworthy of a modern society.[10] If someone was in need, it was usually their community of origin (their so-called *Heimatgemeinde*), rather than their municipality of residence (*Wohnsitzgemeinde*) that was liable to provide support. This meant that many who needed welfare or poverty relief were forced to return to their *Heimatgemeinde*. In view of this, and because for many the acquisition of municipal citizenship was a costly affair, this system tended to impair people's freedom of movement, and hence the kind of economic freedom that liberals had demanded in the name of progress and national integration.[11]

Few things mattered more than money when it came to retaining communal agency. In shouldering much of the cost of economic liberalization, the *Gemeinden* did much to defend themselves as legitimate and meaningful entities.[12] Although city councils (as well as many tax-paying citizens) often bitterly complained about their financial obligations towards new residents, they also drew confidence from their considerable financial responsibilities. In this less conspicuous part of the story, they thus capitalized on the part they played in oiling the wheels of a series of far-reaching economic and institutional reforms. Estimates suggest that around 1900 German localities spent considerably more on social support and poor relief than did either the federal states or the imperial state.[13] Many urban reformers seem to have been well aware that, certainly when it came to making economic liberalization work, the nation was little more than the sum of its municipal parts.

What we see, then, is not the demise of the *Bürgergemeinde* in the face of advancing modernization.[14] Such a perspective not only rests on an idealized view of the imperial past.[15] It also dramatically underestimates the creative energies and regenerative powers of urban communities, and the part they play in the construction of institutional networks and structures beyond the local level. There is of course no doubt that, from the mid-1860s, most state authorities sought to install residence as the basis for pauper relief. Yet since they were unwilling to pick up the bill for their modernizing agenda, the municipalities' capacity to shape developments according to their own preferences was not fundamentally diminished. It was against this backdrop that many towns began to fashion a series of strategies to defend what they deemed their right and proper interests. These ranged from means tests and expulsions at one end, to franchise restrictions at the other end of the spectrum. Restricting access to citizenship became one of the key mechanisms in this contest between the state and the local communities.

Naturalization was often highly expensive.[16] Although from the middle of the century various states imposed a maximum limit on what municipalities could charge, naturalization fees continued to vary significantly. For the less-well-off, including unqualified workers and single or widowed women, they remained substantial throughout the nineteenth century.

What varied much less was the purpose of citizenship fees, which was to exclude the poor and incorporate the well-off residents, if necessary through compulsion. German municipalities had no interest in granting citizenship to the poor, mainly because such a policy would have undermined their vision of the self-sufficient *Bürgergemeinde* of independent heads of family.[17] As late as 1896 the eminent scholar of constitutional law, Max von Seydel, criticized what he saw as the anachronism of Bavaria's citizenship and social relief law: the fact that, with its emphasis on *Heimat*, rather than *Wohnsitz*, it imagined a largely sedentary population, at a time when the situation in Bavaria's industrial centres was much like in Prussia.[18] Meanwhile, commentators from the political left lamented the widening of the gap between political rights and socio-economic duties. As the Social Democrats Paul Hirsch and Hugo Lindemann wrote in an influential publication in 1905: 'The number of those whose rights rested on ancestry began to pale in relation to the number of migrants who, although they contributed their fair share to the life of the municipality, would remain without any influence on its direction.'[19]

At one level, of course, these concepts simply denote differences in legal status: a citizen of a municipality enjoyed particular economic and political rights there by virtue of his legal status as a *Gemeindebürger*. Yet to contemporaries, and particularly to the citizens of a particular municipality, these concepts evoked different kinds of imagined community and concomitant visions of place. Put simply, at least in the context of local citizenship, *Heimat* stood for a community that was both stable and closely knit, while *Wohnsitz* had gained prominence in the era of the potential wanderer, to use Georg Simmel's poignant phrase. While *Heimat* evoked an exclusive place, *Wohnsitz* was reflective of the functional conception of space according to which municipalities were to be little more than elements on a national map. Throughout the nineteenth century these conceptions of community remained in tension with one another.

In spite of similar challenges, however, towns employed different strategies as they sought to reconstruct the *Bürgergemeinde*, the community of citizens. Thus, as we shall see in relation to civic inclusion, the economically more conservative Ulm acted much more progressively than the highly industrialized Ludwigshafen. But the real lesson appears to be much more radical than that. It is not just that the two tendencies sometimes complemented each other, resulting in a constellation that Reinhart Koselleck has described as the *Gleichzeitigkeit des Ungleichzeitigen*. It is, rather, that the defence of the status quo in one area could be *conducive to* far-reaching reforms in another.

Just as significant, and at least as visible, were the efforts by various groups of residents to open up new avenues of civic inclusion. For citizenship was not only about the remaking of towns as integrated places. It was also about people—such as men and women who began to organize themselves in *Bürgerrechtsvereinen* and in various kinds of consumer cooperatives—creating a place for themselves in the towns which they inhabited. Up to a degree, their efforts represent an explicit response to the exclusionary tendencies of local citizenship. Just as important, however, they constitute attempts to widen the realm of citizenship, not primarily via legal reform but through increasing the spectrum of recognized civic participation. In one sentence: by creating more spaces and places for civic inclusion.[20]

3
Citizens and Residents

On the list of imperial laws whose impact on our practical lives is not always advantageous,…the Imperial Residence Relief Law occupies a preeminent place.

Article entitled, *Unterstützungswohnsitz oder Heimatrecht*, Ulmer Tagblatt (1878)[1]

Let us declare unmistakably that…we would see in…the abolition of the institution of the feste Heimat *a great danger not only for the municipal household but for the life of our municipality.*

Magistrate of Augsburg (1877)[2]

Instead of the Unterstützungswohnsitz *Bavaria has her* Heimatgesetz…*This* Heimat *is to bind the state citizens to their fatherland; the Bavarian is to possess a place where he is permanently at home, receives welfare support in time of need, a place from which nobody can expel him.*

Franz Josef Ehrhart, leading SPD politician in the Palatinate and fierce critic of the Bavarian *Heimatgesetz*, Ludwigshafen (1901)[3]

In 1852 Ulm's then mayor, Julius Schuster, reminded the members of the citizens' committee (*Bürgerausschuss*) that both the world and Germany were changing. In particular, he noted, the 'material unification of Germany' had become a reality in the course of the 1840s, with far-reaching consequences for the dozens of states and thousands of municipalities that dotted the German lands.[4] The free movement of goods and people, which for Schuster were hallmarks of the new era, had heightened both prosperity and poverty. Starting in Saxony and parts of Prussia, the shock waves of economic liberalization had now reached southern Germany with a vengeance. One way to absorb them, and one which the mayor thought best suited to local circumstances, was to protect existing industries 'against outside competition.' Yet protectionism in itself would not do according to Schuster. Instead, any protectionist measures had to be combined with a reform of municipal citizenship and poor relief. Most of all, the mayor recommended, Ulm had to tackle the challenges that lay ahead in a spirit of co-operation and openness, of inventiveness even. Only through 'the combined efforts of state, corporations and private means of support' could the threat of financial ruin be averted.[5]

Having affirmed that the situation was serious rather than hopeless, the mayor urged his colleagues to look for outside inspiration. As far as he could judge, states had adopted two contrasting strategies to cope with the financial impact of economic liberalization. The first, practiced in Prussia and Switzerland, was to boost economic mobility by introducing the freedom of residence for citizens of the same state. Schuster felt no need to explain that, were such a regime introduced in Württemberg, the guilds would lose their remaining powers to control access to labour markets. The second strategy, practiced in Hannover and Austria, tied the right of trade to municipal citizenship. Württemberg, Schuster noted with a sense of relief, had so far chosen a path that lay somewhere in between these two 'diametrically opposed systems': While its citizens were free to reside wherever they chose, its *Gemeinden* were nevertheless entitled to confine trading rights to the holders of municipal citizenship; the law also entitled them to refuse citizenship to certain categories of applicants.[6]

Letting go of *Heimat*

As the reflections by Ulm's mayor indicate, the pressures on south-German municipalities to reform their practice of citizenship and poor relief had become acute at least two decades before unification. From the mid-1860s the balance that Ulm's mayor had been hoping for, between offering people the liberty to settle freely and allowing municipalities to control access to economic resources, began to tip in favour of the former. With the *Gemeindeordnung* of 1862, the guilds were formally abolished. In the same year, a new state law regulating poor relief came into force, further shifting the financial responsibility from place of origin (*Heimat*) to place of residence (*Wohnsitz*). As § 1 of the new law decreed: *Die bürgerliche Armenpflege ist Aufgabe der Gemeinden* ('Poor relief is the responsibility of the municipalities.').[7] Württemberg's municipalities, and particularly the well-endowed towns drawing most of the labour migrants, sought to oppose this wherever possible. Thus, in 1863, Ulm's council lamented that 'the larger urban communities in particular' were bound to suffer from the new law. This was because Ulm's population already included a disproportionate number of 'poor people who are not citizens;' by placing the burden of financial responsibility on the *Wonsitzgemeinde*, the community in which a migrant had taken up residence, the 'influx of such people' was set to increase even beyond current levels.[8]

An examination of citizenship applications in Ulm during the 1860s proves instructive in this regard. It shows that decisions were determined almost exclusively by financial considerations, while religious or confessional allegiances proved virtually irrelevant. Discrimination occurred mainly on economic grounds. Of the 142 applications submitted in 1864, for instance, only four were unsuccessful. Among the unlucky applicants was the butcher Conrad Angele. His example shows that moral considerations sometimes mattered, particularly where a moral blemish came on top of financial unreliability. Thus, Angele's application was turned down not only because of his proven 'financial liabilities' (the municipal records describe him as incapable of proper 'housekeeping'), or because he had proposed to marry a local girl who had the misfortune of lacking a dowry. What also appears to have influenced the council's decision was that his first marriage was divorced due to several instances of adultery. What made Ulm's councillors reject Angele's application, then, was that they deemed him untrustworthy on a number of counts.[9]

Angele's fate at the hands of the local authorities was by no means exceptional. Not even citizens could expect to receive preferential treatment if they entered into a marriage that was judged financially unviable. Thus, when the wagon-maker and Ulm citizen Friedrich Vogt decided to marry Barbara Moorath, who already had two illegitimate children, the council granted her citizenship but denied the same right to her children.[10] The organist Ludwig Diffenbacher, like Vogt a citizen of Ulm, met the same fate when he sought to acquire citizenship for his fiancée and future wife, Lisette Kochendörfer: While Kochendörfer's fortune was considered too small for comfort, as a musician Diffenbacher had to rely on an irregular income. The council concluded that the application could only be endorsed if Diffenbacher could provide 'detailed evidence of his financial circumstances.'[11] Yet these unsuccessful cases represent exceptions that confirm the rule. Of the 138 applications for municipal citizenship submitted in 1865, the only unsuccessful one was turned down after the applicant, one Barbara Roth, had failed to pay the mandatory citizenship fee of 47 gulden.[12] There is little reason to doubt that these examples, drawn from the years 1864 and 1865, are indicative of a broader pattern: on the whole, only people who possessed the required means applied for local citizenship, resulting in a success rate of close to one hundred per cent.

But the real challenge derived from the implementation of the imperial Relief Residence Law, which in Württemberg entered into force in April 1873. In line with the new law, municipalities were obliged to provide social relief for recent arrivals who fulfilled the two-year residence requirement. That the new imperial law was binding for Württemberg's municipalities was obviously significant. Equally important was the moral weight it had gained by virtue of its association with national unification. National liberals in particular, despite harbouring reservations about the law's impact on their town, proved reluctant to challenge an imperial law in public. Those further to the left, including many democrats, expressed their misgivings more openly, particularly once the moral frenzy surrounding unification had receded.

Whatever differences may have separated Württemberg's political factions, however, from the mid-1870s at the latest concerns about the principle of residence began to be expressed irrespective of party-political affiliations. Citing Bavaria's stance as proof of their assertion (it was not until 1917 that the traditional Bavarian citizenship law, based on someone's origin or *Heimat*, was replaced by the imperial *Unterstützungswohnsitz*), many critics of the new residence law claimed that there was simply no contradiction between the traditional *Heimatrecht* and the freedom of movement. That there was one had of course been the central argument in favour of making residence the new touchstone of social relief entitlements.[13]

Ulm's response to the 1875 Württemberg state survey brings out some of the most salient criticisms raised against the new law. Among the various lamentations the town's mayor expressed in his detailed report, financial ones weighed particularly heavy. Migrants were accused of opportunism. Many people, von Heim noted, would try their luck in Ulm because the support they received there was both more lucrative and more secure than was the case in municipalities lacking private charities.[14] The result was a dramatic increase in the pressure on the town's private support networks. To alleviate matters, von Heim recommended a number of measures. These included the expansion of the local insurance scheme for the particularly vulnerable group of domestic servants, the establishment of pension funds for the elderly, and the provision of additional orphanages by the state. The

logic of the mayor's argument is unmistakable: in promoting economic liberalization, the state had created new financial burdens for the municipalities; state authorities were therefore morally obliged to help the communes.[15]
A decade later, similar complaints resurfaced in relation to the 'large increase
in expenses' for illness and poverty relief as a result of free movement and
liberal residence legislation; and all this at a time, so the argument ran, when
the imperial social insurance legislation was still a long way from making a
difference.[16]

What the city council objected to most strongly was the two-year qualifying period envisaged by the imperial law, which many councillors regarded
as unduly short. Württemberg's municipalities thus responded with relief
when the Reichstag rejected a petition demanding the reduction of the
residence period by another year.[17] Yet towns such as Ulm did not simply
wallow in self-pity. Trying to make the best of what many perceived as a
bad situation, they sought to obtain a precise picture of the different categories of residents. Particular attention was paid to the whereabouts of new
residents. Their dates of arrival and departure were now registered as a
matter of course. With this information to hand, local authorities could
proceed to drawing up lists of people they considered an actual or future
financial liability. What had encouraged them to identify potential targets
for expulsion was a paragraph in the imperial law about free movement. It
stipulated that new residents who were incapable of supporting themselves
and their families could be expelled, as could those who had applied for
social welfare support before fulfilling the mandatory two-year residence
period. State authorities could thus not simply bully the *Gemeinden* into
submission. Not that they would have hesitated to do so; but they also
knew that the municipalities were the financial pillars of the state's new
economic regime.[18]

In May 1874, the head of Ulm's police force asked the town's social relief
officer to give his men access to all available records concerning poor relief.
In assessing this information, the municipal police hoped to identify actual
or potential recipients of financial support that could be expelled without
violating existing laws.[19] Ulm's *Stadtpolizeiamt* produced its first list of candidates for expulsion in the summer of 1874. It contained the names of 212
local residents: 75 workers (a category that included day labourers as well
as factory workers) represented the largest contingent; they were closely
followed by a substantial number of craftsmen; the list also featured over
80 women, including many widows, as well as several laundresses and

seamstresses.[20] We have little reason to doubt that most of the entered individuals were expelled shortly before they reached their two-year period of residence.

As the case of the spinster Josepha Pfeilmaier shows, however, the state authorities failed to endorse some expulsion orders. Pfeilmaier had moved to Ulm from neighbouring Flohberg in 1887 because, according to her own testimony, she had been 'too embarrassed' to give birth to her child 'in [her] own Heimat.' Unimpressed by the young woman's plight, in 1889 Ulm's local welfare committee recommended her expulsion to prevent her from qualifying for social relief payments. After hearing the statements of both Josepha and her father, however, the district court confirmed the state authorities' decision against her expulsion. The fact that Josepha's father, a well-to-do optician and engraver, was about to set up his business in Ulm may well have reassured the authorities that she was unlikely to become a burden to the local purse.[21] Others, like the domestic servant Engelbert Schwarz, were less fortunate. He was expelled from Ulm for a minor criminal offence. In 1882, Schwarz, who had his *Unterstützungswohnsitz* in Ulm, where he had lived for 19 years, had been sentenced to 50 days in prison for theft. As he was not a citizen of Ulm, he did not possess the unconditional right of residence, which alone would have protected him from expulsion. The municipal authorities' decision to expel him by virtue of the 1833 state citizenship law did therefore not violate the imperial law about free movement.[22]

Not that a town such as Ulm would have refused, in principle, to support individuals and families who fell into poverty. What its authorities sought to avoid, however, was that poor people whose municipality of origin was elsewhere, gained a permanent entitlement to social relief. Most of the short-term residents who became needy were supported, rather than expelled. For unless a recipient of support had been legally resident without interruption for at least two years, town councils could pass on the costs they had incurred to the recipient's previous community of residence, which usually was his or her municipality of origin (*Heimatgemeinde*). The result was a proliferation of conflicts, often mediated by state authorities, over financial liability.

The case of the 43-year-old widow Ursula Liebert from Langenau is one among many.[23] In 1877, three years after her husband had died in the poor house of Langenau, Liebert decided to move to Ulm because it offered better employment opportunities. Of her three children, the younger two remained in Langenau, where they lived with another family. Her oldest son accompanied Liebert to Ulm, where he worked as a day labourer. From 1878, Ursula Liebert, whose health had begun to deteriorate soon after her arrival, received roughly 60 marks per annum to supplement her modest monthly income of about ten marks. The amount was paid out by Ulm's social relief committee (*Armenverband*), which would then bill the municipality of Langenau, where Liebert possessed her *Heimat*. But, in 1882, for the first time the social relief committee in Langenau refused to reimburse Ulm for the support of Ursula Liebert. It justified this by claiming that she had now earned her residence relief in Ulm. Ulm's social relief committee refused to accept Langenau's position: having received income support there during her two-year qualifying period, Liebert had failed to acquire her relief residence in Ulm.[24] The district court decided that Langenau would have to pay Ulm the outstanding amount of 160 marks, but that Ulm would henceforth be responsible for the support of Ursula Liebert.[25]

For municipalities, protracted conflicts over financial liability pointed to a serious problem of information and control, one that they could ill-afford. Many towns, including Ulm, responded with a reorganization of existing arrangements for social relief and poverty. The support of poor residents through local funds was of course no invention of the 1870s. Yet before the Relief Residence Law entered into force, the situation had been relatively straightforward. Thus, Ulm's 1861 regulative on poverty relief (*Armenordnung*) singled out three categories of residents as legitimate recipients of support: first were the full citizens enjoying social as well as political rights; then came those possessing the *Heimatrecht*; and, lastly, the so-called *Beisitzer*, long-standing residents of relatively low status.[26] All recipients of welfare payments, named *Hausarme*, were obliged to receive one of the local poor guardians and to offer them 'insight into the household' and 'to respond truthfully to all his inquiries.' Poor guardian (*Armenrat*) was an honorary office, open to 'respectable citizens and residents endowed with the necessary intellectual and moral education.' Up to the 1860s, many poor guardians had belonged to a guild. Those who received poor relief had 'to act on the encouragements and reprimands' of the poor guardian in charge of their case. Recipients of poor relief who were able but unwilling to work could be forced to accept employment offered by the local authorities. Those who refused could be deprived of their meal rations for a certain period.[27]

With the reform of the town's *Armenordnung* in 1874, Ulm's authorities explicitly responded to the imperial Relief Residence Law.[28] Reflecting on the reforms carried out locally over the previous five years, Mayor von Heim noted in 1880 that 'municipal poor relief' had mostly developed 'under the authority of the imperial law concerning the *Unterstützungswohnsitz* of 6 June 1870.'[29] But just as important as the state's directives was local self-interest: high levels of labour migration, along with the dwindling of *Heimat* as the accepted touchstone for defining social relief entitlements, meant that towns that failed to reform ran the risk of seeing their budgets spiralling out of control. In an environment where most municipalities strove to improve their mechanisms of control, failing to do likewise could have costly consequences.[30]

In Ulm as elsewhere, a key part in the reform process consisted in the creation of a new municipal body, the so-called social relief and welfare commission (*Ortsarmenbehörde*).[31] While the municipal council retained overall responsibility for the administration and allocation of funds for poverty relief, the practical work was delegated to a specially established social relief committee (*Armendeputation*). Its members included the mayor, the deans of the Protestant and Catholic churches, the priest of the local hospital, as well as four councillors, three members of the *Bürgerausschuss*, and 17 poor guardians. The mayor and the dean of the Protestant church acted as joint chairs of the social relief and welfare commission, whose members met fortnightly on Monday afternoon. In practical terms, the most important part of the commission was the cohort of poor guardians, the so-called *Armenräte*. Appointed for a period of six years, the poor guardians were required to be of 'charitable spirit,' and their aim 'to serve in the interest of a good cause.' Their ranks received a massive injection of manpower (no women were appointed to the office) during the 1870s. There were 197 poor guardians in Ulm in 1886. Each was allocated a single urban district within which they had to carry out regular checks among welfare recipients; and to hand out funds to those whom the commission deemed worthy of support.[32]

The poor guardians were recruited from the respectable citizenry. Thus, in 1876, nearly half of them were independent craftsmen (especially bakers and confectioners), while a little over 20 per cent belonged to the trading profession. The army of nearly two-hundred poor guardians also included several teachers (whose number would increase from the 1890s), doctors, civil servants, clerics, as well as several people of independent means. Each poor guardian was on average responsible for 170 inhabitants, resulting in a very dense net of social control. Ulm's support network was denser, for instance, than were those of Stuttgart (950 inhabitants per poor guardian), Elberfeld (290), or Cologne (270).[33] They would check at regular intervals whether the recipients of support payments fulfilled the criteria stipulated in § 8 of the town's statute for public poverty relief: that they did not have sufficient means to support themselves, nor the capacity to earn their own living. As a municipal body, the *Armendeputation* was charged with maintaining a precise record of all the recipients of social welfare support. Annual checks were carried out to ensure that those on the lists continued to meet the criteria for receipt of relief payments. The chief social relief officer, called *Armenpfleger*, had to notify the authorities when someone was in breach of the rules. This could be because a claimant had obtained financial assistance from external sources, or because they were in a position to sustain themselves through their own work.

The trajectory of expenses devoted to poor relief between 1875 and 1886 suggests that Ulm's efforts had been effective. During the course of this period, which had seen both heightened social mobility and an economic depression affecting both consumer spending and tax revenue, the annual expenditure on social relief only rose from 52,654 to 70,970, hence by less than 2000 marks per year.[34] Encouraged by these figures, *Armenpfleger* Wolfenter concluded that there was reason to believe that 'the malicious consequences of the *Unterstützungswohnsitz*' had reached their high-water mark.[35] Significant challenges—including the close to 20,000 of unemployed journeymen that passed though Ulm every year during the 1880s and 1890s, or the high cost to be paid for rental accommodation due to shortages in the housing market—would remain. But these only prompted new reform efforts. From the turn of the century, the *Gemeinde* became even more active in providing social welfare and employment to its inhabitants.[36]

Making them *Heimat*-worthy

The question of municipal citizenship occupied an equally central place in a young industrial town like Ludwigshafen where the question of local citizenship was also seen primarily from the point of view of pecuniary and economic needs. For, while its political elite proved adept at attracting energetic entrepreneurs—the merchants and traders of the 1850s and 1860s were followed by the industrialists that from the 1870s shaped the city's economic trajectory—Ludwigshafen lacked significant financial assets. Certainly compared with more established towns such as Ulm and Augsburg, which relied on a dense network of public and private charities, Ludwigshafen was rather poorly equipped on this score. Already in its year of foundation as an independent municipality, a Bavarian state official noted that Ludwigshafen's tax revenue was insufficient to finance even the most necessary reforms:

> Whereas the representatives of communities that evolved over centuries have been able to extract revenues and accumulate a certain degree of wealth, aided by extended periods of peace, rich harvest and the growing prosperity of the population, here everything needs to be created from scratch if a state of destituteness in all spheres of life is to be avoided.[37]

Thus, while Ludwigshafen's leading entrepreneurs and politicians habitually portrayed their town as a 'German Chicago'—as a space under construction rather than a place where well-off pensioners could enjoy a walk in the park after concluding their *Kaffeekränzchen*—they resorted to metaphors of place and of status when it came to constructing the city as a civic community. In Ludwigshafen as in many other German towns of a similar ilk, civic exclusion became the flipside of extraordinary economic growth.[38]

As early as 1858, the mayoral office informed the state authorities that Ludwigshafen was 'experiencing an influx of foreign and domestic working-class families.'[39] Attracted above all by the rapidly expanding building firms and the mechanical workshops near the railway station (which specialized in the manufacturing of train carriages), these new arrivals put Ludwigshafen's financial resources under considerable strain. Besides, as far as the liberal-dominated council was concerned, their presence hampered the creation of an effective urban infrastructure. The report mentioned schools in particular. Ludwigshafen's attractiveness to labour migrants was described as deceptive: Many migrants were lured by the comparatively high wages offered to both skilled and unskilled workers.[40]

But if the local wages were above-average, the report pointed out, so were the living costs, making it difficult for new arrivals to make ends meet. Many families were therefore 'in danger of falling into poverty,' with some of the poorest having to be 'expelled from the town at the expense of their *Heimatgemeinde*' (which before the introduction of the imperial Relief Residence Law in 1871 was legally permissible). Overall, the mayor's report concluded, a worrying 'discrepancy' had opened up between the number of 'actual citizens and well-off inhabitants' on the one hand, and that of the working classes on the other.[41] By discrepancy the mayor did not mean the imbalance between the minority of citizens and the mass of the disenfranchised residents. What really worried both him and the majority of the city council was not the question of political exclusion as such (although some liberals no doubt felt uneasy about this too). What prompted their concern, rather, was its cause: the feebleness of Ludwigshafen's middle classes; the fact that the *Bürgergemeinde*, the civic core of relatively-well-to-do citizens, was small compared with the have-nots who paid little tax, and lacked social and political entitlements.

These problems persisted well into the twentieth century. As late as 1911 the city government (which now included several SPD councillors) lamented that, of a tax-paying population of 17,785, almost 80 per cent had annual salaries of less than 2000 marks. While the 'young and productive forces' would often turn their back on Ludwigshafen after a short period of residence, the 'economically weak elements' tended to settle there for good. Indeed, many individuals who had taken up residence in Ludwigshafen, the report noted bluntly, belonged to a 'rural underclass' hailing from the town's immediate hinterland. For all these reasons, the 'character of the local population' had to be called 'proletarian.'[42]

In sharp contrast, the qualified workers employed on permanent contracts— the report mentions the locksmiths, turners, foundry men, carpenters, surveyors, and masters: in short, the upwardly mobile candidates for the envisaged middle-class core—often 'lived in the countryside,' where they had bought a house and 'enjoyed the health benefits' of rural living. Meanwhile, the most qualified and most highly paid employees—the technicians, scientists and office personnel working for the large companies— rarely lived where they worked, with Mannheim presenting a particular magnet for middle-class professionals. The result was a considerable loss in tax revenue and hence in civic substance.[43] Whereas Ludwigshafen's economic contribution extended far beyond its geographical boundaries, it was left bearing the cost of a social relief system fit for a city whose core was the industrial working class.[44]

The state's legislative framework did not make things easier for a town like Ludwigshafen. What rendered Bavaria exceptional was not that its citizenship law had traditionally been founded on the principle of *Heimat*, rather than residence. As pointed out earlier, this had been true for most

German states outside Prussia up to at least the 1860s. What made it unique, rather, is that it managed to rescue this system into a period in which the rest of Germany had begun to adopt, mostly through gritted teeth (and much open envy for Bavaria's exceptionalism) the imperial Residence Relief Law. While the latter made social welfare rights contingent on a minimum period of residence (*Wohnsitz*), in Bavaria they continued to be tied to people's community of origin.

Yet, in spite of the formal retention of *Heimat*, in the course of the 1880s and 1890s Bavarian citizenship law was undergoing a series of revisions, making it increasingly difficult for municipalities to exclude or include according to their own preferences.[45] The reform of 1896 indicates the decisive step in this process. In effect, it increased the emphasis placed on residence at the expense of *Heimat*, thereby closely aligning the Bavarian law with the imperial *Unterstützungswohnsitz*.[46] In its reconstructed form, the Bavarian *Heimatrecht* enabled municipalities to demand the naturalization of erstwhile residents who had moved to another *Gemeinde*. A qualifying period of two years was now sufficient for a town to submit an application for naturalization on behalf of a former resident, regardless of an individual's knowledge or consent. After this period, the responsibility for social relief lay with someone's municipality of residence, unless his or her former *Heimatgemeinde* had failed to submit an application.

The situation was even more straightforward for individuals whose *Heimat* lay outside Bavaria, as was the case for many recently naturalized Bavarians. Responsible for this was the imperial law about free movement, which decreed that (unlike the longer-established Bavarians) new Bavarian citizens could not be forced to adopt a new *Heimatgemeinde*. What proved increasingly controversial in Bavaria was that, after four years of residence, such recent Bavarians acquired the *Heimatrecht* automatically in their municipality of residence.[47] Ludwigshafen's council responded by reinforcing an already restrictive approach towards potential new citizens. As one of the fiercest critics of this policy, the Social Democrat Friedrich Ehrhart chastised the local bourgeoisie for its obstructive practice: 'The army of have-nots, which is growing day by day in the towns and on the countryside, has become the horror of our honourable, otherwise very "patriotic" and "philanthropic" bourgeoisie.'[48] The first SPD councillor in Ludwigshafen's history, Ehrhart knew what he was talking about. As in many other southern-German towns, Ludwigshafen's authorities endeavoured to prevent the less-well-endowed inhabitants from becoming citizens.

From the late 1850s, in a first line of defence, the town council asked for increased 'financial securities' from new arrivals whose solvency it had reason to doubt. Those belonging to this category were asked to pay a deposit, 'the size of which [was to be] calculated according to the number of family members' taking up residence.[49] Here Ludwigshafen had little choice but to follow Mannheim's example, where a similar system had been in place for a number of years. New residents who did not possess their *Heimat* there had to pay a deposit of 500 gulden upon first registration, which at that point was considerably more than an average worker could earn in a year. It was this particular regime that for a few years had made Ludwigshafen an attractive destination for people with little or no means. As far as Ludwigshafen's mayor was concerned, copying Mannheim's example was therefore the only way 'to protect the interests' and 'promote the welfare' of the city. This aim could only be achieved if the majority of its population consisted of 'elements that can be expected to take a warm interest in Ludwigshafen's prosperity.' As Ludwigshafen's first mayor lamented, however, this was not the case at present.[50] For almost a decade, the state authorities went along with Ludwigshafen's practice of taking a deposit from new residents. In 1858, the state official in charge even suggested that, as an additional precaution, the town council might wish to 'demand an appropriate school fee' from families who did not possess the *Heimatrecht* in Ludwigshafen.[51]

The maxim whereby a candidate's solvency mattered most to the outcome of his or her citizenship application continued into the imperial period. The purchase of a house could sometimes alleviate existing doubts, as in the case of the shoemaker Johann Caspar Hasselbacher from nearby Neustadt. While Hasselbacher's initial application was rejected, he was nevertheless encouraged to reapply as soon as 'he saw himself in a position to take up residence in Ludwigshafen.'[52] Another applicant, the tailor Emil Görlitz, hailing from Weimar yet resident in Mannheim, was less lucky. He was rejected outright due to a 'lack of means,' and because he showed no intention of making Ludwigshafen his permanent place of residence.[53] More affluent applicants, such as the merchant Adler from Oberginzern, or the tradesman Adolph Jacquet from Frankfurt am Main, were granted citizenship without further ado. Each was simply asked to pay the statutory naturalization tax of 80 gulden, make a donation to the hospital of 140 gulden, and to prove that they had renounced their former *Heimatrecht*.[54] The records offer no indication that factory workers were being discriminated against when it came to granting citizenship. So long as they fulfilled the statutory residence requirements, had proved themselves 'capable' at work and were flawless in their 'moral conduct,' their applications would be approved.[55] The logic applied was above all a pecuniary one, while social and cultural criteria did not sway the council either way.

The fees imposed were thus both a means to control immigration and to generate much-needed financial revenue. While the 38,034 gulden that Ludwigshafen earned between 1853 and 1873 from charging naturalization fees may strike us as rather modest, this is not how contemporaries saw it. The sum was equivalent to twice the city's total municipal tax revenue for 1872, and hence to approximately ten per cent of its annual revenue from direct taxation.[56] Its significance for the municipal budget explains why the city council endeavoured to set the naturalization tax (the so-called *Bürgereinzugsgeld*) near the maximum permissible level. Thus, at one of its first meetings, in June 1853, its members agreed on the following fees: 200 gulden for Bavarian citizens; 220 for members of other German states; and 260 for non-Germans. The highest fees were designed for municipalities in a position to offer their citizens the use of common land (the so-called *Allmende*), or scholarships and other special grants funded by local charities. That Ludwigshafen could not grant any such benefits to its citizenry did not prevent successive councils from setting its fees at the upper end of the scale, however. If the Bavarian government nevertheless went along with the council's proposals, at least for a while, this was because it recognized the lucrative employment opportunities the young trading town offered its inhabitants.[57]

The Bavarian state's leniency in this area ceased in the course of the 1860s, however. It was at this point that influential sections within the state bureaucracy began to regard free population movement and economic liberalization as vital means to strengthen Bavaria's position within Germany. In 1868 (the year in which the guild system was officially abolished in Bavaria) the state reduced the permissible maximum fees for naturalization in Ludwigshafen to 100 gulden (171 marks) for Bavarian citizens, 150 for non-Bavarians, and 200 for foreigners. By the late 1890s these fees had been reduced even further, to 85 marks for all applicants irrespective of their state citizenship; and in 1903 the common fee for naturalization was set at 50 marks.[58]

Yet the municipal authorities were quick to adapt to changes of the legal status quo. This became evident in 1868, for instance, when the distinction between *Heimatrecht* and *Bürgerrecht* (which unlike the former entitled its holder to take part in local elections) was abolished in the Palatinate, but not in the rest of Bavaria. This reform did not stop Ludwigshafen's council from asking citizenship applicants who had acquired their *Heimatrecht* before the law's enforcement to pay the full statutory citizenship fee. In other words, they refused to transfer the *Heimatrecht* to full municipal citizenship unless an extra fee was forthcoming. It was in this spirit that, as late as September 1886, the town council instructed the mayoral office to compile lists with the names of residents falling into this category. These were then asked to pay the *Einzugsgeld* of 102 marks, the fee the municipality had been entitled to charge new citizens before 1868.[59] A register that was created on this basis in the mid-1880s featured more than one hundred people; and of those, the mayor reported at a council meeting, 93 had agreed to pay the citizenship fee, while 23 had filed a complaint with either the mayoral office or the district authorities.[60] On several occasions, the council even threatened to retract the *Heimatrecht* from those who refused to pay the requested fee, a threat subsequently declared illegal by the district authorities.[61]

Of the roughly 20 long-standing residents who refused to pay the fee demanded by the council, nearly all worked for the *Pfälzische Eisenbahn*. They justified their stance by pointing to the terminable nature of their contract as railway employees and the highly mobile nature of their occupation. Their taking up residence in Ludwigshafen could therefore not be counted as a voluntary act. Rather, what had prompted them to live there was their contractual obligations as railway employees; there was consequently no guarantee that they would not be moved elsewhere at short notice. The city council did not accept this line of argument, however. What mattered, its liberal majority professed, was the very 'act of taking up residence' in a particular municipality, while the 'nature of the employment contract' was irrelevant to judging someone's intentions.[62] As the request by the train driver Franz Joseph Büchler shows, only in exceptional cases did the council accept a plea for exemption. When Büchler claimed that he had moved to Speyer in 1884, subsequently bought a property there, and that he was likely to be asked to acquire the *Heimatrecht* in that municipality, the council granted him an exemption on condition that he could offer 'instant proof of having acquired the *Heimatrecht* in Speyer.'[63]

Unsurprisingly, Ludwigshafen's authorities were equally reluctant when it came to granting citizenship free of charge. In order to be eligible, applicants had to have been resident for a minimum of ten years from the age of majority. Anyone who had received welfare support during this period, been out of work or moved to another municipality, even if only temporarily, forfeited their eligibility. But even where these conditions were met, the council's approach was marked by circumspection. One way to lower the number of potential recipients was by determining that only those who had both worked *and* lived within the town's jurisdictional boundaries would be eligible. This was particularly effective in relation to workers employed by the BASF, as some of its production plants were located in Friesenheim, which before its incorporation into Ludwigshafen in 1892 formed a separate municipality. However, where the BASF's management was able to prove that a candidate had worked for the most part within the boundaries of Ludwigshafen, the town's finance commission tried to be co-operative. Thus, in 1886, after some initial resistance, it agreed to grant citizenship free of charge to 19 BASF workers. Three applications were none the less rejected: two because the candidates had already paid the naturalization fee of 171.43 marks, which was taken as proof that they were ineligible to receive citizenship free of charge; and one because the candidate in question failed to offer 'proof of having been in uninterrupted employment as a wage labourer.'[64]

Of those who sought naturalization free of charge, civil servants were most likely to succeed. Thus, in 1883, 'several civil servants employed here for more than ten years' claimed that they were eligible for an exemption. The council's initial reaction was to contact other Palatinate towns to find out if there existed a shared practice in relation to this category of public employees. Speyer, Neustadt, and Pirmasens all replied that they knew of no exemption for city employees; Kaiserslautern reported that it had recently decided to grant the *Heimatrecht* free of charge to 'all police officers whose *Heimatgemeinde* was not Kaiserslautern'; meanwhile, Zweibrücken informed Ludwigshafen that 'several civil servants' had indeed recently benefited from a special provision. Based on this information, Ludwigshafen's authorities decided to adopt a case-by-case approach.[65]

Thus, in October 1894, the council considered whether a group that included the municipal school inspector Wagner, the director of the private girl's school Vollert, the town's public construction officer Höh, and the municipal registrar Günther should be granted citizenship free of charge. It decided that, in accordance with Bavarian law, Wagner and Vollert were entitled to free citizenship by virtue of their employment as town civil servants; Höh and Günther were granted the same right due to their 'faultless service' over an uninterrupted period of ten years.[66] Yet when, towards the end of the same session, the SPD councillor Ehrhart proposed that all those permanently employed by the town be granted the *Heimatrecht* free of charge and 'without imposing the usual waiting period,' his request was rejected by all votes against one on a recommendation of the finance commission.[67]

Making *Heimat* stick

Ludwigshafen was not alone among Bavarian towns in seeking to defend its authority over local citizenship. Due above all to its substantial (and increasingly struggling) textile industry Augsburg's population included a significant portion of relatively poor factory workers and domestic servants, many of them women. Being fairly well endowed with private and public charities, the city was also an attractive destination for poor migrants from Swabia and further afield. Even though the situation appears to have been slightly more favourable than in either Ulm (where the imperial Relief Residence Law heightened financial pressures) or Ludwigshafen (where the distinction between *Bürgerrecht* and *Heimatrecht* was abolished in 1868), an increase in poor residents raised the spectre of a rise in municipal tax.

Already in 1863, Augsburg's council passed an ordinance stipulating rules for the registration of new residents. It drew a clear distinction between those who were deemed respectable by virtue of their occupation, and those who were not. Civil servants, of whom the capital of the government district of *Schwaben und Neuburg* had a great many, were exempt from applying for the required residence permit. Meanwhile, 'other distinguished personalities,' including 'pensioners and privateers' were singled out for a facilitated registration procedure. They did not, for instance, have to turn up in person at the local registry office. Thus they were spared from having to display their paperwork and offering explanations to inquisitive clerks.[68]

The revised local ordinance of 1868 offered further guidance on these matters. It determined that all 'alien persons' had to register with the police authorities within nine days of their arrival. This category (*Fremde*) comprised all those who 'neither originate from Augsburg nor hold citizenship rights there.' In other words, it included all those who possessed neither social nor political rights in Augsburg. Applicants for a residence permit had to register their name and address, as well as their marital status, age, former place of residence, and place of origin (*Heimatort*). They were also

obliged to inform the authorities about the purpose and prospective duration of their stay. Like in the 1863 ordinance, certain professions were
exempt from having to undergo this procedure. These included employees
of the Bavarian state, of the church, the town administration, as well as those
working for charitable organizations.[69] Residents who had lived in Augsburg
for a minimum of five years at age of majority could apply for the *Heimatrecht*,
provided they were Bavarian citizens and had paid both direct tax and their
contribution to the local treasury and welfare office. Applicants who had
claimed welfare support during those five years saw their qualifying period
extended; those who had failed to reach a certain tax threshold had to wait
for ten years until they could apply.[70]

The fees imposed depended on an applicant's origin and profession, and
they also changed over time. Thus, in 1868, applicants from Augsburg who
got married had to pay 41 marks if they were day labourers, and 61 if they
belonged to a profession that received a monthly wage. Bavarians from outside Augsburg had to pay 61 marks if they were workers, and 82 if they
belonged to a wage-earning profession. 'Foreigners' had to pay double these
amounts. In 1884, the fee for applicants for municipal citizenship whose
Heimat was in Augsburg (many of them native Augsburgers) was calculated
according to their tax status: those who paid more than 6.86 marks in direct
tax were charged 128 marks, while those who paid less were charged 85
marks. Applicants from other German states had to pay 171 and 114 marks,
respectively.[71] The next revision took place in 1896, after the Bavarian
Heimatrecht had undergone a radical reform. Now all German citizens,
including Augsburg natives, had to pay a naturalization fee of 40 marks.
Foreigners (which by that point referred exclusively to non-Germans) were
charged 160 marks.

Between 1870 and 1875 Augsburg's combined annual revenues from fees
for *Heimatrecht* and *Bürgerrecht* was close to 40,000 marks, equalling ten per
cent of the city's annual expenses for poverty relief.[72] These fees thus constituted a relevant source of municipal income. More important, certainly in
the long run, was their use as a device for shaping the socio-economic profile of Augsburg's population. The hurdle for those intending to acquire
their *Heimat* in Augsburg was to be considerable, and high for those seeking
to become *Bürger*. This is why the city government steadfastly opposed
reductions in fees. From its point of view, low fees, or the provision of
exemptions, made a town attractive to the wrong sort of people. While certain exemptions had to be granted by law, the local authorities tried to

keep the pool of eligible candidates small, as evidenced in the debate over which professional categories would qualify for a fee waiver. They also sought to create a more elaborate system of surveillance and control. The 1868 local ordinance already reflected these intentions. It determined that the members of certain professional categories, including domestic servants and unskilled workers, were entitled to acquire the *Heimatrecht* free of charge, provided they had resided in Augsburg for at least ten years without interruption, and had not committed any criminal offences.[73]

But who exactly constituted a wage labourer (*Lohnarbeiter*) or an unskilled worker (*Gewerbsgehilfe*) remained a matter of considerable debate. In 1883, the magistrate and council of Regensburg inquired how Augsburg's authorities handled these matters.[74] Their reply was as follows: a bricklayer who was self-employed for part of the year did not qualify, whereas a 'fireman working for the gas works or a machine minder working for the state railways' did. As a rule of thumb, applicants on a fixed income were not deemed eligible, unlike those who were paid on a daily or weekly basis.[75] Working from this principle, the town council in 1896 refused to grant a dyeing assistant who had lived in Augsburg since 1884 the *Heimatrecht* free of charge. The applicant had not, the magistrate noted, been employed as a wage-worker for seven years prior to the new law entering into force. Drawing on police records, the council therefore concluded that, having been self-employed between 1892 and 1896, he had forfeited his eligibility.[76] The authorities' scrutiny further intensified during the 1890s. In the case of domestic servants, for instance, the council sometimes consulted the records of the municipal health insurance, and the *Dienstbotenbuch*, the document domestic servants had to produce when they took up a new place of residence; in relation to factory workers, too, police information was often used to ascertain someone's duration of residence.[77]

But administrative scrutiny did not reduce the potential for uncertainty and discord. In 1902, for instance, Augsburg's magistrate exchanged information with a number of other cities, including Munich and Nuremberg, about the eligibility of tramway conductors. Were they eligible to be exempted from the normal fees? Munich's response was straightforward: tram conductors belonged to 'the category of urban residents who were entitled, after a prescribed period of residence, to acquire the *Heimatrecht* free of charge.'[78] A few days later, the magistrate approached the directorate of Augsburg's tramway company with a number of additional questions: did tramway conductors receive a monthly salary for their services? What were the contractual rules guiding their appointment and dismissal? Were tram-way workers employed on the same terms as the tramway conductors?[79] The directorate of the privately run tramway company replied that both the tramway conductors and the drivers received a monthly salary, and that their period of notice was 14 days. In contrast, those doing less qualified work, including cleaning staff and repair workers, were paid weekly.[80] Based on this information, the magistrate decided that 'tram conductor Bran is not eligible for the acquisition of the *Heimatrecht* free of charge.'[81]

It is not surprising, therefore, that the 1896 reform of Bavaria's *Heimatrecht* went down badly with Augsburg's liberal-dominated government. Like their counterparts in Ludwigshafen, they much resented its three core inno-vations: after only three months, new residents were entitled to receive some basic poor relief from their municipality of residence; after two years of resi-dence, their former municipality could submit applications for *Heimatrecht* on their behalf; and after four years, recently naturalized Bavarian citizens who did not have their *Heimat* in Bavaria acquired the *Heimatrecht* auto-matically in their municipality of residence.[82] Like other Bavarian towns, Augsburg's council complained that the right of *Gemeinden* to rid them-selves of their poor by applying for the *Heimatrecht* on their behalf mainly benefited rural communities at the expense of the larger towns. It was rela-tively easy, Augsburg's 1896 petition to the two Bavarian houses of repre-sentatives stated, 'to hang around' in a town for three months by drawing on private welfare without being noticed by the authorities.[83] It was also 'absurd,' the council complained in another submission, to assume that, hav-ing resided somewhere for a mere three months, a 'person would feel more attached to his community of residence than to their *Heimatgemeinde*.'[84]

But once the 1896 law had been took effect, Augsburg's authorities had little alternative but to make the best of a difficult situation. Like other municipalities having to operate in a more complex legal environment, Augsburg's first step was to upgrade its mechanisms of registry and control. Like elsewhere, this was done with the aim of gaining a clearer picture of the pool of actual or potential applicants for *Heimatrecht* or *Bürgerrecht*: their date of arrival (and, wherever possible, of departure), their address, their civic and professional status, their financial circumstances, and so on. This information was vital not least because it enabled Augsburg to apply the principle of reciprocity: municipalities that had submitted an application on behalf of their former residents could expect to be treated in kind, while those who had not done so would be left alone.[85]

Towns that had refrained from making use of this provision in relation to Augsburg included Munich, Nuremberg, Würzburg, Aschaffenburg, Regensburg, Bamberg, as well as Donauwörth and a few others. These towns were listed and their future actions carefully registered.[86] But this was only the beginning. In April 1897, police officer Sänger was asked to 'create a list containing all those towns which have made use of § 7a of the *Heimatgesetz* in relation to Augsburg residents.'[87] A mere two days later Sänger's men submitted the requested list, which included the names of 43 towns of various size, including Fürth, Kempten, Neu-Ulm, Nördlingen, Rottenburg, and Schwabmünchen.[88] Less than a week was to pass before Augsburg's magistrate decided to establish a register containing the names of people who, while they possessed their *Heimatrecht* in Augsburg, had resided in other Bavarian municipalities for a minimum of four years.[89]

At the same time, the existing social relief system underwent a process of expansion and modernization. In 1896, for example, the magistrate recommended that applicants and recipients of poor relief be dealt with by one and the same administrative body, irrespective of whether they possessed the local *Heimatrecht*.[90] This would have significant staffing implications.[91] Treasurer Frey highlighted the problem when it first arose. While his department at present dealt with about 2400 applications every year, this number was likely to rise to roughly 3600 if the suggestion was put into practice. This was all the more serious, he warned, as the workload within the *Bureau der Armenpflege* had already increased dramatically. His men had begun to target family members of poor relief and social welfare recipients whose financial situation had improved. As well as making people more reluctant to apply for poverty relief in the first place, these efforts had generated more than 20,000 marks each year over the past half-decade. Frey calculated that 'two further efficient office clerks' would be needed in the first instance. He also recommended that a full-time administrator be appointed to oversee and direct the variegated activities of the local almshouse. Frei also reminded the magistrate that the *Armenanstalt* (for which his department was also responsible) provided temporary housing for 'close to 200 individuals,' employed no less than '40–50 workers,' and had an annual turnover of 90,000 marks.[92]

Frey's next request for further staff appointments came in 1902, when he reported 'a massive increase' in the workload of the municipal welfare office. As well as 'a proliferation in the number of the urban poor,' a great deal of time and effort needed to be devoted to the mentally ill, to collecting welfare payments from other municipalities, and to dealing with orphanage cases. Yet while the workload had gone up 'enormously,' staff numbers had remained stagnant. To this Frey added an observation about the working conditions he and his staff had to endure on a daily basis:

> Work in the almshouse places great demands on its staff, for a number of reasons. Consider, for example, that those working here have to deal with a wide range of people, many of whom are less than decent. Among those who seek our advice are some very debauched individuals, and some of the people that we see, and who cause trouble the moment they come through the door, are also extremely dangerous. Consider, too, that several times a year we are engaged in large administrative procedures (especially in relation to applications for fuel and for rental support), and all this on top of the usual stream of applications and the time that we have to devote to keeping our books in good order.[93]

Equally revealing is the discrepancy that appears to have opened up between the magistrate and council on the one hand, and the administrators working at the frontline on the other: While the elected politicians defended the Bavarian status quo to the hilt, from the turn of the century some frontline civil servants began to point out the practical flaws of the Bavarian *Heimatrecht*. As far as they were concerned, the continued linkage between social entitlement and someone's place or origin had caused administrative problems of grave proportions.

Among the fiercest and earliest defenders of the existing legislation were Mayor Fischer and his allies on the town council. Fischer played the decisive part in the successful opposition to the Bavarian government's 1867 proposal to facilitate the acquisition of the *Heimatrecht* for new residents.[94] In 1877, Augsburg's mayor declared in the *Deutsche Gemeinde-Zeitung* (after that periodical had invited a statement on the pros and cons of the Bavarian *Heimatrecht*) that the Bavarian laws regulating citizenship and poor relief had 'proved sensible in all respects.' Augsburg would therefore 'see in the introduction of the North-German Relief Residence Law...a great danger not only to the municipal budget but also to the life of the *Gemeinde* more generally.' The great advantage of the Bavarian *Heimatrecht* over the imperial *Unterstützungswohnsitz*, Fischer asserted, was that it provoked far fewer conflicts over liability. According to the mayor, Augsburg was involved in only one or two such conflicts in an average year.[95] And when the 1896 reform was on the horizon, the magistrate fiercely condemned the 'mixing' of the principles of *Heimat* and *Unterstützungswohnsitz*, origin and residence.[96] In its petition to the Bavarian Landtag the town magistrate likewise opposed the proposed changes on the grounds that they were 'irreconcilable with the principle of the *Heimatrecht*.'[97]

Yet the battle lines over citizenship began to shift decisively following, as a result of proportional representation, a sharp rise in the SPD's influence in Augsburg. Thus, in 1911, neither poor relief officer Heuberger nor treasurer Frei, in confidential reports submitted to the magistrate, had anything positive to say about Bavaria's *Heimatrecht*. Heuberger was particularly blunt in his assessment of the situation, which in many ways echoed opinions that had been expressed previously by various exponents of the political Left.[98] Bavaria's existing citizenship legislation, he noted sarcastically, dated from the 'medieval' period, when the bulk of the population had been immobile; such a law was therefore incommensurate with 'the heightened mobility' that characterized the modern age. Even in its current state, Bavaria's social relief legislation was inspired by 'the patriarchal idea of sedentariness.' More importantly, Heuberger argued, in enabling town and country to share the cost resulting from poverty, sickness, and old age, the full adoption of the imperial Relief Residence Law would benefit Augsburg financially.[99]

His colleague, treasurer Frei, although adopting a more diplomatic tone, shared this basic assessment. He too came to the conclusion that the larger towns would 'undoubtedly benefit' if Bavaria abandoned its anachronistic *Heimatrecht*.[100] The latter, he added, had been 'severely punctured' ('*erheblich durchloechert*') by the reform of 1896. There was therefore little reason, Frei noted, for the pessimistic scenarios painted by some opponents of the proposed reform.[101]

The contrast between Augsburg's elected politicians and its two most senior welfare officers is revealing. What appears to have prompted Heuberger's and Frei's departure from the traditional consensus is not so much ideological reservations about the principle of *Heimat*. What heightened their scepticism, rather, was that they had to face, on a daily basis, great complexity and a self-defeating workload. Towns such as Augsburg, having to cope with a fluctuating population, found it much harder to keep track of those of its poor that had left the town than did the small, rural communities. This put them at a considerable disadvantage, not least because they could only dispense themselves of their responsibilities once a former resident had acquired the *Heimatrecht* somewhere else. This often only happened if their former municipality of residence applied on their behalf, which in turn presupposed that the towns had a precise understanding of the whereabouts of its residents, past and present. Quite frequently, however, that information was hard to come by.

4

Remaking the *Bürgergemeinde*

Let me note, finally, that I was asked how it was possible that the meeting had been placed under surveillance, given that the Heimat- und Bürgerrechts-Verein *did not debate public affairs, and considering that the meetings of a very similar association, one that was close to the Centre Party, were not being monitored.*

Police official to Augsburg Magistrate, 1906[1]

Against one Wilhelm Stallman from Griehlsheim near Worms, who is reportedly not only unable to work but also had to be admitted to hospital...is issued an expulsion order on the basis of the existing law on free movement.

Minutes of Ludwigshafen City Council, 1887[2]

It is to be hoped...that a great many will acquire local citizenship rights via the easier route provided by the new law; otherwise one might have to fear a certain ossification in the life of the Gemeinden.

Karl Schefold, Chairman of Ulm's *Deutsche Partei*, 1885[3]

If one challenge to the established *Bürgergemeinde* emanated from the imperial Residence Relief Law, another derived from the invention of national mass politics, in the shape of universal manhood suffrage, in 1867/71. With a new national franchise that included all males of 25 years or older (with the exception of soldiers on active service, prisoners, and paupers), the previously prevalent link between municipal citizenship and direct political participation had been broken.[4] All of a sudden, a large part of Germany's adult male population could take part in the election of a national parliament, in direct and secret balloting, while most of them continued to be excluded from local political participation, with most state elections continuing to rely on an indirect or otherwise restricted franchise. With the introduction of universal manhood suffrage for national elections, the notion of disenfranchisement assumed a new meaning and political urgency.

It is only through a discussion of its crucial political implications, then, that we can begin to grasp the broader significance of citizenship for the remaking of German communities during this period. The two processes, while closely related, did not go hand in hand. Admittedly, town authorities endeavoured to align the socio-economic substance of an urban population as closely as possible with its political enfranchisement. It is that balance that many had in mind when they lamented the fate of their *Bürgergemeinde*, the community of municipal citizens. As we have seen, however, achieving this balance became more difficult from the 1860s, as free movement and economic liberalization ceased to be mere rhetorical devices. Confronted with a new situation, towns began to engage in exclusionist practices. With the introduction of a national political franchise that (by contemporary standards) was highly inclusive, however, efforts at political exclusion that continued to rely on a vision of community that emphasized differential status became increasingly hard to justify. Just as the institution of the *Unterstützungswohnsitz* configured Germany as a national space (rather than as a conglomeration of localities), the imperial franchise defined Germany as a national political culture (rather than as the sum of local political cultures).

The local franchise restrictions that existed in the imperial period—the three-class franchise in Prussia and an often restrictive practice of *Bürgerrecht* in much of the German South—have understandably influenced historians' judgment of German liberalism. According to an influential interpretation, they enabled urban liberals to develop a split political personality by shielding themselves from the conflicts and struggles that came to define imperial political culture.[5] There is no denying that, for many liberals, German politics after 1867/71 smacked a little too much of democracy and of the masses. In the view of many urban liberals in particular, the majority of the newly enfranchised groups were lacking in education, sophistication and proven ability; the fact that most of them possessed little or no property served to justify these reservations. How could someone who had no material stake in his or her community act responsibly and rationally? How could they be deemed fit to influence the distribution of power, let alone the course of urban reform, in the same way as were liberal-minded property owners? That most German liberals were not democrats had become apparent already during the 1840s, and liberal views changed only slowly (and as a result of external pressure) on this issue over the decades leading up to the First World War.[6]

A more positive picture has been painted in a number of recent works on urban liberalism. Its main exponents have stressed the positive consequences of a relatively exclusive municipal franchise. German municipalities, according to this interpretation, provided liberals with the protected sphere they needed to pursue their progressive reform agenda in areas like housing, social insurance, education, hygiene reform, or the professionalization of municipal administration. Rather than function as a refuge of traditional notable politics, the exclusive political culture of urban liberalism here tends to be associated with administrative skill, political pragmatism, and progressive reformism.[7] In a similar vein, some historians concentrating on the cultural aspects of urban liberalism have highlighted its innovative impact on cultural education or on modern design and architecture. Challenging a body of established works on this subject, whose authors have questioned liberalism's progressive credentials, these historians have insisted on the many and often ambivalent modernities characterizing liberal politics and culture.[8]

A comparative approach reveals the practice of citizenship as more varied than it has often been portrayed in accounts that, explicitly or implicitly, set out to confirm or challenge the *Sonderweg* view of German history. Associating efforts to revive and reconstruct the *Bürgergemeinde* during the era of industrialization and free movement with either modernity or reaction may prevent one from recognizing some of the most intriguing and unexpected aspects characterizing this process. This chapter will demonstrate, for example, that a relatively open economic climate could be attained at the price of political exclusion; or that economic conservatism could go hand in hand with political inclusion. As we shall see, the persistence of a (however reconstructed) corporatist tradition, embodied in the 'hometown spirit' of a town such as Ulm, could be more conducive to civic inclusion than an economic climate whose hallmark was anti-corporatism, the pattern that characterized Ludwigshafen am Rhein. At the same time, in the later nineteenth century local citizenship got entangled with areas of human activity that lay outside the political sphere narrowly conceived. One such area, which will be the focus of the final section, concerns the activities of consumers.

A 'community of trust'

The most remarkable trajectory of the three *Bürgergemeinden* considered here was that of Ulm. The legislative context played a crucial role in this.

Exceptionally liberal by German standards, between 1849 and 1885 the local franchise in Württemberg was tied to residence, rather than municipal citizenship. This meant that citizens of Württemberg could take part in local elections where they were legally resident, irrespective of whether they were citizens or possessed the *Heimatrecht* there. The only condition was that they had paid their local tax in the three years preceding a municipal election. Citizens of other German states, provided they offered Württemberg citizens the same right were treated likewise in return. This arrangement appears to have raised few eyebrows in Ulm during the 1850s and 1860s, when the cohort of state citizens who were not also municipal citizens was still relatively small. This changed with Württemberg's adoption of the imperial Relief Residence Law in 1873, however, a move that was greeted with considerable public dismay. As late as 1896, a district report concluded that economic liberalism and freedom of movement had not only called for great financial sacrifice. These developments had also spelled the end of the 'old *Bürgergemeinde*.'[9]

The adoption of the imperial *Unterstützungswohnsitz* was bound to change the culture of municipal politics, certainly in Württemberg. For the first time, all new male residents of a certain age (rather than just Württemberg citizens) not only had the right to take part in local elections after a period of three years; but these new voters were now also entitled to poor relief, adding pressure on the municipality's resources.[10] The financial implications of this change prompted much explicit concern. Yet, as some of the objections raised indicate, the implementation of the imperial law also touched deeper layers of communal self-understanding. What was at stake in the eyes of many citizens was the recognition to be gained from being a *Bürger*. Several local commentators expressed anxiety that the new law would undermine the status of the traditional *Bürgergemeinde*, that civic core of the municipality. Its defining principle was the reciprocity of rights and duties among the community of citizens. In guaranteeing residents the same political *and* social rights that municipal citizens enjoyed by virtue of their being *Gemeindebürger*, the imperial residence law had in effect devalued this fundamental principle of give and take.

The view that the imperial legislation had undermined the spirit of mutual obligation became widespread. This spirit had underpinned social relations under the *Heimatrecht*, where origin, not residence, had defined a person's civic status. Whereas before the adoption of the imperial residence law, municipalities had relied on close bonds between members of the same family, friends or close acquaintances—people who were tied to each other by a sense of mutual responsibility—the former rested on the impersonal links that defined a community of strangers: an 'alien body,' to cite one commentator.[11] Indeed, many saw in the frequent 'disputes between various municipalities' over who was responsible for the needy as 'a sad testimony' that poverty relief had been 'robbed of all ethical content.'[12] What these conflicts demonstrated in the eyes of many longer-established citizens was that communal solidarity as people had known it had broken down irreversibly. As long as the traditional *Heimatgenossenschaft* had been intact, the poor had not faced the suspicion to which they were now often subjected as they sought to join communities where they had neither roots, nor relatives, nor friends.[13] In many rural gemeinden in particular, thus went a common complaint, the imperial residence law had prompted the locals to resort to reprehensible practices. It had become usual, one editorial noted, for 'non-indigenous families' to be forced to leave a municipality just a few weeks before they fulfilled the two-year residence requirement.[14]

This perception was by no means confined to a particular political milieu or party. In the spring of 1881, Count von Varnbühler, one of the leading proponents of economic liberalization in Württemberg, demanded in a motion to the Reichstag that the *Heimatrecht* be reinstated, citing sentiments of 'disorientation, unease and dissatisfaction' with the present situation.[15] Varnbühler's intervention should not be read too quickly as a liberal's turn to the right. What had prompted him to intervene, rather, was the perception that, as one of the politically more inclusive German states, Württemberg had been particularly short-changed by the imperial *Unterstützungswohnsitz*. Just a few years later, during a swearing-in ceremony for newly-elected town councillors, Mayor von Heim struck an even more dramatic note when he lamented the decline of the traditional citizen. As far as Ulm's mayor was concerned, this state of affairs owed much to the demographic shifts of the preceding last two decades. Of the 419 marriages concluded in the previous two years, he reminded his audience, only 73 had involved a husband who was a born-and-bred Ulmer; 263 of the newly-wedded men had hailed from other Württemberg municipalities; 45 from Bavaria; 31 from other German states; and 7 from foreign countries.[16]

But the problem was not migration as such. The problem, for von Heim and the majority on the city council, was that the new arrivals had acquired substantial rights without having to become citizens, that, with the introduction of the imperial Residence Relief Law, the incentive for becoming an Ulm citizen had been effectively removed. The *Bürgergemeinde* as his own generation had known it was likely to be doomed: 'If this trend continues, then everything we used to associate with the *Bürgerrecht*, its legal and factual significance, will have lapsed before long.'[17]

A glance at applications for municipal citizenship before and after German unification shows that Ulm's mayor was not engaging in a nostalgia-driven fantasy. Once the imperial Relief Residence Law had been enforced, naturalization figures began to drop sharply. Thus, while in 1869/70 55 men, 92 women, and six children were granted citizenship, generating a total revenue in fees of 12,180 marks, in 1870/71 the respective figures were 31, 21, 1 and 8310; and by 1883/84 the 20 men, one woman, and four children that acquired local citizenship in that year generated a revenue of just 2700 marks.[18] As the previous chapter revealed, this was not because the acquisition of citizenship had become more difficult: the success rate both before and after unification was nearly 100 per cent. The conditions for a successful application were relatively transparent, and all the indications are that, with few exceptions, only those who met the stipulated conditions, and who could pay the relatively modest naturalization fee, submitted an application.

With the imperial law on the horizon, however, residents no longer felt the same need to apply for local citizenship in the first place. The material incentive for doing so, if it had not disappeared completely, had considerably weakened. Even though explicit statements on this question are hard to come by, a look at the number of citizenship applications submitted during the 1860s and 1870s appears to confirm this view. While throughout the 1860s the council had received an average of between 140 and 150 applications per annum—in 1870, the last year before the introduction of the imperial law about the *Unterstützungswohnsitz*, 142 people applied—numbers dropped off sharply thereafter: from 142 in 1870 to 52 in 1871, to 31 in 1875, and 15 in 1879.[19] All this must have confirmed Ulm's established citizenry in their belief that the *Gemeindebürgerrecht*, once a mark of belonging to a distinctive community, had lost much of its moral purpose and former prestige.

These developments provoked widespread concern, as well as a clear sense of frustration among exponents of Ulm's civic community. Yet the new situation also engendered inventive political action on a number of levels. In expressing their dissatisfaction with the imperial law and its consequences, for example, Württemberg's municipalities put pressure on the

Landtag, whose members, one must not forget, were themselves citizens of a *Gemeinde*. One of the outcomes of the ensuing debate was a new state law, the *Gesetz über die Gemeindeangehörigkeit* of 16 June 1885, a clear manifestation of the strength of municipal sentiment in Württemberg. Its effect was to tie the local franchise back to the possession of municipal citizenship.[20] This restriction did not violate the imperial residence law, whose focus was on social relief. As far as municipal citizenship and political inclusion were concerned, the *Gemeinden* remained in charge. The immediate consequences of this legislative reform was dramatic: In Ulm alone, the implementation of the 1885 law led to the temporary disenfranchisement of over 2000 residents, the equivalent of nearly 50 per cent of potential voters.[21] Thanks to a remarkable turn of events, however, the impact of the 1885 law on Ulm would remain minimal. How can this be explained?

The short answer is that, Ulm's council (whose majority had supported the 1885 reform) did not wish to see the town's citizenry decline in proportion to its total resident population. Thus, shortly before the 1885 state law entered into force, the city authorities invited all residents to apply for local citizenship at the reduced (and, essentially, symbolic) rate of only 3 marks. The announcement concluded with detailed practical instructions on how to proceed: people were encouraged to make their way to 'room 19 of the city council,' bringing along their tax receipts for the years 1882/83, 1883/84 and 1884/85.[22] Councillor Ebner, a local solicitor, democrat councillor and member of the *Württemberg Landtag*, even gave a series of public lectures on the new law.[23] As he explained, in his first public speech on the consequences of the 1885 reform, to an audience of several hundred:

> Everyone who has hitherto been entitled to vote in local elections without being a municipal citizen—that is to say, everyone who paid communal tax for longer than three years—is entitled to acquire municipal citizenship against a one-off payment of 3 marks. In so doing, they will gain citizenship rights not only for themselves but, also for their wife and children.[24]

That this inclusive approach was likely to benefit Ebner's party does not sufficiently explain the democrats' efforts on behalf of civic inclusion. What influenced their stance, apart from political expediency, was an established narrative of communal self-description that appears to have exerted considerable influence on contemporaries. As Ebner kept insisting in front of the various audiences he addressed in the space of a few weeks: the larger the group of citizens entitled to take part in the political process, the greater the resulting 'community of trust' on which the citizens' representatives could lean as they made their decisions in difficult times.[25] For the exponents of the democrat *Volkspartei* (founded in 1864), a key player on Ulm's political stage, the question of political legitimacy was an unalienable pillar of urban life. Mutual trust could not flourish in the absence of a high degree of political inclusion. Seen in this light, Ebner and his party stood for a broad local movement intent on rescuing part of a holistic hometown culture with democratizing consequences. But Ulm's reformed corporatism—economically conservative and politically inclusive—was driven not by nostalgia, but by a spirit of pragmatic reform.

If the democrats took the lead, the other local party of importance, the liberal *Deutsche Partei*, followed suit. At a party meeting devoted to the issue, advocate Karl Schefold maintained that only at first glance did the restriction of the local franchise pose a 'great danger' to Ulm as a community; for in offering inhabitants the opportunity to acquire citizenship at a reduced rate during a limited period, the council had taken measures that would alleviate the problem. Like the *Volkspartei* democrat Ebner, the National Liberal Schefold encouraged eligible residents to make use of this special provision; and like his democrat counterpart, he argued that reinstating the link between political rights and citizenship would strengthen Ulm as a *Bürgergemeinde*. In this way, he opined, communal citizenship would 'regain in substance and appeal,' and hence strengthen 'the life of the community.' The more residents would make use of this opportunity, the smaller the danger that 'public life' would grow 'stale.'[26]

Ebner's and Schefold's efforts on behalf of political enfranchisement proved consequential. By the end of 1888, the number of citizens had risen to over 3500, which in relative terms was close to the situation that had presented itself before the 1885 law had entered into force.[27] After the three-year period had passed, the fee for acquiring local citizenship was set at 40 marks. This was still a fraction of the amount that Augsburg and Ludwigshafen had charged their applicants for civic naturalization in the 1880s. Consequently, by 1890 close to 70 per cent of Ulm's male residents who possessed the national franchise could vote in local elections. This was a far larger proportion than in either Augsburg or Ludwigshafen; it was also significantly above the German average.[28]

If civic inclusion was an undoubted ambition, however, levelling was not: social differentiation remained one of the pillars of Ulm's civic culture. Indeed, from the very outset, the concerted effort at incorporating as many residents as possible into a self-governing community was coupled with attempts to retain specific distinctions of status and entitlement. Dividing residents into three categories, Ulm's 1885 municipal code (*Gemeindeordnung*) offers a reflection of this broader civic agenda. Proceeding from the bottom to the top, there were first the *Gemeindeeinwohner*, the residents without citizenship for whom the imperial legislation had brought improved social rights; next came the *Gemeindebürger* or municipal citizens, who in addition to the usual social relief entitlements had the right to take part in local elections; at the top of this hierarchical pyramid were the to so-called *Stiftungsbürger*, who, in addition to the social and political rights they shared with the *Gemeindebürger*, were also eligible for a series of specific funds and scholarships: hence, the composite of *Bürger* and *Stiftung*, citizen and charity. In many ways, the *Stiftungsbürger* enjoyed the full range of entitlements that until the invention of free movement and *Gewerbefreiheit* had been the preserve of the municipal citizen. But while long-standing citizens possessed these entitlements by virtue of seniority and descent, new citizens could acquire them through payment of an extra fee: 80 marks on top of the 40 they were required to spend in order to acquire citizenship.[29]

There are no indications that the logic underpinning this differentiation of municipal citizens into different categories was perceived as unwarranted when it was first announced in 1885. Thus, the democratic councillor Ebner, in one of his public lectures on the new *Gemeindeordnung*, insisted that the differential fees proposed found their justification in the quality and range of Ulm's charities, particularly in the field of education. The total endowment of Württemberg's charitable trusts, he noted, amounted to some 73 million marks; and, in Ulm alone, the funds that the various trusts—ranging from the family trusts of the Besserer, Gassold, Karg, and Kraft to the public trusts that were mostly in Evangelical hands—had put aside for educational purposes were 300,000 marks. Many Ulmers who wished to embark on a degree in higher education, Ebner reminded his audience, would continue to rely on these funds. As a recently completed survey had shown, a degree in theology cost about 2900 marks, while most other degrees necessitated an investment of about 1600 marks on average.[30] It was therefore only right, Ebner concluded, that the municipality had decided to set the fee for those wishing to become *Stiftungsbürger* at 80 marks on top of the 40 they had to pay for the regular citizenship. In terms of the total capital resulting from its charitable foundations, Ulm was the richest municipality in Württemberg. With 7.4 per cent of the state's total capital from such organizations, Ulm lay ahead of

Biberach (6.2), Ravensburg (3.3), Stuttgart (3.2), and Heilbronn (1.3).[31] Ebner, who represented Ulm as a democrat in Württemberg's *Landtag*, spoke for many when he insisted that these fees were a modest price to pay in view of the honour and entitlements to be gained from becoming an Ulm citizen.

Forging a 'solid citizenry'

The task of Ludwigshafen's liberal elite was not so much to protect an established *Bürgergemeinde* from diminution as to literally *create* such a community from relatively feeble foundations. At least initially, efforts at civic closure had no place in this project. This became evident as early as 1857, when a number of local craftsmen requested that corporatist interest be placed at the centre of communal development. It was in that year that master saddlers Brubacher and Fotter, who were citizens of Ludwigshafen, filed a complaint with the state commissariat against the naturalization of one Ries from Baden. Ries, who did not possess a master's diploma, had been granted citizenship 'almost unanimously and after only a short debate' by the local council. Brubacher and Fotter outlined the time-honoured arrangement to the authorities: two masters (they were referring to themselves), who together employed a maximum of three assistants, were in control of the city's saddler trade. It was therefore with great misapprehension that they had learned of the council's granting 'the privileges of citizenship and mastership' to someone who in their estimation was 'a foreigner.' The success of Ries' application struck them as all the more puzzling as he had 'proved incapable of acquiring such rights in several other municipalities, including Durlach, Bruchsal, Karlsruhe, Heidelberg, or Mannheim.' By naturalizing a journeyman from another state, they insisted, the council had set a bad example.[32] Although its decision might 'benefit the municipal purse,' it threatened to ruin those who had contributed so much to Ludwigshafen's prosperity. For not only had they and other master craftsmen made 'substantial sacrifices' by establishing their businesses in Ludwigshafen a decade before the town's official foundation; just as important in their view, by refusing to join the radicals in 1848, they had also demonstrated their moral judgement and political moderation. However, Brupacher and Fotter did not succeed with their petition. Instead, the state authorities supported the council's decision, stressing that it was 'up to the council to protect the interests of its citizens.'[33]

What the council and the city's mayor initially regarded as more conducive to Ludwigshafen's interests than civic closure was controlled expansion,
if necessary via forced naturalization. One problem they faced was that
many residents had no wish to become citizens in the first place. This is true
in particular of people who felt relatively secure in their livelihood, and
who therefore often valued mobility more than socio-economic security.
For residents falling into this category, the cost of acquiring local citizenship
often appears to have outweighed its potential benefits. The merchant Carl
Bähr offers a case in point. In 1858, the city council asked Bähr, who had
been 'resident in Ludwigshafen for several years,' to accept municipal citizenship, subject to the prior payment of 220 gulden. Bähr refused to comply,
maintaining that this request violated the spirit of *Gewerbefreiheit* and free
movement: as a citizen of the Palatinate, Bähr claimed, he was entitled to
'conduct his business anywhere in the Palatinate without acquiring local
citizenship.' But the Bavarian state authorities, instead of accepting his point
of view, confirmed the mayoral office's decision, asking Bähr to 'either
accept Ludwigshafen's *Bürgerrecht*' on the terms offered 'or else leave the
town' for good.[34]

Bähr's case points us to what remained a central feature of Ludwigshafen's
citizenship policy: The council's persistent efforts to compel well-to-do
residents to become citizens by asking them to pay a relatively hefty citizenship fee, one that amounted, on average, to several times the monthly salary
of a teacher or lower civil servant. Bavarian law left room for forced natu-
ralizations of this kind—what its critics called *Zwangseinbürgerung*—provided the targets were Bavarian citizens. This was because the Bavarian
Heimatrecht of 1868 decreed that Bavarians who resided in Bavaria had to
have a *Heimat*. This did not apply to non-Bavarians, however, who enjoyed
legal protection from forced naturalization, as this practice was in violation
to the imperial law about free movement.[35]

The consistency with which Ludwigshafen's authorities pursued this
strategy in the final decades of the nineteenth century is therefore truly
striking. At a meeting in 1867, the town council decided that it was in the
interest of 'fair and equal treatment' that a certain category of residents be
charged the *Bürgereinzugsgeld*, if necessary under compulsion. This included
long-standing residents who, despite conducting a business or owning property in Ludwigshafen, had not yet become citizens. The council then considered a list with the names of 41 residents from the Palatinate, and
concluded that they be asked to pay the naturalization fee of 60 gulden.[36]

Yet this decision no longer met with the unqualified approval of the district authorities. There was nothing wrong in principle, the district official noted, with asking long-standing residents (most of whom possessed a *Heimatschein* of another Bavarian *Gemeinde*) to pay the citizenship fee; yet the running of a business could not, in itself, be taken as an indication of someone's wish to take up permanent residence. The spirit behind the law concerning *Gewerbefreiheit*, the state official lectured the council, had been precisely to 'do away with importunate restrictions of this kind;' the disassociation of business activity from local citizenship was therefore at the very heart of a modern market economy based on free movement of goods and, above all, of people. The only criterion on the basis of which the council could force someone to acquire citizenship was 'property ownership of a sufficient kind.'[37]

Ludwigshafen's councillors learned quickly, however. In April 1867, the mayoral office presented the council with a list containing the names of 51 residents. Of these, 41 had their *Heimat* in the Palatinate, and 10 were from other parts of Bavaria or from other German states. Those who had been included in the list either owned a house in Ludwigshafen or were in permanent employment and thus relatively solvent. The district authorities accepted the list, except for the ten residents who originated from outside the Palatinate.[38] Several of those who were subsequently invited to pay the citizenship fee of 60 gulden asked that the fee be waived. Some requests were discussed in a council meeting in September of the same year. Rudolph Deutsch, a businessman from Mossbach, maintained that his house, having been paid for by his mother in law, was 'not really his property.' But the council refused to accept his claim. Leopold Herz, a merchant from Ruchheim, had migrated to America 'without permission' (!) and was therefore outside the reach of Ludwigshafen's treasury. Johannes Schlosser, fireman from Hochdorf, and Nicolaus Wilhelm Schmid, railway official from Pirmasens, while they were given a temporary exemption, were asked to pay the fee as soon as their financial situation allowed. Six other residents were also granted an extension until 1 October 1868, during which period they had to either offer proof of having renounced their present state membership or expect to be evicted from Ludwigshafen.[39]

In July 1871, the council majority reiterated its long-standing conviction that 'inhabitants who either entertain a business or purchase property' were liable to pay the *Bürgereinzugsgeld*; and, once again, it justified its viewpoint by pointing to the need to create 'equity in relation to existing citizens.'[40] While this procedure was legally sound in relation to Bavarian citizens (who according to paragraph 5 of the *Heimatgesetz* of 16 April 1868 had to acquire a *Heimat* in Bavaria), however, the council also applied it to non-Bavarians, many of whom refused to pay the requested fee of a little over 200 marks. These included Tobias Beyer, a warehouse worker, and Wilhelm Gast, a small trader from Obergen. Both informed the mayoral office that they had no intention of giving up their Württemberg citizenship.[41] Others justified their refusal on economic grounds: Peter Hähn, a blacksmith from Bruchsal in Baden, insisted that his house was burdened with debt, and that the requested naturalization fee would only add to his financial difficulties.[42] Thomas Pfeiffer, a railway official from the Palatinate, claimed that he intended to sell his house, while worker Max Rapp informed the town mayor that, while he had 'always wished to become a citizen of Ludwigshafen,' he would have to move elsewhere should his employer go bankrupt.[43] In September 1871, the district authorities informed the mayoral office that its practice of forced naturalization of non-Bavarians violated the imperial law concerning free movement.[44]

Henceforth and throughout the imperial period, the local authorities employed a two-pronged strategy: simple imposition of the naturalization fee in relation to Bavarian citizens, and a formal request of naturalization in the case of non-Bavarians. The list that was compiled in the summer of 1871 strictly adhered to this logic: 28 Bavarian citizens, mostly traders, merchants, civil servants, artisans, railway employees, as well as representatives of the local *Kleingewerbe* such as butchers, bakers, and inn keepers, were given a short period within which to pay the naturalization fee of 100 gulden. At the same time, 17 non-Bavarians were invited to pay the slightly higher amount of 156 gulden.[45] Aware that Ludwigshafen's authorities could not compel them into acquiring the local *Heimatrecht* (which in the Palatinate included the *Bürgerrecht* and hence the franchise), however, many non-Bavarians refused to comply. Conceding that the imperial law about *Freizügigkeit* rested on the principle of reciprocity (Bavarians could not be forced to acquire citizenship by non-Bavarian municipalities either) Ludwigshafen's council nevertheless expressed great disappointment at this state of affairs:

> Only a solid citizenry (*eine gediegene Bürgerschaft*) ... can serve as the pillar (*Stütze und Basis*) of both the *Gemeinde* and the state. In Ludwigshafen such a citizenry could only be engendered through the path of compulsion. The revenues thus generated, complemented by voluntary contributions of various kinds, enabled [the town] to create the common institutions that serve the

public. The Bavarians have no option but to pay, while all the others, who enjoy the same rights as the latter, get everything for free. This leads to an inequity that is widely experienced as aggravating.[46]

One of the major ironies of the Bavarian situation was indeed that its *Heimat*-based citizenship legislation had the effect of privileging non-Bavarians over Bavarians: While existing Bavarian citizens had to have a *Heimat* within Bavaria, migrants from other German states who had recently acquired Bavarian citizenship did not. The number of new Bavarian citizens without a *Heimat* in the state was particularly high in urban, industrialized regions. With the 1896 reform, these *heimatlose Bayern* acquired the *Heimatrecht* more or less automatically as a legal entitlement after a four-year waiting period, provided they had fulfilled their tax obligations and not received any welfare benefits during this time. As Ludwigshafen Mayor Krafft complained in 1901: 'The non-Bavarians literally acquire the Heimatrecht in their sleep, after four years of residence, something that is irreconcilable with the spirit of the [Bavarian] Heimat law.'[47] The mayoral office, while it recognized the resulting discrimination of Bavarian citizens, insisted that the way to resolve it was not by abolishing fees across the board, but, rather by ceasing to give preferential treatment to *heimatlose Bayern*.[48]

When it comes to making sense of the trajectory of Ludwigshafen's *Bürgergesellschaft* in the second part of the nineteenth century, legal obstacles to incorporating middle-class residents who were not Bavarians are just one important factor to consider. Another concerns the liberal-dominated council's reluctance to facilitate naturalization for industrial workers. Of the 20,000 inhabitants Ludwigshafen had in 1884, for instance, only 509 were citizens; and in 1889, only 51 out of 1091 citizens were factory workers.[49] The resulting levels of disenfranchisement were much higher than, for instance, in Ulm. Thus, of the 5897 residents who in 1890 were entitled to take part in elections to the Reichstag, only 1091 possessed the local franchise. In other words, more than 80 per cent of Ludwigshafen's male population of 25 years or older was effectively disenfranchised at this point. By 1899 (the year in which the SPD experienced its first political breakthrough in the city, winning seven council seats when it used to have just one) the rate of disenfranchisement had declined to approximately 60 per cent. The largest expansion of the franchise occurred in the first decade of the twentieth century, when the SPD gained the majority in the town council: By 1909, 80 per cent of those who could vote in national elections possessed the local franchise.[50]

Both the long-standing closure and the sudden opening-up of Ludwigshafen's citizenry around 1900 find their explanation in the town's early history.
The city's founding fathers, who for nearly half a century dominated urban
politics, were entrepreneurs of various kinds, as a glance at the town's mayors
up to the 1890s reveals.[51] The first mayor, Heinrich Wilhelm Lichtenberger,
inherited his father's trading firm in 1836 at the age of 24.[52] His successor,
Carl Huss, began as a partner in Lichtenberger's firm before setting up his
own shipping business in 1850.[53] It was in line with Ludwigshafen's economic transition from a trading to a factory town that the three mayors that
followed—Josef Hoffmann (1868–71), Georg Kutterer (1871–1889), and
Wendel Hoffmann (1889–1891)—ran large local construction firms, while
the last unpaid mayor, Dr Carl Grünzweig, was the director of a chemical
factory. It was not until 1896 that the council decided to employ a full-time
mayor, which tells us something about the self-understanding of this particular circle of national-liberal entrepreneurs-cum-politicians. Unlike their
counterparts in more established towns, whose administrative procedures
had been modernized soon after mid-century, Ludwigshafen's elites drew
no clear distinction between private and public affairs. To them, the task of
governing a town was not fundamentally different from running a large
business. Of equal importance are the town's contrasting political temporalities: While in Ulm the revolutionary events of 1848/49 had created a
precarious balance of power between liberal nationalists and particularist
democrats, in Ludwigshafen the national-liberal entrepreneurs, the town's
founding fathers, ruled almost without opposition until the turn of the
century.

Yet the local liberals could be in no doubt that, sooner or later, the legitimacy of their rule would be contested. Witnessing the national political
rivalries of the 1880s and 1890s, they were aware that Ludwigshafen's long-
term demographic trajectory favoured their political opponents; that time
was working in favour of the Social Democrats, who would easily surpass
them once most industrial workers possessed the municipal franchise. It is
the recognition of the inevitability of this trend that in part explains why
civic exclusion assumed such a pivotal function in the liberals' fight to retain
power and influence. The abolition of the distinction between *Heimatrecht*
and *Bürgerrecht* in the Palatinate in 1868 further reinforced liberal intransi-
gence in this area, for it meant that one potential hurdle to full political
participation had fallen. It may explain, too, why Ludwigshafen's liberals
clung on to any device available to restrict the existing community

of citizens, for example by preventing working-class applicants from acquiring citizenship free of charge.

A few examples, all drawn from the 1880s, must suffice to illustrate this point. The first concerns the 32-year-old Christian Heckmann, printer and father of a four-year-old son. In 1886 Heckmann requested to be granted the *Heimatrecht* free of charge, on the grounds that he had been a resident of Ludwigshafen for ten years. But his application was rejected out of hand. According to the council, Heckmann had failed to provide evidence of his period of residence; besides, he had only just become a Bavarian citizen.[54] When his ten-year period as a Bavarian citizen was confirmed, the council demanded proof of his ability to earn a living and of his lack of a criminal record during the previous ten years.[55] The case was closed after both the district authorities and the government of the Palatinate confirmed that Heckmann had no legal claim to being exempt from paying the naturalization fee.[56] The bricklayer Johannes Maunsmann was more fortunate. Being unable to offer proof of going without a criminal record and of having been employed without interruption over a period of ten years, he saw himself rejected on his first attempt.[57] Only when the district authorities supplied witness reports, which confirmed Maunsmann's uninterrupted employment, did the council finally give in.[58]

Another example is offered by a collective application by several railway workers. In April 1888, the railway employee Heinrich Klag submitted a petition in which he demanded that he, along with 13 colleagues, be granted the *Heimatrecht* free of charge. Klag claimed that he and his fellow railway men fitted the category of *Gewerbsgehilfen*, which according to the Bavarian *Heimatgesetz* of 1868 was exempt from the normal fees (along with domestic servants and others not employed on a monthly salary). Predictably, the mayoral office's initial reaction was to reject Klag's request, insisting that collective applications were not permitted; and because railway workers were classified as (wage-earning) state employees, rather than *Gewerbsgehilfen*.[59] Yet the district authorities, drawing on a report from the directorate of the *Pfälzische Bahnen*, which confirmed that Klag and his colleagues fitted the category of *Gewerbsgehilfe*, supported the petitioners. Ludwigshafen's council appealed against the state's decision, describing the issue at stake as of the 'utmost importance' in view of the 'large number of railway and factory workers, as well as all sorts of assistants' who would see in petitioner's victory a sign of encouragement. But the government of the Palatinate threw out the appeal.[60]

The late 1880s were significant in yet another respect: In 1889 the Social Democrat Franz Josef Ehrhart not only became a citizen of Ludwigshafen after paying the statutory 171.43 marks in naturalization fee; but he also joined the council as the first SPD delegate.[61] Ehrhart, who emerged as the Palatinate's leading SPD politician, would be instrumental in breaking the liberals' stranglehold on power after 1900. He was also one of the most vocal critics of the Bavarian citizenship law. In 1901, at the fifth conference of Bavaria's larger towns (an event he attended jointly with Ludwigshafen's liberal Mayor Krafft), Ehrhart rallied support for a petition against the status quo. In the speech he delivered to justify his stance, he described the premise that every citizen had to 'have a place where he is permanently at home'— the pillar of the Bavarian *Heimatrecht* which Bavarian liberals and conserva- tives defended with equal commitment—as incommensurate with the reality of an industrial society.[62]

Most of all, however, Ehrhart and his allies chastised the political dis- crimination that the Bavarian law had helped maintain. His intention, Ehrhart explained, was 'to change the relation of residents to citizens.' The exclusivity of local citizenship had resulted in the disenfranchisement of the majority of the local population, and hence in a 'contrast between rights and duties' that was now widely regarded as 'indefensible.'[63] For Ehrhart and his increasingly large political following, there was a high price to pay for moulding a working-class city like Ludwigshafen according to the dream of liberal respectability and predominance. As far as the social- democratic left was concerned, the Bavarian *Heimatrecht* reflected a social fantasy, one that belonged to a bygone era.

The prestige of an 'acquired *Heimat*'

In Augsburg, meanwhile, the citizen-to-population ratio was around six per cent in 1875. More instructive is, once again, the relation between local and national enfranchisement: In 1885, 14,000 of Augsburg's then roughly 60,000 inhabitants could take part in elections to the Reichstag, but of those only 3500 could vote in local elections. The resulting rate of disenfranchisement, which oscillated between 60 and 70 per cent, remained largely unchanged until the turn of the century.[64] The authorities' charging of an extra levy for those wishing to add the municipal citizenship to the *Heimatrecht* ensured that political inclusion remained low.[65] Thus, between 1869 and 1875, the number of citizens had risen by a mere 83: from 2923 to 3006.[66] Unlike the political establishment in Ulm (or of Bavarian cities such as Fürth or Nuremberg), Augsburg's ruling National Liberals did not regard the small size of its *Bürgergemeinde* as a problem that needed correcting. Thus, when, in 1878, the magistrate of Nuremberg expressed concern about the constant decrease of 'the number of citizens in relation to the number of residents,' Augsburg's authorities responded by supplying the relevant figures, but without flagging the issue as a matter of concern.

What facilitated Augsburg's restrictive approach was that, like in the rest of Bavaria (but, unlike the Palatinate), its authorities were able to distinguish between *Heimatrecht* and *Bürgerrecht*. Thus, in 1884, the cost of acquiring municipal citizenship for applicants who already had their *Heimat* in Augsburg ranged between 85 and 128 marks, depending on their tax status (those who paid more than 6.86 marks in direct tax had to pay the higher fee). Applicants who did not have their *Heimat* in Augsburg had to pay between 114 and 171 marks.[67] These fees may have been small beer for middle-class residents keen to acquire the local franchise, but they could act as a disincentive for people on low incomes, all the more so as the profession of the *Heimatrecht* entitled them to poor relief if they became needy.

When in the course of the 1890s a series of reform proposals were submitted in Bavaria, in an attempt to remove existing disincentives for working-class applicants intent on acquiring local citizenship, Augsburg's government sounded the alarm bells. In this respect, the 1894 proposal by Lerno and Geiger to the Bavarian Landrat, which asked that the maximum local citizenship fee be set at 24 marks, was deemed particularly worrying. As Augsburg's magistrate informed the district government, this measure would 'significantly facilitate' the acquisition of citizenship through working-class residents, which the magistrate regarded as entirely 'undesirable.'[68] The 1896 reform of the Bavarian *Heimatrecht* put many of the larger towns on their guard. In part, of course, these concerns derived from the challenge the reform posed to the city's budget. But that was not all. As far as the dominant liberals were concerned, finance and politics were two sides of the same coin. For in Augsburg, like in the rest of Bavaria, the *Heimatrecht* was the first step on the road to full citizenship. This explains, among other things, why Augsburg's authorities had for some time shown an interest in the political leanings of citizenship applicants. Thus, in 1896, the magistrate asked police official Saenger to 'conduct his investigations on whether applicants were members of the SPD as unobtrusively and secretly as possible.' Saenger replied that the relevant investigations would henceforth be conducted by a 'special reconnaissance patrol' and not, as had hitherto been the case, by ordinary policemen.[69]

Spying on applicants suspected of socialist leanings was coupled with a restrictive citizenship policy, particularly towards working-class applicants, the majority of whom were Catholics. The example of the veterans of the 1870/71 war is particularly instructive here. In 1895, on the occasion of the 25th anniversary of the battle at Sedan, six Augsburg war veterans— two factory workers, two day labourers, a turner, and a locksmith—invited the magistrate to 'follow the example of other towns' by offering war veterans citizenship free of charge.[70] Ten days later, the magistrate replied in the negative. Specifically, the veterans' request was judged as 'going too far' in view of the 'large number of persons' who fell within the same category.[71]

A second (equally unsuccessful) plea by local war veterans reached the magistrate in 1899.[72] Some uncertainty over the right approach apparently persisted, prompting further inquiries on the financial implications of the war veterans' request. Drawing on information thus generated, the magistrate estimated that 'approximately 220 members of local veteran associations' might desire local citizenship rights, but that the real number might be much higher, as many veterans did not belong to any such association.[73] A state-wide inquiry showed that Augsburg's intransigent approach was out of step with the practice of such cities as Nuremberg, Würzburg, or Bamberg. In each of these towns, war veterans could acquire both citizenship and *Heimatrecht* at significantly discounted rates. Instead of following their example, however, Augsburg's government decided to emulate Munich's compromise solution to the problem: war veterans already in possession of the *Heimatrecht* at the outbreak of the war in 1870 were eligible to acquire citizenship at a much reduced fee; those who did not could acquire local citizenship at a moderately reduced rate.[74]

A further example concerns the treatment of mid-ranking civil servants, which in a district capital such as Augsburg constituted a sizeable group. Here too, Augsburg's magistrate strove to gain an adequate overview of the situation before moving to a decision. To this end, in 1902 it sent an inquiry to the magistrates of Munich, Erlangen, Nuremberg, Fürth, Würzburg, Bamberg, Bayreuth, Regensburg, Landshut, and Kempten. Did these towns offer discounted rates to resident civil servants seeking citizenship?[75] The incoming replies highlight the full range of approaches Bavarian towns applied to cope with the political demands of this particular group of residents. At the restrictive end of the spectrum, Munich and Kempten did not offer any preferential treatment to its public civil servants.[76] The most generous terms were offered by two of Bavaria's most dynamic towns: Nuremberg and Fürth. Members of the local police force who were natives of Nuremberg and had served for a minimum of seven years, acquired citizenship free of charge. Nuremberg also offered its *Bürgerrecht* free of charge to members of the voluntary fire brigade, provided they had served for at least ten years. The same held true for 'active members of the voluntary first-aid service after 15 years of uninterrupted service.' Similarly favourable terms were offered to civil servants, including teachers and members of the professional fire brigade, provided they had served for a minimum of ten years.[77] An even more generous attitude could be found in Fürth, where everyone possessing the *Heimatrecht* was invited to acquire citizenship free of charge. Lower civil servants from other German states, who had been resident in Fürth for a minimum of four years, were eligible to acquire citizenship at the modest rate of 18 marks.[78]

Where did Augsburg position itself? The members of the voluntary fire brigade, a traditional bastion of urban liberalism, were granted citizenship free of charge, provided they had served without interruption for at least 15 years; local civil servants who had been employed on a permanent contract for at least five years enjoyed the same privilege, as did female teachers on a fixed-term contract. In 1903, moreover, the magistrate decided to afford female teachers on full-time contracts (after they had submitted a motion requesting equal treatment) the same right that their male counterparts had enjoyed for some time. Henceforth, they too would acquire the *Heimatrecht* (but, not the municipal citizenship) free of charge, a decision that was justified with the 'low financial risk' to be incurred by offering female teachers such favourable terms.[79] Revealingly, however, Augsburg's council and magistrate refused to extend this right to female teachers working for confessional schools. Unlike their colleagues working for interdenominational schools, the magistrate considered those teaching at confessional schools as 'unlikely to take an interest' in this matter anyway(!).[80] A fortnight later the chairwoman of the *Lererinnengruppe* Augsburg thanked the magistrate on behalf of her colleagues. The female teachers considered their being granted the *Heimatrecht* as a sign that their achievements as teachers had been recognized. As the chairwoman of Augsburg's Women Teachers Association expressed in her note of gratitude: 'Quite aside from the legal advantages to be gained from possessing the *Heimatrecht* in Augsburg, the female teachers feel particularly honoured because of the ethical value of "acquired" *Heimat*, and of the prestige which it bestows on its holder, which is greater than in the case of its "inherited" counterpart.'[81]

In spite of these concessions to specific professional cohorts, the distinction between *Heimatrecht* and *Bürgerrecht* was painstakingly upheld. Even the welfare officers Heuberger and Frei, who in 1911 spoke out in favour of adopting the imperial *Unterstützungswohnsitz*, did not wish to see the distinction abolished. Nor did they believe that the acquisition of citizenship should be facilitated. In fact, Frei justified his stance by emphasizing that the distinction between *Heimatrecht* and *Bürgerrecht* would remain in force even if Bavaria chose to adopt the imperial Residence Relief Law. Not only did this civil servant designate municipal citizenship as the 'more noble form' of the Bavarian *Heimatrecht*. He also expressed hope that the resulting shortfall in revenue from fees for the *Heimatrecht* would be compensated for by 'increased revenue from citizenship fees.'[82]

Although the liberals' restrictive citizenship policy had for some time caused resentment among political opponents, it was not until the mid-1890s that these complaints were followed by deeds. In 1896 the *Verein zur Erwerbung des Heimat- und Bürgerrechtes in der Stadt Augsburg*, an association of Social Democrats, was founded with the aim of turning working-class residents (as well as 'small traders and lower civil servants' who felt insufficiently represented by the ruling liberals) into citizens. To facilitate this process, members committed themselves to making weekly savings of between 10 and 20 pfennigs. The magistrate immediately classified the association as a political organization and put it under police surveillance, to the protestations of the association's executive.[83] At a subsequent meeting, Landrat Loewenstein criticized the discriminatory elements of the state's *Heimatgesetz*: not only were the fees imposed often very high, but in many Bavarian towns, two-thirds of the residents did not possess the *Heimatrecht*, and only about one sixth was in possession of municipal citizenship.[84] The meeting concluded with the chairman's announcement that the association had now 34 members. This was followed by the election of the executive, to be composed of two master shoemakers, two master carpenters, and one factory worker.[85] In 1906, a speaker from Thüringen argued that Bavaria's high citizenship fees had a similarly exclusionary effect as the Prussian three-class franchise. Although Bavarian municipalities were free to offer the *Heimatrecht* and *Bürgerrecht* free of charge, few, and least of all Augsburg, actually did so. But the numerous challenges that confronted German towns—the speaker mentioned the local tax system, the introduction of interconfessional schools, and social housing—could only be resolved satisfactorily if the working classes were given the vote.[86]

It is indicative of Augsburg's confessional landscape that in 1899 ultramontane Catholics set up their own association, the *Katholischer Heimat- und Bürgerrechts-Verein für die Stadt Augsburg.* The association, which was open only to 'Catholic men,' entertained close links with the local Centre Party and the Catholic *Neue Augsburger Zeitung.*[87] Its executive consisted of two typesetters, a master tailor, a newspaper man, a sexton, an iron turner, two small traders, and an office clerk. While the association's central aim was the same as that pursued by its social-democratic counterpart, it was less explicit in its critique of the liberal regime. Members had to pay a joining fee of 0.75 mark, and later a monthly fee of 1 mark. Its main purpose, of course, was to enlarge the contingent of Catholic voters participating in local elections. The tight link with the Centre Party becomes apparent in a 1914 announcement: 'Those members of the Centre who do not yet possess local citizenship rights are urged to join the association. Every man of the Centre should acquire these rights before the next local election, as only citizens are entitled to vote!'[88]

Like their counterparts in Ludwigshafen, but in contrast to their colleagues in Ulm, Augsburg's political leaders defended the *Heimatrecht* to the hilt. They did not think they were engaging in an anachronistic fantasy as they pursued this particular agenda. Yet in doing so, they inadvertently helped increase the pressure within the urban-civic arena. While the house did not burst under the strain, cracks did result, making people look for alternative fields in which to put their civic energies to use.

A place for the consumer

The case of associations fighting for a more inclusive local franchise offers a first reminder of the limitations of top-down perspectives on citizenship. Or as Geoff Eley has recently noted: 'Each new logic of governmentality… simultaneously entailed its new fronts on citizenship.'[89] Some of these new fronts were not restricted to the political narrowly conceived, for the struggle over political inclusion cannot be confined to its more formal political operations. Notwithstanding the centrality of the local franchise, legal citizenship rights constituted only one of the means by which towns reproduced themselves as civic communities. Another, and one that would assume an equally significant place in the latter half of the nineteenth century, concerns the self-organization of people in consumer co-operatives, or to use the most widely used German contemporary term: *Konsumvereine*.

Whereas the debate and practice surrounding local citizenship tells us much about the objectives town councils pursued, the history of the consumer co-operatives shows that the remaking of urban communities involved creative agencies that operated outside the field of formal politics. Indeed, the co-operatives can help remind us that communities were the product of different kinds of political practices and types of mobilization. They also reveal the extent to which the interests and concerns of everyday life began to shape civic affairs.[90] In a period in which many a German council sought to navigate change through conventional strategies of civic exclusion, consumer associations offered those without political participation rights (including women) an alternative avenue for shaping the life of their chosen community of residence.

Although they quickly became a self-evident feature of Germany's urban landscape, consumer co-operatives were, in fact, a foreign invention. The role model was England's Rochdale co-operative. Yet this process of emulation and selective borrowing proceeded at high speed. By the beginning of the First World War, Germany's co-operative movement came second after Britain's in terms of size of membership and volume of business.[91] The first *Konsumvereine* and *Konsumgenossenschaften* were founded in Saxony, Schleswig-Holstein, Rhineland-Westphalia, Bavaria, and Berlin in the 1850s and 1860s.[92] Counting only those that belonged to a national umbrella organization, there were 111 consumer co-operatives in Germany in 1870, rising to 263 by 1890, and reaching 1563 by the outbreak of the war. The largest increase occurred after 1889, when a new imperial law was introduced that limited the personal financial liability of the associations' members.[93] The real number of consumer associations must have been far higher, however. In 1895, for example, the chairman of the board of Ludwigshafen's consumer co-operative, Rudolf Schmitt, estimated that between 1866 and 1895 the number of consumer societies in Germany had risen from 199 to 9934.[94]

What was most visible about the co-operatives was admittedly their economic function: to provide their members with a range of essential goods, particularly what contemporaries called *Viktualien*, groceries such as flour, rice, grain, milk, meat, and bread. The *Konsumvereine* sought to accomplish this aim by buying large quantities from suppliers. The larger co-operatives that sprang up in the last two decades of the nineteenth century often ran their own bakeries and butcheries. Many were founded with the explicit aim of improving the choice available to consumers who were restricted to local markets. This partly explains why the majority of co-operatives founded between 1860 and 1890 were located in small- and medium-sized towns that lacked department stores, and where the relatively small number of grocery-selling establishments limited variety, while keeping prices comparatively high. Members would buy vouchers from their consumer society, which they would then use as payment in local shops that had agreed to accept its terms of trade.

Many co-operatives were run part-time by members of the self-employed middle classes. Middle-class associations of this kind, which were inspired by the founder of the co-operatives movement in Germany, the left-liberal Schulze-Delitzsch, also pursued a moral and educational agenda. People were to be lured away from the deeply engrained habit of buying their groceries on credit at the local shops. A jurist and deputy from Saxony, who was familiar with the world of small industry and artisanal production, Schulze-Delitzsch saw the co-operatives as filling the economic and social void left by the disappearance of the guilds. In the 1850s, he asserted that *Konsumvereine* would play as 'powerful a role in the social development' of German communities as the vanishing guilds had done in the life of previous generations. This was necessary, Schulze claimed, at a time when 'the monstrous development of big industry threatens the independence of our *gewerblicher Mittelstand*'.[95]

A rather different type of co-operative was gaining ground from the 1890s. Its main purpose was to offer affordable goods to its mostly lower-middle and working-class members. Co-operatives of this second type aimed at empowering the consumer by rationalizing distribution and achieving competitive prices for basic foodstuffs.[96] They often chose their suppliers from outside the locality, from other German states, or even from abroad. Some began to establish production units (particularly for basic groceries such as vegetables, bread, or flour) in order to improve the terms of trade for customers, or because certain local producers (especially bakers or butchers) had chosen to boycott them. Organizations of this kind became particularly common in the large industrial towns with sizeable working-class populations.[97]

Both kinds of co-operative provided arenas for civic participation outside the confines of conventional politics. Both shaped the reconstruction
of urban communities. But, whatever their conspicuous similarities, they
did so in different ways. The first type of co-operative, which existed in
Ulm, tended to reinforce established social hierarchies. Its leading members
envisaged their town as an integrated whole, as an established place rather
than as work in progress. The second type, which came to predominate in
both Augsburg and Ludwigshafen, drew its justification from the reality of
a class society. Its exponents envisaged the town in which they operated not
as an integrated whole but as a functionally differentiated space. What separated these two kinds of organizations was not the choice between stasis and
movement. Rather, each one was informed by a different vision of communal development that favoured a distinctive practice of place-making: as
a specific configuration of status in the former case, and as the result of a
journey in the latter.

Ulm's first consumer co-operative was founded in 1866 with an initial
membership of slightly over 200.[98] Officers of the garrisoned troops and
lower civil servants had been instrumental in its creation. The co-operative's
first chairman was the major Adolf von Hügel, who in 1872 was succeeded
by a district judge by the name of Breitling. The 1872 executive also comprised a district court clerk, a secondary school teacher, Ulm's chief police
inspector, a cavalry captain, and a war commissioner. The co-operative's
membership was even more diverse than its executive. Although until the
1880s its core can be described as thoroughly middle class, members also
included factory owners, religious ministers, and day labourers. It was only
from the turn of the century that workers came to dominate the co-operative, at least numerically.[99]

It did not take long before the organization got into the firing line for
the first time. In 1869, by which point the co-operative had achieved an
annual turnover of 59,000 gulden and become a recognized player in the
local economy, Ulm's *Gewerbeverein* sent a formal note of complaint to the
municipal council.[100] Signed by ten of its leading exponents, the petition
conveys a sense of the frustration many local traders and shopkeepers seem
to have felt at the co-operative's activities. These had now reached an extent,
the petitioners complained, where they threatened to 'destroy the liveli-
hood of local businesses.'[101] There are several reasons why Ulm's *Gewerberverein*
regarded the *Konsumverein* as a threat. The fact that some of the shopkeepers who joined the association had offered discounts to non-members was

one. This, they protested, was in breach of the co-operative's statutes. Another concerned the 'purchasing power' exercised by the association. What was even more worrying, however, was the large number of high-ranking civil servants and military officers among its leading members. As its critics openly admitted, that the co-operative was 'overwhelmingly in the hands of these classes' gave it respectability in the eyes of the larger public. There was only a short step, the petitioners asserted, from prestige to popularity; and an even shorter one from popularity to lasting economic success. Many a local craftsman or small trader, they complained, now saw himself forced to accept unfavourable conditions, 'including the granting of discounts.'[102]

Yet, the petitioners did not restrict themselves to airing their dissatisfaction. While they knew that prohibiting the co-operative would have violated imperial law, they still expected to be adequately protected from the effects of its commercial activities. It was in this spirit, at any rate, that they approached the local authorities. Their central demand was taxation. For, in their view, the consumer co-operative 'represented nothing less than a trade organization.' As far as its business activities were concerned, it had always resembled 'a joint stock company' more than a charity or mutual-benefit-society. In view of this, the petitioners insisted that it should be 'subject to trade income tax.' To this they added a moral argument about the role of public office holders in an urban municipality such as Ulm. Ulm's most important resource—trust in the impartiality of its civic institutions—was under threat as long as civil servants played a central role in the *Konsumverein*. Civil servants, they demanded, should be barred from joining a consumer association as card-carrying members:

> One might think of a post office clerk who catches sight of trade samples or of commercial notifications; or of a customs officer who might use his judgement concerning the nature of goods, prices or sources of supply to further the interests of his association; one might think of a post-office clerk exploiting telegraphic messages of a commercial nature to the same end. It is largely irrelevant whether these fears are well founded or not. All that is required for a most unhappy state of affairs to evolve, all that is needed for the trust in the integrity of the civil service to become permanently damaged, is that suspicions of this kind are allowed to develop and take hold among the public at large.[103]

Ulm's mayor replied the very same day. He began by pointing out that, with the enforcement of *Gewerbefreiheit* in the 1860s, economic competition had indeed become the legally accepted norm. Neither the state nor the municipality was therefore in a position to impose undue restrictions on the economic activities of a consumer association as long as it complied with existing law. Nor could the town authorities prevent local traders from doing business with such organizations. At the same time, von Heim recognized that the new economic order had caused financial damage to many businesses, emphasizing, however, that the protests should not be directed against 'those who exploit the new legislation to further their own interests.'[104]

That Ulm's mayor shared the petitioners' central accusation is evidenced by the circular he sent to the town's senior civil servants. In it, he asked them either to cancel their membership altogether or at least refrain from buying goods that were also available, albeit at slightly higher prices, in local shops. That the co-operative's activities had caused 'rancour' within a sizeable part of the local business community was only too understandable according to von Heim. He left no doubt that he considered membership in the consumer co-operative incommensurate with the office of a municipal civil servant.[105] Heim's successor as mayor, the moderate liberal Wagner, was much less guarded in expressing his reservations about the *Konsumverein*. In a letter sent to all civil servants in July 1890, he accused the co-operative of selling certain goods at higher prices than were charged in some local shops.[106]

The co-operative's development from 1869 onwards suggests that, at least initially, the impact of the agitation by the *Gewerbeverein* and later the *Schutzverein* (an association whose declared purpose was the defence of the local *Mittelstand*) was considerable: The co-operative's treasurer resigned at one of its first meetings, while another member of its executive let it be known that he saw himself 'forced to resign due to professional reasons.'[107] Moreover, after a second wave of public agitation against the *Konsumverein* in 1872, chief police inspector Reich and war commissioner Kraus, while expressing their willingness to remain in the association's executive, resigned from their seats on the politically sensitive finance committee. The executive decided to replace Reich and Kraus with members who 'do not occupy any public office.' One member's suggestion, that the co-operative respond to the 'public agitation against the *Konsumverein*' with a concerted information campaign, failed to be endorsed for fear of escalating a latent conflict.[108] Moderation would remain the co-operative's main public strategy throughout this period of controversy.

Internally, however, the arguments of the opponents of the co-operative were subjected to a rigorous debate. Thus, in 1892, the charge of selling at exorbitant prices (made by the right-wing *Schutzverein* and then explicitly endorsed by Mayor Wagner in a series of statements) was thrown out at once. If true, Ulm's public would not buy at the co-operative; besides, the business community for which the association posed a threat was small 'compared to the much larger number of workers, minor civil servants, widows, etc.' who had to live on a very small income.[109] Only on one occasion, when Mayor Wagner sent out his critical circular directly to the civil servants, did the co-operative's members decide to submit a formal complain to a higher authority.[110]

In the medium to long term, however, the *Konsumverein* was thriving in spite of the enmity it attracted. After a moderate increase of its membership during the 1870s (from 308 in 1869 to 368 in 1877), numbers began to rise sharply: to 491 in 1880, 646 in 1884, 861 in 1888, 1090 in 1890, and 3000 in 1899.[111] The co-operative also appears to have flourished as a community that took pride in its achievements. Thus, when in 1899 its director Weishaar reached 25 years of service, its members not only celebrated his anniversary, but presented him with a gift of 500 marks.[112] In the same year, Weishaar invented the custom of presenting employees with Christmas presents, ranging from 100 marks for long-serving employees to 5 for recently appointed ones. Revealingly, duration of service was the only factor determining the level of the sum to be awarded: Thus, the long-serving warehouseman Müller was offered twice as much (namely 100 marks) as the recently appointed master baker Jung, a decision Weishaar defended when it was queried at a general meeting.[113]

At the same time, however, the co-operative's total turnover was growing less fast than its membership. Thus while the latter roughly quadrupled between 1868 and 1890, the former less than doubled within the same period, which suggests that Ulm's *Konsumverein* had begun to restrict itself to the sale of a limited range of goods, possibly ones offered by local traders and shopkeepers.[114] At the very least, the co-operative seems to have been prevented from exhausting the considerable economic potential it had indicated during its first years of its existence. In spite of the increasing popularity the working-class co-operatives enjoyed from the 1890s onwards, the *Konsumverein Ulm* remained faithful to the middle-class vision orginating with Schulze-Delitzsch. Thus when, in 1902, dozens of consumer co-operatives in Württemberg left the *Deutscher Genossenschaftsbund* after it had expelled organizations that had allegedly violated the ethos created by Schulze-Delitzsch, Ulm's co-operative refused to follow suit.[115] When it came to the crunch, its leading exponents did not follow the path of the working-class societies. When push came to shove, they defended the place-reinforcing ethos that had inspired the *Konsumverein*'s foundation against the place-transcending vision of the working-class co-operatives.

Augsburg's early consumer associations also remained firmly within the parameters defined by Schulze-Delitzsch. The declared purpose of the city's first organization of its kind, named *Augsburger Konsumverein*, was to 'acquire potatoes and peas' and sell them on to its members. Founded in 1855, the association was chaired by the book trader George Jaquet. Its executive consisted of 15 members, including Mayor Forndran, two surgeons, a factory owner, a newspaper editor, a spice trader, a master shoemaker, a book binder, and a basket maker.[116] Although the available records offer no confirmation either way, the *Konsumverein* appears to have represented one of the numerous co-operatives that either disappeared after little more than a decade of their existence, or whose impact remained too marginal to generate much public interest.

A more ambitious agenda informed the city's second co-operative. The *Verein zur Anschaffung nöthiger Lebendbedürfnisse* received a positive welcome in the press when it was founded in 1859.[117] One report described its previous activities as 'brisk and most useful.' It had been steadily growing in size thanks to its ability to supply its members with a large range of goods 'at very moderate prices.' It was therefore high time, the report suggested, that the public familiarize itself with all the services the co-operative had to offer to new members.[118] Encouraged by its initial success, in 1863 the co-operative's executive sought to achieve expansion by requesting permission to sell to non-members as well.[119] Augsburg's magistrate, however, declined the request.[120] The co-operative ceased to exist in 1876, when 105 members decided to dissolve it after it had incurred heavy losses during the previous year.[121] Several affluent businessmen, some of them members of the co-operative, stepped in to settle the matter.[122] The premises, including machinery, horses, carriages, and furniture, were quickly sold off to furniture manufacturer Woerle and the director of the brewery school, a man by the name of Michel.[123] The ease and speed with which the co-operative was dissolved is intriguing. Although the evidence does not allow for a clear-cut conclusion, it appears that the executive's ambition to expand the association's customer base beyond its immediate membership had made it more controversial, and hence more prone to incurring financial losses. When it began to struggle, a number of local entrepreneurs were ready to strike.

Only one of Augsburg's consumer associations proved too strong for its numerous opponents. Founded in 1893, the *Allgemeiner Konsumverein Augsburg* was a co-operative of the second generation, one that catered above all for the needs of the city's working and lower middle classes.[124] Unlike its Ulm counterpart, Augsburg's *Konsumverein* left the German *Genossenschaftsbund* in 1902 after its executive had expelled 99 co-operatives it deemed in violation of its stipulated rules.[125] By 1897 the co-operative had three outlets in the city, rising to five by 1900. What marked it out as a co-operative of the new kind was that, rather than confining itself to buying and selling a range of products, with the setting up of its bakery in February 1900 it crossed the threshold to self-production. Its membership multiplied as a result, from 95 in 1891 and 174 in 1895 to 923 in 1900. By 1901 the *Allgemeiner Konsumverein Augsburg* had 1434 members. Of those, approximately 80 per cent were factory workers, mainly from the Wertach districts. By that point the association was run by 24 members of staff, including an executive director, a master baker, a warehouseman, three journeyman bakers, and three delivery girls. During the same period (between 1891 and 1901), its total turnover increased from 17,730 to 242,551 marks, and its profit from 767 to 27,009 marks.[126]

As the co-operative's executive chairman described the purchase of the property that would come to house its bakery: 'The thought of possessing one's own home must fill every co-operative member with a sense of pride.'[127] There was also no doubt, he noted, that 'the idea of the co-operative has begun to make significant inroads into all strata and professional classes.' Yet the core of the membership continued to consist of residents from the working-class districts, for whom the co-operative emerged as a source of pride and collective identification. They took pride, for instance, in the fact that their *Konsumverein* appeared to be in tune with the times; that it could be held up as an embodiment of norms that characterized the modern age. Thus, after noting the great efforts that had been required to set up the *Allgemeiner Konsumverein Augsburg* in 1891 and then bring it up to its present standard, the acting chairman invoked the bakery as the symbol of the co-operative's modern spirit:

> Our bakery, the pride of the co-operative, fulfils all the technical and hygienic requirements of a modern bakery. Its light and airy premises, coupled with the rigorous sense of duty guiding its staff, reassure our dear members that they can consume our products with the greatest appetite.[128]

The example of Ludwigshafen shows that the emergence of new strata (particularly of the new middle classes of public-service workers and civil servants) often favoured the emergence of a co-operative. The city's first consumer association came into being in 1873, on the initiative of employees of the BASF, the Pfalzbahn and the railway carriage factory. These companies not only provided it with the necessary premises for the storage and sale of goods. They also sought to ensure that its governing body remained in the hands of people with national-liberal convictions at a time when the trade unions and the SPD had discovered the consumer societies as a means to gain supporters.[129] In line with this conservative orientation, the co-operative took great pains to avoid posing a threat to local businesses. In fact, up to the turn of the century, one of the main incentives of membership was to purchase goods from local businesses at discounted prices using vouchers. For many years, this so-called *Fremdgeschäft*, the trade between members and local businesses, produced a larger turnover than that which the co-operative achieved through direct sales.

By 1888, the co-operative's annual turnover was 323,320 marks, resulting in a profit of 21,890 marks. By that time the total membership had reached 1063, reflecting an increase of over ten per cent on the previous year.[130] By comparison, the total turnover of Ulm's consumer co-operative in 1886 was 127,553 marks, and its membership 678; and all this in spite of the fact that, with a population of approximately 35,000, Ulm in 1886 was still considerably larger than Ludwigshafen (whose population was well below 25,000 at that point).[131] It is revealing that even Augsburg's co-operative, despite being located in the largest of the three towns, could not match the annual turnover of its Ludwigshafen counterpart. Yet, not only did Ludwigshafen's consumer association grow much faster than those of either Ulm or Augsburg. It also reacted with greater confidence to external criticisms. Thus, when from the mid-1890s several national interest groups (including the *Zentral-Verband deutscher Kaufleute*) began to lobby the Reichstag in an attempt to restrict the activities of the consumer co-operatives, Ludwigshafen's executive decided to make their views heard at the national level. Rudolf Schmidt, the then chair of its governing body, stressed the co-operative movement's positive 'social and educational impact' on German consumers. In encouraging individuals to organize their households in a more orderly fashion, and to pay for their purchases in cash, the co-operatives had benefited society as a whole. Curtailing their activities would therefore represent 'a step backwards: socially, morally, and economically.'[132]

In 1896 two members of Ludwigshafen's *Konsumverein* even took on the critics of Germany's co-operative movement. In a contribution published in the *Organ des Allg. Verbandes deutscher Erwerbs- und Wirtschafts-Genossenschaften* (the association founded by the pioneer of the liberal consumer movement, Schulze-Delitzsch), they contended that the problem did not lay with the consumer co-operatives, but, rather with the congestion of the local small-trade sector with people who were lacking in both skills and qualifications.[133] As they pointed out, in Ludwigshafen 180 small traders and shopkeepers were active in a town of roughly 35,000 inhabitants, amounting to one trader per 39 families. But of those, the authors estimated, 'hardly more than 30 are properly qualified tradesmen.' The rest were 'small grocers' known for storing their merchandise in their living and bedrooms without giving much consideration to issues of hygiene and cleanliness. Many, the report continued, sold their products at inflated prices to customers suffering from a lack of choice. All this was in marked contrast to the town's consumer co-operative, which conducted its activities in an orderly and professional manner, and which, through its very existence, had helped to stabilize prices for essential goods.[134]

When in 1906 the Social Democrats gained the majority on its governing body, Ludwigshafen's consumer co-operative joined the *Fortschrittlicher Zentralverband deutscher Konsumvereine*. This resulted in the creation of numerous new salesrooms across the city, as well as in a significant increase in annual turnover. It also increased tensions within the existing consumer association. Most middle-class members responded by resigning and setting up their own organization, the *Warenbezugs- und Sparverein Ludwigshafen*.[135] Unlike in Ulm, then, where middle-class members managed to retain their grip over the association's executive, in Ludwigshafen the numerical predominance of workers led to a split within the town's co-operative movement. As in Augsburg, but on an even grander scale, the place-transcending working-class co-operative would take a pivotal place in the life of the city whose inhabitants prided themselves on living in a 'German Chicago.'

The local franchise and the consumer co-operatives each offer a window into the ways urban residents remade their communities during this period. Starting with the exploration of municipal citizenship, what is particularly revealing is the variety of potential practices and courses of action people pursued. Yet what we see is not unlimited contingency. What imposed a certain logic on the complexity of urban life are the place-making visions that informed the practices of local actors as they grappled with the challenges they encountered.

The investigation of municipal citizenship revealed different degrees of inclusion and exclusion. By the standards of the time, Ulm's approach to municipal citizenship was extremely inclusive. What enabled this inclusiveness was not in the first instance the subscription to some progressive (Western) political ideas. What proved crucial, it appears, was the adherence to a specific ideal of the *Bürgergemeinde*. This ideal was not a priori. It was embraced in an effort to cope with the brave new world of economic liberalization and free movement. To no small degree, it drew inspiration from the normative universe that Mack Walker termed the German hometown. In essence, the home towns represented an attempt to amalgamate two seemingly contradictory principles: exclusion and inclusion, privileged status and egalitarianism, each in relatively hefty concentration. As Walker observed, the classical home towns were intolerant of the presence of non-citizens because they 'needed no class of mobile, dismissible, unskilled labour of the kind that found place in city and countryside.'[136] The apparent paradox lies in the fact that under different circumstances, this exclusive impulse could breed inclusion. In the post-unification context, as imperial legislation prohibited the exclusionary policies practiced in most German municipalities at least until the middle of the century, the hometown's inclusive impulse evidently still carried weight. Indeed, it could still inspire civic reform. The way in which Ulm's leading political actors responded to the 1885 state law offers a powerful demonstration of this. But this was not the static and inward-looking hometown Mack Walker described. The city's reformers imagined Ulm as a place that was the result of work in progress— not a configuration of status. In the late nineteenth century, the aim of remaking the town as an integrated whole could only be realized with the aid of a dynamic vision. This was in contrast to the much more industrialized Augsburg and Ludwigshafen am Rhein, where, at least in relation to local citizenship, the emphasis was on the town as a well-ordered place: as a configuration of status. Compared with Ulm this was a defensive conception. In both Augsburg and Ludwigshafen, civic exclusion prompted those at its receiving end—above all the socialist and Catholic working-classes, as well as women—to join associations that fought for the extension of the local franchise.

However, the real analytical purchase results from exploring how these two alternative avenues to civic inclusion—embodied, respectively, in the

Figure 7. Pedestrians and shopkeepers on the Hirschstraße in Ulm, circa 1910. © Stadtarchiv Ulm.

practice of municipal citizenship and in membership in consumer co-operatives—interacted with each other. What this analysis suggests is that they complemented each in compensatory fashion. That is to say, civic exclusion on one level appears to have favoured the emergence of practices of inclusion on the other. Thus, while Ulm proved highly inclusive in relation to political citizenship, its consumer co-operative proved ultimately place-reinforcing. Its priority consisted in the integration of established sections of the local economy—butchers, bakers, grocery stores, artisans, and small traders of various kinds—into the *Konsumverein*. What informed this practice was not a conservative notion of community, but the mostly implicit conviction that too much socio-economic segmentation would undermine the urban community. This was in contrast to both Augsburg and Ludwigshafen, where a different kind of consumer co-operative came to prevail. Rather than socio-economic integration for the sake of communal holism, its declared aim was the support of affordable consumer goods for those who could least afford them. Rather than place-reinforcing, its socio-economic practices were place-transcending. Its exponents tended to envisage their city in terms of a journey, not as a well-ordered place.

PART III

Rhythms

Prologue

In and Out of Sync

If he walks a little faster than others, he will prosper. But as soon as he lags behind, his own destruction will follow.

Friedrich List (1841)[1]

For Mayor Fischer, the nation's fate would be decided in towns such as Augsburg. In September 1871, almost a year to the day after the German victory over France had been sealed on the battlefields near Sedan, Fischer decided once again to preach to the converted. The liberal public he addressed shared his view about the detrimental impact of the pope's intervention on Germany. So did most members of Augsburg's magistrate and council, irrespective of their religious allegiance. Like their mayor, they regarded the confessional conflict between the state and the Catholic Church as a question of life and death for the German Empire. But were they up to their historic calling? Fischer seems to have doubted that they were. As he instructed his audience: 'What we must demonstrate before the world is that, here, in our good town of Augsburg, there exists an understanding for those larger questions; we must demonstrate that we are worthy members of a great nation-state.'[2]

Liberal nationalists like Fischer were not alone in emphasizing the close links between the local and the national spheres of life. Yet liberals felt more inclined than others to experience their town through the normative lens of the time traveller: as a stage on which the dramatic struggle between backwardness and progress was enacted daily. Many therefore demanded, in public rather than behind closed doors, that backwardness was to be extinguished in the name of a new synthesis of the national and the local. Indeed, liberals were more likely than others to claim that the separation of local and national affairs was deeply immoral. Their preoccupation with progress was thus inspired, at least in part, by the nationalist idea. Nationalism supplied them with a moral-emotive code of considerable weight. For the task they had set themselves was a large one: urban spaces were to be transformed; new places were to be created. The pulse of local life was to be quickened in the name of *Fortschritt*.

This was not the retreat from the pitfalls of modern mass politics that some historians have located;[3] nor was it a cynical adaptation of nationalism in the service of practical ends. The nationalist code appealed to liberals for reasons that were more intuitive than instrumental. Recurrently, rather than permanently, it evoked near-unimpeachable authority. Above all, it appeared to afford liberals with the status and recognition they believed they deserved by virtue of their education, their expertise in various fields, their work ethics, and their patriotism. The new nation-state promised a society in which the liberal middle-classes would be the natural educators of the people.[4] As part of this moral-emotive constellation, nationalism began to influence the dynamics and rhythms of communal life, with consequences that proved difficult to control.[5]

As social spaces, towns are invested with a multitude of (often competing) rhythms. They influence the remaking of urban communities in crucial ways, as we've seen in the preceding chapters. In the chapter on the local economies, for instance, an Ulm daily lamented the marginal role of commuter traffic. What it was lamenting, in other words, was that the pulse rate of Ulm's economic life was too low compared to, for example, Reutlingen or Heilbronn. Conversely, for many an inhabitant of Ludwigshafen the city's economic dynamism, sustained by constant population movement, constituted a source of great pride. In the field of elementary schools, furthermore, the move from three large classes to six or more age-related classes represents another attempt to alter the rhythm of instruction and learning. The tramway timetables—in the last third of the nineteenth century, many German cities significantly increased the service frequency in this domain of urban life—offer another example of this equation of progress with an increase of frequency and speed. A case in point is the description of the new tramway schedule that appeared in Ludwighafen's *Stadtgeschichte*, published on the occasion of the city's 50th anniversary:

With regard to the current timetable, let us note that on the main lines—
Rheinbrücke-Bahnhof-Anilinfabrik—a five-minute service (5 *Minutenbetrieb*)
will operate between 7.15 am and 9 pm. However, between 5.30 am and 7.15
am and between 9 pm and 11 pm a ten-minute service (*10 Minutenbetrieb*) will
be in operation on these lines. Furthermore, between 6 am to 10 pm a ten-
minute service will be in operation between the train stations of Ludwighsafen
and Mannheim. A 20-minute service (*20 Minutenbetrieb*) will be established,
until further notice, on the lines Bahnhof-Friedhof, Anilinfabrik-Friesenheim,
Kaiser Wilhelmstrasse-Mundenheim.[6]

This is, admittedly, as close as urban reformers came to insisting that local
life was, and indeed ought to be, underpinned by particular rhythms. Like
many phenomena of real significance, the theme of rhythm appears to have
made few headlines. German contemporaries hardly ever used the word. Yet
hidden rhythms were almost everywhere, shaping social relations and leaving their imprints on the urban landscape. The chapters of this part develop
this theme from different empirical vantage points: chapter 5 looks at the
liberal apostles of progress, focusing in particular on struggles over the urban
theatre and public health; chapters 6 and 7 explore the same theme through
an examination of Sedan Day parades and Corpus Christi processions.
Culture (theatre), Nation (Sedan), and God (Corpus Christi) all had their
own pilgrimages in the late nineteenth-century city.

If liberals came to develop a veritable obsession with the rhythms of
communal life, this was in part because their nationalist morality made them
prone to bouts of impatience and doubt.[7] German liberals were, in the
words of David Blackbourn, 'men in a hurry, engaged in an internal civilizing mission in a latecomer nation state.'[8] This accounts for the missionary
zeal with which they pursued their chosen task. It also explains why they
tried to remake their towns in a national image, in areas ranging from public
hygiene to the theatre, and from urban growth to the *Volksschule*, and why
this prompted those who disagreed with the liberals to propose alternatives
of how to remake urban space.[9]

In practice, however, the rhythms of life affected everyone. The difference
was that, in insisting that *Fortschritt* was to be accomplished come what may,
urban liberals lifted it out of the unconscious realm and made it a topic in a
public struggle. As far as they were concerned, many disturbing inadequa-
cies continued to hamper, even threaten, the young imperial order. That the
imperial state had not succeeded in putting an end to internal opposition—
the conflict between the state and the Catholic Church was followed by

the assault on the socialist left—or that its impact overseas continued to lag
behind its economic prowess, was an unsettling experience for the nationalist
majority within the liberal movement. It matters little, when it comes to
explaining local agencies, whether historians consider Germany more 'modern' than some of the proponents of the *Sonderweg* have made us believe.[10]
What matters is whether a significant portion of the Empire's most ardent
advocates doubted the resilience and adequacy of its public life and
institutions.

Doubts about the stability of the new order also go some way towards
explaining the centrality the *Kulturkampf* would assume in the liberal imagination. This struggle served to dramatize, in the words of Geoff Eley, the liberals' commitment to a society centred on a particular vision of progress.[11]
Fought under the banner of imperial nationhood, its official measures had the
effect of affronting ordinary Catholics, turning, according to some historians,
a socially diverse denominational community into a relatively homogenous
'Catholic milieu' whose members subscribed to 'ultramontanism'—a decidedly anti-liberal, Rome-orientated and emotional interpretation of Catholic
faith, with a strong preference for religious practice.[12] In this process of negative integration, an allegedly diverse community of Catholic 'milieu managers,' consisting of Catholic priests, editors of ultramontane newspapers and
leaders of Catholic associations, is sometimes attributed a crucial role. Most
importantly, the German culture war, rather than accomplishing its purported
task of closer nation integration, divided the nation along confessional lines.
According to some historians, it created 'not one nation, but two.'[13]

The chapters on Sedan Day and on Corpus Christi will offer a rather
different reading of the German culture war. They will show those who
participated in these important events engaged in a complex dialogue
with each other—in something that resembled a competitive dance rather
than a battle. A consensus was never attained, to be sure, but then nor was
it intended. As acts of public worship, Sedan Day parades and Corpus
Christi processions constituted two of the major public mass rituals during the era marked by nationalism and the *Kulturkampf*. Both were
dynamic, rather than static rituals, reflecting the tastes and preoccupations
of the people who practiced them. Both can be seen as powerful dramatizations of both the contrast and the correspondence between the sacred
and the profane. Those who physically took part signalled their commitment to a particular conception of time and place. They also performed a
particular temporal routine.[14]

But the differences separating them are at least as important as the parallels. Sedan Day represented a recent invention, while the origins of Corpus Christi Day lay in the late-medieval period. Sedan Day was at once more narrow and more encompassing than Corpus Christi. While Sedan Day was devoted to one particular nation, Corpus Christi, at least in terms of its central religious message, transcended geographical location and national affiliation; and whereas the Sedan Day parades embodied the German nation worshipping itself, the Corpus Christi processions only included Catholics as active participants. Yet in spite of the indubitable differences separating Sedan Day parades and Corpus Christi processions, in the praxis of urban communities they did not represent mutually impenetrable worlds. Rather, they acted as symbolic vehicles enabling a dialogue that brought ultramontane Catholics and liberal nationalists closer together. The rhythms they followed proved admittedly different—but not irreconcilably so.[15]

5

Apostles of Progress

Augsburg is no doubt flourishing and progressing. As our city is growing, however, so is the number of tasks that our citizenry may struggle to do justice to. The decisions on how to meet those requirements...will lead us down a path of either progress or regression, rise or decline...

Editorial in support of liberal candidates at the 1878 council elections,

Augsburger Neueste Nachrichten[1]

These tasks are more pressing than we may today believe, and we therefore need to undertake them if we are to keep up with the raging progress of our time, if we are to avoid, that is to say, falling behind our state's other striving towns.

Speech held by Councillor Oswald in 1890 during a meeting of the committee preparing the election of Ulm's new mayor[2]

Even though it is the youngest,
It is not the slightest
Of the cities of the Palatinate.
It has no equal,
Since none of the others has achieved
What it has become—all on its own.

Inscription on postcard ('Ludwigshafen am Rhein'), 1890s[3]

The apostles of progress have not been treated too kindly by historians. National Liberals in particular have often been depicted as those who sacrificed their liberalism on the altar of Prussian power politics—as that opportunistic lot who, while it clung on to liberal rhetoric, had in fact taken a turn to the right, with its members ending up as political conservatives, misogynists in disguise, or right-wing nationalists.[4] As a consequence, historians studying the mindsets and motivations of liberal nationalists often felt it necessary to legitimize their endeavour. At the outset of his classic on Marian apparitions in nineteenth-century Germany, for instance, David Blackbourn justified his decision to devote a separate chapter to leading intellectuals of the *Kulturkampf* by reminding his readers that the 'martinets of modernity' (he was referring to Rudolf Virchow and other champions of the culture war) mattered just as much as the humble Saarland villagers that were the true protagonists in his story.[5]

Engaging with some of the negative readings of German liberalism, more recently some historians have begun to stress liberals' contribution to the modernization of German society and culture. They have usually concentrated on a single city, examining liberal (and left-liberal) politics in the broadest sense. Differences in approach and emphasis notwithstanding, one of the central conclusions emerging from this research is that liberals, in spite of their growing political conservatism, had often been in the vanguard of local reform movements in the arts, in education, or in the area of social welfare or public health. Some historians have further demonstrated that urban liberals operated in a local environment that was much more politicized than previous research had made us believe.[6]

Instead of asking whether the actions of German liberals ought to be classified as progressive or reactionary, this chapter examines how urban liberals employed a nationalist moral code in an attempt to alter the rhythm of communal life and the shape of the urban landscape. Through investigations of the controversies surrounding the urban theatre and public health, these dynamics are brought into view.

Political cultures

Partisan politics played a part wherever *Fortschritt* became a topic of vigorous debate, but its role and impact varied considerably from one place to another. Of the three towns considered here, Augsburg developed by far the most antagonistic political culture. Its franchise was particularly restrictive (only around 20 per cent of those who could vote nationally possessed local citizenship). It was exclusive not only in terms of the number of people who could take part in municipal elections, but also regarding the way in which votes were translated into seats in the municipal council. District-based majority voting worked in the liberals' favour. These restrictions served to solidify the predominance of the National Liberals in the town's legislative and executive bodies; unsurprisingly, the extent of liberal predominance in a town whose majority consisted of Catholics with ultramontane leanings proved a persistent source of tension.

These tensions were inextricably linked to the national question. Indeed, the antagonism between liberalism and (Catholic) conservatism in Augsburg grew out of the conflict the city experienced over the German constitution of 1849. Up until March 1849, Augsburg's citizenry had been relatively united across denominational lines in its endorsement of the German constitution.[7] But when, on 21 May of that year, the city's conservative mayor, Georg von Forndran (who had been elected in 1847 as the candidate of the Catholic middle classes) refused to support the motion of no-confidence against the Bavarian government that the liberals submitted to the Bavarian Landtag, this split Augsburg's bourgeoisie into two competing factions: one liberal and pro-unification, the other conservative and pro-Bavarian.[8] After the outbreak of a major cholera epidemic in 1854, which struck some of the town's Catholic districts particularly hard, the National Liberals became the strongest group in the municipal council. From 1860 they also constituted the majority in the city magistrate, the town's political executive presided by two full-time mayors. Augsburg's three dominant political figures of the mid-1860s—the advocate Joseph Völk, the banker Hans von Stetten, and the then deputy mayor Ludwig Fischer—all belonged to the pro-Prussian wing of Bavaria's Progressive Party.[9] Most importantly, the National Liberals who assumed power in the 1860s were to rule the city without interruption until 1908, when proportional representation put an end to their hegemony.

The injection of a new political style into Augsburg's political life owed much to Ludwig Fischer (1832–1900). A Catholic lawyer and the son of the radical Stanislaus Fischer, he was one of Bavaria's leading exponents of the *Fortschrittspartei*. Born in 1832, Fischer attended the *Gymnasium* in Augsburg before studying law in Munich and Berlin. After being elected deputy mayor in 1862, in 1866 he succeeded the conservative Johann Georg Forndran (1807–1866) as the town's chief civil servant, a position he continued to occupy until his death in 1900. The Bavarian government did as much as it legally could to prevent Fischer's political rise. After his election to the office of deputy mayor in 1862, for instance, it took the ministry more than a month to confirm his appointment. Once established in his post, Fischer's actions did little to alter the state authorities' views on his suitability for the office of mayor. In fact, the district governor's reports on Fischer's impending re-election as deputy mayor read like a plea for his dismissal. Not only was Fischer castigated for his allegedly 'unashamed coquetting with the town's working-classes,' for not having missed a single 'meeting of the *Nationalverein* and of the *Schleswig-Holstein Verein*' since becoming deputy mayor in 1862, and for having exacerbated 'confessional quarrels' in the town. It was because of Fischer's 'party-political bias,' the governor noted, that he had felt it appropriate to award him grade III in his testimonial in the previous year, a grade that indicated Fischer's 'unsuitability to be mayor of the town of Augsburg.' As the official conceded with an air of resignation, however, refusing to confirm Fischer's appointment was out of the question in view of his and the liberals' popularity with the urban electorate.[10] Three years later, when Fischer was re-elected as deputy mayor, Munich's written endorsement took four months to arrive. When he was unanimously elected to the office of *Oberbürgermeister* the following year, it took the Bavarian government more than three weeks to endorse his appointment.[11] These acts put a strain on Fischer's relationship with the Bavarian state for decades to come. They also confirmed him in his belief that the *kleindeutsch* nation-state was the only reliable guarantor of *Fortschritt*.

Fischer's political career is interesting not least because, as a Catholic and liberal nationalist, he defies simplistic interpretations of the *Kulturkampf* as a confessional conflict and of German nationalism as an inherently Protestant phenomenon. In 1891 Fischer joined the executive of the Pan-German League, a radical nationalist and imperialist pressure group. Conservatives of either confession rejected the political style that Fischer and his associates embodied, while Protestant and Catholic liberals formed the bulk of his supporters.[12] Like many other members of the liberal ruling elite of the 1860s and 1870s, Fischer was not rooted in the town's traditional networks of notable politics. In contrast to the Protestant Nikodemus Frisch, who as deputy mayor became Fischer's right-hand man for more than 30 years, Fischer had none of the airs and graces of the old urban bourgeoisie. His long-standing membership of the German *Reichstag* and of the Bavarian *Landtag* altered little in this regard. Despite his formidable political pedigree, and his recognized skills as an administrator and politician, Fischer never ceased to act like a new man. His style was informal, populist and antagonistic, rather than polished and conciliatory. In his 1862 inauguration speech as deputy mayor (he was 30 years old at the time), which was widely noted, Fischer went immediately on the offensive, outing himself as a liberal conviction politician whose guiding principle was progress rather than compromise:

Figure 8. Erster Bürgermeister Ludwig Fischer, circa 1885.
© Stadtarchiv Augsburg.

Gentlemen! I shall never forget that I am a servant of the *Gemeinde*, not its ruler. My sole duty lies in the promotion of the town's welfare on the basis of the constitution and the laws of the land. Starting from this premise, however, I shall never lose sight of the fact that we live in the second half of the nineteenth century, and that progress means life while stagnation represents death. Wherever I recognize a real need for reform I shall express my beliefs with frankness. While I respect everyone, notably every religious conviction, it remains my firm belief that whenever a state or municipal administration endorses the position of a particular confessional party, it does so at the expense of the welfare of the wider community.[13]

Towards the end of his speech, just in case anyone had missed the gist of his message: 'It is therefore by adhering to such convictions and intentions that I am assuming this office: trusting in the support of my political allies, hoping to gain the respect of my honest opponents, unconcerned about the judgment of the unprincipled and the sycophants, moving ahead with boldness and guided by the will to do good.'[14]

From the mid-1860s Fischer was the undisputed leader of a powerful liberal circle whose members aimed to overcome what they saw as backwardness rooted in clerical tutelage. By Augsburg's standards, this was

'politics in a new key.'[15] What made it so was less the campaigning techniques than the antagonistic language employed by its exponents. Even
more than their actual policies, it was this style that set them on a collision
course with various parts of Augsburg society. Of course, the liberals could
not simply discard other interests and opinions. But there were limits to
their willingness to engage with those who challenged their political
agenda. The conflict with political Catholicism in particular would prove
systemic to their rule. Given Augsburg's confessional composition, with
Catholics accounting for between 60 and 70 per cent of its resident population between 1852 and 1910, and the presence of numerous Catholic
clergy and several influential Catholic newspapers, this is hardly surprising.
By 1880 the locally centred *Neue Augsburger Zeitung* had over 10,000 subscribers, making it Germany's Catholic daily with the highest circulation
rate, while the nationally influential *Augsburger Postzeitung* had between
5000–6000 subscribers.[16]

Indeed, the existence of an extremely effective Catholic network of
communication explains why it would take the SPD so long to make inroads
into the Catholic electorate. At least in the older parts of town (much less
so in the working-class districts in the city's north-western part), a high
degree of geographical segregation between the confessions was common.
As late as 1873, Wilhelm Heinrich Riehl claimed that, in Augsburg, religion
was still the main factor shaping social relations.[17] The strength of Augsburg's
political Catholicism also accounts for the relentlessness with which Mayor
Fischer and his allies pursued their modernizing agenda.[18] From the 1860s
onwards, the competition over progress that ensued between urban liberals
and ultramontane Catholics carried all the hallmarks of a modern political
contest.[19]

The inextricable nexus between local and national progress in the
liberal imagination became particularly evident in the 1884 elections,
which in Augsburg were fought simultaneously at the national and
municipal levels. From the liberals' point of view, these elections were
about stemming the ultramontane tide in the Empire and in Augsburg
alike. While Augsburg's National Liberals knew full well that they stood
no chance of beating the Catholic-conservative candidate within the
electoral district, Ludwig Fischer's strong showing among the urban electorate (of the 9929 urban votes cast, Fischer received 4711, with 'only'
3694 going to the Centre candidate) prompted ecstatic celebrations in
the liberal camp. Fischer's strong performance in Augsburg, under

conditions of universal manhood suffrage, was widely judged as having saved the honour of the liberal party against a disciplined and well-organized opponent. As the *Augsburger Neueste Nachrichten* noted: 'The [Centre Party's] ballot machine worked well, as was to be expected, and it is due to its efficiency that knight Biehl will now move to Berlin. But he will not be able to act as the representative of the town of Augsburg, and to have been able to prevent this we deem our greatest achievement.'[20] About one month later, after the liberals had defeated the Centre in the municipal elections, the same newspaper exclaimed:

> Victoria, victory is ours!…Yesterday, after being given the first firm signs of victory, Augsburg's entire liberal citizenry breathed a sigh of relief—as if it had just been liberated from a nightmare, as if it had just woken up from a bad dream! For it was a very bad dream that we had been dreaming of late! Thank God it was just a dream![21]

Ulm's liberals congregated in the *Deutsche Partei*. Founded in 1866 after the Prussian victory over Austria, its supporters faced their strongest opponents in the anti-Prussian *Volkspartei*. Established in 1864, the People's Party emerged as the organizational focal point of Württemberg's democratic movement. Ulm's relatively inclusive franchise (more than 50 per cent of those entitled to vote nationally could take part in local elections) played in the People's Party's favour, while it prevented the National Liberals from dominating decision-making in the council. Both parties had emerged from the 1860s split of Württemberg's Progressive Party into a *kleindeutsch*-liberal and a *grossdeutsch*-democratic faction.[22] This division of the liberal movement found its exact replica in Ulm. When in August 1866 supporters of Württemberg's *Deutsche Partei* petitioned the King to enter into peace talks with Prussia, the *Ulmer Volksverein* (a loose liberal-democratic association founded in 1865) split into various factions. The association finally dissolved in January 1867, just a few days after some of its former members had founded a local branch of the *Deutsche Partei*. In November 1869 the left liberal elements within the former *Volksverein* established the *Freisinnig Grossdeutscher Verein*, a coalition of anti-Prussian democrats and Catholics loyal to a greater Germany. However, the German victory over France sounded the death knell for the association.[23]

After a year or two of keeping a low profile due to the stigma it had acquired because of its anti-Prussian stance before the outbreak of war, the *Volkspartei* regained its former strength. By the mid-1870s, Ulm's democrats, often in alliance with lower-middle-class Catholics and Protestants, were once again able to challenge the pro-Prussian liberals. Indeed, as early as 1871 the majority of Ulm's electorate refused to lend its support to the candidates of the *Deutsche Partei*. Especially in the more important of the two representative bodies, the Municipal Assembly (*Gemeinderat*), the candidates put forward by the *Bügerverein* were more likely to be elected than those proposed by the *Deutsche Partei*.[24]

Yet in Ulm, too, the National Liberals were a force to be reckoned with. German unification had undoubtedly strengthened their cause, at least as long as nationalism's normative weight could not be questioned. Had the proponents of the *Volkspartei* not sought to absorb the nationalist code to some extent—in the sense of endorsing the German nation-state and removing the blunter versions of Württemberg particularism from their rhetorical arsenal—they could hardly have survived beyond the year 1871. Nor would they have done as well as they did in national elections in Württemberg soon thereafter, and particularly during the 1880s and 1890s, when they became the region's strongest party. In Ulm itself, the *Deutsche Partei* and the *Volkspartei* battled for hegemony. As the liberal *Ulmer Schnellpost* described the entrenched rivalry between the city's leading political parties:

> Yesterday the town's two competing electoral associations, the *Verein der deutschen Partei*, whose programme is *deutschnational* through and through, and the *Bürgerverein*, whose members belong to a range of different parties united in their opposition to the *Deutsche Partei*, held their meetings in different inns to deliberate the forthcoming municipal elections. The association of the *Deutsche Partei* met in the *Sonne*, while their opponents gathered in the *Petersburger Hof*.[25]

The existence of deeply engrained democrat loyalties offers one reason why Ulm proved difficult terrain for a party that was so markedly pro-Prussian. Another concerns liberal nationalism's open support for the *Kulturkampf*. Not that relations between Catholics and Protestants had been entirely free from tensions. Yet in Ulm, confessional matters were mostly discussed behind closed doors. The impact of this strategy on the Catholic community is difficult to estimate. It did certainly not prevent the emergence of an associational network of some significance. By 1886, 121 journeymen had joined the Catholic journeymen's association (founded in 1852), and the Catholic Lehrlingsverein (founded in 1888) had 173 members by 1908.[26] The first newspaper promoting the interests of political Catholicism, the *Ulmer Volksbote*, was founded as late as 1898. Also,

Father Magg, the spiritual leader of Ulm's Catholics throughout the 1880s and 1890s, was more interested in cultivating ties with the (mostly Protestant) local authorities than in creating a large and tightly integrated Catholic milieu.[27]

For the local democrats and their Catholic supporters, the liberals had shamelessly imported a national conflict into local affairs. In part, this charge arose from the intensity with which Ulm's National Liberals campaigned during national elections. Thus, before each election to the Reichstag, the executive of Ulm's *Deutsche Partei* formed an electoral committee. That many of its candidates during the 1870s and 1880s were fervent supporters of the *Kulturkampf* only added to its unpopularity with the *Volkspartei* and its voters. As a Protestant reader of the *Ulmer Tagblatt* expressed his disgust at statements made by Dr Römer, the National Liberal candidate in the 1874 election: 'Mr Römer's party uses a language that is not far away from the call, "Get him, for he's a Catholic!" A political style that is so bereft of any humanity deserves only one fate: thorough defeat, brought about by the Catholic voters.'[28]

With the exception of Ulm's *Oberbürgermeister* von Heim (1877–81) and Hildesheim's mayor Gottlob Friedrich Riekert (1881–84), both of whom joined the Berlin Reichstag as Free Conservatives, several of the National Liberal candidates elected to the Reichstag in the district during the 1870s and 1880s—particularly the lawyer and geologist Robert Römer (1871–77), and Augsburg's mayor Ludwig Fischer (1884–90)—were fierce *Kulturkämpfer*. And as the democrats kept pointing out, the complete absence of Catholics on the *Deutsche Partei*'s municipal ballot papers indicated a deep-seated anti-Catholic bias. In 1877, for example, the *Ulmer Tagblatt* criticized the said party for not having 'brought it over itself' to include a single Catholic in its electoral list, despite the fact that 7000 of Ulm's population were Catholics.[29] Throughout the 1880s Ulm's *Katholischer Bürgerverein* tended to team up with the left-liberal *Bürgerverein*.[30]

The National Liberals were also criticized for not paying sufficient attention to 'personal ability' and 'economic interests.'[31] It was such criteria that guided the *Bürgerverein*'s electoral committee in its selection of candidates, as a meeting it held on the eve of the 1879 municipal election reveals. Its sole purpose was to reach agreement on a list of candidates. As the chairman explained as he went through the proposed list, name by name: The 'merchants' were represented by the candidates Eckstein and Ebner, the skipper guild by Mr Heilbronner, the timber merchants by

Mr Ruess, the brewers and economists by factory owner Mr Mayser, the small traders by furniture manufacturer Mr Forstner, the innkeeper guild by 'their chairman, Mr Ebert,' and the 'construction trade' by Mr Hillenbrand. As the chairman concluded : with 'barrister Sänger we have done justice to the wishes of the Israelites,' and 'in Mr Hillenbrand and Mr Eckstein the list also contains two Catholics.'[32]

What we see here is a veritable clash of political styles. For the liberal *Bürgerverein* the representation of the various economic and religious interests was absolutely crucial. The liberal nationalists' approach appeared to undermine a political culture that had proved conducive to Ulm's development as a cohesive community. The *Bürgerverein* did not favour tradition over progress. What it stood for, rather, was an alternative political culture, one that sought to accommodate different cultural identities and economic interests.

The second half of the 1880s at first appeared to bring a rapprochement between the various groups competing with each other in local elections. Thus, most of the electoral lists put forward now contained members from more than one electoral association, with candidates who only figured on a single list standing little chance of getting elected. There were even some efforts made to agree on a joint list. In 1885, for example, four candidates appeared on the lists of the *Bürgergesellschaft* (which in 1883 for the first time had allied itself with the *Deutsche Partei*) and the democratic *Bürgerverein*, including master butcher Wollinsky, a man well known for his national-liberal views.[33] But some of the liberal candidates were regarded as *personae non grata* by the other side. Thus, the *Bürgerverein* refused to open its list to liberal candidates who were known for their antagonistic style. One individual who apparently fell into this category was the bookshop owner Frey, who proved unacceptable to the democrats and their supporters.[34] In 1887, the National Liberals and the *Bürgerverein* once again failed to agree on a joint list.[35]

The election of a new *Oberbürgermeister* in 1890—the Free Conservative von Heim resigned on health grounds after 27 years of service—appears to have marked a turning point for Ulm's political culture. The election of the 33-year-old Heinrich Wagner as von Heim's successor became possible after a broad coalition comprising moderate liberals, democrats, and Catholics had formed in explicit opposition to the *Deutsche Partei's* official candidate.[36] Wagner's success followed a highly divisive national election campaign. Although it had resulted in the defeat of the National Liberals in both the district and in Württemberg generally, the campaign itself had strained the political climate in Ulm. Wagner, a skilled administrator from a relatively modest background, had acquired an impeccable reputation for pragmatism in his capacity as Ulm's head of the police service during the late 1880s. These virtues he stressed in the presentation he gave as part of his candidature in front of more than 1,500 of Ulm's citizens.[37]

At the same event, Wagner's main rival, the 36-year-old district judge and Ulm-born Dr Korn, declared himself an 'enthusiastic advocate of Kaiser and Reich,' with a heart that was beating 'for the greatness, power, and reputation of the beloved German Fatherland.'[38] On the eve of the election, members of the *Deutsche Partei* published a flysheet that portrayed Korn, a high-flying district judge, as the superior candidate. By contrast, Wagner was described as a mere 'administrator' whose lack of a university education made him unsuitable to act as mayor of a town of Ulm's importance.[39] This strategy badly backfired. On the same day that the city's liberal nationalists described Wagner as unsuitable for the office of mayor, his supporters leaked a letter by the widely respected von Heim, in which he explicitly endorsed Wagner's candidacy.[40]

The process leading up to Wagner's election is interesting for at least two reasons. First, all the candidates who put themselves forward for election were asked to express their willingness to refrain from seeking a seat in the Reichstag. In part, of course, this concession was sought because Ulm's citizens wished to appoint someone who, once installed in his post, would not spend a substantial amount of his time pursuing his political ambitions in the Berlin Reichstag. Other towns of similar size employed a deputy mayor and a board of magistrates that, at least in part, consisted of full-time civil servants. Ulm's mayor not only carried an exceptionally great range of responsibilities by comparison. He was also expected to be visible as the city's highest civil servant. At a salary of 6000 marks, excluding free accommodation in a sizeable *Dienstwohnung*, this was only fair.

But this is only part of the reason why the candidates for Ulm's office of mayor were asked to forfeit their national political ambitions. It is noteworthy, for example, that the committee organizing the election of the new mayor did not regard taking up a seat in Württemberg's *Landtag* as a problem. This was not merely because of Stuttgart's proximity. More important was the view that compromise rather than conviction politics offered the best guarantee for the Ulm's prosperity and continuous progress. At the first meeting of the committee charged with organizing the election of von

Heim's successor, the new incumbent was profiled as a pragmatist able to prevent Ulm from falling further behind some of Württemberg's 'up-and-coming towns.'[41] What Ulm needed, several committee members agreed, were further infrastructural reforms. The priorities enumerated included the removal of the suffocating fortification walls, the relocation of the municipal cemetery to the city's periphery, the building of a multi-purpose town hall and public baths and a power station for industrial purposes.[42]

Two years after his election, during the habitual swearing-in-ceremony for new council members, Wagner pointed out that in the previous year Ulm had been 'untroubled by the party-political quarrels and fierce infighting' that had been 'the norm in many of Württemberg's municipalities.' Instead, Ulm's citizens had been engaged 'in a friendly competition,' whose driving motive had been 'the realization of practical aims in the interest of the common wheel.' If this spirit persisted, then 'Ulm's prosperity was not in danger.'[43]

In Ludwigshafen, the deeply entrenched political alliances that we identified in both Augsburg and Ulm only emerged around the turn of the century. Up to the 1890s, the lack of any serious political rivals meant that Ludwigshafen's liberals could exist as a relatively diffuse group whose behaviour was gregarious, rather than determined by the rules and techniques of modern party politics.[44] The 20 plus councillors who were elected between 1850 and 1899—before 1869 only the 30–50 per cent of citizens paying the highest taxes were eligible anyway—tended to represent broadly liberal positions on questions ranging from cultural and economic policy to franchise reform. After 1868 the Municipal Assembly was entitled to choose the town's mayor from amongst its members. In line with Palatinate law, moreover, before 1896 the mayor did not receive any salary for his services, but carried out his duties as an honorary office. Up to that point, the town's mayors had consisted of well-to-do or affluent notables without prior training in public administration. This changed with the appointment of the lawyer Friedrich Krafft in 1896. Ludwigshafen's first professional mayor and like his predecessors a National Liberal, Krafft was a seasoned civil servant.

The city's administrative infrastructure developed rather slowly, too. As late as 1877 there were only nine full-time policemen in charge of maintaining the public order of a town of roughly 13,000 inhabitants; by 1890, when the population had risen to around 25,000, the number of full-time policemen had reached 27; but it was not until 1897, when the population exceeded 40,000, that the town was divided up into six police districts, each of which was allocated a contingent of ten policemen.[45]

More importantly, as long as municipal citizenship was restricted to a select group of middle-class residents—up to the turn of the century the city's proportion of local to national voters was below 20 per cent—the style of liberal politics was conciliatory, rather than antagonistic. Various lists of candidates were submitted before an election. Some candidates appeared on the lists of several electoral associations, a common strategy designed to widen an individual candidate's appeal by bringing him to the attention of a range of economic interest groups—including artisans and craftsmen, small traders, and shopkeepers, and so on—rather than to the followers of one particular party. Following the party line was no precondition of success in a context in which a broad liberal orientation could almost be taken for granted.[46]

The ways in which municipal elections were fought, particularly the electoral lists that the various associations printed and then distributed, reinforces this impression. For example, on the occasion of the 1879 election one list simply defined candidates in terms of basic socio-economic categories, with an indication of how many names should be included under each heading.

Figure 9. Postcard of Ludwigshafen am Rhein, with a poem praising its industrial and civic achievements, circa 1910. © Stadtarchiv Ludwigshafen am Rhein.

The headings were: BASF (six candidates), *Pfälzische Eisenbahnen* (five candidates), craftsmen (six candidates), other trades (four candidates), workers (three candidates), other (three candidates).[47] The BASF and the *Pfälzische Eisenbahnen* promoted candidates who were educated (ranging from skilled workers and office personnel to university-educated scientists and directors) and decidedly National Liberal in orientation. This pattern did not change significantly over the course of the next ten years. The five electoral lists that were on offer in 1889 still featured similar socio-economic categories as their main criteria for distinguishing between candidates.

But something significant did change in that very same year—something that signalled the beginning of a new era in local politics. For it was in 1889, the year before the laws against the socialists were abolished, that Ludwigshafen's leading Social Democrat, the prolific and widely respected Franz Josef Ehrhart, held an election meeting in one of the city's inns. Its purpose was to mobilize working-class and lower-middle class voters through a campaign that focused on the council's reluctance to grant citizenship rights to workers and other less-well-off sections of the urban public. These tactics paid off, at least for Ehrhart. Having been featured on three electoral lists, he gained the first Social Democrat seat on Ludwighafen's town council, a seat he would retain until his death in 1908.[48]

Ludwigshafen's eventual transition to modern party politics occurred in 1894, when the SPD, as well as stepping up its mobilizing efforts, for the first time put forward its own electoral list. The local association of the Catholic Centre Party also organized several meetings to promote its candidates. What is remarkable is that SPD candidates could now be found on some of the other lists, except those controlled by the BASF and the *Pfälzische Bahn*, which both remained reserved for liberal candidates. A total of ten election proposals were submitted, mostly in the form of adverts in newspapers. Attempts by the BASF to influence its workforce—workers were guided to the ballot box by their foremen, provoking fierce protests from the SPD—confirm that from the mid-1890s Ludwigshafen's political culture was turning more antagonistic.[49] In 1899, the SPD and the Centre Party agreed on a joint list comprising ten candidates from the SPD, nine from the Centre, and 16 liberals and independents. It was advertised in the SPD daily, the *Pfälzische Post*, as well as in a Centre Party election pamphlet. Both parties now endeavoured to appeal to the town's petit-bourgeois voters, as well as to the workers of the various industrial factories. These efforts paid off for the SPD in particular, which won 7 of the 27 council seats. The election resulted in a near-complete rejuvenation of the existing council: only four of the previous councillors (including the Social Democrat Ehrhart) were re-elected.[50]

In 1904, SPD and Centre once again agreed on a joint list; and for the first time, this provoked a concerted response from the various liberal groupings, which now united under the banner of National Liberalism. Modern mass politics, pioneered by the Centre and the SPD, had finally arrived in Ludwigshafen. The SPD managed to increase its weight in the council, winning 11 seats, while four went to the Centre, four to the National Liberals, and seven to independent middle-class candidates.[51] The final step towards a more modern style of politics in Ludwigshafen occurred with the introduction of proportional representation in 1908. From now on electoral coalitions would be a thing of the past. Of the 26 council seats, the SPD gained 13, while the National Liberals won a total of seven; the Centre failed to improve on its four existing seats.[52]

It is unlikely that the introduction of a more antagonistic style, influenced by national themes and strategies, would have been delayed for so long in Ludwigshafen had political Catholicism assumed only half the significance that it enjoyed in and around Augsburg. Not only did Ludwigshafen lack established confessional networks comparable with those present in Augsburg or Ulm, but it also boasted an unusually fluctuating population in which young working-class men were the dominant element.[53] No doubt things improved from the 1880s onwards: a Catholic journeymen's association was founded in December 1887, with 43 members and close to a hundred adult members;[54] but by the end of 1891, the 'number of active members' had dropped to 18, despite the introduction of a more stringent regime of discipline and control designed to improve attendance at the monthly meetings.[55] The association set up to promote the establishment of a clubhouse for Catholic journeymen, founded in 1894, albeit tightly integrated and fiercely doctrinal in orientation, remained small.[56] Meanwhile, on the political plane, Ludwigshafen's large Catholic population for the most part disregarded its confessional allegiance when it went to the polls. The vast majority of Ludwigshafen's Catholics (who in contrast to portions of the Protestant working classes remained completely inaccessible to the lures of National Liberalism) supported the Social Democrats in both national and local elections. Meanwhile, in contrast to both Augsburg and Ulm, Ludwigshafen's Centre Party tended to fare best among middle- and upper-middle-class Catholics.[57]

Stadttheater

The theme that had preoccupied Augsburg's population the most in recent times, the city magistrate's weekly report noted in February 1873, was 'the question of whether or not a new municipal theatre ought to be built.' Yet the decision that had been taken—namely, to close the old theatre temporarily due to growing health and safety concerns—prompted critique from both the supporters and opponents of the new theatre.[58] Few people in Augsburg, it seems, doubted whether the city needed a theatre. But the question was what kind.

When it comes to delving deeper into the liberals' love affair with progress as they understood it, the *Stadttheater* provides a particularly rich field of investigation. Looking at the municipal theatre—its allocated role and its public reception, its performances, its cost to the municipal purse, to mention just a few of the relevant issues—enables us to shift our focus from political constellations to the normative and moral dynamics driving urban reform. Even more than the study of urban politics, the theatre offers insights into how urban actors endeavoured to reconfigure urban space by changing existing and creating new places of recognized significance. Certainly for its many advocates, the municipal theatre constituted an important part within a broader project of cultural reform. Over and beyond that, however, and particularly for the liberal movers and doers, it served as a mirror of individual and collective status and prestige.

'Show me our *Stadttheater*, and I tell you what we're worth.' This sentence sums up how many educated Germans appear to have felt about their city's theatre: as something that offered pleasure and enjoyment, to be sure, but also as something that reflected on their own place in the worlds they inhabited; on the public recognition they enjoyed as a status group; on their own self-worth even. Directly or indirectly, the theatre was relevant to many people's *Lebenswelt*, which is why it stirred up such heated debate. For if one section of an urban population demanded that the theatre be improved as a cultural institution—be this by putting on different, more 'sophisticated' kinds of performances, or by building an entirely new *Stadttheater*, as was the case in Augsburg—this could be experienced as humiliating, even offensive, by others. The theatre was more than an urban cultural institution. It also served as a projection foil for debates that touched on questions of a more existential nature. For the champions of *Fortschritt*, the theatre was a very serious matter indeed.

Augsburg's first *Stadttheater* was built in 1776. Financed by the municipal social welfare bureau, it was located in the Jakoberstadt, a district in the town's east end traditionally inhabited by craftsmen and day-labourers.[59] The theatre's early years were promising: in 1787 it saw Mozart's opera *Don Giovanni*, to be followed, in 1793, by the *Zauberflöte*. Yet the theatre's architectural style was as modest as was its location, leading Wilhelm Heinrich Riehl to the conclusion that it resembled an almshouse or chapel more than it did a temple of the arts.[60] The theatre's directors, who like many of their German colleagues in other cities ran the institution as cultural entrepreneurs, tried to make ends meet by offering a programme designed to please the tastes of a broad section of the population. In addition to the more demanding classical plays, they put on a large number of adventure plays and comedies, as well as performances by magicians that often drew considerable crowds. It was only from the 1850s that a more elevated cultural vision began to take hold in Augsburg, one more in tune with the tastes and sensibilities of the town's educated bourgeoisie. The result was a division of labour in the provision of theatrical performances. Whereas in the *Stadttheater* comedies were increasingly replaced by classical dramas and operas, the town's various fringe theatres continued to cater for more popular tastes.[61]

Yet the *Stadttheater*'s transition towards greater sophistication did not fulfil everyone's expectations. In 1859, for example, one of the town's liberal newspapers lamented that while works of 'inferior or even dubious quality' had often filled the house, 'musical and dramatic masterpieces' attracted only a dozen or so people.[62] Numerous performances provoked scornful comments from the local press. In 1872, for instance, after a staging of *Figaros Hochzeit*, one liberal daily bid good-bye to one actress, and requested the departure of another: 'The raging sea demands its sacrifice! One has already been devoured. Miss Hummler is no longer. Yesterday she wiped Augsburg's plentiful dust off her small feet and boarded the train with the necessary resignation. We have been waiting for a while to hear the same news about Miss Link!'[63]

In the course of the 1860s these criticisms gained currency. By that time all of Augsburg's liberal dailies had begun to run special columns devoted to the strengths and, more frequently, the perceived weaknesses, of the *Stadttheater*. There is no doubt that public expectations concerning the quality of the performances on offer had risen continually since the middle of the century. Thus, when in 1862 the liberal *Augsburger Neueste Nachrichten* took stock of the past theatre season, its arts editor did not spare his praise;

but he also noted that, if the overall quality had been satisfactory or even high on some occasions, this had been due, above all, to 'guest performances by a number of celebrated artists from outside.'[64]

After German unification, Augsburg's liberals adopted an even more robust approach when debating the state of the city's theatre. Emboldened by their local predominance, they now argued that the theatre faced a crisis, one whose resolution required radical steps. The outbreak of a fire in the mayoral box on 1 January 1876 no doubt buttressed their cause. For a socio-cultural milieu that was preoccupied with progress, the fusion of these two sets of concerns—the health and safety of the public, and the status of the theatre as a cultural institution, a *Bildungsinstitution* of central significance—created a potent brew with which to nourish their campaign in support of a new *Stadttheater*. What Augsburg needed, they insisted, was a theatre commensurate with the cultural vision of a prosperous and ambitious town: large, centrally located, and featuring state-of-the-art equipment. The city that had evolved over the previous century or so had only little in common with the Augsburg of the present day. 'Improved schools and the mass-circulation of serious literature' had created a need for 'genuine intellectual entertainment.'[65]

The thirst for culture and sophisticated forms of entertainment, some pointed out, was no longer confined to the rich and the educated. This new need for cultural engagement had begun to affect, in the words of one commentator, sections of the urban public that until a few years ago 'could have attended a puppet show or a religious recitation in the Catholic men's association to satisfy their intellectual urges.' Augsburg, so this particular newspaper report continued, was no longer populated almost exclusively by 'pious linen weavers and cotton-spinning machines.' The days when culture, education, and the arts had been subordinated to material interests had gone for good. It was now widely recognized that a theatre was an educational institution, a *Bildungsanstalt*, and a very important one at that.[66] During the previous decades, due in part to the influx of new people into the town (including, the report noted, many Jews), the 'circle of art lovers' had not doubled, but quadrupled. The only adequate response to this situation was the building of a new theatre.[67] Augsburg's cultural life was deemed wanting, in terms of quality and range above all, but also in terms of the quality and frequency of performances on offer.

For the supporters of the project, Augsburg was in the process of becoming a different place. Anticipating the stormy reception their proposal would receive, the city's liberals did not stop short of ridiculing the numerous opponents of the new theatre. Given the centrality the town's educated strata ascribed to public cultivation (*Bildung*) through art, ridicule appeared as a means that was both legitimate and appropriate to their cause. It was in this spirit that one of the foremost liberal dailies described the controversy that had ensued over the *Stadttheater* as a struggle which pitted the 'educated' (*Gebildeten*) against the 'philistines' (*Pfahlbürger*). For the latter, the editors complained, culture was a low priority. It only entered their minds 'once the last cobblestone has been replaced by a new one and each alleyway has been connected to a sewage pipe.'[68]

If playing on the theme of cultural inferiority was one of the strategies the advocates of the new theatre adopted, pointing to the financial weight of Augsburg's community of art lovers was another. Many of those who had recently settled in one of the city's more affluent neighbourhoods (in the 1880s only about 30 per cent of the residents of the bourgeois districts were born in Augsburg) regarded the status quo of the city's cultural offerings as unsatisfactory: 'A town that seeks to grow must ensure that it provides a minimum degree of cultural entertainment for those who are free to consume their wealth anywhere they choose.'[69] One of the main arguments of those who opposed the projected new *Stadttheater*, namely, that it amounted to a monument to the town's affluent strata, a cultural temple designed mainly for bourgeois enjoyment and self-worship, was roundly rejected. The new theatre, liberals contended, would benefit all of Augsburg's inhabitants. While at present the more affluent season-ticket holders were guaranteed a seat, those who relied on affordable tickets from the box office frequently had to be turned away due to a lack of available seats. With the new theatre in place, this sorry state of affairs came to an end.[70]

Crucially, Augsburg's liberals saw in the controversy over the future of the *Stadttheater* a conflict that was part of the much larger struggle over progress and, ultimately, over the rhythms shaping public life. What endowed this conflict with such emotional energy was precisely that a tangible local concern had been fused with a powerful nationalist morality. In the rhetorical hands of certain liberals a *Stadttheater* became an indicator of the nation's cultural state. The implicit logic of this argument was unmistakable: urban politicians and executives had a duty to invest in a city's cultural life. For Councillor Keller and his associates, Augsburg had been left in a state of dormant neglect by those who should have been its leading reformers, with the 1854 cholera epidemic marking the low point in the city's recent history.

The political leaders who had governed the town up to the early 1860s—Keller spoke of the old 'calamitous regime'—had failed to promote Augsburg's collective interests, with disastrous consequences. Thus, in the three decades leading up to the 1860s, Augsburg had irrevocably fallen behind towns like Nuremberg or Fürth. In the liberal narrative of urban reform, the economic prosperity and cultural dynamism of these cities appeared as a reflection of the patriotism of their respective populations.[71] Seen in this light, a cultural institution like the theatre appeared of crucial symbolic and practical importance. As Keller elaborated in his final plea for the new *Stadttheater*:

> The science that deals with the economy of nations teaches us that it is only decadent nations that regard luxury as infelicitous. We should not like to think that only a few years after the great events of 1870 and 1871 we have become one of those decadent nations. In fact, I believe that, on the contrary, those great events will lead us to a level of prosperity that far exceeds our expectations, a degree of prosperity from which all classes of society will benefit and which will create new life not only in our nation, but also in our town.[72]

The controversy over the theatre was of course also a conflict over the influence of different social and political groups on the town's configuration as a cultural space. In his counter-plea, the speaker for the opposition thus not only criticized what he regarded as the excessive cost of the proposed project. He also doubted that the kind of *Stadttheater* that the liberals envisioned would fulfil its allotted educational role. Popular plays, so he predicted, would be sidelined by operas, as was already the case in the present theatre. As Catholic Councillor Naegele summed up:

> You keep talking of the need to educate the public. But only plays educate the people, and thoroughly so, a fact which you refuse to accept. The *Stadttheater* has not seen good actors or actresses in a very long time because you keep favouring the opera over everything else. But let me say to you, gentlemen, that I do not recognize the opera as a suitable means of popular education in the same way that I do recognize the theatre as an educational institution [*Bildungsanstalt*]. If you were able to offer me something that I could rightly regard as popular education, I would be the first one to come on board and support your proposal.[73]

The socio-economic background to the conflict is underlined by the view of another member of the opposing camp, who also pointed out that, in spite of proclamations to the contrary, the proposed *Stadttheater* reflected the interests of the liberal bourgeoisie, while it offered little for the majority of

Augsburg's population. His statement culminated in a scathing critique of what he deemed the negative picture the liberal speaker had painted of the local *Gewerbestand*. Whereas parts of the liberal press had labelled the city's petit-bourgeois small traders and craftsmen as roadblocks on the path to modern progress, one councillor accused Augsburg's bourgeoisie of a lack of loyalty to local producers. 'There are several people in Augsburg who just cannot be pleased. They get all the things they need from Munich, or even from Paris. Avoiding the local crafts and trades is unlikely to benefit Augsburg's *Gewerbestand*.'[74]

Designed by the famous Viennese architects Ferdinand Fellner and Hermann Hellner (the pairs' credentials included theatres in Budapest, Hamburg, Prague, Vienna, and Wiesbaden), the new theatre was completed in the autumn of 1877. Built in the style of the neo-renaissance, the theatre could house a maximum audience of 1,400. Positioned on an imposing site at the northern end of the newly constructed Fuggerstrasse, the demonstrative grandeur of the new *Stadttheater* was widely visible. The theatre's interior was conspicuous for its numerous statues and ornamental and figurative paintings. On the first floor a Corinthian order of columns caught the visitor's eye. These were complemented by statues of Goethe and Schiller beneath marble busts of Mozart and Beethoven. The ceiling of the auditorium was covered in allegories symbolizing the arts of dance, tragedy, poetry, epos, satire, and rhetoric. The first time the theatre-going public could acquaint themselves with all these marvels was on 26 November 1877, when the theatre opened with performances of Weber's *Jubelouvertüre* and Beethoven's *Fidelio*.[75]

Ulm's first *Stadttheater*, which remained in operation until its destruction during the Second World War, was built in 1781 at the cost of 16,000 gulden. It was located in the centre of town and could be accessed via six separate entrances. In spite of its rather cramped location between the barracks and a laundry, with 750 seats the theatre was deemed respectable for a town whose population at the end of the eighteenth century was roughly 11,000. On a gross floor space of 40 × 16.5 metres, it contained an entrance hall, a parterre, a space for the orchestra, two loges, an amphitheatre, a gallery, and a number of rooms for actors and staff. During the course of the first half of the nineteenth century, the heavily-used building required considerable maintenance work. The locker rooms and the space for the orchestra were extended, and in 1857 gas lighting was installed in response to long-standing complaints about the poor visibility of the performances. This was followed,

Figure 10. Stadttheater Augsburg after its completion in 1877.
© Stadtarchiv Augsburg.

in the latter part of the century, by the installation of a new heating system as well as electric lighting.[76]

Ulm's theatre, too, proved an occasional focal point of controversy. Some regarded it as an unnecessary extravagancy. Thus, just a few years after its completion in 1781, numerous citizens accused the council of misgovernment, arguing that the long-envisaged building of a jail should have been given priority over the creation of a *Schauspielhaus*. The question even came before an imperial court in 1785, which endorsed the city council's decision to favour a theatre over a prison. Four years after the judges had passed their verdict, the new theatre opened its doors to the public. During the first few decades of its existence, public demand for theatrical performances seems to have been relatively modest, too modest, at any rate, to justify the appointment of a permanent group of actors and technical staff: As late as 1836, instead of employing its own theatre cast, the city relied on touring theatre

Figure 11. Stadttheater Ulm, Theatergasse 8, around 1890.
© Stadtarchiv Ulm.

companies, which would give performances throughout the winter months. Only relatively few performances were offered in the period between spring and autumn.[77]

In spite of these modest beginnings, however, in the second half of the nineteenth century the theatre began to establish itself as an integral part of Ulm's cultural life, thanks in large part to the cultural ambitions of the city's educated middle-classes. The season now ran from October to April, with a weekly programme that included plays, concerts and, from 1870 onwards, operas and operettas. As in Augsburg and many other German cities, the town council employed a full-time director who, as well as bearing sole artistic and financial responsibility, had to satisfy the expectations of both the town council and the public. In this way, the city's authorities limited their own financial risk by treating the director as a private entrepreneur of sorts (of sorts because the council fixed ticket prices at a relatively low level). As a tenant, he had to pay rent, as well as cover other expenses such as heating costs. The director of Ulm's *Stadttheater* was provided with an annual sum of 4500 marks. He was asked to pay a deposit of over 1000 marks, to be withheld in the case of a breach of contract or in case of damage to property or theft. During the season of 1878/79, for example, a staggering 142 performances were given, most of them operas. Demanding a relentless pace, the council ensured that it got its pound of flesh from the directors it appointed over the years. This arrangement between the city and its theatre directors was problematic in several ways. Not only did it prompt most directors to leave after only one or two years of service. It also ensured that the theatre came regularly under the spotlight. Given that putting on even a modest opera was very costly, many directors found it difficult to recuperate their expenses through ticket sales. Some, like Benno Timansky, who served as director from 1881 to 1885, tried to improve their precarious income by putting on children's matinees.[78]

All local newspapers ran columns on the theatre's offerings. That the tone of these reports was often harsh and unforgiving did not make the directors' task any easier. Operas in particular were a frequent target of the city's numerous art critics. It seems that, from the middle of the century, Ulm's theatre directors had been contractually obliged to offer operas, mainly because they were popular with the middle classes who regarded them as the most sophisticated form of high culture. However, operatic performances were also very expensive to run, all the more so as they were often poorly attended, threatening to drive directors into financial ruin. Moreover, there developed a sense among the more demanding portions of the urban public that what they were being offered was mediocre. The newspaper reports, and the readers' letters that the performances provoked on a weekly basis, speak a clear language in this respect. Some argued that the town authorities ought to accept that there were limits to what a provincial town could offer in terms of artistic standards, and that the opera in particular was too demanding an art form to be practiced at a satisfactory level in Ulm.

Others maintained that the same pragmatism should be applied in relation to classical drama. Staging plays such as Schiller's *Don Carlos*, Hauptmann's *Die Weber*, or Göthe's *Faust* appeared simply too demanding for the actors of a provincial stage. Some commentators took this line of argument to its harsh conclusion by insisting that being offered no performances was preferable to being subjected to poor ones: 'We have to give up on the opera, and we should, given the quality of our actors this season, also give up on classical drama. The ladies on their own, however talented and eager they may be, are not capable of performing a drama like Schiller's

Don Carlos in a suitably dignified manner.'[79] The views expressed continued to be antagonistic, however, with no consensus emerging. Much of
what was said remained contradictory. For just after they had recommended that both opera and drama should be abandoned, the editors of
the very same liberal daily argued that director Stickshould concentrate
on drama, rather than opera. They also suggested that the pulse rate of
cultural life be lowered:

> A town of Ulm's size can expect to be able to offer good dramatic perform-
> ances, which in a way are much easier to bring on stage than even a mediocre
> opera. One, at most two, opera performances per week would be more than
> enough. Besides, we may ask ourselves with some justification if five, and
> sometimes even six, offerings per week are not too much for a town of
> medium size, in the same way as seven performances recently proved to be
> too much for Stuttgart.[80]

Adding to these problems, at least from the point of view of Ulm's cultural
elite, was popular culture, the fact that it far outweighed the theatre in
terms of public appeal. Indeed, to the great dismay of Ulm's bourgeois lovers of art, given the choice, most Ulmers would have opted for the circus
instead of getting involved with highbrow culture. Thus, in September
1878, just a week before the theatre season opened, Ulm's authorities
granted a licence to Circus Wulff, which enjoyed a first-class reputation all
over Germany. In the course of the following weeks, the city's residents
flocked to the circus in their droves. The director of the theatre, seconded
by season-ticket-holding members of the educated public, criticized the
council for having invited the circus into town at the height of the theatre
season. This had created a competitive situation in which high culture was
bound to lose out to the more simple pleasures catered for by the circus.
According to these critics, the council was faced with a simple choice
between either supporting the city's theatre by 'protecting it from competition that is bound to undermine it;' or else abandon the entire concept of
a *Stadttheater*. This was, of course, a rhetorical proposition, given that a
theatre was a *sine qua non* for a town of Ulm's size, certainly from the point
of view of its liberal bourgeoisie. As far as the council was concerned, however, urban culture had to reflect a variety of tastes and preferences. Instead
of giving a promise of protectionism, it merely reminded the director of his
contractual obligations. These not only ruled out the possibility of reducing the number of weekly performances, but also of concentrating on dramas at the expense of opera performances.

The contrast of opinion on public culture found expression in the local press. While the national-liberal *Ulmer Schnellpost* endorsed the highbrow culture favoured by the educated, the democratic *Ulmer Tagblatt* began to style itself as the champion of the Circus Wulff, encouraging readers to attend its shows. As it countered calls to prohibit circus performances during the theatre season: 'The excellent attendance rate of the circus Wulff...should convince a sober-minded theatre direction that gaining the favour of the public is not that difficult at all. But it requires the direction to stop expecting the public to accept, without a hint of protest, its demands and desires.'[81] In suggesting that the theatre serve the paying public, rather than the other way round, the *Ulmer Tagblatt* (and many of its readers who contributed to the debate with letters they sent to the editors) was implicitly challenging the educational ambitions of Ulm's liberal bourgeoisie. Meanwhile, responding to recent expressions of dissatisfaction by the public, the council insisted that director Brauer fulfil § 2 of his contract by offering not only plays and dramas, but also operas. When Brauer, whose financial situation seems to have become dire by that point (and who tried to supplement his income by simultaneously acting as director of the theatre at Metz), did not comply, the town council terminated his contract, retaining his deposit of 1714 marks. Brauer committed suicide in January 1878.[82]

The council's stern line towards the directors of the *Stadttheater* corresponded with popular attitudes concerning the role of urban culture. Particularly since the controversy over the circus, many began to challenge the champions of high culture, demanding that the future director of the theatre be forced to offer a more attractive and varied programme. In particular, people began to ask for the inclusion of comedies to complement the more high-brow plays favoured by the director and his supporters. The circus, too, continued to capture the public's imagination. As a newspaper editorial summed up the public discussion in the autumn of 1877: 'Ulm's public is currently split into two rival camps and everywhere—notably around the tables of the town's pubs and inns—the question being debated is 'circus or theatre?'[83]

But the problem with low attendance rates continued even when the theatre faced no competition from the circus. As Ulm's leading liberal daily observed: 'The theatre is going through a difficult spell. Complaints can be heard from all corners...Our public has long demanded an opera, but now that it possesses one which is on a par with the best operas Ulm has seen, attendance is abysmal.'[84] When in 1886 the city council appointed a new director, his contractual obligations included the staging of operettas and plays. The classical operas that had so engaged the liberals' cultural aspiration were no longer listed as mandatory. At the same time, the number of performances was limited to a maximum of six per week. There was now a recognition, it seems, that while Ulm was a regional leader in the field of higher secondary education, it could not compete with Stuttgart, let alone Munich, on the theatrical stage.[85]

Ludwigshafen's *Kulturleben*—measured by its ability to offer a cultural life that could satisfy the tastes of the urban middle-classes—was a far cry from that of the older, more established towns of Ulm and Augsburg. Was there a place for the theatre in this 'German Chicago'?

Perhaps unsurprisingly, a *Stadttheater* was not a priority in an industrial town that had little alternative but to pour almost all its energies and resources into the creation of an infrastructure commensurate with its rapid economic and demographic development. Unlike Ulm and Augsburg, Ludwigshafen did not build a municipal theatre that could have offered demanding dramas and operas. It is doubtful whether there would have been much demand for this sort of cultural activity before the 1880s. Besides, the proximity of Mannheim, whose cultural life was extraordinarily rich (it was in Mannheim's *Nationaltheater* that Schiller's drama *Die Räuber* experienced its debut performance in 1782, thus establishing its reputation as one of the foremost stages in Germany), led to a division of labour in the cultural sphere.

While Ludwigshafen's elite may have regarded Mannheim as an unpleasant rival on the economic plane, in the fields of culture and education it undoubtedly served as a magnet. Not a few of Ludwigshafen's entrepreneurs and directors lived in Mannheim or Heidelberg;[86] many more sent their children to private schools across the Rhine, at least until Ludwigshafen featured its own range of private schools from the 1870s. More importantly, when the bridge over the Rhine was opened in 1867, this considerably shortened travel times for commuters. Henceforth, Ludwigshafen's educated middle classes could reach Mannheim's *Nationaltheater* (as well as many others of its venues of culture) in little more than half an hour. Harsh though it may sound, when it came to culture and matters of advanced education, Ludwigshafen's liberal middle classes did not regard their city as an interesting investment opportunity. High culture was not among the things they thought their city could, or indeed should, be expected to provide. In these and other respects, then, they treated their town as a functional space, rather than a place to be invested with meaning and dense sociability.

Yet theatres, albeit of a different kind to those offered in Augsburg or Ulm, did take root in Ludwigshafen. Their advocates were the culturally-minded sections of the lower-middle and working classes. There were, for one thing, the travelling theatre companies that stopped by in Ludwigshafen to entertain the public. In an announcement dating from 1853 to promote the summer performances of the Tivoli theatre, for example, it was repeatedly stressed that the theatre 'was merely to entertain and to amuse the public,' mainly through 'comedies, Vaudevilles, and burlesques.' In addition, readers were reassured that innkeeper Deutsch, 'the owner of the new beer cellar,' would make 'every effort to supply the public with good food and drink.'[87] More important, not only as a venue for plays, but also for social events more broadly, was the town house, the so-called *Gesellschaftshaus*, which opened in 1882. Privately financed and run, the town hall was a multi-purpose building that emerged as a centre of social and cultural activity.[88] While the ground floor was taken up by various restaurants, a garden with a bowling alley and public baths, the first floor contained a large auditorium (Saal) with a maximum capacity of 1000 people.[89] Its rooms and offices were used by local associations for meetings and informal gatherings, while the larger halls and the auditorium served as a venue for comedies, plays, and concerts of various kinds. Contemplating the town hall's impact on Ludwigshafen's cultural life, the *Ludwigshafener Anzeiger* drew an enthusiastic conclusion: 'The large rooms were always crowded with happy people who after a day's hard work were keen to meet up with friends and acquaintances to enjoy themselves. Everyone agreed that the evening concerts represent a real need in the cultural life of our town, which during the summer months is not exactly spoiled with cultural treats.'[90]

So did Ludwigshafen's liberal movers and doers not pursue an educational mission? Did they not try to cultivate the town's population, which in its majority consisted of industrial factory workers? Did they not believe that economic growth and *Bildung* had to go hand in hand, that they were two sides of the same coin, and that the theatre and other cultural institutions played a crucial role in educating and cultivating the public? Did Ludwigshafen's bourgeois elite not believe that their town had to make its contribution to the German *Kulturnation?* Did they not subscribe to the conviction that the state of the town's cultural life was a reflection of its status within the German nation? These questions are not easy to answer. There can be little doubt that Ludwigshafen's cultural and political elite on the whole subscribed to the same cultural values and aspirations as their

counterparts in Ulm and Augsburg, and indeed all over Germany. Thus the
concept of *Bildung* was a key component of bourgeois self-definition and,
consequently, of their definition of German national identity.[91]

What is even more instructive than these parallels, however, are the features that set Ludwigshafen apart. Among these, the fact that its elite rarely
displayed the degree of local rootedness and urban patriotism that we have
encountered in Ulm and Augsburg strikes me as the most important. For it
was sentiments of local patriotism that engendered the competitive spirit, as
well as the public controversies, that to an important degree inspired cultural life in these three towns. If Ludwigshafen's cultural elite did barely
engage themselves in such heated discussion—with the exception, as we
saw, in the field of elementary education—this was because its own cultural
aspirations were less closely linked to a particular place than was the case in
Augsburg and Ulm. It is this particular disposition that Friedrich Burschell
was referring to when he argued that in the town of his childhood 'a great
deal of money was earned that was then spent elsewhere, in nicer and more
elegant towns, such as nearby Heidelberg, where the industrialists and councillors of commerce began to have their villas built, which with their towers
and pinnacles looked like castles.'[92]

Even though in theory the town's liberal bourgeoisie could have cultivated such patriotic sentiments, the conditions on the ground were not
fertile for them to emerge in the first place. To begin with, the opportunity costs for setting up a cultural infrastructure comparable with more
established cities would have been extremely high in an industrial town
dominated by a highly fluctuating working-class population; moreover,
Mannheim's proximity, whose cultural life was eminently accessible for
Ludwigshafen's middle classes, meant that the incentive for doing this
was extremely low. Just as crucial is another point, one that brings our
story back to the local-national nexus: From the point of view of
Ludwigshafen's liberal elites, their town was comfortably in tune with
the normative prerogatives of Germany's new nationalism and its powerful manifestation, the German Reich: What they may have lacked in
terms of cultural sophistication and institutions, they possessed, to a far
greater extent than most other cities, in terms of industrial might and
dynamic inventiveness.[93]

Nor, it seems, was this particular disposition restricted to the town's elites.
There was very little, Adam Ritzhaupt noted in his childhood memories,
which could have inspired the town's inhabitants with a sense of 'pride,
reference, and admiration.' The bourgeois spirit that existed in longer-

Figure 12. Postcard entitled *Gruss aus Ludwigshafen*, 1907. As well as containing a panoramic view of the city at the top, the card zooms in (from left to right to bottom) on three landmarks of urban communication and commerce: the postal office, the railway station, and the market square. © Stadtarchiv Ludwigshafen am Rhein.

established towns had not really existed in the Ludwigshafen of the *Kaiserreich*, mainly, so he concluded, because Ludwigshafen had 'no past.' In Ritzhaupt's telling of the story, 'retrospection' was a rare habit in a town in which only few people harboured the intention of settling permanently. In the Ludwigshafen of his own memory, people had 'lived…decisively in anticipation of the future.' The Ludwigshafen of his childhood, so Ritzhaupt maintained, was a town with an aura that 'educated people perceive as soul-less' at best, and as 'disdainful, chaotic, and ugly' at worst. Ludwigshafen was a town of 'forceful restlessness.' To the middle-class mind, Ludwigshafen appeared disorderly and unpredictable.[94] Describing a trip to Speyer he undertook as a child during the 1890s, the Ludwigshafen-born writer Friedrich Burschell singled out the contrast in the rhythms of life as the most distinctive feature separating the two cities: 'Whereas in my home-town people seemed always to be in a hurry, and their faces signalled impatience and taciturnity, in Speyer people seemed to walk the streets out of pure enjoyment…'[95]

It would be tempting to regard such thinking as indicative of a cold mentality that left little room for the emergence of a strong local identity, let

Figure 13. Ludwigsstraße in Ludwigshafen am Rhein, circa 1910.
© Stadtarchiv Ludwigshafen am Rhein. Compare this illustration with
illustration 7 (Hirschstraße in Ulm). Both illustrations date from 1910. In Ulm's
Hirschßtrasse the tramway rails are single while the Ludwigstraße has double-
tramway rails. Both sides of the Ludwigsstrasse are densely packed with shops,
and the pavements are crowded with men, women (many with pushchairs) and
children. Indeed, while in Ulm's Hirschstraße pedestrians neither keep to the
pavement nor seem to follow prepared routes (nor do they appear to be in a
particular hurry), those who leave the pavement in Ludwigshafen are either
crossing the Ludwigstraße or waiting for the tramway approaching in the
background. Even though we don't know on which day of the week the two
pictures were taken, the impression that one is looking at different rhythms of
life is almost tangible.

alone a sense of urban patriotism. The fabric of urban life, one might conclude, was not as densely invested with meaning and close social relations in
Ludwigshafen as was the case in Ulm or Augsburg. Yet such reasoning
would be simplistic. Rather than the absence of rootedness, Ludwigshafen
might stand for a different pattern of forging a sense of belonging out of
existing structures and available narratives. For many a resident of
Ludwigshafen—not only for its liberal proponents of *Reichsnationalismus*—
the glorification of movement and of restlessness, rather than undermining
a sense of place, appears to have been its constitutive agent.

Life and death

Succeeding a discussion of a cultural institution with an investigation into questions of urban health—shifting from operas to sewage pipes, as it were—may seem more than a little odd. Not necessarily so, however, if our central concern is the liberal pursuit of *Fortschritt*. Of all possible indications of a town's position on the backward-progressive continuum, hygiene and public health were just as important as *Bildung* and *Kultur*, certainly for the liberal apostles of progress. Rather than as two unconnected spheres, many saw them as variations on the same theme. Besides, debates over public health had become usual long before the Wilhelmine period. That early-modern cities could be veritable death traps had become common knowledge well before the French Revolution. As far as Augsburg's liberals were concerned, what may have been normal for the sixteenth century was unacceptable for the nineteenth. Besides evoking feelings of impurity and disease, for the liberal movers and doers in particular, high mortality rates signified decadence and helplessness, and hence the very absence of progress.[96] Here, then, is another theme that enables us to probe beneath the spectacle of political rhetoric and into the practice of urban reform, a theme, furthermore, that raises questions about the use of urban space and the pace and rhythm of communal life.

Augsburg faced a particular challenge on this front. The town had experienced cholera epidemics in 1854 and 1873. The first outbreak in 1854 had been especially vicious, killing more than 1000 inhabitants, with the death toll being particularly high among less well-off Catholic artisans living in the town's older, densely populated areas. It was during these decades that Augsburg gained a reputation as an unhealthy place. As Max Pettenkofer described the situation in a working-class neighbourhood when he visited Augsburg during the first epidemic: 'In House no. 214 five out of nine persons died, while the others fell ill.—Neither a yard nor a toilet; on the floor there was a dirty urinal made out of wood. All nine inhabitants belonged to the same family. The 16-year-old son worked as a metalworker in the factory of engineer Haag...Like many of his colleagues working at the Haag factory, he had fallen ill while at work.'[97]

The second outbreak, in 1873, was somewhat less consequential, not least because the authorities had taken measures to prevent public gatherings of any kind. For example, the city magistrate decided to cancel the planned public procession on Sedan Day, restricting activities to the flagging of public buildings.[98] Yet although the 1873 outbreak cost fewer lives, the liberal take-over in the 1860s meant that that the normative climate had changed. Now even an epidemic of limited proportions was perceived not as an inevitable fate, but as a sign on the wall, as a stain on the city's drape that needed eradicating. Fears of a renewed outbreak remained acute for decades to come. In 1892, for instance, a leading exponent of the Wertach branch of the liberal *Bürgerverein* warned that the recent cholera outbreak in Hamburg posed a 'big danger' for Augsburg, too. As well as urging the inhabitants of his district to observe rigorous standards of cleanliness, he also asked the magistrate and council to finally deliver on their promise of connecting all the houses left of the river Wertach to the public sewage system, and to ensure that the rubbish would be collected, once a week, at the town's expense.[99]

The 1873 cholera outbreak in particular prompted a debate on urban hygiene that persisted until the turn of the century. Two years after the epidemic had struck, the district physician, Wilhelm Kuby, gave a lecture in the main branch of the liberal *Bürgerverein* on 'Public health from a political vantage point.' Its main focus was the high mortality among Augsburg's children. As Kuby explained, 43 out of 100 children died in their first year, but in the *Hettenbachvorstadt* (another of Augsburg's working-class districts), only 18 out of 100 children survived their first year.[100] By 1877, when the town's average mortality rate was still 41 out of 1000 inhabitants, the topic had begun to permeate the town's liberal press. This was, as one newspaper had it, an issue the people of Augsburg would 'prefer not to address.' But given that the town's 'unfavourable mortality rates' had begun to 'attract the world's attention,' silence, on this occasion, was 'not gold but the absolute opposite.' The entire issue had become embarrassing, even humiliating: 'Well-meaning friends from both near and afar express their commiseration because we live in the unhealthiest town in the whole of Europe. The disadvantages a town of such notoriety may have to experience sooner or later are unimaginable.'[101] High mortality, thus the conclusion, undermined not only a community's reputation, but also its development prospects. It thus represented a very costly kind of shame.

From the 1870s onwards it became more and more common in Augsburg to place mortality rates in a national and, increasingly, international context. For the town's leading liberal daily, England offered the most instructive case of comparison. As its editors noted, large industrial towns such as Manchester, Oldham, Salford, and Liverpool had mortality rates of 29.1, 29.3, 31.8, and

27.5 out of 1000 inhabitants, which was 'considerably better than Augsburg.'[102] What partly inspired the growing internationalization of the debate on health and hygiene was the existence of an imperial state whose bureaucracy produced a constant stream of statistics. The information thus generated only confirmed what Augsburg's liberal nationalists had been preaching all along: that Augsburg formed part of a much larger and more powerful entity, and that the status and honour of town and nation were inextricably linked. Most of all, however, the imperial figures confirmed that Augsburg was falling short of its task. It was in danger of becoming an embarrassment not only to itself, but to the rest of a new Germany destined for progress and power in the name of civilization. As an editorial in the *Augsburger Neueste Nachrichten* explained with biting irony:

> Ever since the *Reichsgesundheitsamt* publishes, on a weekly basis, statistical surveys on the mortality rates of the large cities of Germany as well as those of all other culture states [*Kulturländer*], complete with a brief characterization of its causes, everyone will notice that, of all the larger towns in Germany and central Europe, Augsburg features the highest mortality rate. Almost without exception, Augsburg ranks just ahead of the Indian metropolises of Madras and Bombay, but only rarely do we find the odd German town, such as Munich, ranked in close proximity.[103]

While the comparison with Bombay and Madras could serve as a subject of amusement, the German comparisons left no room for any kind of escapism. What was especially alarming was that Augsburg's average annual mortality rate of over 40 per 1000 inhabitants during the 1870s was considerably higher than that of Nuremberg, which rarely rose above 30, while Stuttgart, Frankfurt am Main, Karlsruhe, and Wiesbaden tended to have rates in the twenties. There was no doubt about what had caused this variety. The gap that separated Augsburg from cities such as Nuremberg, Frankfurt, or even Stuttgart, so all local commentators were agreed, would only be small if it was not for the city's extraordinarily high rate of child mortality. In the first half of the 1870s the annual death rate among Augsburg's newborn children was 43 per cent. This meant that 50 per cent of all deaths that occurred in a single year concerned children in their first year.[104]

What was responsible for these high mortality rates, and what could be done to improve the situation and get Augsburg moving up the imperial league tables? The answer, most experts concurred, was poor hygiene as well as poor water quality. Both were attributable to the city's inadequate infrastructure. Between 1871 and 1880, Augsburg's population grew from 51,220 to 61,408, or by approximately 19 per cent over a ten-year period. Fertility was exceptionally high during these ten years, but so was mortality as a result of serious problems with hygiene.[105] The first step in a programme of infrastructural improvements was taken in 1879 with the building of the new water works and the laying of new water pipes across much of the city. This allowed for the closing down of all wells, a main cause of typhus and dysentery and hence of the high death rate among children.[106] The building of a modern sewage system and a new way of disposing of faeces in the 1880s also brought improvements. The last of these measures was particularly controversial, especially among the city's home owners, who had to carry the cost of the necessary installations. When the magistrate in charge of the project discussed the shortcomings of the existing system at a meeting of the liberal *Bürgerverein*, this provoked fierce resistance from a group that included a master carpenter, a treasurer, a brewery owner, as well as the trustee of the municipal hospital. They all complained about what they regarded as the exorbitant cost of the envisioned reforms for home owners and insisted that the present custom, which was to dispose of the waste in sewage tanks every six weeks, had worked well in the past.[107]

In spite of initial resistance, however, matters seem to have improved significantly by the 1890s. In a lecture on public hygiene and health in Augsburg over the previous 20 years, which was attended by close to 100 people and reported in all the local newspapers, the then district physician, Dr Dorfmeister, was able to present a story of nearly unbroken progress.[108] There was no longer any foundation, Dorfmeister claimed, for the 'extremely bad reputation' Augsburg had gained due to its wanting sanitation infrastructure. Thanks to the new water works and to the introduction of a much-improved system of waste disposal, Augsburg's mortality rate had dropped to the level of other German cities of similar size. Since 1865 the death rate for typhus had fallen from 14.4 to 4.7 per cent in 1880, reaching 0.3 per cent in the previous year, with child mortality having significantly decreased as a result.

What made humbling news, however, were the data concerning tuberculosis. Drawing on the latest imperial statistics, Dorfmeister reported that, out of 62 towns of similar size, only seven showed a higher death toll resulting from this infectious disease. While deaths from tuberculosis were falling in Munich and Berlin, developments in Augsburg were less favourable, with the working-class districts in particular continuing to give cause for concern. To reverse this trend, Dorfmeister recommended the construction of a new abattoir, a disinfection ward, an association for the promotion of public health, as well as a sanatorium to cure those affected by the illness.[109] He concluded his lecture by reminding his audience of the 'economic value of public health' and of the 'large losses caused by high mortality.'[110]

In Ulm, too, mortality was relatively high throughout the 1870s, particularly among babies and toddlers, although the overall situation was better than in Augsburg. As late as 1882, out of 100 children born alive, 35 died in their first year, a situation that only improved, albeit slowly, from the mid-1880s. In 1885, it was still 29 out of 100 children that died in their first year, at a time when the average for the German empire was around 24, a level that Ulm would not reach until the early 1890s, although subsequent years would bring further improvements.[111] Conversely, Ulm's general annual mortality rate was more in line with the imperial average, and in the course of the mid-1880s it even fell below the national level.[112]

As in Augsburg the most serious challenge facing Ulm's authorities was the high mortality among newborn children, with unclean water being its main cause. Like there, the ability to secure plentiful supplies of fresh clean water was seen as a sign of being up with the times. Although a whole series of artificial waterworks using wheels and cisterns had been built in Ulm between the fifteenth and seventeenth centuries, the population increase that occurred in the nineteenth century led to shortages in available drinking water. Efforts to compensate for these, such as using water from the Blau river, had an adverse effect on the water quality, as did the building of new houses near wells.[113] One observer, a professor from Tübingen, having sipped water from one of Ulm's wells, complained in an 1860 letter to a local pharmacist that never before had he tasted water of such 'disgusting and abhorrent' quality.[114] While the direct influence of his observation is difficult to ascertain, the building of a new water works (which became operational in 1874) suggest that Ulm's authorities had come to share the professor's judgment.[115] As well as improving the quality of the town's drinking water and eliminating potential sources of contamination, between 1875 and 1889 the authorities renewed and expanded the existing sewage system.[116]

Yet what was at least as instrumental in bringing down child mortality from the 1880s, it seems, was the creation of a nursery in the 1870s. Certainly, of all the factors driving this project and bringing it to fruition, concerns about hygiene and mortality carried most weight.[117] The original initiative for the project emanated from the town's diocesan synod. A committee for the founding of a *Kinderkrippe* (consisting of members of Ulm's Protestant elite, the committee also included the wife of principal mayor von Heim) was established shortly after Christmas 1876. On 11 September 1877, the birthday of the queen of Württemberg who acted as trustee and sponsor, the nursery opened its doors to the public.[118] Although the nursery project was warmly welcomed by the authorities and received much praise in the local press, it was run as a charity and relied on the generosity of private donors and the revenues from various charity events. Children between six weeks and three years of age were eligible, but at least initially demand far outstripped supply. A deaconess and two maids took care of the children; they would call on the service of a medic for advice on hygiene and in case of children falling ill.[119]

The various efforts to improve public hygiene and reduce mortality among both children and adults apparently began to bear fruit from the 1880s. As in Augsburg, Ulm's authorities, and particularly the liberal-minded public, became eager consumers of the annual statistics published by the imperial health ministry in Berlin. Whenever the news on Ulm was encouraging, local liberals would contrast its performance with that of other well-known regional towns, particularly ones that grew faster and were more industrialized than Ulm. What these comparisons appeared to prove, at last, was that there were other indications of progress than steep population growth, the number of weekly train tickets sold to migrant workers, or the proportion of the population employed in factories. To offer just one example for this kind of reasoning, taken from an 1889 newspaper editorial: 'The Imperial Ministry of Health's mortality statistics for the month of February contain extremely encouraging news for Ulm. The average mortality rate for this town, calculated over the year, was 13.3 per 1000 inhabitants, placing it well ahead of Stuttgart (19.9), Gmünd (27), Augsburg (27.6), Cannstatt (27.9), and Reutlingen (45.8).'[120] Imperial statistics also served to rebut false rumours on the spread of infectious diseases. As the *Ulmer Tagblatt* informed its readers regarding the impact of the seasonal flu on urban mortality:

A fairly common view has it that, because of the impact of influenza, Ulm's mortality rate in January had been particularly high. That is not the case. While the town suffered 74 deaths in January 1889, the figure for January 1890 was 73. In other words, while in many towns this year's influenza outbreak caused a marked rise in mortality, in Ulm the number of deaths occurring during the same period decreased by one.[121]

It appears that the efforts to enlighten the public on hygiene, along with the concrete measures taken to improve the situation, were not entirely in vain. Thus, when in 1893 the editors of the same local newspaper looked back on four decades of initiatives to improve public health, the overall picture they painted was one of steady progress:

> It is only a few years ago that, when a civil servant or an officer and his family were relocated from the lowlands to Ulm, this caused considerable grief among the relatives, who felt pity at seeing their beloved next of kin moving to notoriously unhealthy Ulm. Today things are different: Malaria is as good as unknown; typhoid is very rare among the bourgeois population; and the overall state of health has improved beyond recognition. In the period from 1858 to 1868 the number of deaths per thousand inhabitants stood at 32.5, between 1879 and 1887 the average was 24.5, and between 1881 and 1890 it further decreased to 22 per thousand. In fact, with 20.6 per thousand residents, last year's ratio was even better. If we compare these figures to those of other towns, such as Augsburg (28.2), Würzburg (25.2), Heidelberg (26), and Heilbronn (23.1), *then Ulm can rightly regard itself as one of the healthiest German towns.*[122]

The most characteristic feature of the debate surrounding public health and hygiene in Ludwigshafen am Rhein is the virtual absence of arguments that link these problems, so far as they manifested themselves locally, with the theme of progress and civilization, which in Augsburg and (albeit in less marked and pugnacious a manner) in Ulm were rather common.

Not that there had been no cause for concern on that front. While we lack reliable data for the 1870s and 1880s, what we do know is that child mortality in Ludwigshafen was still relatively high at the beginning of the twentieth century (as was the town's average birthrate). The worst killer in late-nineteenth-century Ludwigshafen was tuberculosis, which accounted for more than 20 per cent of all deaths. As late as 1906, 22 per cent of all children died in their first year, which was about 5 per cent above the average for the Palatinate as a whole, and about 3 per cent above the average for Palatinate towns. But it was still considerably lower than in the district capital of Speyer (where the average rate was 27 per cent) and also considerably below the average child mortality for Mundenheim (incorporated into Ludwigshafen in 1898), where it was around 40 per cent as late as 1906. In the years immediately preceding the First World War, Ludwigshafen's average mortality among children in their first year declined still further, to around 15 per cent.[123]

The improvements that did occur, as well as reflecting changes in diet and personal hygiene among an overwhelmingly working-class population, can be attributed to reforms of the existing infrastructure. Here again, the most important relate to sanitary improvements. Due to the town's high ground water levels, residents for a long time had obtained their drinking water from a number of wells, some of them equipped with pumps.[124] That this was potentially detrimental to the quality of available drinking water is not really surprising, not if we consider that the town's pit latrines were located in close proximity to the wells. Another, even more serious, problem was that Ludwigshafen's ground water was high in iron and manganese, and that, by general consent, it tasted horrid. Indeed, at an 1878 council meeting complaints were expressed that 'foul-smelling water' was 'posing a risk to the population's health.'[125] The fact that the chemical factories covered all their water requirements from the Rhine may explain why it took until 1895 for the first water works to be opened in Ludwigshafen, with 715 households connected, a figure that would increase four-fold over the next ten years.[126]

The problems of drainage and waste disposal had been tackled slightly earlier. A number of spillways had been built in the 1870s for the drainage of rainwater, but at high watermark these represented a potential source of contamination as they carried polluted water from the Rhine back to the centre of town. This is why the construction of the first effective sewerage system in the town's southern part had to wait until the mid-1880s. Regarding the disposal of waste and human faeces, the main problem was the existence of the widespread use of latrines in all part of town (there were 2100 such latrines as late as 1913), and more specifically, that until the 1880s the most common way of emptying the latrines was for peasants to collect their content and using it on their nearby fields, thereby further adding to the risk of degrading the quality of drinking water. To reduce the risk of contamination, in 1886 the council commissioned a private company that henceforth emptied the thousands of pit latrines twice a year.[127]

Ludwigshafen highlights some of the dynamics and motivations influencing the remaking of German communities in the second half of the nineteenth century. Its liberal movers and doers were just as fervent advocates of progress, and of the German Reich, as their counterparts in Ulm and Augsburg. In spite of this, however, they did not on the whole feel a need to connect practical concerns with urban hygiene and mortality to these larger themes. The fact that their town did not fare badly compared with more traditional cities may partly explain this. That progress came at a cost in a town that appeared to embody it in its raw, undiluted form was a view shared by the reform-minded public. The conviction that Ludwigshafen was different in a positive sense—less sentimental and more brittle than some of Germany's established towns, whose core was solidly middle-class; that it was somewhat more in sync with modern times seems to have entered the mindset not only of the local bourgeoisie. That problems existed did not make people question its progressive credentials. Nor did it challenge its self-ascribed status as an incarnation of the new, powerful Germany.

The example of urban health throws a sharp light on the links between progress and nationhood in the liberal imagination. The apostles of progress were most numerous, as well as most vocal, in Augsburg. The cholera epidemic of 1854, which was followed by a smaller outbreak in 1873, left a profound trace on the collective memory of the city. As an event, it appears to have disturbed the liberals in particular, serving as a catalyst for their reformist nationalism. While it would go too far to ascribe their ascendancy during the 1860s to this experience, it undoubtedly helped them gain popular support among the middle-class citizenry. For the city's liberals around Ludwig Fischer, these epidemics represented manifestations of backwardness in a society that was destined for glory both at home and abroad. Disease and mortality on this scale were unworthy of the Germany that was to embody their own aspirations. They were incommensurate with the vision of national grandeur they had cultivated for some time. While both Ludwigshafen and Ulm had reasons to worry about public health and hygiene, neither city had seen people starve on the streets and in their houses on a large scale in their recent past. As a consequence, it seems, death and disease were less subject to the kind of intense politicization than they were in Augsburg. Although themes of public concern, they were less impregnated with fear. Above all, they were not hijacked by the nationalist code.[128]

   The emotional energies that were thus released or contained had consequences for place-making activities in other fields, as the debate surrounding the urban theatres has highlighted. Augsburg's new *Stadttheater* was built at a small yet safe distance from the densely populated core of the city. As a cultural institution embodying always-fragile liberal hopes and expectations, it was set apart, if only slightly, from the world that only a few decades ago had seen mass death born out of ignorance. If it was put on a pedestal, this was not only to show off the cultural power of the new Augsburg, but also, it seems, to protect the splendour of the building and its interior from the threat of pollution. The prospect of renewed shame could never be ruled out; nor could a slowing down of the pace of cultural life. In striking contrast, Ulm's theatre was hemmed in between old houses in an inconspicuous part of town. Not that Ulmers failed to take their theatre to task on various pretexts. Some lamented the dim lighting, while a great many others criticized either individual actors or entire performances, and often both. Many chose to go to the circus instead. On the whole, however, the theatre in Ulm was supposed to be a place that could integrate various tastes and interests, as well as different rhythms of life: a broad church, rather than a colonizing institution. Meanwhile, the liberals of Ludwigshafen, instead of creating a place for a *Stadttheater*, took advantage of Mannheim's rich offerings on the theatrical front. In the 'German Chicago,' most people projected their visions of progress, as well as their nationalist aspirations, onto other spaces and places: the chimneys rising up from the BASF production halls; the ships that were discharging their cargo before embarking on their downstream journey; the young men and women, and even their children, all of whom seemed accustomed to a different pulse of life.

6

Sedan Day

Tomorrow, Sunday, Ulm's population will celebrate the memory of the Battle of Sedan. What moves the heart of the nation on this special day is a deep sense of gratitude towards providence. If this gratitude finds its preferred object in Sedan Day, it is because it was on this day that our people's struggle for national unity ended in magnificent triumph, thus enabling our Fatherland to take its rightful place in the world.

Ulmer Tagblatt (1887)[1]

The German nation does not celebrate 2 September as a day of battle – as it has been accused in certain quarters—but as the day of the rebirth of the German empire, an empire of light and truth, resurrected from the ruins of an empire of lies and faithlessness.

Ludwigshafener Anzeiger (1876)[2]

Let us, in view of tomorrow's Sedan Day celebrations, once again appeal to our town population's patriotic spirit. May the people of our town demonstrate by richly decorating their houses that Augsburg continues to be an honourable bastion of German nationhood.

Augsburger Neueste Nachrichten (1894)[3]

For Germany's champions of the Second Empire, 2 September 1870 was set to become Germany's national holiday. After all, this was the day when the news of the defeat of French troops in a decisive battle that culminated in the capture of Napoleon III and his army had reached the German population. On Sedan Day the German people were to worship their nation through participation in a comprehensive journey (embodied in the urban parades) along a number of significant places (including churches, town squares, schools, and other places of local significance). Just as the battle of Sedan helped Germany to find its place in the world, Sedan Day was to find its place in the heart of the German people.

Best known is the imperial part of the story. In June 1872, the Pietistic priest Friedrich Wilhelm Bodelschwingh, who had played a leading role in the victory celebrations in Berlin in the previous year, demanded in a much-noticed plea, that the day of the Battle at Sedan be henceforth celebrated all over Germany as a national holiday.[4] Yet although several German states (including Prussia and Württemberg) soon elevated 2 September to a public holiday for schools and universities, Sedan Day failed to receive the official blessing of either the Kaiser or the Reichstag. What prompted Wilhelm I's objection was not the choice of date or the event to which it referred. Rather, the elderly monarch had little time for national festivals. Like other Prussian aristocrats of his generation, he was deeply suspicious of public mass ceremonies centred on national, rather than dynastic authority. On the same grounds the Kaiser turned down a petition, submitted by liberal Protestant circles in the spring of 1871, to commemorate 18 January, the day when the Empire was proclaimed at Versailles, as the founding day of the German nation.[5]

Not that its lack of official endorsement had prevented Sedan Day from being celebrated in all parts of Germany.[6] Although no uniform template existed for commemorating the event, in many German towns the festivities soon proceeded according to a distinctive script. Its components ranged from familiar practices to more spectacular displays: houses were decorated with black-white-red flags (often in combination with the flags of the state and the municipality); pupils attended celebrations and listened to speeches given by their teachers in front of their schools or in the classroom; parish priests held special church services for their congregations; and there was, and this usually marked the highpoint of the day, a large parade in the after-noon, composed of numerous school classes, including, where such schools existed, the students of the local grammar schools, as well as school girls dressed in white. Among those who processed *in corpora* were the members of the various singing and veteran associations, of the former guilds, as well as the various branches of the municipal administration and executive. The final hours of the celebrations were spent with people congregating in vari-ous local inns, or in a specially prepared fairground off the city centre, where once again music performances and speeches were offered to the gathering crowds.[7]

As historians have pointed out before, however, as a national festival Sedan Day remained contested. Overall, it proved more appealing to urban than to rural folks. The celebrations drew their most enthusiastic support from local liberals. Sedan Day was not popular with the majority of German Catholics (except for liberal Catholics), who tended to associate the event with the *Kulturkampf*. It also had few enthusiastic supporters among democrats and groups further to the left. Socialists in particular regarded the celebrations as a jingoistic device in the hands of the dominant classes. These critical voices have often been taken as evidence for the nation's lacking popular appeal, for its representing an obsession confined to the educated middle-class public. Yet, as other scholars have emphasized, when it comes to national mass events disagreement can be more productive than an apparent consensus born from indifference. As long as the celebrations on Sedan Day drew large crowds, controversy made it more, not less, effective as a national festival.[8]

What I want to suggest, however, is that Sedan Day can point us towards something rather more fundamental. What the open or behind-the-scene controversies that beset the celebrations from the outset reveal is not so much the presence or absence of nationalism, however locally mediated and reconstructed. What they bring to the fore is the unease that many people felt—and it was mostly sentiments and instincts that seem to have mattered here—as they saw themselves confronted with the hegemonic aspirations of *Reichsnationalismus*. As far as the champions of imperial nationalism were concerned, Sedan Day was to set the stage for a comprehensive restructuring of people's sense of time and place. This was an attempt to impose a new rhythm on the life of Germans irrespective of their political or religious affiliations, and regardless of where they hailed from or happened to reside.

The numerous sceptics and opponents of Sedan Day appear to have grasped that something much larger was at stake than having to put up with a large national festival once every year. They appear to have noticed that, albeit operating at a more abstract symbolic level, Sedan Day was connected to the project of *Fortschritt* whose more concrete manifestations we have investigated in the previous chapters. Many appear to have realized that Sedan Day's deeper ramifications went beyond its constituting a day in the nation's calendar. They recognized, it seems, that it bore an intimate connection with a series of schedules operating in various spheres of life—including economic production, educational performance, the consumption of culture, or public transport—that had come to underpin a certain vision of progress.[9] It is a sign of this cognizance, and of the misgivings it often caused, that many began to try to reconfigure the festive practice through a series of creative interventions and disruptions. Many of these disruptive acts—such as preventing a municipality from getting involved in the celebrations every year, moving the celebrations from a normal working day to a Sunday, or by refusing to have church bells rung on this special day—can be read as efforts to fashion an alternative rhythm of life. Although those who engaged in them may have viewed themselves as defenders of the status quo against an overbearing imposition, their project was, in fact, a creative, rather than merely a defensive one. As a result of their endeavours, the homogenizing conception of nationalist time and space gave way to a more pluralist pattern.[10]

Before Sedan

There were local cultures of nationhood that predated the Sedan Day celebrations. Judging by the reports the district commissioner dispatched to his superiors in Munich at regular intervals, in Augsburg the national question had become a topic of public controversy in the wake of the 1848 revolutions. Things looked all right to begin with, at least as far as Bavaria's state official was concerned. Throughout the 1850s, most people in Augsburg appear to have imagined Germany through a *grossdeutsch* lens. The commissioner's reports on external events, such as the war in Italy in 1859, are especially instructive in this regard. Augsburg's population, he noted, had not only followed events in Sardinia and Lombardy with 'the greatest interest,' but many inhabitants had also expressed their 'German national sentiment' on several occasions. What the commissioner took as unmistakable manifestations of such sentiment were essentially pro-Austrian and anti-French attitudes. Not that people had been uncritical of Austria—'the drawbacks of her administration and the need for reforms were recognized' even by its supporters—but their misgivings about Prussia had been more pronounced than the reservations they had felt towards Austria. Only a small liberal minority, represented by the *Augsburger Anzeigeblatt*, had frequently raised its voice against Austria, without however expressing any sympathies for Prussia.[11]

This perception would change in the course of the 1860s, however. At the outbreak of the war between Austria and Prussia, the official still described the public mood in Augsburg as 'patriotic and *grossdeutsch*;' and when Austria's defeat at Königgrätz emerged as an undisputable fact, the prevalent attitude he found among the Swabian population was apparently one of disappointment and consternation. But all was not well at this point.

Thus, in Augsburg itself, the district official remarked with a sense of fore-boding, the reactions to the war had been mixed. Whereas the city's popula-tion had taken part in collections in support of the wounded soldiers from lower Franconia, the liberal-dominated magistrate had failed to join a dec-laration of sympathy for the defeated troops. While the returning Bavarian soldiers had received a warm welcome almost everywhere in the district, Augsburg's authorities had treated them 'with the same indifference' as dur-ing the war.[12] Liberals known for their close links to the *Nationalverein* had even taken things to a new level. Instead of simply adopting an attitude of distance towards the returning Bavarian troops, they had used Austria's defeat as a welcome opportunity to out themselves as *kleindeutsch* national-ists. Indeed, many had begun to put 'all their eggs in the basket of the North-German Confederation.'[13]

As the events surrounding the 50th anniversary of the battle of Leipzig indicate, however, the divisions over the national question had become visi-ble well before the Prussian victory at Königgrätz. On 14 September 1863 Augsburg's city council received an invitation from the organizing commit-tee (composed of the magistrates of the cities of Berlin and Leipzig) to take part in the anniversary, to be held in Leipzig on 18 and 19 October. The let-ter, dispatched to all German state and district capitals, expressed the convic-tion that 'only a general national festival' could do justice to the 'most glorious day in German history.'[14] On 19 September, Augsburg's magistrate, then still in the hands of pro-Austrian conservatives, turned down the invitation, emphasizing that Augsburg would stage its own festival. In view of this inten-tion, the town's participation in the planned festival in Leipzig was described as 'inopportune.' The magistrate's justification was one that would become *de rigueur* for municipalities opting out of large national festivals that had attracted some interest elsewhere. It emphasized that its stance represented the rule, rather than the exception. Augsburg had not been alone in deciding against sending a delegation to Leipzig: Munich, Landshut, Nuremberg, and Regensburg had done likewise.[15] Yet the municipal assembly, where liberals had recently gained predominance, had other ideas. Its majority insisted that Augsburg fulfil its 'patriotic duty' by sending a delegation to the main cele-brations in Leipzig. On 25 September, this position was unanimously endorsed in a public meeting attended by more than 200 citizens known for their liberal conviction; and on 4 October, a mere fortnight before the cel-ebrations in Leipzig were to begin, the conservative magistrate succumbed to liberal pressure.[16] Two days later the municipal council settled for a delegation composed of two magistrates (including the city's *zweiter Bürgermeister*, Ludwig Fischer) and two municipal councillors (the banker Albert Erzberger and the estate owner Johann v. Stetten).[17]

Encouraged by this favourable turn of events, Augsburg's liberals ensured that their city would commemorate more lavishly than originally planned. The festivities came to centre on a few significant places, some private, but most of them public. On the eve of the main festival, numerous inhabitants began to decorate their houses with wreaths and flags in the Bavarian and in the German colours. A torchlight procession got under way in which more than a thousand inhabitants took part. The participants included the fire brigade in uniform, the gymnasts, as well as numerous citizens, veterans, and the members of several choral societies. If liberal sources are to be believed, the procession attracted 'masses of spectators.' Participants were treated to patriotic speeches and to a choral performance of Arndt's song, *Des Deutschen Vaterland*, which preaches national expansion in open disregard of state borders.[18] This was followed, the next day, by services in several of Augsburg's churches, with a special service being held in the town's synagogue. For the secular part of the celebrations, the municipal authorities, representatives of the Bavarian state government, as well as officers and contingents of soldiers from the garrisoned troops were all in attendance. After the singing of the *Uhlandlied*, the liberal councillor Joseph Völk (a Catholic who in 1863 had founded the Bavarian *Fortschrittspartei*) and the then first mayor Forndran (a Catholic and fierce supporter of Bavarian autonomy) each gave a speech. While Völk drove home the *kleindeutsch* interpretation of German history, Fordnran's speech was *grossdeutsch* and conservative in spirit.[19] Whereas Völk portrayed the battle of Leipzig as a violent outburst of popular sentiment and as the starting point for closer national integration, Forndran claimed that what rendered Leipzig a 'truly national victory' was that it had seen Prussia and Austria united.[20]

By the mid-1860s, the conservative voices found themselves increasingly on the defensive. This became evident at the Festival of Bavarian gymnasts, in 1865, and the Festival of Bavarian sharp-shooters, in 1867, both of which took place in Augsburg. In each event, Augsburg's liberals partly succeeded in turning an established Bavarian festival into a platform for promoting their *kleindeutsch* agenda. At the Festival of Bavarian Gymnasts in July 1865, more than 900 gymnasts from 70 Bavarian towns and villages congregated onto Augsburg where they found the streets decorated in a sea of flags. Some of them featured the Bavarian colours of blue and white, but most of the decorations on display bore the colours of either Augsburg or Germany. Of the municipal authorities, the then Deputy Mayor Ludwig Fischer and a dozen other representatives were in attendance. Principal Mayor Forndran, whose health was deteriorating (he would die the following year), had left Augsburg for a six-week holiday a mere two days before the start of the festival. The report conveys the utter gloom a loyal Bavarian state official appears to have felt at the scenes that were unfolding. While the sight of 'a good number of Bavarian flags' pleased the commissioner, he nevertheless expressed his astonishment at the fact that, on the occasion of a festival organized by and for Bavarian gymnasts, 'not a single word' had been 'dedicated to the Bavarian fatherland or the Bavarian king.'[21]

The Bavarian sharp-shooting festival of 1867 offers further confirmation of the gap that now separated liberal nationalists and Bavarian loyalists. What outraged the district commissioner was the organizing committee's decision to allow contestants from all over Germany—and not, as custom would have dictated, only the Bavarian marksmen—to aim at the discs labelled 'Bavaria' and 'Augsburg,' respectively.[22] The executive of Augsburg's rifle-shooting association must have been well aware that their decision was highly symbolic. Some of the contestants left no doubt that they saw this as an unacceptable dilution of the festival's Bavarian character.[23] When the two associations of Traunstein and Munich filed an open protest, the organizers gave in and reinstated the traditional format.[24] But this did not deter Mayor Fischer (who had succeeded Forndran during the previous year) from beating the nationalist drum in the festival speech he delivered on the final day of the event: 'We need to keep reminding ourselves that we are but parts of a large people that strives for unity and that is entitled to a pre-eminent place in the world.'[25] The conservative magistrate Aichinger struck a different note in a speech he gave at the concluding awards ceremony. Aichinger, who did not mention Germany once, ended with a toast to the King of Bavaria, triggering shouts of enthusiasm among the assembled marksmen from outside Augsburg.[26]

Austria's defeat in 1866 had undoubtedly emboldened Ludwig Fischer and his allies to come out in support of the North German Confederation. Both Fischer and Völk insisted that a strong Customs Union was 'a prerequisite to the future of the German fatherland.'[27] Ultramontane Catholics responded by mobilizing the rural Catholic population. The elections to the *Zollparlament* of 10 February 1868 gave liberals a foretaste of how a direct election based on universal manhood suffrage might affect their prospects of political leadership. To the great dismay of Augsburg's liberals, Ludwig Fischer was roundly defeated by his Catholic-conservative opponent.[28] But their retaliation was swift: When Bavaria prepared to commemorate the 50-year-anniversary of the state's constitution on 26 May 1868, Augsburg's magistrate, in a letter sent to all Bavarian magistrates, announced that it had decided to abstain because 'the necessary festive spirit' was missing, and due to a lack of available funding.[29] The state official described the magistrate's justification as inconsistent at best. There had been no shortage of means, he noted, when it came to celebrating events that suited Augsburg's National Liberals, such as the meetings of the Bavarian Teachers Association, and the various gatherings of the folksingers, the gymnasts and the fire fighters. At the same time, the liberals would boycott any event likely to 'strengthen the Bavarian-particularist cause.'[30] In the end, a small celebration did take place, with minimal official involvement; only Augsburg's Catholic Casino made a real effort to celebrate the event.[31] In August 1870 the district commissioner observed that 'German national attitudes and sentiments' had now taken root among larger sections of the town's population, a trend that was likely to intensify as the war continued.[32]

The means by which the German nation could become a self-evident point of reference for townspeople varied considerably. What helped bring it to Ulm was the almost uninterrupted presence of federal troops. Ever since the city had become part of the Kingdom of Württemberg in 1810, soldiers (mainly from Württemberg, Bavaria, and Austria) were among the most visible features of its townscape. With the creation of the German Bund in 1815 these military contingents became integrated into the federal army. Encounters with federal troops, whether in one of the town's inns, or on the occasion of one of their numerous manoeuvres, were frequent. There were four military barracks in Ulm in 1831, providing accommodation for 2000 soldiers, at a time when the population was just under 15,000. Yet this level of provision proved often insufficient, particularly during the large troop concentrations in the run-up to military manoeuvres or at times of social and political upheavals (1848/49) and war (1859, 1866, and 1871). The building of the *Bundesfestung* between 1842 and 1859 on the initiative of the German Confederation further reinforced the presence of federal troops in Ulm. Thus, while for most of the 1840s there was on average one soldier for every ten inhabitants, by the end of the nineteenth century that figure had almost doubled.[33]

Ulm's population was less than united in its attitude towards the garrison troops and the fortress. An 1848 petition by 'several citizens and inhabitants of Ulm' to the National Assembly in Frankfurt shows how the presence of the fortress helped conjoin local and national concerns in the minds of the urban public. The petitioners urged the Paulskirche delegates to provide binding regulations for the system of national fortresses in the constitution they were in the process of drafting. Large military fortresses, they pointed out, placed a heavy burden on a town's resources and often severely hampered its potential for expansion and hence for economic growth.[34] Ulm's fortress was portrayed as a living example of the flawed policies of the German Confederation. Driven by the 'interests of a few great powers' (a clear reference to Prussia and Austria), these policies had failed to do 'justice to the nation as a whole.'[35] The only way to protect Germany from attacks from the West, the petitioners recommended, was by building fortresses along her western borders. Within a truly national system of defence, Ulm's fortress would be part not of the first but of 'the third line;' its purpose would then be 'to concentrate surrendering and scattered troops.'[36]

Large-scale billeting during manoeuvres and at times of war provided another cause for controversy. In 1848, for example, several Ulm citizens sent letters to the municipal council to protest against the reduction of the daily allowance for billets.[37] The town authorities swiftly forwarded these complaints to the district government, which contacted the ministry in Stuttgart, which discussed the matter with representatives of the German Bund or of Austria.[38] Billeting and other impositions on municipal resources continued to be a cause of concern to both Ulm's public and the town authorities. In April 1859, when war in Italy looked almost inevitable, Ulm's council begged them to protect the 'civic rights' of the town's population, drawing their attention to some of the negative by-products of large troop concentrations: the requisitioning of important public buildings for military purposes without adequate financial compensation; the threat of epidemics due to inappropriate accommodation and sanitation; prevention of trade, communication and industry over an extended period of time. In order to protect the public from such hazards, the municipal council suggested that a sufficient number of temporary barracks be built at the outskirts of the town.[39] In October 1860, after another negative experience with Austrian troops participating in the Italian campaign, the city council asked the ministry in Stuttgart to ensure that the overall burden from billeting and requisitions be, henceforth, shared out more evenly among Württemberg's towns.[40]

But if the presence of federal troops had endowed Ulm's inhabitants with a national perspective, the events leading up to unification raised the more pressing issue of national loyalty.[41] Like many other German towns during this period, Ulm witnessed a sharpening of divisions between political rivals. In Württemberg, these divisions were defined, at least initially, more by political ideology than by confession or religion. The democratic *Volkspartei* and its followers were in their majority siding with Austria, not because they particularly liked Austria's domestic and foreign policies, but mostly because she appeared as the only power capable of keeping much-resented Prussia in check. Democrats also sought to defend local and regional autonomy in the face of increasing pressure exerted by both the Württemberg state and Prussian-led northern Germany. After the Prussian victory of 1866 Ulm's most influential democratic daily missed no opportunity to shoot off its arrows against Prussia and Bismarck. As late as December 1869, its editors concluded that Prussia's constitutional deficits and its conscription regime meant the southern German states were 'less inclined than ever to establish a closer allegiance with the North.'[42] Prussia, so they kept insisting, was trying to impose its militaristic culture—its *Soldatentum*—on the rest of Germany. As it was put in an 1870 *Volkspartei* appeal against closer military integration with Prussia: 'Instead of 4600 recruits the *Land* [by which they meant Württemberg] is now asked to provide 5800. Instead of 3,700,000 gulden it has to pay 5,300,000 gulden for its military...'[43] The liberal *Deutsche Partei*, which supported the alliance with the North German Confederation, was described by the editors as 'Prussia's dogsbody in Württemberg.'[44]

Württemberg's National Liberals had begun to embrace Prussia after its victory over Austria in 1866. Thus the liberal *Ulmer Schnellpost*, rather than portraying Prussia as a menace, called the North-German Confederation 'the doctor that heals us.' The key medicine supposed to cure the nation's ailments was the 'unity of legislation.' The editors thus explained the difference between the noisy nationalism of the pre-unification period and the energetic nation-building they expected from the new Reich: 'Just a few years of [common legislation] will take us further than a hundred years of festival activity by the choir societies, sharp-shooters, and gymnasts ever will.'[45] The same Ulm daily similarly summed up the duty of the people of Württemberg in a future German nation-state in October 1870, at a point when Germany's military victory over France was no longer in doubt: 'Illegitimate are all the peculiarities that prevent the Württemberger from feeling German first and foremost; legitimate all those, which can guide him in that very direction.'[46]

But Ulm's liberals were up against a formidable opponent. Thus, in the 1868 elections to the Customs Union parliament, the anti-Prussian *Volkspartei* performed strongly, garnering three times as many votes as the *Deutsche Partei*. In Ulm itself, however, liberals and democrats were more evenly matched both in 1868 and throughout the imperial period. It was only after unification that the odds shifted, for a brief period, in favour of the liberal nationalists.[47] Meanwhile, in Württemberg more generally, the *Deutsche Partei* formed the strongest political force in the first two decades after unification (with the exception of the period between 1877 and 1884, when the pro-Prussian *Deutsche Reichspartei* gained an even greater share of votes). However, by the late 1880s the democrats had regained their former strength, while the Catholic Centre and the Social Democrats began to establish themselves as significant political movements within the state.

Yet in Ulm and Württemberg, too, the years 1870/71 mark a caesura in the political realm. Broadsides against Bismarck or Prussia disappeared completely, at least for a few years. As the *Ulmer Tagblatt* noted rather soberly after the military victories of September 1870: 'The sense of a newly found vigour and the nation's rightful pride coalesce in the wish to consolidate the momentous victory into the future. This is to be achieved through a closer alliance between the South and North.'[48] But even though Ulm's democratic daily lost its anti-Prussian bent, with reports on local and regional issues dominating its pages for a few years (and with weather forecasts taking up ever greater space), the editors did not take a U-turn. For what changed was less the substance than the focus of their critique: Bismarck and Prussia were replaced by a more general preoccupation with questions surrounding legislative change at imperial level; polemics gave way to pleas for understanding, and for the right to defend regional and local interests. There were also moments of undisguised nostalgia, as when the editors discussed the new uniforms for Württemberg's troops, which would resemble the Prussian uniform in all but a few minor details: 'Whether this change will be for the good of our military? Time will tell. No doubt they will miss their old cap when they feel the heavy helmet pinching their heads; nor is the Prussian bonnet, which doesn't have a screen, a particularly beautiful sight.'[49]

No such nostalgia haunted the mouthpiece of the town's liberal nationalists. Its editors insisted that the war against France represented a just cause, and that its higher purpose was to make the Germans recognize their true 'calling' as members of a powerful nation and as a civilizing force in the world: 'As long as the German people are not united, as long as it does not occupy the position that befits it alongside other nations, it will remain hampered in doing justice to the high calling that it is destined to fulfil among the peoples of this earth.'[50] In view of the German victories on the battlefield in September, Ulm's National Liberals had little time for those who demanded that Württemberg be granted constitutional exemptions in the forthcoming negotiations with the imperial authorities. Württemberg was not to follow Bavaria's predictable example. Instead, its editors demanded, quite simply, that 'the constitution of the German nation must be the same for North and South.'[51]

One reason why Ludwigshafen's liberals did not feel a great urge to import national politics into local political affairs—at least not in the demonstrative way we have encountered in Augsburg and, to a lesser extent, in Ulm—appears to concern the traditions of the Bavarian Palatinate. The Palatinate's alliance with the Bavarian state was recent, a product of Napoleonic power politics. Compared with the population of the Bavarian heartlands, people in the Palatinate remained reluctant Bavarians.[52] This, in turn, made them more susceptible to the idea of German nationhood than was the case in many other German states. There were, one might say, fewer intervening factors than existed in either Württemberg or Bavaria proper. Less energy had to be mobilized to convert people to becoming loyal Germans than may have been necessary in states where the bond between monarch and population was more firmly established, or warmer, or both. For these reasons, it seems, in the Palatinate there was less need to beat the nationalist drum.

Along with the Protestant parts of Franconia, the Palatinate represented the exception in this regard within the Bavarian state. There was a marked degree of symmetry in this respect between Ludwigshafen and its hinterland. Thus, unlike Augsburg, which witnessed a sharp divergence in the distribution of political power between the district and the town itself, Ludwigshafen, like the district of Speyer-Frankental and the Palatinate in general, in the course of the 1860s developed into a bastion of national liberalism.[53] This was to have a decisive impact on municipal politics. Unlike their counterparts in Augsburg, Ludwigshafen's liberals had little reason to adopt the kind of frontier-group mentality that liberals began to adopt in other parts of Germany (such as parts of Baden or confessionally mixed regions of Prussia) in the course of the 1860s. They were consequently less prone to embrace a patriotic vision in which the nation appeared to be threatened from within. They did not see their calling in becoming the chief defenders of an embattled German Reich.

Besides, as a young industrial town experiencing large-scale migration, Ludwigshafen lacked the resources other towns could put aside for public festivals and commemorations. Its predominantly entrepreneurial elites were rather slow in developing a taste for grandiose national fetes and commemorations; just as its highly fluctuating population found it harder to develop the sense of place, and the related sentiments of local patriotism, that characterized the residents of longer-established cities. There is no evidence, for example, that Ludwigshafen participated in the 50-year anniversary of the Battle at Leipzig that took place in 1863; and it is rather unlikely that a celebration took place in the town itself, let alone that the authorities dispatched a delegation to the main celebrations in Leipzig. Furthermore, municipalities of Ludwigshafen's size and significance—for even as a centre of the chemical industry, Ludwigshafen was only really coming into its own in the course of the 1880s—were rarely invited to take part in prestigious events of this kind. The only town in the Palatinate that received an invitation from the organizers to take part in the celebrations in Leipzig was the district capital of Speyer.[54]

If the 50-year anniversary of the Palatinate's unification with Bavaria in 1866 (which took place just a few weeks before the outbreak of the war between Prussia and Austria) is anything to go by, then Bavarian celebrations were a slightly different matter. But even on that occasion, Ludwigshafen's city council only learned of the planned celebrations after receiving a circular letter from a festival committee in Kaiserslautern. The preparations were apparently well advanced by this stage. In the letter, the organizing committee urged several smaller towns of the Palatinate to join the celebrations. As far as most councillors were concerned, Ludwigshafen was 'in no position to carry out a large festival on its own;' but since they nevertheless wished to 'demonstrate their loyalty to both the Bavarian royal house and to Germany,' the councillors decided unanimously to send a delegation to Kaiserslautern to join the celebrations in what at that point was the district's largest city. That the members of the delegation could not expect any financial contribution towards their expenses was justified on patriotic grounds. 'Every true patriot,' so the liberal-dominated town council concluded, regarded it as 'a matter of honour' to be part of a delegation celebrating the

Palatinate's bond with Bavaria. At the same time, the council used the occasion to convey in no uncertain terms the city's firm allegiance to the German nation, entitling its delegation to join a resolution that rested on four essential elements: a solemn declaration that the Palatinate was feeling German and wished to remain German; unqualified opposition to a German *Bruderkrieg*; self-determination for Schleswig-Holstein; and, lastly, a German parliament. It was through the display of a copy of the resolution that the delegation had to demonstrate its right to take part in the commemorations in Kaiserslautern.[55]

The *kleindeutsch* orientation was strengthened further in Ludwigshafen after Austria's defeat in 1866. With the *Ludwigshafener Anzeiger* and the *Pfälzischer Kurier* both setting up their headquarters there, Ludwigshafen became the centre of liberal nationalism in the Palatinate.[56] That the National Liberals also dominated municipal politics became clear on 27 October 1867, when the town council issued a formal note of protest against the perceived threat of an abolition of the existing contract between the North German Confederation and Bavaria.[57] At the elections to the *Zollparlament* in February 1868, 246 Ludwigshafen voters supported the candidate Röchling, who represented the National Liberal *Fortschrittspartei*, whereas his Catholic-conservative opponent Römmich would receive 151 votes. However, in the predominantly rural district of Speyer-Frankental as a whole, Röchling suffered a devastating defeat, thanks in large part to the overwhelming support his opponent had received in the mostly Catholic canton of Speyer.[58] The event appears to have reinforced Ludwigshafen's alliance with national liberalism. What mattered even more in this respect was the military encounter with France in 1870, which, given the Palatinate's geographic location, had a significant impact on public perceptions across the region. From 1868 until the turn of the century, small-German nationalism thus became the ideology of choice not only for Ludwigshafen's entrepreneurs but also for the majority of its citizens.[59]

Commemorations

Unsurprisingly in view of the foregoing, Ludwigshafen's liberals quickly endorsed Sedan Day. Indeed, the first attempts to commemorate the battle of Sedan got under way in 1871. Rather than emanating from the local authorities, however, they took the form of spontaneous initiatives by a vocal minority. On its front page the liberal *Ludwigshafener Anzeiger* published a poem entitled 'Zum 2. September,' along with an editorial explaining the battle's course and pointing out its historic significance for Germany's present and future.[60] From another report in the same daily we learn that the musical society *Frohsinn* gave a performance in the garden of one of the local inns.[61] Yet, after the hoped-for endorsement of Sedan Day by the Kaiser had failed to materialize, nothing much seems to have happened the following year.

The debate over whether to commemorate Sedan Day, and if so, how, only began in earnest in 1873. The impetus came from outside. On 19 June the city council discussed an appeal by a committee representing the cities of Langenburg, Bonn and Düsseldorf, which encouraged other towns to join the movement in favour of an annual Sedan Day celebration. The council responded with a qualified endorsement, expressing its willingness to act on the appeal's recommendation as soon as 2 September had 'assumed the status of a national holiday.'[62] But this did not satisfy Ludwigshafen's leading liberal voices. On 24 August, Mayor Georg Kutterer called an extraordinary meeting to discuss if the battle of Sedan should be celebrated every year. There was general accord concerning the event's central importance. The day on which German armies had defeated the French troops at Sedan represented, in the words of one councillor, an event that, albeit bloody, had turned out to be 'highly beneficial' for Germany. Several councillors remained more lukewarm, however, noting that 'neither the Reich nor the individual state governments' had come forward to endorse Sedan Day. Besides, doubts were raised if, in the 'present political climate,' 2 September would enjoy everyone's approval. Some noted that the Catholic clergy was unlikely to give permission for a special religious service to be held on Sedan Day, while others expressed concern about the likely cost of a festival and its implications for the local tax burden.[63]

Confronted with these reservations and objections, Sedan Day's most outspoken supporters found themselves initially on the defensive. But they recovered quickly. Many began to challenge the view that, when it came to Sedan Day, the municipalities had to wait until they were given the green light by the Empire. Some argued that, even though 2 September had not been endorsed by the Kaiser, in reality many German towns were already treating it as a national holiday. It was therefore a question not of if, but when, Sedan Day would assume official status. Nobody 'endowed with true German patriotism,' they insisted, would be able to oppose the 'celebration of this glorious day.'[64] Concerns about the possible damage to confessional relations were likewise judged as entirely unfounded. As one of Sedan Day's proponents maintained, what set Ludwigshafen apart from many other German towns was precisely that 'the members of the various religious denominations' were mostly supportive of the festival, that not only Protestants and Jews, but also Catholics thought that Sedan Day should be afforded a place in the city's festive calendar. For all these reasons, he continued, Ludwigshafen should take the lead in promoting Sedan Day as a national holiday within the Palatinate.[65]

However, 'after much lively debate,' the majority on the municipal assembly opted for a compromise. Instead of taking the lead among Palatinate cities, the council decided to hold an informal public meeting to discuss the festival's organization and raise the necessary funds.[66] Held in the hotel *Drei Mohren*, the meeting began with the setting up of a small festive committee; this was followed by the launching of a collection to be continued until the day of the festival. The event had, in the words of a local daily, offered testimony of the 'patriotic spirit' and 'healthy thinking' of Ludwigshafen's population. It had also convinced the champions of Sedan Day that the city did not provide fertile soil for 'anti-national endeavours.'[67]

Although the first Sedan Day celebrations in Ludwigshafen proceeded at a relatively modest scale, they provided an opportunity to experiment with a set of symbolic places and practices that would undergo only few alterations in future years. They started with a torchlight procession that set off from the market place at 8 o'clock. Among the participants were the municipal fire brigade, the marksmen and gymnasts, the four leading choral societies (whose respective names were *Caecilia, Frohsinn, Bavaria*, and *Concordia*), and the town's war veterans. The editors of the *Ludwigshafener Anzeiger* counted 210 torchlight and 24 lampion carriers. The procession lasted for about an hour before returning to its starting point at the market square. There the celebrations continued with the choral societies singing the *Deutsches Lied* by Johann Wenzel Kalliwoda, with elementary-school teacher Roehrig acting as conductor. A patriotic speech by the town's Jewish teacher, Dr David, concluded the event.[68]

But 1873 was the first and last time that the celebrations took place without the municipality's official involvement. Encouraged by the enthusiasm the festival had generated in other parts of Germany, the mayor's office, in close collaboration with a special festive committee, took charge of the event. In 1877, the municipal council even decided that Sedan Day should henceforth be celebrated at the town's expense.[69] Four members, including the mayor, were entrusted with the festival's organization.[70] From the mid-1870s, moreover, the celebrations followed a pattern that would remain unchanged until the turn of the century. To begin with, Sedan Day was commemorated in two separate festivals, one in the city centre and the other at the Hemshof, the industrial district near the BASF's production plants. In 1874, the celebrations in both parts of town consisted of canon salutes detonated early in the morning; pageants proceeding along the main roads; and of musical performances, as well as speeches and social events taking place throughout the day. From 1875, after the council received permission from the Bavarian government, a special church service was held in the Protestant (but not in the Catholic) church. In addition, from 1882 local schools played a prominent role, with teachers distributing pretzels to their pupils before treating them to lectures on the historic significance of Sedan Day.[71]

On several occasions—including 1876, 1879, and 1890—Ludwigshafen commemorated Sedan Day more lavishly in a joint celebration with Mannheim. A number of further, less spectacular, modifications to the established pattern are more revealing. One concerns the day on which the celebrations were to be held. Although Sedan Day was usually celebrated on 2 September, from the 1880s, whenever 2 September fell on a weekday, the festivities were moved to either the preceding or subsequent Sunday. Like in Ulm (but unlike in Augsburg), these adjustments were introduced after local entrepreneurs had complained about the disruptions public festivals caused to the working week. The entrepreneurs, then, while they let the nation into the town, only did so on their own terms. To them, the town was first and foremost an economic space, one whose functionality was not to be undermined by an event that celebrated national unity. Rather than allowing the working week to be disrupted by a national event whose significance they did not deny, they sought to control the temporal rhythm of local life. National time, while legitimate, was not to colonize the city, not even for a day or two a year.

What part these entrepreneurial interventions played in the festival's loss of its initial stature in the course of the 1890s is difficult to ascertain. From that point on, however, it was above all the local veteran associations that fought to keep Sedan Day going as a public event. In 1893, for instance, 'a small circle of German men' provided the *vanguard* of the urban celebrations. In the words of the *Neue Pfälzische Kurier*: The 'thousands' of the 1870s had been reduced to 'hundreds,' mostly veterans, who, although they had visibly aged, had lost

Figure 14. Newspaper advertisement for the 1877 Sedan Day celebrations in Ludwigshafen, held jointly with Mannheim. Photo: OZ.

Fest-Programm

zur

Feier des 25. Gedenktages des Sieges von Sedan

in Ludwigshafen am Rhein.

Samstag, 31. August 1895.

Abends 8 Uhr: **Festbankett** im großen Saale des Gesellschaftshauses mit Festrede und Vorträgen hiesiger Gesangvereine. Die militär. Vereine sammeln um 7¼ Uhr in ihren Vereinslocalen.

Sonntag, 1. September 1895.

Früh 6 Uhr: Musikalischer Weckruf.

„ 7 „ Festgeläute und Böllerschießen.
Antreten der im nördlichen Stadttheile wohnenden Mitglieder der militär. Vereine und der Sanitätscolonne auf dem **Fabrikplatze,** der übrigen Mitglieder auf dem **Ludwigsplatze.**

„ ½8 Uhr: **Abmarsch** der militär. Vereine und der Sanitätscolonne vom Ludwigsplatze mit Trauermusik nach dem Friedhofe, woselbst

„ 8 Uhr: **Gedächtnißfeier** und Schmückung der Kriegergräber.

Vorm. ¼10 Uhr: Kirchgang unter Betheiligung der Vereine in die kath. und protest. Kirche des südl. und nördl. Stadttheiles.

„ ½10 Uhr: Gottesdienst; in den protest. Kirchen **Festgottesdienst;** im **südl. Stadttheil** mit Festgesang durch den Verein für classische Kirchenmusik.

„ ½11 Uhr: **Schulfeier** mit Sedanschriftvertheilung für die Schüler und Schülerinnen der 5. mit 7. Volksschulclasse in der Turnhalle des Schulhauses an der Oggersheimerstraße.

„ ½12 Uhr: Bretzelvertheilung an sämmtliche Schüler und Schülerinnen der Volksschule in **ihren Classenlocalen.**

Nach dem Gottesdienste: Parade der militär. Vereine auf dem Platze über dem Viaduct (Sängerfestplatz) nebst Parademusik bis 12 Uhr.

Mittags 12 Uhr: Festgeläute und Böllerschießen.

Nachm. ½3 „ **Im Stadttheile Friesenheim:** Gedenkfeier am Kriegerdenkmal mit Festrede ꝛc.

Abends 7 Uhr: Festgeläute und Böllerschießen;
Aufstellung der militärischen, Gesang-, Turn-Vereine ꝛc., **ohne** Fahnen und der Feuerwehr auf dem Ludwigsplatze zum **Abmarsch im Lampionzuge nach dem Rheinufer.** Abgabe der Lampions erfolgt auf dem Ludwigsplatze.

Abends nach 8 Uhr: **Festliche Brückenbeleuchtung** mit Feuerwerk.
Festliche Auffahrt von beleuchteten Schiffen; während des Feuerregens Absingen der „Wacht am Rhein" und „Deutschland über Alles" gemeinsam mit den jenseits aufmarschirten Mannheimer Vereinen unter Musikbegleitung.

Am Sonntag den 1. September. Beflaggung der städt. Gebäude und der Rheinbrücke, und wird die verehrliche Einwohnerschaft höflichst gebeten, auch ihrerseits durch Flaggenschmuck u. s. w. zur Erhöhung der Feier beizutragen.

Ludwigshafen a. Rh., den 23. August 1895.

Im Auftrage des Fest-Ausschusses:

Der 1. Vorsitzende:

Lauterborn,

J. V. des Bürgermeisters.

Figure 15. Newspaper advertisement for the 1895 Sedan Day celebrations in Ludwigshafen, showing that the festivities had been brought forward to a weekend (31 August/1 September). Photo: OZ.

none of their 'youthful vigour,' let alone their 'passion' for the occasion.[72] The municipal council remained actively involved in the organization of the festival, but public interest had waned compared to the 1870s and 1880s. Thus, in 1897, when on 6 September the prince regent visited the city just a few days after Sedan Day, it was once again the 'war and veteran associations' who put the stamp on the occasion.[73] For them at least, the connection to German nationhood had remained a deeply personal affair.

In Ulm, too, the first celebrations of the battle at Sedan were triggered by the immediacy of the event itself. The town's liberal and other pro-Prussian circles took the initiative, with their efforts clearly benefitting from the enthusiasm that accompanied the German victory, one to which South German troops had made a salient contribution. The resulting mood appears to have left little room for staying aloof, let alone for the noisy discord Sedan Day would occasionally provoke in later decades. In the evening of 3 September 1870, after news of the German victory had reached Württemberg, a church service was quickly arranged in the *Ulmer Münster*. Upon completion of the service, the large crowd congregated in front of the nearby town house, where people listened to patriotic songs performed by the local choir societies. Thereafter, ten members of the council marched to the garrison to congratulate its governor on the German victory.[74] Later on that evening, led by their headmaster, the pupils of Ulm's *Gymnasium* carried out a torchlight procession through the streets of the town.[75]

With time, however, spontaneity gave way to reflection and a fair amount of discord. During the following two years Ulm did not see any celebrations comparable to the ones that had taken place spontaneously just a few days after the battle of Sedan in 1870. As in Ludwigshafen, the lack of imperial endorsement in 1872 seems to have left many in Ulm, including the supporters of Sedan Day, in a state of uncertainty. But not for long. In 1873, during a meeting of the municipal council, a group of local liberals demanded that Sedan Day be granted official status.[76] A mere week before the date of the battle returned for the third time, *Oberbürgermeister* von Heim raised the 'question concerning the holding of a national festival on 2 September.' The mayor made much of the fact that Stuttgart, Esslingen as well as other Württemberg towns and cities had recently expressed their intention to carry out a festival to commemorate the battle of Sedan. There was no doubt in von Heim's view that Württemberg's second city ought to follow their example. He ended his plea with a proposal on how the festivities were to be conducted. His list of suggestions included the decoration of the town with flags; the ringing of bells at the *Schwörhaus*; the playing of a chorale from the *Münster*; and finally, a local school holiday on the day of the celebrations.[77]

Von Heim must have anticipated that his proposal might be controversial, but he could hardly have predicted the concerted nature of the response it provoked. The two leading democrats on the council insisted that the authority in questions of German nationhood lay with the Empire: So long as Sedan Day was not 'endorsed by the Reichstag as the only true representation of the German people,' it could not really be described as a national holiday. They also pointed out that Stuttgart's decision to celebrate Sedan Day, which the mayor had cited to buttress his plea, had been reached by a majority of a single vote, and that the envisaged participation of local schools was contingent on permission by the state's cultural ministry. Last but not least, Ulm's democrats queried the moral appropriateness of the event itself. 12 May, the day on which the peace treaty with France had been signed, provided a more suitable date for a national festival than a day that evoked 'the memory of a bloody battle.' For all these reasons, they recommended that Ulm postpone any decision on the issue until the members of the Reichstag had made up their mind.[78] Responding to these reservations, two members of the *Deutsche Partei* stressed the significance of the event for Germany's present and future. 2 September, they once again lectured the sceptics, was the day when 'German arms' had gained a historically momentous victory. But, to their dismay, they found themselves defeated in the subsequent ballot.[79]

Only four days later, at another council meeting, the balance appeared to shift, yet again, in favour of the Sedan Day enthusiasts. Mayor von Heim, who again acted as chair, informed the assembled councillors that the cultural ministry in Stuttgart had just proclaimed a general school holiday for 2 September. As the mayor sought to reassure his colleagues, this was not a one-off permission, but a permanent decree.[80] Von Heim chose his words carefully. He merely suggested that the news from Stuttgart ought to pave the way for 'a simple yet dignified celebration' in Ulm. At the same time, he condemned the executive of Ulm's *Deutsche Partei* for having addressed the public in a 'passionate and highly inappropriate announcement.' In the last week of August, the party had asked Ulm's population to decorate their houses with flags and to take part in both the pageant and the church service in the *Münster*.[81] The chairman of the citizens' committee (*Bürgerausschuss*) accepted Heim's criticism, but insisted that the members of his party could

not be held collectively responsible for the actions of its executive. Like
Ulm's mayor, he argued that the proclamation of a general school holiday
for 2 September had created a new situation. Now that Württemberg's
youth had been given 'the right to keep alive the memory of those great
events,' Ulm's authorities should cease to stand aside.[82]

But the democrat councilors were not easily swayed, pointing out that
Ulm's population, much like the rest of Germany, was 'deeply divided'
over Sedan Day. In the final ballot, Heim's proposal was defeated by just
one vote, with all six democrats on the council voting against it.[83] But
2 September would be commemorated in some style despite the lack of
official endorsement. This was due to the initiative of a committee of liberal
citizens, most of them members of the *Deutsche Partei*. The proposal they
submitted to the council entailed a request for landlords to decorate their
houses with flags. It also included an application to hold a large pageant
from the market place to the Protestant Cathedral, where a church service
would be held, as well as a series of more informal festive activities (such as
speeches and choir performances) to be held in the afternoon.[84]

If the period from the early 1870s to the turn of the century is judged as
a whole, then the 1873 debate in the council looks particularly turbulent
and controversial. Even thereafter Sedan Day never really settled into the
routine the city's liberals had tried to establish. Thus, in 1874, just a year after
their initial defeat, Sedan Day's supporters managed to persuade the city
council to act as official sponsor. Whether Heim's strategy of linking the
celebrations with the inauguration of the city's new *Gymnasium*—the grammar schools, both the school buildings and its teachers and pupils, became
one of Sedan Day's central agents—facilitated this move is difficult to say.[85]
What is evident is the emergence of a pattern during this period for conducting the festival: the ringing of church bells at 7 a.m. signalled the start
of the festivities, which was followed, at 8 o'clock, by the blowing of a choral from the cathedral tower, at which point a large public pageant set off
from the City Hall to the *Ulmer Münster*; this was followed, at 9 a.m., by a
church service in the cathedral, with a series of speeches that were delivered
in the town's grammar school concluding the official part of the celebrations; the afternoon was reserved for more informal activities to be held at
the Friedrichsau.[86]

But Sedan Day's fusion with local officialdom would not be permanent.
Democrats in particular continued to express reservations about the celebrations. It was 'not through celebrations and processions,' the democratic

Ulmer Tagblatt wrote in 1875, that one showed a deeper understanding of the true significance of 2 September, but rather through one's 'firm commitment to participate in the formation of a vibrant and free German *Bürgertum*' one that would be willing to 'bring the ultimate sacrifice to transform the German Empire into a free German Empire, a homestead of genuine civic virtue.'[87] On 19 August 1880, just two weeks before Ulm celebrated the 10th anniversary of Sedan Day in a festival attended by several state officials, the council decided to restrict the town's official involvement to once in every five years.[88]

This remained valid until the turn of the century. What kept Ulm's Sedan Day celebrations going from the late 1880s were above all the veteran associations, who used the event to raise money for their ageing members. What also prevented the event from dying down completely was that, twice in a decade, the town authorities endorsed it officially, which proved conducive to its public appeal. In 1895, for example, as well as acting as organizer, the authorities subsidized the festival with a sum of 1500 marks. Even on that occasion, the mixed organizing committee found it difficult to agree on a date: While some, especially the National Liberals, favoured 2 September, others, above all local entrepreneurs keen to avoid unnecessary stoppages, insisted on 1 September. More than a decade later than their counterparts in Ludwigshafen am Rhein, several of Ulm's factory owners and merchants had begun to challenge the conventional view of how national historic events were to be commemorated. While they did not dispute the significance of great historic events, they too made it clear that the life of a modern nation was to be defined, to an important degree, by the rhythm of economic life.[89]

Augsburg's first celebrations of the battle of Sedan occurred just days after news of the event had reached Swabia. Public and private buildings were decorated at once. Around noon a group of Augsburg citizens formed a procession heading for the homes of Mayor Fischer and advocate Dr Völk, Swabia's two leading representatives of the *Fortschrittspartei* and of Bavaria's branch of the *Nationalverein*. The two men were then treated to a standing ovation in recognition of their continual efforts on behalf of the national cause. The state official who observed the scene noted that the German victory had convinced Augsburg's liberals that henceforth 'everything was possible.' As he wrote to the district government on the emotional atmosphere he had just witnessed: 'People have stopped thinking. They just want to celebrate.'[90]

The following year saw a more elaborate celebration of Sedan Day, and this time the local veterans association (*Königlicher Veteranenverein*) was in the vanguard. Possessing 136 full and 130 honorary members, the association had for some time acted as a champion for a *kleindeutsch* Germany, as demonstrated by its annual commemoration of 18 October, the day of the battle at Leipzig. Encouraged by the influx of a large contingent of new members in the wake of the 1870/71 campaign, its executive declared 2 September the association's new 'day of honour.'[91] On 2 September 1872, the veterans attended a church service in the Protestant and Catholic churches at Heilig Kreuz. In the course of the association's evening festivities, Ludwig Fischer extended a toast to the German Kaiser, while another guest toasted to the king of Bavaria.[92]

Although the celebrations in 1872 were of a more informal nature than those of subsequent years, the liberal magistrate was eager to create an impression of officialdom by having city hall covered in German and Bavarian flags.[93] Shortly thereafter, the 'municipal council endorsed the magistrate's decision to celebrate 2 September as a national holiday.'[94] From the summer of 1871, moreover, the city council had begun to lobby for the building of a war monument, bearing the names of Augsburg citizens that had lost their lives in the war.[95] Encouraged by the public support for the project, on 17 June 1871 the magistrate decided to acquire the *Frohnhof*, a large square encircled by state buildings on one side and the Catholic cathedral on the other. In January 1872, the city council seconded the magistrate's decision to have a war memorial constructed on the site.[96]

A few months later, the magistrate proposed to put aside 20,000 and 25,000 gulden for the project. Yet with a total cost of 42,000 gulden, the monument turned out almost twice as expensive as originally planned. This was a very large sum to spend on a municipal monument by contemporary standards, even for a town of Augsburg's size. One reason why the doubling of the originally projected sum provoked virtually no opposition might be the fact that the monument expressed the theme of local sacrifice for a national cause, thereby fusing local and nationalist concerns and sensibilities.[97] After a controversy over its symbolism had settled down–the eminent Munich sculptor Zumbusch opted for a classicist style, while some members of the council demanded that the warrior at the centre of the monument be given a more martial expression[98]—the new monument was inaugurated on 2 September 1876.[99] The plaque that was attached to the monument carried an inscription by Augsburg's school inspector Bauer:

Aus Kampfes Nacht	From the Night's Battle
Stieg auf die Macht	Emerged the Might
Der Sonne gleich	Like Sunlight
Das deutsche Reich[99]	The German *Reich*.

There soon evolved a script—consisting of a number of significant places, actors, and practices—according to which the celebrations would henceforth be conducted. Some of its elements (including the church services, the flagging of private and public buildings, or the staging of a procession) had already been present in previous years, while others (such as the speeches delivered in front of the new war monument) were added to the mix. Overall the pattern that emerged in Augsburg in the course of the 1870s was denser than that which characterized the celebrations in either Ludwigshafen or Ulm, reflecting the liberals' desire for the nation to colonize urban space for the duration of the event.

On the eve of 2 September, the municipal buildings and many private houses would be decorated with German, Bavarian, and Augsburg flags, with the veteran associations holding services in both Christian churches. Choral music would be played from the Perlach tower at the break of dawn and again later in the evening. In the afternoon, a commemorative service would be held in front of the monument of fallen soldiers at the Protestant cemetery, an event that was accompanied by the singing of religious psalms, and which concluded with a patriotic speech by the minister conducting the service. Upon conclusion of the cleric's speech, the Protestant veterans associations would place wreaths at the steps of the monument. The event would be attended by a number of private associations, including the association of journeymen, as well as by the children of the city's orphanage and almshouse. On the day of the festival, the richly decorated war memorial on the *Frohnhof* would be covered with wreaths and serve as a magnet for both the solemn and the passers-by. The same applies to the graves of fallen soldiers, which would be covered with flowers and wreaths, offering an 'honourable testimony to those who died for the Fatherland and to the pious and patriotic sensitivity of the donors.'[100] The more informal part of the festivities, such as the performances and social gatherings in public places and in various inns, would begin in the later afternoon and stretch far into the night.[101]

In subsequent years, and particularly from the 1890s, it was above all the local veterans associations that kept the celebrations afloat in many towns, while the authorities often shifted into the background. The only constant sign of official recognition was the decoration of the municipal buildings (including the monument on the *Frohnhof*) with German and Bavarian flags. Yet the habit of private landlords decorating their houses in similar fashion seems to have continued more or less unabated throughout the entire period.[102] At a time when the municipal authorities sought to refrain from issuing announcements and conducting speeches, the liberal newspapers contributed even more to informing the public of the various festive activities and encouraging participation. For example, on 1 September 1894, one local newspaper reported that there had been few announcements so far about festive activities on Sedan Day. This the editors attributed to the fact that 'all larger festivals had been postponed to next year, when we shall celebrate the 25th anniversary of the Reich's resurrection.'[103] On the eve of the festival, the same newspaper addressed its readers thus: 'Let us, in view of tomorrow's Sedan Day celebrations, once again appeal to our town population's patriotic spirit. May the people of our town demonstrate by richly decorating their houses that Augsburg continues to be a veritable bastion of German nationhood.'[104]

The quest for recognition

How did the champions of Sedan Day cope with its bumpy reception, compounded by the fact that it was denied imperial recognition? One of their coping strategies was to create a virtue out of a need. Urban liberals, who almost everywhere were in the vanguard, kept stressing that Sedan Day was the people's festival and that it was therefore ordinary Germans, rather than the state, who had to take the initiative. Some liberal observers went so far as to claim that it was the conviction which held that the celebrations should 'evolve from the people' that had prevented the Kaiser and the Reichstag from investing 2 September with official authority. Sedan Day, to be worthy of its purpose, had to flow from a collective emotional need.[105] In this way, the opposition that Sedan Day provoked among the public gave way to an interesting reconfiguration of political moralities. While liberals began to praise the virtues of spontaneous mobilization in the name of nationhood, local democrats (often in alliance with left liberals and, as in Ulm, with the support of conservative Catholics) argued that the Empire had to provide the lead. Whereas liberal nationalists began to imagine the German nation as a work in progress, the product of popular energies and dispositions, Sedan Day sceptics associated it with the authority of the imperial state.

No doubt liberals on the whole believed in the ideal according to which genuine national festivals should emanate from an emotional need instead of being imposed from above. Yet for many, the festival's lack of official recognition was a source of deep disappointment. It was disappointing, most of all, because it strengthened the cause of their opponents. As mentioned previously, Württemberg democrats and Bavarian conservatives made much of the fact that the Reichstag had failed to endow 2 September with an official stamp of approval. Having opposed Prussia right up to the war against France, both had to tread carefully in the immediate aftermath of unification. Each of them had to prove their loyalty to the new empire. Yet by failing to embrace Sedan Day, the imperial authorities unintentionally released some of the pressure on the former opponents of *Kleindeutsch* unification. Worse still as far as many urban liberals were concerned, Sedan Day's non-official status created a space for democrats and conservatives of various kinds (including Catholic conservatives) to reclaim public space by querying the legitimacy of the festival. Meanwhile, the liberals found themselves in a predicament, for they could not criticize the Kaiser and the Reichstag for failing to declare Sedan Day a national holiday, at least not publicly.

Yet this still left liberals with the option of criticizing their own city authorities for failing to join the wave of popular support that had begun to carry Sedan Day. As the liberal *Ulmer Schnellpost* noted pithily in 1873: There was 'not a single town around Ulm' that had failed to embrace Sedan Day, including Geislingen, Biberach, and Blaubeuren, let alone Stuttgart. But 'while almost everywhere the council is setting a patriotic example by providing both encouragement and organization,' the 'council of the garrison town of Ulm, the state's second city,' had 'repeatedly refused to participate in the celebrations.'[106] In 1881, moreover, the author of a reader's letter complained bitterly about the city government's objection to granting the festival official status. All the more so as Sedan Day had become 'second nature' to most of Ulm's inhabitants, just 'like Christmas, or Easter, or any other religious festival.'[107] When in 1891 the local veteran association asked the municipal council to play a more active part in the festival's organization (as it had done in 1885), the latter refused, promising that it would get involved again in 1895, a promise it indeed honoured.[108]

When in 1900, however, Sedan Day returned for the thirtieth time, it was the veteran associations, rather than the town authorities that organized the celebrations and invited the public to attend.[109] The festival never lost its popularity among certain sections of the public, to be sure. Nor did it fulfil the nationalists' hopes that it would be able to transform people's sense of place and time, bringing national and local rhythms into a seamless dialogue; and that it would fester a sense of community in which locality and nation would be amalgamated to the extent where the distinction between them became entirely meaningless.

Responding to an initial reluctance on the municipal council's part to endorse Sedan Day, Ludwigshafen's liberals too insisted that the commemoration of 2 September reflected a popular need: 'The towns that have come out in favour of celebrating 2 September include Munich, Leipzig, Breslau, Stuttgart, and Nuremberg. Will Ludwigshafen abstain? We should not like to think so.'[110] At least on this occasion, the message was unambiguous: those who used formalist arguments to prevent Sedan Day from becoming a datum in the urban festive calendar showed a shameful lack of German patriotism. For the local liberals, the authorities' reluctance, justified with the festival's potential to divide, was all the more regrettable as the Catholic district capital Speyer had drawn a different conclusion:

> In yesterday's meeting, the city council of Speyer has concluded to honour Sedan Day with an official festival. The council justified its decision by pointing to the large number of German cities that recently endorsed Sedan Day; and because 2 September, not because but despite its representing a day of battle, had to be regarded as the day when the rebirth of the German nation had begun.[111]

Overall, therefore, the festival's lack of imperial endorsement strengthened the liberals' resolve to gain recognition for Sedan Day locally, in the towns where they were active as citizens, entrepreneurs, consumers or members of local associations. In fact, this was the ultimate motive behind their claim that the celebrations were popular among the German people. Their determination increased in proportion to the resistance they experienced. Thus, when in 1873 Ulm's council voted against official involvement, or when in 1880 the same body decided to confine its participation to once every five years, this caused considerable resentment within the ranks of the *Deutsche Partei*. Calls for declaring Sedan Day an official municipal festival began to abound in the local press. Thus, in 1873, a reader aired his frustration at the council's decision in a letter to the *Ulmer Schnellpost*, but not without revealing the ambiguity with which he and others appear to have perceived the matter: 'The quarrel over whether to celebrate Sedan Day has now reached

Ulm as well. Although initially we sympathized with a degree of scepticism, now that Germany's largest cities and many of its small towns have recognized 2 September as a national festival, the persistent quarrelling and our falling behind strike us as entirely inappropriate.'[112] The pressure on municipal councils mounted after Württemberg's cultural authorities declared 2 September a school holiday, even listing it as an official day of remembrance in the royal Württemberg calendar. Now that Sedan Day featured in the state's cultural calendar, liberal nationalists in Ulm and elsewhere felt emboldened to urge their own municipalities to get their act together.[113]

What some of Sedan Day's supporters resented just as much as lack of official endorsement was calls to postpone it. Such postponements became common in many German cities from the 1880s, whenever September 2 fell on an ordinary workday or, as was the case in 1876 in Ulm, on a traditional market day (in this case a Saturday). As the *Ulmer Schnellpost*, which advocated a purist position on the celebrations, noted sharply: 'The decision of the *bürgerliche Kollegien* to celebrate Sedan Day, but not, as is customary everywhere except in Ulm, on 2 September, is a welcome sign to all those in Germany for whom Sedan Day offers no cause for joy.'[114] Even in 1895, when Ulm's authorities were officially involved in the festival's organization, 2 September was not declared a public holiday, with many shops remaining open until 3 p.m.;[115] and the workers choral society, the *Arbeitersängerbund*, decided against participation.[116] In Ludwigshafen, too, pressure exerted by employers led to Sedan Day being celebrated on either a Saturday or Sunday. This was in contrast to Augsburg, where throughout the imperial period Sedan Day was commemorated on 2 September. In a city with numerous large factories, this must have reduced the number of potential participants.

On those occasions when Sedan Day was celebrated with the authorities' involvement, the tone of the liberal reports were the often optimistic and conciliatory, and at times even joyful. Such was the case, for example, in Ulm in 1875: 'It has now become evident that the real enemies of the firmly established, unified and great German *Reich* constitute but a tiny minority; and moreover, that they do not attack the Empire as such but rather specific institutions and occurrences. What all this means is that Sedan Day has been accepted as Germany's national holiday.'[117] In 1877, after the *Gemeinderat* had voted unanimously in favour of an official celebration, the *Ulmer Schnellpost* predicted that the hoped-for normalization of Sedan Day would lead to a more sober attitude towards France, and hence a national pride less reliant on enmity: 'The more our hearts are freed from national hatred, the greater and purer may be our joy on Sedan Day.'[118]

Conversely, the tone of the reports gained in triumphalism whenever the local authorities appeared to distance themselves from the festival. Thus, in 1881 (after the council had agreed on a quinquennial rhythm), the same liberal daily that just a few years previously had expressed hope in a reconciliation with France responded to the charge, made by democrats, Catholics, and socialists, that celebrating Sedan Day would only serve to deepen Germany's enmity with France, that the German victory had served humanity as a whole: On Sedan Day, they claimed, France and Europe had been rescued from Napoleon's banditry.[119] In 1884, the front-page editorial described the Battle of Sedan as 'the great turning point,' as the event 'through which the French nation had to hand over her century-long position as the world's first power to the German nation.' 'The handing over of the Kaiser's sword to the Prussian King represents the symbol of the shift of world power from the French to the German people.'[120]

In Augsburg, magistrate and council officialized Sedan Day in a meeting on October 1872.[121] Given the magistrate's support of the *Kulturkampf* throughout the 1870s and beyond, this caused ill-feeling among Augsburg's large Catholic population.[122] As the Catholic *Postzeitung* commented in 1872: 'The commemoration of Sedan Day, announced with a great deal of fuss in some quarters, has by and large failed to generate the expected enthusiasm.'[123] When in the same year Ulm's council denied the festival official status, the *Augsburger Postzeitung* was quick to inform the public of the decision by Swabia's old imperial city.[124] For the editors of one of Germany's leading Catholic newspapers, Ulm's case offered proof that Sedan Day did not have to be a public demonstration of anti-Catholic sentiment. As the *Postzeitung* was keen to point out, Württemberg had proved the only state where Sedan Day could be called a *Volksfest*:

> Only in Württemberg, where the war between the state and the Church is largely inexistent, did the celebrations gain a popular character, because both state and Church took part in a spirit of relative harmony. Everywhere else, and particularly in Bavaria, the commemorations turned into a no-confidence vote against the ruling National Liberals. Public buildings were decorated with flags on the instruction of the distinguished magistrates and civil servants, with national-liberal-minded house owners and free masons swiftly emulating their example. The Munich correspondent of the *Frankfurter Zeitung* was able to spot a single (blue-white!) flag in that city, while in Augsburg itself,

the liberal public was almost alone in following the order of the ruling National Liberals. In Würzburg, the correspondent of the *Fränkisches Volksblatt* counted 72 flags in spite of the council's decree, while in Nuremberg the bells were rung and the flagging was almost universal. Only in the Palatinate did people remain less offish than for example in Frankfurt and Mainz, where the attempt to manipulate true public sentiment failed miserably. To be sure, and as the *Frankfurter Zeitung* was keen to report: the bells rung quite beautifully in the latter town, the canons thundered 101 times, and nor was there a lack of the inevitable chorale delivered from one of the church towers. But the flagging of the houses was sparse, not to say squalid. Barely a fifth of the city's population took part in this party festival of the National Liberals.[125]

As far as the *Postzeitung* was concerned, then, Sedan Day had been more popular where liberals had shown no interest in the purification of public space in the name of the nation. For that was, in effect, how many Catholics read the liberal actions and rhetoric that inspired the *Kulturkampf*. As an attempt to rid German towns of the things that were seen as incommensurate with the liberals' understanding of *Fortschritt*, as an effort to colonize public space in the service of altering the rhythm of people's everyday lives. This was why, according to Augsburg's most influential Catholic newspaper, Sedan Day had little prospect of becoming the self-evident ritual liberals had hoped for.

There can be little doubt that Sedan Day's popularity relied to some extent on the support and recognition it received from municipal and state authorities. The more conspicuous the authorities' involvement, the greater the material support the organizers could hope to receive. In 1895, Augsburg's industrial and trading community alone donated over 16,000 marks in funds, bringing the total of private funds to more than 25,000 marks.[126] Estimates concerning the number of participants varied between 20,000 and 30,000, but given that the total consumption of beer ran to 430 hectolitres, the latter figure sounds more realistic.[127] The 1895 event also suggests that, once the festival crossed a certain threshold, the hype and emotional involvement could assume new heights. It also favoured the emergence of a competitive spirit among the population. Thus, in the run up to the 25th anniversary celebrations, several Augsburg inhabitants complained that their district lay outside the route of the festive procession, but their request for inclusion was turned down on the grounds that the veterans would be unable to march long distances, especially should the weather turn out to be warm.[128] The 1895 celebrations were accompanied by another incident which shows that, whenever the celebrations involved a mass public, they unleashed competitive dynamics on the ground. On this occasion, the participants were shop owners, and the issue was closing times. Thus, when the shop-owners of the *Karolinenstrasse* decided to close their businesses on Sedan Day, those of the other main commercial roads quickly followed suit.[129]

Meanwhile, in Ludwigshafen the domineering position of urban liberals and the relative weakness of their opponents seem to have prevented the obsessive preoccupation with Sedan Day that was so common elsewhere. It was not until 1876, when the celebrations were held jointly with Mannheim, that the authorities began to take a more active stance. From then on, however, the municipal council, and particularly the mayor's office were calling the shots, albeit in consultation with a special festive committee. So much so, in fact, that on 1 September 1887 the district government had to remind the mayor that Bavaria's law of association prescribed that the authority over the festival lay not with the council, but had to be delegated to a special festival committee. To this the mayor replied that, in Ludwigshafen the festival committee and the municipal authorities were 'one and the same.' The latter would make all decisions in this respect, although he and his aides would often seek advice from municipal councillors and the provosts of the town's military organizations. The term 'festival committee', so the mayor declared with astonishing candidness, had been invented to retain an appearance of 'parity,' even though such a committee did 'not really exist.'[130]

The most persistent opposition to the celebrations emanated from ultramontane Catholicism. Particularly during the height of the *Kulturkampf* in the 1870s and early 1880s, Catholics felt themselves on the defensive in a society many of them experienced as hostile. A society, moreover, whose political, economic, and cultural parameters seemed largely defined by liberals who used the nationalist card to prove that their vision for achieving progress was superior to anyone else's. Of the three towns examined, Augsburg's Catholics were most open in their opposition to Sedan Day. As long as the religious feelings of Catholics were insulted in the most blatant manner, the *Augsburger Postzeitung* concluded early on, the demand for Catholics to take part in the celebrations amounted to a 'bitter mockery.'[131] In 1873, as the liberal endeavour to establish Sedan Day as new routine became evident, the city's Catholic Casino decided to take a passive stance towards a 'political festival' at a time when developments 'left every Catholic heart with a deep sadness.'[132]

Announcements of this kind only served to enrage Augsburg's liberal nationalists. In 1874, for example, Mayor Fischer condemned Bishop Kettler of Mainz for having declared that Catholics had a duty to distance themselves from the Sedan Day celebrations. As Fischer exclaimed in front of a large crowd of supporters: 'I would like to remind the man in question, who was not ashamed to describe the duty of German Catholics in this way, of God's commandment that says you shall honour your mother and father, a commandment that he violates when he repudiates the fatherland whose air he breathes, and rebuffs mother earth who nourishes him (stormy and long applause).'[133] The bishop of Augsburg chose to express his reservations against the Sedan Day celebrations more discretely. Thus, when in 1876 the municipal authorities invited him to the inauguration of the new war monument on Sedan Day, he let it be known that he was scheduled to undertake a three-week tour of his diocese, for which he would need to set off just a few days prior to the planned inauguration.[134]

In Ludwigshafen, too, where Catholics made up half of the resident population, Sedan Day had a clear confessional component. This became evident in the differential involvement of the two parish churches. Unlike its Protestant counterpart, the Catholic parish church did not offer a special church service on Sedan Day.[135] It would take 20 years until the authorities expressed their dissatisfaction at this state of affairs. In 1890, the mayor asked the Catholic parish priest if he would mind having the church bells rung on Sedan Day, as did the Protestants. The priest replied that such a step could not be taken without prior authorization by the bishop, who in turn let it be known that such a move would require the consent of the Bavarian government. After letting the matter rest for the next few years, Mayor Krafft renewed his request in 1895, when Sedan Day was again celebrated jointly with Mannheim. This time he approached the bishop directly, reminding him that the Protestant parish had already given permission to having the church bells rung at 7 a.m., 12 noon, and 7 p.m. Could the Catholic parish be expected to do likewise?[136] The extent of his frustration is tangible from a separate letter he sent to the bishop:

> It does not look in the least favourable if one of the two parish churches has their bells rung while the other does not. It also prompts all kinds of speculations about the causes for this discrepancy among a population whose majority finds it hard to understand why the two Catholic churches do not ring their bells on the day. Perhaps this is something your Episcopal Honour might wish to take into consideration when he enters into deliberations on the matter.

This time the mayor's intervention bore fruit, and the bells of the town's Christian churches were rung simultaneously: on 27 August the vicar informed the mayoral office that Ludwigshafen's Catholic parish would be instructed to ring its church bells at the requested times.[137]

In Ulm, where Catholics amounted to less than a third of the population, the confessional dimension of Sedan Day revealed itself more subtly. On the whole, the debate over the meaning and significance of the celebrations was indeed less affected by confessional antagonism than was the case, for instance, in Augsburg. This is not to say, however, that the *Kulturkampf* had not affected the celebrations. In 1882, for instance, the *Ulmer Schnellpost* commented: 'All our schools celebrated Sedan Day, with one exception.'[138] Subtle tensions were visible throughout the 1870s. Thus in a festival speech, the director of Ulm's *Gymnasium* spoke of his 'pain' in view of the fact that there were still Germans 'who do not rejoice in the Reich's welfare, nor lament its short-comings and afflictions.' These Germans, by which he no doubt referred to Catholics and Socialists, were 'unlikely to contribute towards, let alone bring sacrifices on behalf of, [the Reich's] continued existence and progress.' He then continued in the same vein: Their attitude 'may sadden us, but it must not surprise us, and we certainly must not allow it to instill in us anger and hatred against those Germans who still are un-German.'[139] As far as the direc-tor of Ulm's grammar school was concerned, scepticism towards Sedan Day was incommensurate with loyalty towards the nation.

But in Ulm such broadsides were relatively rare. The attitude of influen-tial Catholic figures seems to have been conducive to fostering a more benign climate. Significantly, following the Protestants' example, the Catholic parish offered its members a special church service on Sedan Day. Even liberal observers enthused at the fact that all three religious communities— Protestants, Catholics, and Jews—held special church services to honour this historic event.[140] What distinguished the Catholic service, however, was that it took the form of a requiem in memory of Germany's fallen soldiers. By comparison, the Protestant services were more explicitly centred on Sedan and its purported historic meaning. Ministers used their sermon to emphasize the lessons to be drawn from the historic event itself, often depicting it as a sign of divine providence.[141]

Aside from this difference in style and emphasis, the Catholic parish left no doubt that it remembered Sedan Day as a separate community. This meant, above all, commemorating it in a separate place. Ulm's Cathedral, the city's largest building by far, would have offered ample space for a joint

Christian service. Yet, at least on this occasion, the priest politely declined the offer of being submerged into a seamless national community. The pageant of school children demonstrates this very clearly. After the pageant's completion, the Protestant children would attend a ceremony in the *Ulmer Münster*, in the course of which a few songs were performed, followed by an edificial speech. In 1878, the festival committee encouraged the local priest to let the Catholic children take part in this event, encouraging him to address his flock in a separate speech. His reply was as friendly as it was unmistakable—after the completion of the pageant in the Cathedral, the Catholic children would congregate in the Catholic *Wengenkirche* for a 'church service in memory of the German soldiers who died in the last war.'[142] A slightly different approach was adopted a decade later, however. While Catholic and Protestant children still attended separate church services, the Catholic service now included an *Erinnerungsfeier*, a commemoration of Sedan as an historic event.[143]

Overall, however, the liberal uncertainty about the status of Sedan Day remained considerable. This uncertainly only buttressed the quest for the festival to gain the widest possible recognition. One of its manifestations was a preoccupation with decorations and flags. For the proponents of Sedan Day, the national flag was more than a symbol of nationhood. The flags on display were also components within a larger effort to nationalize urban space. The more places that could be marked out by national flags, the more the distinction between locality and nation would be revealed as a delusion. Irrespective of whether the celebrations were organized by local committees or whether the authorities themselves lent a helping hand: a few days before the festival the inhabitants were usually invited by public announcement to decorate their houses with flags. The editors of newspapers supportive of the festival, and sometimes their readers as well, would then keep a watchful eye on whether the public would heed these calls.[144] As early as 1874, the *Augsburger Neueste Nachrichten* reported that most houses had been richly decorated for the festive occasion.[145] Three years later, the same newspaper went into much greater detail: 'Many flags were on display on the eve of the festival, and when dawn broke most of the remaining landlords could be seen decorating their houses, so that in the end all of the town's roads, with very few exceptions, were covered in German and Bavarian flags.'[146] And when Sedan Day's fortunes began to wane in the 1890s, the preoccupation with festive decorations became even more marked:

> It would go too far if we tried to name everyone who decorated their house in a particularly beautiful way. Even so, it was above all the shopkeepers who

distinguished themselves on this occasion. We would like to mention in particular the decorations we saw at Kröll and Nill, Brothers Guggenheimer,
Spanier, Passage Untermayer, and so forth. Of the private houses, we would
like to mention, apart from the buildings in the Maximilianstrasse, the houses
in the *langen und alten Gassen, dem oberen, mittleren und unteren Kreuz, dem
Hunoldsgraben, Philippine Welserstrasse*, etc.[147]

In Ludwigshafen in 1876, meanwhile, a liberal editorial identified discrep-
ancies in the density of the decorations between the town's central part,
where the established middle classes prevailed, and the *Hemshof* in the north,
the location of the BASF and its workforce:

> When it comes to the illumination of buildings, the citizens of the centre
> could have made a bigger effort, but even here we need to single out the
> house of Mr. W. Hoffmann near the market, which was very nicely illumi-
> nated. By contrast, many landlords at the *Hemshof* endeavoured to dignify the
> festive experience through the use of fireworks, illuminations, emblems, etc.
> But it was the direction of the BASF that made the biggest effort of all.[148]

In 1890, the streets with the most elaborately decorated shop-windows were
named, as were the owners of the shops. Special mention was afforded to
'nursery von Schmitts in the Kaiser-Wilhelmstrasse.' Of the shops along the
Bismarckstrasse, those of 'milliner Misses Spatz,' 'merchant Georg Coblenz,'
'barber Geiss' and 'modiste Graf' were especially mentioned.[149]

In Ulm meanwhile, the liberal *Schnellpost* tried to teach the public in the
proper use of national symbols. In 1878, one of its commentators complained that many people had pegged out their national flags the wrong way
round, with the red at the top rather than at the bottom of the flag. Such
'thoughtlessness would be inconceivable' at France's national holiday, where
even 'in the remotest village' people would know how to peg out the national
flag.[150] But they also extended praise for the lengths to which some private
landlords had gone in decorating their houses in honour of Sedan. 'The
town's streets were covered in flags, many shop-windows were decorated,
and the streets were filled with crowds endowed with a festive spirit.'[151] On
the occasion of the 1886 celebrations, too, the fact that 'the public and many
private buildings had been decorated with flags' was deemed worth men-
tioning.[152] Again in 1887: 'Goldsmith Göbel has exhibited a large painting of
the Battle of Sedan in his shop window, adorned with a wreath of flowers
by nurserymen (Kunstgaertner) Wolfenter and Schults.'[153]

★ ★ ★

The liberal middle classes' quest for recognition, of which the preoccupation with festive decorations provide a particularly colourful manifestation, was born out of the tension and uncertainty they experienced in a society they wished to remake in their own image. During Sedan Day this liberal impatience translated into attempts to nationalize a town's significant places, ranging from schools over churches to town squares and shop windows, at least for a day once every year. But this was not a struggle between the champions of nationhood and those who were indifferent or outrightly hostile to the national order. The critics of Sedan Day challenged the integral nationalist conceptions to which many liberals subscribed, and which went hand in hand with a homogenizing approach to urban space. In seeking to delimit a town's official involvement in the celebrations, or in refusing to turn a church into an active component of the festive procedures, the sceptics in effect contributed to the elaboration of alternative rhythms of communal life. In doing so, they engaged with the national frame of reference, while at the same contributing to the weaving of the fabric of nationhood. In this way, antagonism and the sense of non-recognition acted as engines for the reshaping of both local and national communities. This dialectic of antagonism and accommodation, a drama in which liberal nationalists and ultramontane Catholics were the protagonists, will come into even sharper relief in the subsequent chapter, which looks at Corpus Christi processions.

7

Corpus Christi

Every true Catholic will happily take part in this public demonstration of his faith, in accordance with the divine Redeemer's monition: 'Whoever acknowledges me before men, I will also acknowledge him before my Father in heaven.' Thus come along, you Catholic youth, you Catholic men, women and virgins, come along in your droves to accompany the holiest of Sacraments.

Neue Augsburger Zeitung (Catholic), 1872.[1]

On Thursday, 31 May Ludwigshafen's Catholic parish community celebrates Corpus Christi in a public procession that will proceed along the streets of our town. We trust that all of our inhabitants will follow this Catholic cult with the consideration and respect that we owe one another in exercising our religious duty.

Katholischer Fabrikrat Ludwigshafen am Rhein, 1888[2]

Yesterday the Catholic parish church celebrated the most glorious of religious festivals, Corpus Christi, in the traditional way. Attendance at the procession was extremely high.

Ulmer Volksbote (1900)[3]

On a sunny day in June 1897, the Augsburg councillors Kusterer, Doll, and Martin joined the town's main Corpus Christi procession. Given that the three men represented the Centre Party in Augsburg's liberal-dominated city council, their taking part in this most important of Catholic religious feasts was by no means exceptional, as each year thousands of inhabitants either joined the Corpus Christi procession or lined the streets as bystanders. In the local press, both liberal and Catholic newspapers covered the event in the usual way, noting, among other things, that the town's garrisoned military had lined the route of the procession, or that 'many houses' had been decorated 'with birch branches, wreaths, and images.'

They also mentioned, without further ado (and without naming names), that 'three councillors' had joined the procession. None of the newspapers covering the event reported that anything extraordinary, let alone improper, had happened before, during, or immediately after the procession.[4]

As we learn from the controversy that ensued, however, what was unusual was the three Catholic councillors' choice of dress: that they had decided to participate in the procession wearing their office holders' livery, the so-called *Amtstracht*, apparently marked a departure from established custom. At the council's next meeting, the three men were thus promptly reminded by Chairman Stolz that by wearing their councillors' livery at a religious festival, they had violated the dress code that was adopted in the late 1860s for such occasions. A Catholic and the editor-in-chief of the liberal *Augsburger Abendzeitung*, Stolz insisted that any councillor attending an event devoted to a single denominational group did so in an entirely private capacity, and from hence arose the need for councillors to wear normal dress rather than official garb. Aware that he was representing the view of the liberal majority, Stolz concluded by asking the three Centre Party members either to play by the rules henceforth or file a motion in favour of changing them.[5]

Augsburg's leading Catholic voices responded swiftly to what they perceived as yet another demonstration of liberal arrogance and insensitivity toward the town's largest denominational community. The editors of the *Neue Augsburger Zeitung* condemned the 'schoolboy-like dressing down' of the three Catholic councillors in a public meeting, describing the behaviour of 'Stolz and his backers' as 'intolerant' and 'ruthless, a 'brutal violation' of the religious feelings of Augsburg's entire Catholic population. Whereas liberal councillors routinely wore their livery at the festivals of local veterans associations or of the firefighters, as well as on Sedan Day, they refused to dispatch an official representation when the 'Catholic bishop' invited them to take part in the Corpus Christi procession.[6]

The incident appears to confirm the view that Germany in the late nineteenth century was split into two separate emotional communities, with liberal nationalists on one side and ultramontane Catholics (and conservative Protestants) on the other. There is no doubt that divisions existed, or that Catholic milieu managers were active in each of the three towns. For example, from the 1850s some of Augsburg's Catholic clergymen sought to ensure that the children of mixed marriages were brought up as

Catholics. The bishop instructed the city's parish priests to make their permission of marriage contingent on parents' consent 'to educate all their
children in the Catholic faith.' Up to the 1880s, couples intending to marry
were asked to make a vow to that effect.[7] Local priests were asked to report
parents living in mixed marriages who intended to bring up their children
as Protestants. This was more than a play of words. Thus, a Protestant father,
who in 1883 wanted to send his seven-year-old daughter to a Protestant
school, was prevented from doing so by the bishop because he and his former wife (a Catholic) had committed themselves to bringing up their
daughter a Catholic.[8] In 1889 moreover, the bishop asked Augsburg's parish
priests to create registers detailing mixed marriages conducted in the period
from 1878 to 1887.[9]

But intentions are not the same as outcomes. What is commonly
described as confessional milieus represented work in progress, more project than *fait accompli*.[10] In and of itself, for example, the preoccupation with
mixed marriages is neither a sign of an integrated milieu, nor does it
necessarily point to deep-seated confessional antagonism. In fact, one
might just as plausibly argue that efforts to prevent Catholics from mar-
rying non-Catholics indicate the relative fluidity of social associations
during this period. Admittedly, standing at roughly five per cent during
the imperial period, intermarriage rates between Catholics and Protestants
were modest indeed.[11] Yet these aggregate rates reflect above all existing
opportunities: throughout the nineteenth century most Germans lived
in small municipalities that were relatively homogenous in confessional
terms. Low aggregate intermarriage rates should therefore not be taken
too readily as evidence for confessional segregation. In middle-sized
towns with denominationally mixed populations, marriages between
Catholics and Protestants were quite common: the rate stood at around
25 per cent on average in Ulm, 38 per cent in Ludwigshafen, and between
10 and 15 per cent (depending on the urban parish in question) in
Augsburg.[12]

The Corpus Christi processions can help put this fluidity of religious life
into sharper relief. Catholics who participated in them celebrated the tangible existence of the holy in the world, manifested in a particular chronology and through a series of sacred objects and places, which, in addition to
churches, included hosts and altars. The Catholic processions followed a
specific itinerary and produced a particular fusion of time and space.
Consciously or not, those who processed on Corpus Christi performed a

particular rhythm of life. For the self-appointed apostles of progress, on the other hand, the schedules of modern progress (symbolized, for instance, by the urban tramway) were worthy objects of protection. The rhythm of the processions was thus markedly distinct from the nationalist temporality embodied by the Sedan parades. Yet while the rituals performed respectively on Sedan Day and Corpus Christi differed, they proved not incommensurate. What the Corpus Christi processions reveal is that contestation was conducive to staying engaged as members of distinctive yet closely related emotional communities. Beneath the rhetorical battles characterizing the German culture war, there hence emerged a quest for a shared rhythm of life. Its main inspirations were the languages of nationalism and of Christianity.

Genesis

Established in 1264 by papal decree, by the fourteenth century the processions had become a 'universal feast.' Conducted in a variety of ways, their central purpose was to venerate the Holy Sacrament.[13] Taking place ten days after Pentecost, the Feast of Corpus Christi represents the liturgical enactment of the doctrine of transubstantiation – the view, that is, that when the bread and wine are consecrated in the Eucharist, they cease to be bread and wine and become instead the body and blood of Christ, a transformation made possible by the Holy Spirit. Its embodiment is the consecrated Host carried in procession by a representative of the church.[14] In the wake of the Reformation, the processions turned into public dramatizations of one of the central doctrinal differences between Roman Catholicism and Reformed Protestantism.[15] The processions served as journeys to mark out and sacralize the territory of communities. As Rubin has noted: 'In Germany the custom of beating the boundaries of a village was particularly common, and the procession with the host stopped at numerous important places—trees, mills, crosses, bridges—and blessed them in turn,' creating 'ritual occasions in secular spaces of towns and villages.'[16] In mixed confessional regions and towns, the processions could become 'occasions for violent confrontation.'[17]

The enthusiasm the Corpus Christi processions prompted among Catholic lay folk was seldom shared by the clergy and those who served under its auspices. When the Council of Trent (1545–1563) put the mass at the centre of a reformed Catholic liturgy, this elevated the office of the priest. Yet like any other ritual carried out with such frequency, mass threatened to grow into a routine. Clerical complaints about the lay folk attending the ceremony in a spirit of mere obedience became common. Many believers began to show a preference for liturgical forms that allowed them to play a part in sacramental acts.[18] Public processions fulfilled this need for participation and status recognition. Even after the Catholic Reformation had passed its violent peak, the Corpus Christi processions retained a central role in communicating the doctrinal and liturgical differences between Protestants and Catholics. With the formation of nation-states in the nineteenth century, moreover, the processions were frequently drawn into the 'lengthy and unusually intense conflict over public space.'[19]

In the second half of the nineteenth century (and particularly after unification) Germany experienced a proliferation of Corpus Christi processions. Many existing processions grew considerably in size. Moreover, Catholic communities that had conducted the processions inside the church until quite recently—including those of Ulm (1853), Ludwigshafen am Rhein (1881), or Karlsruhe (1896)—requested permission to hold them under the open sky.[20] Yet, as a survey conducted by the Baden state authorities in 1904 shows—they sought to ascertain if the interruption of public transport was a common occurrence during the processions—the picture remained multi-faceted. Of the eight municipalities that responded to the survey, three (Darmstadt, Heidelberg, and Stuttgart, all mainly Protestant) reported that the feast of Corpus Christi was conducted inside the town's Catholic churches; two (predominantly Catholic Freiburg im Breisgau and Mainz) informed that the tramway traffic was suspended for a few hours during those cities' large public processions; Strasbourg small procession caused no disruption to the public's free circulation, while in Mannheim (where the Protestant majority was moderate) city representatives complained about the regular interruption of commercial traffic during the event; finally, in Frankfurt am Main (where Catholics supplied little more than a fifth of the urban population) the Corpus Christi procession was confined to the cathedral square.[21]

For pious Catholics the Corpus Christi processions offered an opportunity literally to preach the right doctrine (transubstantiation) and way of life (a demonstrative and emotional religiosity that culminated in public rituals) to those of other faiths. Moreover, at a time when established forms of association had come under threat—most clearly in the abolition of the guilds around the middle of the nineteenth century—they continued to uphold a corporatist ideal of society, one in which clergy and lay folk, men and women, school children and guilds, as well as the various secular and religious associations constituting the procession each occupied a separate place: not as anonymous parts of an abstract society, but as components of an integrated and tangible social body. In a cultural climate in which the remaking of established spatial arrangements was habitually praised, the processions maintained the ideal of society as a well-ordered place.[22]

If the processions offered a means to preach to members of competing faiths, they were also attempts to sacralize public space. Those who broke the rules provoked harsh reactions. On the Catholic side, this could take the form of reprimands directed at bystanders who failed to take off their hats as the Host was passing, or of expressions of outrage prompted by liberal refusals to cease all public transport while the procession was in progress. Meanwhile, for the more fervent exponents of liberal nationalism, the very sight of a Corpus Christi procession could evoke a longing for a purified public space, one in which goods and people could circulate freely. This purifying urge could be triggered, for instance, by the sight of a procession expanding beyond its pre-allocated route. After all, in contrast to the Sedan parades, which were often moved to the weekend when 2 September fell on a workday, Corpus Christi processions followed a strictly religious temporality. That they would not succumb to the rhythm of the modern factory was part of their very *raison d'être*.

This contrast became especially tangible whenever the processions brought the tramway to a temporary halt, which for some liberal nationalists was the closest thing to constituting a sacrilegious act. The tramway was seen as one of the embodiments of progress. From the mid-1890s, Ludwigshafen's residents could expect a tramway every six minutes.[23] When the 1884 procession in Augsburg necessitated a disruption of the normal tramway traffic for approximately two hours, the executive of the Augsburg Tramway Company announced the alternative timetable in the local papers: 'During tomorrow's Corpus Christi procession the routes Frauentor-Perlach and Perlach-St. Ulrich will be suspended. The line Königsplatz-Göggingen will be running again normally from 7.30. The first carriages from Göggingen will be available from 7 a.m. All other lines will be running normally.'[24]

Ulm witnessed its first Corpus Christi procession under the open sky in 1853. Previously, the procession had been conducted inside the church. It

was not until the mid-1880s, however, that the annual Corpus Christi procession began to capture the attention of newspaper editors, the local
authorities and the public at large. In 1885, one of the local newspapers
noted that the procession had reached a considerable size and that Ulm was
now 'Württemberg's second largest Catholic community after Stuttgart.'[25]
Between its initiation in 1853 and the turn of the century, Ulm's Corpus
Christi procession had indeed expanded year on year, reflecting the fact that
its Catholic population had increased from 1500 to over 11,000 during that
period, or from less than 20 per cent to about 26 per cent of the town's
population.[26]

In terms of arrangements and organization, the Corpus Christi procession conducted in Ulm in 1899 is rather typical of events of its kind in
Germany at the time.[27] After an early-morning mass at 6 a.m. and a high
mass at 7 a.m., the procession started at 8 a.m. and lasted for about two-and-
a-half hours. Certain groups, including the members of the Catholic Church
and School Council, as well as the Catholic civil servants, were provided
with kneeling benches, which were placed before the altars that punctuated
the route of the procession. The procession itself was arranged in the following order:

1. Boys of the elementary school.
2. Girls of the elementary school.
3. Pupils of the secondary school (lower grades).
4. One detachment of musicians.
5. Associations of apprentices and candidates for catechumen with flag.
6. Association of journeymen and other youth with flag.
7. Pupils of the secondary school (higher grades).
8. Salesmen's Association *Lätitia*.
9. Military.
10. One detachment of musicians.
11. Men with flag.
12. Church choir with flag.
13. Members of the supervisory school authority.
14. Civil servants and military personnel.
15. Girls dressed in white, with symbols and flowers.
16. The Sanctum under the Traghimmel with the clergy; choir flags.
17. On either side of the Sanctum: the Catholic Church Council.

18. Order of Merciful Sisters [Barmherzige Schwestern] with flags.

19. Virgins, if possible dressed in white and carrying wreaths, candles, and flags.

20. One detachment of musicians.

21. Women with flag.

Ludwigshafen's Catholics had to wait more than 20 years after the city's foundation before they could participate in an open-air Corpus Christi procession. At least initially, clerical provision could not keep up with the rapid growth of the urban population, and Protestants and Catholics had to hold their services in the same church.[28] Yet as early as 1855, when there were 1061 Protestants and 1030 Catholics in a total population of 2290, several citizens sent a plea to the Bavarian king asking that the two Christian denominations each be provided with its own parish church.[29] After this wish had been granted (in the 1860s both Catholics and Protestants formed their own parishes and moved into separate churches, selling the original church building to the Jewish community, who converted it into a synagogue, which was opened in 1865), the Catholic parishioners initially continued to hold their Corpus Christi procession inside the church.[30] This was still the case in the 1870s, by which point Ludwigshafen's Catholic community comprised more than 6000 members. It was not until 16 June 1881 that Ludwigshafen witnessed its first Corpus Christi procession under open sky.[31]

In Augsburg, meanwhile, with its tradition of parity between the two Christian confessions, religious festivals had long been an integral part of urban culture, retaining their significance throughout the nineteenth century.[32] Corpus Christi processions had been carried out there for centuries, long before Augsburg became part of Bavaria, where the processions enjoyed quasi-official status. The town's Protestant inhabitants had lost their former demographic predominance in the eighteenth century. By 1880, Catholics made up approximately 70 per cent of the town's population. Although Augsburg's nineteenth-century transformation into one of the centres of German industry affected many areas of religious life, it did not undermine the pivotal place of religion in the lives of most inhabitants. The annual Corpus Christi processions, in particular, continued to act as a potent reminder of the sheer strength of ultramontane Catholicism in the city. The main procession constituted the largest and most spectacular event of the

Figure 16. Main Corpus Christi procession in Augsburg, circa 1870.
© Stadtarchiv Augsburg.

year, attracting thousands of participants throughout the period of the
Second Empire.[33]

Protagonists, participants, and absentees

Attracting thousands of active participants and thousands more as spectators,
the processions served as powerful vehicles of Catholic self-assertion. So
who acted as their protagonists, who attended them, in what capacity, and
who abstained?

In terms of their constitution, the processions were both top-down and bottom-up affairs. The church hierarchy, and above all the bishops, could play a central role, as did the editorials of various ultramontane newspapers. Just as significant were the parishioners themselves, who sometimes demanded that processions be held come what may, putting considerable pressure on local parish priests keen to maintain good relations with the authorities.

If Ludwigshafen is anything to go by, the influence of the church hierarchy seems to have been stronger where the Corpus Christi processions were barely established. Thus, in 1857, at a time when the town had little more than a thousand Catholic residents, the bishopric in Speyer for the first time raised the issue with Expositus Stock, the cleric then responsible for the town's Catholics. The bishopric left no doubt that it expected Stock to take the required steps so that, in the foreseeable future, Ludwigshafen could carry out its first Corpus Christi processions 'on the streets of the town.' As the priest was being reminded in 1857, the staging of open processions had been requested by papal decree in 1838.[34] In 1876, the bishopric asked Stock's successor, parish priest Hofherr, for an update on the situation: 'The Reverend is kindly requested to send us a report on whether, and if so, how, the magnificent procession was conducted in your parish this year.'[35] His reply was that, as in the past, the procession had been conducted inside the church, and that 'four altars have been erected and decorated in the most dignified fashion.'[36]

Hofherr's response only prompted further investigations by the bishop, along with a fresh set of questions: Why did he believe it impossible to conduct the Corpus Christi procession outside the church, as was established practice 'almost everywhere else.'[37] Hofherr offered two reasons why he thought a public Corpus Christi procession was currently not feasible in Ludwigshafen. The first had to do with a lack of the required equipment. There was, he explained, a 'complete lack of flags and standards' on the part of the corporations that would join the procession. As well as lacking a 'capable choir,' his own parish church only owned 'two ungainly flags and standards.' If the requested procession were to be conducted at present, Ludwigshafen's parish priest therefore concluded, 'it would leave an altogether miserable impression;' and given the scarcity of funds in his own parish, it was unlikely that things were to improve in the near future.[38]

Hofherr also identified a number of attitude problems affecting the would-be processants, and here his list of deficiencies was particularly long. There was very little prospect, he noted, of getting together 'thirty to forty men who would not feel ashamed to head the procession carrying lit candles.' Not all members of the Catholic *Fabrikrat*, and not a single of the town's Catholic civil servants—none of whom had attended the bishop's 1874 visit to Ludwigshafen—had joined the last Corpus Christi procession that was held inside the church. Meanwhile, the bulk of Ludwigshafen's ordinary Catholics, particularly the factory workers, Hofherr portrayed as being 'under the spell of their liberal and anticlerical superiors.' He concluded his assessment by stressing that his guiding concern was to protect the dignity of the Eucharist in an environment in which levels of ignorance, derision, and potential intimidation were still high, adding that 'a sizeable contingent of deriders may well recruit itself from amongst our own parish.'[39]

The bishopric in Speyer responded within days.[40] Whilst recognizing the 'difficulties related to the introduction of a public Corpus Christi procession in Ludwigshafen,' Hofherr's superiors insisted that 'a combination of perseverance and cunningness' had enabled parish priests elsewhere to overcome problems very similar to the ones he had just described. The bishopric refrained from decreeing that a Corpus Christi procession be held in Ludwigshafen in the following year. Yet it nevertheless demanded that Hofherr intensify his efforts, so that a procession could be carried out 'as soon as possible.'[41] After a controversy lasting for more than two weeks and involving the Catholic parish priest, the town's mayor, the bishop of Speyer, the municipal authorities, the district government, and even the Bavarian Ministry of the Interior, the procession eventually saw the light of day on 16 June 1881.[42] From its inception, the event attracted substantial numbers of people, both active participants and onlookers, and the indications are that they were conducted in an orderly fashion. The following report, dating from 1892, is quite typical: 'Attendance among the members of the Catholic parish churches of the town's southern and northern districts was invariably high. In the streets along which the procession was passing, numerous houses were decorated with flags and flowers. Magnificent altars were placed in front of four houses. A large watched the procession with apparent curiosity.'[43]

When Ulm's first Corpus Christi procession under the open sky was held in 1853, its Catholic residents numbered 4200, amounting to one-fifth of the town's total population. Why did Ulm's Catholics have to wait until 1853 for the first procession of this kind to see the light of day? It was certainly not for a lack of initiative on the part of Württemberg's Catholic authorities. Among the main inhibiting factors, it seems, was the rudimentary nature of the existing clerical infrastructure in Ulm. In 1822, representatives of Ulm's Catholic community reported to the district government that what had prevented an open procession to date was not a shortage of good will on their part. Nor had they experienced any kind of intimidation at the hands of the Protestant majority. On the contrary, Ulm's confessional relations were described as marked by 'mutual tolerance.'[44] The main problem, rather, was insufficient manpower. In particular, the Catholic parish church lacked personnel capable of maintaining public order. This, the authors of the report noted, was 'the only reason' why the procession was still conducted inside the church.[45]

The local priests did not force the issue either. Although the records on the role of the clerical leaders are not as dense as they are for Ludwigshafen am Rhein or Augsburg, what there is suggests that Ulm's parish clergy felt lukewarm about staging a large Corpus Christi procession. As late as 1874, by which time the open procession had become common practice, parish priest Dischinger, in a report to the district government, offered a sober assessment of the Corpus Christi procession in Ulm. Following on from a description of the route of the annual procession, which the authorities had asked him to provide, Dischinger painted a very blunt picture of how the event affected his work as a priest. Not only did he portray the processions as unpredictable affairs whose potential for causing damage to social relations was considerable. He also left little doubt that they owed their existence to popular rather than middle-class demands. To cite the relevant passage in its entirety:

> The said procession sets off from the Wengenkirche and proceeds towards the Gögglinger Strasse, then covers a small distance outside the town that stretches from the Gögglinger Thor to the Neuen Thor, before returning to the Catholic church via the Wengengasse. The procession attracts a large number of curious onlookers; the devotion of the parish members would be greater if the procession was held inside the church; the genteel Catholics tend to abstain. If the procession was not well-established here, then the under-signed would not wish to introduce it. The clergy must always be in fear that some kind of spectacle might ensue. [46]

The popularity of Ulm's Corpus Christi procession—among parishioners above all, but also among the large crowds of onlookers—did not prevent criticism from the more orthodox portions of its proponents. Such criticism became more frequent, it seems, from the 1890s, when political Catholicism was gathering momentum in Württemberg. The founding of the ultramontane *Ulmer Volksbote* in 1897 bears testimony to this development. In 1903, for instance, the said newspaper noted that participation in the procession, especially by men, had been 'as high as never before', even a few civil servants had followed the Eucharist. While the high attendance among military personnel was equally praised, the 'entire officer corps' had 'distinguished itself by its absence.'[47]

In 1904 the officer corps was once more held up as a negative example: 'Several civil servants and the members of the consistory followed behind the Sanctum; but, as far as we are aware, the officer corps has again been absent this year. The Catholic associations had all taken part, with the Catholic Workers' Association for the first time carrying its magnificent new flag.'[48] In 1905, while 'the majority of Catholic inhabitants' had come out to 'demonstrate publicly their allegiance to the Catholic Church,' not a single officer had been seen. 'Are we to assume that the Catholic officer regards public worship as something dishonourable, even though we know that in other garrisons these gentlemen provide a virtuous example in this respect?'[49] While Catholics could not be forced to attend the processions, and although some might have had legitimate grounds for staying at home, the Corpus Christi procession nevertheless represented 'a holy exercise that should not be missed without good reason,' not even, the editors added sarcastically, 'by the upper ten-thousand.'[50] Just a few days before the 1907 procession, the *Ulmer Volksbote* offered its sharpest and most instructive condemnation of middle-class absenteeism:

> There are Catholics who fulfill their duty as Christians both at home and in the church. But when they are to express their faith openly and freely before the world, they get frightened and refuse to take part in an act designed to venerate God. And whilst they endeavour to lead good Christian lives as individuals, they don't bring it over themselves to express their Christian values by taking part in the Corpus Christi procession. 'I could be seen,' goes a frequently-heard comment, 'possibly even by one of my superiors at work,' who is so 'educated' and 'sophisticated' that he is bound to sneer at 'medieval' religious ceremonies which are venerated only by the most 'ordinary of people.' Yes, we have become the subject of ridicule; some have even charged us of backwardness. Hence what prevents many Christians, including those who consider themselves educated, from demonstrating their Catholic faith in public, is their cowardly fear of other humans.[51]

Meanwhile, in Augsburg, the Corpus Christi processions occupied a more self-evident position. This is evident, for instance, in the dynamics and proce-

dures surrounding the annual invitation dispatched to municipal civil servants. For much of the nineteenth century, the Bavarian district government
of Swabia (which was based in Augsburg) acted as host of the annual Corpus
Christi procession. Throughout the 1830s, for example, its president, Baron
von Lerchenfeld, who himself regularly took part in the procession, invited
all members of the magistrate, irrespective of their denomination, to 'join
the royal government' in attending the procession 'wearing either gala uniform or festive dress.'[52]

This pattern of invitation was maintained throughout the 1840s and
1850s, only to be modified in 1860. From that point on, the district government's letter of invitation was exclusively addressed to the Catholic
members of the magistrate. To cite from the invitation letter of 2 June
1860:'Next Thursday, on the 7th of this month, the feast of Corpus Christi
will be celebrated in the usual way. The civil authorities of the district
capital of Augsburg—insofar as they are members of the Catholic religion—are herewith invited to attend the church service in the Cathedral,
which begins at 7 a.m.'[53] The same applies to the invitation circulars that
the city mayor sent to all the magistrates, councillors, and civil servants.
Between 1820 and 1846, the members of the municipal council had been
invited *in corpore* to attend the religious ceremony in the Cathedral and
the subsequent procession. However, in 1859 the mayor's circular for the
first time specifically referred to the 'municipal councillors of Catholic
religion'.[54] Just a few years later, in 1865, Ludwig Fischer addressed his
invitation 'especially to the Catholic sections' of the magistrate, municipal
council, social welfare officers, and district heads, while from 1867 onwards
he simply addressed it to the 'Catholic members' of the various municipal
bodies.[55]

Heightened concern with confessional membership was to be a first step
towards the local authorities' outright detachment from the processions. It
was Augsburg's magistrate that jumped ship first. In 1870, for the first time
magistrate and council no longer attended the church service on Corpus
Christi, let alone the subsequent procession. In his reply to the district government, Mayor Fischer let it be known that in October of the previous
year the Catholic members of the magistrate and council had decided to
cease the practice of attending religious processions in an official capacity.[56]
Two days later the district government replied in a short, angry note, returning to Fischer the copy of the minutes he had sent in support of his declaration.[57] The following year Fischer provided a more comprehensive justification
for the authorities' stance on the Corpus Christi procession:

It has become notorious that the clerics in charge of organizing the feast of
Corpus Christi split from the established Catholic Church and joined the
neo-Catholic faction of the infallibilists; and it is equally notorious that to this
day no member of the magistrate or municipal council has converted to neo-
Catholicism. If the <u>Catholic</u> members of these two municipal bodies therefore . . . feel unable to attend the Corpus Christi procession, this is because,
given the confessional orientation of the clerics in charge, this procession can
no longer be regarded as a religious festival of the <u>Catholic</u> church.[58]

From 1873 onwards the state authorities emulated the practice set by
Augsburg's magistrate and council.[59] Whereas the processions themselves
were protected by Bavarian law and could therefore not be banned, the
liberal-dominated administration in Munich denied them the extent of
recognition they had once enjoyed. Catholic state officials no longer
joined the procession. Henceforth, those who wished to take part would
do so as private individuals. In 1875 even the King abandoned his habit of
marching in the procession. In Augsburg itself, municipal and state buildings were no longer decorated with flags on Corpus Christi (in visible
contrast to Sedan Day). What remained largely unaltered was the presence
of the garrisoned military, which continued to line the procession, thereby
making a crucial contribution to the maintenance of public safety during
the event.[60]

One unintended consequence of the authorities' new stance on the
Corpus Christi procession was to heighten their appeal with the Catholic
public. In his 1872 report to the district government, for example, Mayor
Fischer conceded that the processions had proved highly popular. In fact,
Augsburg's 'clerical camp' now saw them as 'successful demonstrations in
defence of a religion under threat.'[61] For once, the town's Catholic press
concurred with the mayor. In many an editorial, official indifference was
juxtaposed with the annual procession's evident capacity to capture the emotions of ordinary Catholics. Thus, in 1872, after lamenting the lack of any
official representation at the procession, the town's leading ultramontane
daily concluded confidently: 'This was in stark contrast to the massive participation on the part of the Catholic inhabitants, who followed the procession in much larger numbers than had been the case in previous years.'[62] Or
as the *Augsburger Postzeitung* rejoiced in 1871: 'Most houses along the route
were decorated with images, wreaths, flowers, and green branches. The military stood sentinel at the altars and a 24-men-strong guard of honour, led by
an officer, accompanied the canopy.'[63]

The emphasis throughout the 1870s was on the processions as powerful demonstrations of Catholic piety and solidarity. Statements like 'The procession reached an extension as never before,'[64] 'The Catholic population's attendance at the procession was enormous and is growing year by year,'[65] or 'A several-thousand-strong crowd lined the route of the procession,' characterize this tendency. Rather than complaining that the processional route had been too short to accommodate the participating crowd, Catholic commentators put it on record, year after year, that 'participation was so extraordinary and the length of the procession so immense that when its forefront arrived back at the *Fronhof* [the large square that bordered onto the Cathedral] the men that built its tail were only about to leave the Cathedral.'[66]

At the same time, the Catholic public was constantly reminded that there was a crucial difference between taking part in a procession and watching it pass from the sidelines.[67] In the meetings of Catholic men's associations, for example, mere attendance was regularly condemned.[68] The following reprimand, formulated during a meeting of the *Christlicher Arbeiterverein*, offers a typical example: 'Members Beh and Schmöger expressed their disapproval with fellow members who had either not been seen at the Corpus Christi procession or only attended it as spectators. They also lamented the fact that, of those who joined the procession, some had failed to say the prayers in a loud voice.'[69] Some observers, such as the *Neue Augsburger Zeitung*, went beyond condemnation, stressing that Jesus had left no doubt that those who would publicly acknowledge Him were guaranteed redemption. In this reading, the Corpus Christi processions offered an opportunity to access God through a concrete deed. As Augsburg's Catholics were called upon in an 1873 editorial:

> May the Catholic people use this day to avow its Redeemer, and to demonstrate that its faith is alive and well. Nobody will attempt to disturb the Catholic people in expressing its avowal. Make it your honour, you Catholic men, to follow your Redeemer through the streets, He who said: 'I am the way, the truth, and the life.' Accompany, in earnest dignity and without presumptuousness, undeterred by what others may think, say or do, the holy sacrament, which will be your comfort in the hour of your departure from this life, and which is the pledge to a better, eternal life![70]

By the 1890s the processions had not only managed to retain their popularity, but also regained some of the official endorsement they had enjoyed until the 1860s. In 1892, liberal newspaper editors reported of 'several members of the state and municipal civil service' that had been seen marching behind the Sanctum;[71] and in 1898 'a sizeable number of state officials,' plus the council members Kusterer, Martin, and Doll, had joined the procession.[72] In 1897 the *Neue Augsburger Zeitung* even offered its readers an exact head count: 22 state civil servants in uniform, so it claimed, had taken part;[73] and in 1909, the same newspaper expressed hope that the Corpus Christi procession had finally gained the recognition it deserved:

> A several-thousand-strong crowd lined the route of the procession. All those non-Catholics who have preserved for themselves a rest of objectivity cannot but feel respect for this powerful, imposing manifestation of Catholic faith and Catholic conviction; one is bound to feel moral joy, as well as a sense of cultural-historical fulfillment, at this demonstration of religious idealism by the common people.'[74]

Gaining permission

Even where a Corpus Christi procession became established practice, its annual realization was the result of a complex set of procedures and interactions. Above all, whoever wanted to hold a procession required permission from the local authorities, generating a dense correspondence involving both clerical and secular actors. As well as a legal requirement, the permission-granting process provided town governments with important information on a public mass ritual whose consequences remained unpredictable. Given that the processions tended to take place in or near a town's centre and often proceeded along busy roads, they posed a potential risk to both participants and spectators. Quite frequently, the growth of a Catholic community necessitated changes to an existing processional route, or the temporary suspension of public transport on particular roads. While the processions' annual rhythm was defined by Corpus Christi day, their spatial extension was the result of a complex process of negotiation.

From the point of view of the municipal authorities, proposed changes, particularly those necessitating an expansion to the original route, were highly problematic. By sending a procession down a street that had not been included in previous years, or by expanding the overall route, as well as putting pressure on local police contingents, those responsible increased the risk of unforeseeable incidents. By shutting down of public transport facilities, even if only temporarily, they risked being accused of undermining the liberal ideal of progress, defined as unhindered circulation of goods and people. For all the parties involved, the question of permissions therefore raised a number of sensitive issues. While the municipal authorities used them as a means to control the processions, their Catholic organizers took the manner in which their applications were handled as indicative of the status they enjoyed within the urban community.

Württemberg law dictated that the permission to hold a public procession had to be sought on an annual basis from the relevant local authorities. Thus each year, usually a few weeks before Corpus Christi, the representatives of Ulm's Catholic parish would submit a formal request to carry out the procession, along with a detailed specification of the route they were intending to use. The available records suggest that Ulm's Catholic parish priest never failed to seek permission from the city council. Nor do they contain evidence that the latter had ever denied it. In fact, over the years a certain routine seems to have developed in the interaction between Catholic parish priest and municipal authorities. In 1892, however, Ulm's Catholic parish deviated in one small respect from the usual application procedure. Unlike in previous years, the parish requested permission to use the established route not just for the current, but also for future processions. This seemingly minor alteration—the request for a permanent permission (*dauernde Genehmigung*)—did not escape the attention of the city council. In its recommendation to the council, the municipal police committee recommended that the request be turned down, a recommendation the council ultimately endorsed. In its response to the Catholic parish, the council emphasized that the permission would continue to be 'revocable' (*widerruflich*) on an annual basis. It also relayed the police committee's recommendation that the procession 'not experience any further expansion' in future years.[75]

In other words, while the permission to hold the procession was to remain revocable, its maximum spatial extension was to be defined once and for all. There is no doubt that this arrangement, which remained in place until the outbreak of the First World War, conveyed an important message, one that could be understood by all the parties involved: the Corpus Christi processions, reflecting as they did a spiritual need on the part of the Catholic population, were to be tolerated as a legitimate part of Ulm's religious life; at the same time, however, in Protestant Ulm a Catholic procession would continue to be regarded as an 'extraordinary' event and not, as the Catholic organizers would have preferred, an 'ordinary' occurrence. While the processions were clearly deemed legitimate, they were not to be elevated to an established custom in a town that was among the first to embrace the Reformation. In this way, the Protestant majority sought to maintain control over the configuration of urban space.

In Ludwigshafen, it was the introduction of the Corpus Christi procession itself that proved controversial. Conscious of the legal norms guiding religious processions in Bavaria, in May 1881 Father Hofherr informed the town's mayor, Georg Kutterer that his parish intended to hold a procession on the streets near the church at the beginning of June. Only a short while thereafter, the mayor acknowledged Catholics' constitutional right to hold a procession and even offered Hofherr police protection for the duration of the event.[76] Encouraged by Kutterer's response, at the next church service Father Hofherr invited his flock to take part in the Ludwigshafen's first Corpus Christi procession, prompting 'great joy' among those attending the service.[77] From that moment onward, things seemed to run their unproblematic course: on 22 May, the district government of Speyer was informed of the imminent procession;[78] and on 26 May Father Hofherr informed the city mayor that the financial means to erect four altars had been secured and that the procession would therefore proceed along the more extended of the two routes they had discussed in their previous meeting.[79]

But this was not the end of the story. Word of the Catholic parish's intention to carry out the first Corpus Christi procession outside the church appears to have spread immediately after Hofherr had informed the mayor of his intended choice of route. Before long, the liberal press took up the issue. The first newspaper to publish an article on the matter was the *Pfälzische Kurier*, a Ludwigshafen-based newspaper with a regional orientation and readership. In an article entitled 'The Feast of Corpus Christi in Ludwigshafen,' the editors pointed to the unpredictable nature of large public processions, expressing the hope that the city council would prohibit the procession 'in the interest of maintaining peaceful and harmonious relations between our town's different confessions.' To quote the editorial's central passage: 'We sincerely hope that one does not intend to stir up quarrels and frictions nor cause undue inhibitions in Ludwigshafen.'[80]

The council's liberal majority was quick in adopting the views of the *Pfälzischer Kurier*. On 3 June it rejected the Catholic parish's (legally sound) stance that a simple notification would suffice to meet the requirements for carrying out a public procession. Without conducting a proper assessment of the legal situation, the council then decided unanimously that the procession was to be conducted, 'as in previous years,' inside the Catholic Church. The councillors in attendance listed several reasons in justification of their conclusion:[81] that holding a procession on 'busy roads' would inevitably lead to 'traffic holdups' and that an open procession of the kind proposed by Hofherr carried the risk of 'disturbing the generally harmonious relations among the different denominations,' all the more since Ludwigshafen's population was 'largely unfamiliar with Catholic customs and ceremonies.' The councillors insisted, furthermore, that only 'customary processions and pilgrimages' (which they took to refer to processions that were established locally) were not subject to prior authorization by the state.[82]

On 4 June, Father Hofherr wrote to the bishop of Speyer, complaining bitterly that the liberal council was trying 'to impair the town's Catholics in what is their proper right' and asking the bishop for further instructions.[83] He emphasized, once more, the *Pfälzischer Kurier's* consequential intervention. Only a few days before its editors had urged the council to prohibit an open procession, Mayor Kutterer had confirmed to him 'the constitutional right of Catholics to carry out the procession.' It was only at its meeting of 3 June, Hofherr asserted, that the council had overturned the agreement he had reached with the mayor.[84] The bishop proved immune to liberal intimidation. After pointing out that there could be 'no doubt whatsoever' that Ludwigshafen's Catholic parish had Bavaria's law behind it, he issued the parish priest with the following directive:

> You will therefore galvanize at once the *Fabrikrat* into reminding the mayor's office of...the high ministerial decision...and proclaim, once again, that the procession will be held by virtue of this decision. You need to state, too, that the *Fabrikrat* expects that the Catholic community will receive the protection it is entitled to by law, and that the sole responsibility in the event of possible disturbances rests with the mayor and the municipal police authorities.[85]

When the procession was held for the first time in 1881, observers were agreed that the event had been 'extremely well attended,' while the *Pfälzischer Kurier* noted with a mixture of sarcasm and defiance: 'Today the Corpus Christi procession was conducted here in "customary" fashion for the first time. The council's appeal against the governmental resolution of 13 June will be dispatched today.'[86] Once introduced, however, the processions ceased to cause major friction either among the authorities or within the public at large. Even the national-liberal local newspapers generally struck a benevolent note in their reporting on the event. In 1884, for example, the liberal *Ludwigshafener Anzeiger* published a substantial article outlining the meaning and significance of the processions in the Catholic world. As it explained to its readers:

In all Catholic countries, the Corpus Christi procession represents a magnificent, elevating festival in which all the different estates take part. This is most
evident in medium and small communities, where the population takes personal charge of the decoration of the streets along which the main procession
proceeds. On the day of the procession, young and old are busy collecting
bunches of branches and flowers from the woods and from nearby gardens…It
is common in Catholic countries for worldly dignitaries, the high military
officers etc., to attend the processions, dressed in their finest garb, as its purpose is to reveal to the world the glory of the Catholic Church before the eyes
of those of other faiths.'[87]

Augsburg's liberal government accepted with gritted teeth that in Bavaria
the Corpus Christi processions—being classified as 'customary processions'
(herkömmliche Prozession)—did not require legal permission. This made it
impossible to prohibit a procession on the pretext, for example, that it entailed
the risk of traffic obstruction or of causing death by accident. Instead, the
city magistrate had to work with Catholic parishes to ensure that the processions was conducted in a safe and orderly fashion, even where this necessitated the temporary interruption of public transport. Traffic obstructions
were unquestionably an issue in a town whose main Corpus Christi procession attracted in excess of 10,000 people. In 1881, for example, tramway traffic
was suspended on request of the bishopric until 11 a.m. on the day of the
procession on two main lines in the centre of town (between the Königsplatz
and Perlach, and between St. Ulrich and Frauenthor). Given that the alternatives to outright suspension, such as channelling the procession through a
narrow road used by local craftsmen and traders, were even less palatable, this
decision was the result not of political weakness, but of a robust dialogue
between secular and Catholic authorities.[88]

Augsburg's government could take a stricter approach in relation to the
so-called Pfarrleichnamsprozessionen, processions that were confined to a particular urban parish. Taking place on the first Sunday following Corpus
Christi, they were classified as 'non-customary' processions that required
permission from the municipality in its capacity as the district's central
police authority.[89] As the parish processions were smaller than the main
annual procession, the city government sometimes allowed them to be conducted on roads with tramway traffic, provided the organizers had been able
to control things in previous years. Where disruptions occurred, the authorities took a more stringent line, or even threatened to withhold permission
for future years. Thus, when in 1888, during the procession at St. Georg,

tramway traffic had to be suspended on short notice—by the 1890s the procession in this working-class parish attracted close to 10,000 faithful—this led to increased surveillance in future years. On 10 June 1890, for example, the police officer on duty reported that the procession had hindered the traffic on the St. Georgstrasse. To this he added that 'several particularly demanding persons' have noisily lamented the continuation of tramway traffic during the procession. Upon reading the report, a representative of the city magistrate annotated in the margin: 'It will therefore only be right and proper, in view of these complaints, to ensure that this procession will no longer use roads frequented by the tramways!'[90]

In a few instances, applications to hold a *Pfarrfrohnleichamsprozession* were submitted late, as was the case at Heilig Kreuz in 1877. Two days before the day of the planned procession, Dean Dreer and Capitular Hoermann met up with Mayor Fischer to request a change of route in view of the building works currently carried out at Heilig Kreuz. Fischer denied permission, insisting that what the two men had proposed amounted to a different procession to the one that was normally set out from the church at Heilig Kreuz. Instead of the procession departing from the Cathedral as usual, Fischer requested that it be held inside Augsburg's largest church. Faced with this unpalatable choice, a day before the event Dreer and Hoermann came up with an alternative proposition. They kindly informed the mayor that while the church service would be held in the Cathedral for reasons of safety, the procession would set off, as in previous years, from the square in front of the church at Heilig Kreuz. A few days later the police officer on duty submitted his report, which read as follows: 'The procession that took place today between 11.15 and 12 noon, and which was attended by between 6000 and 7000 people, pilgrims and spectators included, proceeded from the church at Heilig Kreuz, via alte Gasse, across the Residenzhof, past the weisse Lamm, and then back to Heilig Kreuz. No disorders occurred. Signed: Ernst.'[91]

That Augsburg's liberals would have liked to ban the processions altogether, including the main ones that were protected by Bavarian law, is beyond doubt. Thus when in 1896 the magistrate of Karlsruhe reported that both the town's Protestant and liberal Catholic population supported a ban on the Corpus Christi procession, asking its Augsburg counterpart for guidance on the matter, Mayor Fischer annotated Karlsruhe's letter as follows: 'Would be very desirable—but is, alas, entirely impossible here!'[92]

In the case of the Corpus Christi procession organized by the parish of St. Georg, the magistrate enjoyed greater leverage. Even in this case, however, banning the procession was not an option given its popularity among the Catholic faithful. Thus in 1883, parish priest Koch literally begged the magistrate to agree to a change of route to minimize the risk of an accident. This was necessary, Koch maintained, because the procession at St. Georg had been growing continuously in size over the years: a total ban would therefore have 'detrimental consequences' for his work as a priest, given his flock's devotion to the event. In the end, the magistrate allowed the procession to go ahead.[93] How much weight both sides placed on semantics is revealed in the correspondence surrounding the 1889 procession at St. Georg. In his renewed request to the magistrate, Koch used the term *herkömmlich* ('customary') as he referred to the Corpus Christi procession at St. Georg. Having spotted Koch's new choice of terminology, the magistrate swiftly reminded him that the status of a *Pfarrfrohnleichnamsprozession* was different from the main procession:

> We should like to expressly point out that this procession, which you intend to conduct outside the church and its surroundings, does not represent a customary procession (*herkömmliche Prozession*) of the kind described in art. 4, paragraph II of the [state] law of 26 February 1850 concerning public meetings and associations, and that it will therefore continue to be subject to a special permission, to be requested annually from the magistrate.[94]

Unexpected incidents

Although the permission-granting process could be protracted, most processions proceeded more or less according to plan. But unexpected incidents did happen in each of the three towns, and this nearly always caused a stir. Even in Ludwigshafen, where the processions remained for the most part rather uneventful, disruptions occured. The most controversial incident was a temporary obstruction of the tramway carriages, which in Ludwigshafen were horse-drawn until 1902.[95] Thus, when in 1891 the Catholic parish priest asked the district government for permission to hold the procession along the usual route, the latter was well aware that this would necessitate a temporary suspension of the tramway traffic in the Bismarckstrasse. The municipal council was not pleased at the request, with a majority insisting that the envisioned suspension of a 'very busy road' had understandably prompted critique from various quarters. In the end, however, the council decided that ceasing tramway traffic for two hours was preferable to rerouting a relatively large public procession on short notice. While no explicit reasons were given in justification of this decision, it seems that the option of rerouting was rejected because it would have posed a new series of risks; and because it would have raised the procession's public profile even further. None of the councillors attending the relevant meeting suggested that banning the procession was an option.[96]

The following year the Catholic parish priest again approached the district government with the same request. Knowing the municipal authorities' reluctance to suspend tramway traffic on the Bismarckstrasse, the parish priest threatened that, should his request be turned down, he would not hesitate to appeal to the ministry in Munich. The district government's recommendation to the town authorities was to 'retain the established practice in the interest of confessional peace,' and because, should they withhold permission, it would have to endorse a certain appeal by the parish.[97] In the event, the town council saw no alternative to giving its consent, coupled with the renewed request that the parish use an alternative route in future.[98]

Other disruptions were of a more symbolic nature. The controversy over the wearing of the municipal garb, which in Augsburg had made its first appearance in 1897, resurfaced again in 1909. At a council meeting in June of that year, the Centre Party faction in the city council proposed that any member wishing to take part in the Corpus Christi procession by marching in his official livery should be allowed to do so. The proposal was defeated again by the liberal majority: four members from the Centre Party, two Social Democrats, and one National Liberal supported the motion, while 24 liberal councillors voted against it; and, once again, the liberal majority justified its stance by pointing to the symbolic meaning of the municipal uniform. The so-called *Amtstracht*, they contended, represented the municipality as a corporation, and since the council members belonged to different denominations, wearing the uniform at a religious festival that represented the beliefs of a single denomination went against the spirit of confessional parity.[99]

It was precisely this final point that Centre Party member Reifert sought to challenge. The real motivation behind the council majority's negative response he located in 'the liberal conviction that it was best to remain indifferent towards religious matters, and that there should be a separation between state and church.' According to the Centre Party members, however, one of the duties of public authorities was to 'cultivate the religious life of both Catholics and Protestants.' It would therefore only be right and proper if the government of a town whose population was 'nearly two-thirds Catholic' was to recognize the Corpus Christi procession.[100] Meanwhile, Councillor Seiwert, like Reifert a representative of the Centre Party, offered a detailed survey of how other Bavarian towns treated the processions. Of the 44 municipalities constituting his sample, 36 allowed councillors to attend the Corpus Christi procession in an official capacity, some of them *in corpora*; six councils took part in an unofficial capacity; and the councils of only two towns, Lindau and Neu-Ulm, had adopted the same approach as Augsburg. Seiwert concluded his exposition with a broadside against the city council's liberal majority:

> Go and take a survey: Augsburg's Catholics will in their overwhelming majority support our motion, and the town's Protestants won't feel offended by it. The Protestants have always been loyal towards us; they do not wish to see our rights diminished. I should point out that numerous Protestants and other non-Catholics decorate their houses especially for the occasion, a sign of kindness that we Catholics greatly appreciate. But how is it possible, I ask you, that the same Protestants whose behavior towards us and towards the Corpus Christi processions is characterized by kindness—how is it possible for them to feel offended at the sight of Catholic council members joining the procession wearing their uniform? Gentlemen, you may squirm as you like, but if our motion is turned down by you, then the Catholics of Augsburg would have reason to feel affronted, even mortified. ("hear, hear!" from the Center benches.)[101]

That an apparently minor occurrence could spark off a controversy is demonstrated by another incident that took place in Ulm in 1895. Its trigger was a small alteration to the official invitation to the annual Corpus Christi procession. Throughout the 1870s and 1880s, such invitations had followed an established pattern: a few days before the event, the organizing committee (consisting of the parish priest and other representatives of the Catholic community) would publish an advertisement on the feast's day of observance, complete with instructions concerning the practical arrangements and the route of the procession. But in 1895, the text of the advertisement deviated in one respect from the established norm: while in previous years the appeal for the decoration of the houses along the route of the procession was directed exclusively at the Catholic population, in 1895 the text explicitly referred to 'all inhabitants.'[102] To cite the key passage:

In expressing its gratitude to the dear inhabitants living along the route of the procession for the attitude they showed in the previous year, as well as for decorating their houses with flags and other items, the Catholic consistory trusts that it can expect the same friendly cooperation from all inhabitants again during this year's procession. The sole purpose of this announcement is to ensure that the feast [of Corpus Christi] can be conducted with the degree of reverence and dignity that it undoubtedly deserves.[103]

This small change of wording—the use of the phrase 'friendly' co-operation from *all* inhabitants' instead of the more common 'from the Catholic inhabitants'—was instantly picked up on by the local branch of the *Evangelischer Bund*. Founded in 1887, the association's membership comprised Ulm's Protestant-liberal establishment.[104]

Just a few days after the 1895 procession, one of the *Bund's* members claimed that 'several Protestant families' had expressed their 'indignation at the insolence' of the procession's organizing committee. Furthermore, as several of the Bund's members lamented during the same meeting, due to 'prolonged stopovers at the altars,' the procession had taken '90 minutes longer' to complete than in previous years. This had resulted in 'a severe obstruction of public traffic' near the railway station. As the chairman of Ulm's *Evangelischer Bund* described the incident to his colleagues during that meeting: 'several members of local trades (e.g., Scherrer the furniture carter and Eychmüller the foreman) had been held up for more than half an hour; access to the main station had been impossible; several pupils had had their hats knocked off their heads.'[105]

The behaviour of the police and of other personnel charged with maintaining public order also came in for considerable criticism. One of the constables preceding the procession was accused of having 'ordered the public to take off their hats;' and, just a few days before the event, the local police had asked several craftsmen to remove building material they had stored near the processional route.[106] Although less emotional in tone than the *Evangelischer Bund*, the Protestant parish council also criticized the advertisement issued by the Catholic consistory, insisting that the maintenance of 'confessional peace' required that the procession not experience any further expansion in future years. Meanwhile, the local police commission noted, rather soberly, that the growth of the procession in recent years reflected 'the substantial increase of the Catholic population' that Ulm had witnessed in previous decades. This was coupled with a recommendation that, in its future announcements, the Catholic consistory refrain from 'any activity that might be regarded as being directed at the Protestant population.'[107]

As another conflict over traffic obstructions in 1901 shows, however, liberals and ultramontane Catholics remained closely engaged in a dialogue. While the event seems to have raised few eyebrows in Ulm itself, it was picked up by the district government (which had apparently caught sight of an article published in the National Liberal *Schwäbischer Merkur*) a full week after the Corpus Christi procession. The article appeared in the said newspaper on 13 June 1901, nearly a week after the procession took place.[108] Responding to the district government's request for a report on the incident, Ulm's police authorities confirmed that traffic near the main station had been 'obstructed for 20 to 30 minutes' after the procession had come to a sudden halt. As a consequence, carts had been unable to travel to and from the main station, and several travellers had had to cut through the procession; yet since cutting through a religious procession was 'rather embarrassing,' only those 'in a great hurry' had mustered the courage to do so.[109] When the district government inquired if the 1901 incident was part of a general pattern, Ulm's police authorities replied that, in a way, it was: traffic obstructions had multiplied since 1893, when the municipal council had agreed to a rerouting that took the procession along the forecourt of the main station.[110]

The discussion that subsequently ensued within the town council is revealing. It shows that the councillors regarded the traffic obstructions that had occurred as less dramatic than the way they had been depicted by the National Liberal *Schwäbischer Merkur*, whose reports had swung the district government into action in the first place. Thus, Ulm's recently appointed mayor, the Protestant and liberal Heinrich Wagner, remarked that when, in 1893, the council had agreed to an extension of the original route, it had done so in the full knowledge that 'the occasional incident' would be unavoidable. As far as Wagner was concerned, the problems that arose were not grave enough to warrant a ban. After the Catholic councillor Hatzel had seconded Mayor Wagner's view, the other members of the council endorsed his inventive solution to the problem. What Wagner had proposed (after a further rerouting of the procession had been ruled out as impractical) was to change the alignment of the procession. Specifically, he recommended that the procession henceforth be divided into rows of six instead of two people, with ample space being left between the rows to ensure that doctors, busy travellers, and even

Figure 17. Bahnhofstrasse in Ulm, with the railway station in the background. 1905. © Stadtarchiv Ulm.

small carts were able to get to and from the train station unimpeded.[111] In this way, a solution was found that struck a balance between Catholic calls for a dignified procession and liberal demands for unhindered movement of goods and people. It was the result not of a consensus, but of a dialogue. Much more importantly, the solution that was found carried at its heart the recognition of the legitimacy of different rhythms of life, even at the risk of disrupting a ritual that, for many Catholics, embodied sacred time.

Another, more indirect, manifestation of the same tendency towards mutual accommodation can be found in the emphasis Catholic men began to place on the centrality of male participation in the processions. A day after the 1872 procession, for instance, a reader of the *Neue Augsburger Zeitung* pointed out that the initial report on the processions 'ought to have pointed out that it was above all manhood that took part in the Corpus Christi procession in unprecedented numbers.'[112] Reporting on the 1874 procession, the *Augsburger Postzeitung* was equally keen to stress that participation had been larger than ever, 'especially among men.' The editors went even further by claiming that the event had revealed an intimate link between

Catholic masculinity and German patriotism: behind the flag of the Catholic Casino had marched the 'members of the Catholic Casino and the Catholic men's association'; three Casino members had been 'decorated with war medals and military insignia,' offering testimony that '"ultramontane" men are able to fight bravely and with dignity for the fatherland.'[113]

The flip side of this positive emphasis on men was an increasingly common denigration of Catholic women, and of the conspicuous role they had come to play in the (public) performance of important Catholic rituals. Many of Augsburg's Catholic men, it appears, felt distinctly uncomfortable with the prominent role of women in religious life. A meeting of Augsburg's largest Catholic men's association, the *Christlicher Arbeiterverein*, in April 1880, offers a case in point. Addressing the approximately 200 members in attendance, the chairman questioned the assertion that 'piety' and religious instruction should be the 'prerogative of the female sex.' He justified his viewpoint by drawing on examples from ancient Egypt, and classical Greece and Rome, as well as from the Old Testament (citing Moses and Jesus as his prime witnesses). A pious religious life, according to the chairman, would continue to rely above all on the preservation of a family life for whose proper rhythm—in terms of conducting the daily prayers, as well as other elements of religious practice—the men were largely responsible. As he concluded his speech on the respective role of men and women in sustaining a pious religious life:

> What emerges from this examination is that it was above all the men who were charged with nourishing and cultivating piety. It was the duty of the man to act as the minister of his family, to attend the church services on Sunday and on religious holidays, and to conduct the morning and evening prayers with his family. It is a great blessing for someone to have had not only a pious mother but also a pious father.[114]

In part, then, this was a question of leadership within the religious life of the family, which Catholic men began to define as the nucleus of genuine Catholic piety. Another example suggests that, for some, it was also a question of women's presence in sacramental acts linked to, for example, a Corpus Christi procession. Such an interpretation is suggested, for example, by the openly misogynist stance of the chairman of the *Katholischer Männerverein Links und Rechts der Wertach*. As he addressed the 48 members who in 1882 attended one of the association's regular meetings, the chairman not only called for a stronger male presence at significant religious events. He also questioned the moral fitness of women to play a leading role in the performance of religious acts. The police official present at the meeting cited the chairman's concluding statement as follows: 'The saying used to be: "Female sex, pious sex!" Yet, in more recent times, one is tempted to say: "Male sex, pious sex! Female sex, bad sex!"' (Shouts of Bravo!).[115]

Historians are now generally agreed that, in Germany and elsewhere, Catholicism had undergone a process of feminization after 1848, both in reality and in terms of how Catholicism was portrayed. In several European societies, the number of women playing an active part in religious life—by joining female religious orders and congregations or by taking part in devotional forms of religion, including hymns, prayers, pilgrimages, and processions—was clearly on the increase.[116] In several German towns, female congregations—Augsburg was a leading centre of female religious orders—played an important, and increasingly controversial role in the provision of educational and other public services. This feminization of Catholic piety stood in contrast to the liberal ideal of a gendered separation between the public sphere and the private sphere. While middle-class men were expected to participate in the shaping of public life, women, according to the prevalent liberal morality, were supposed to fulfil their assigned role as wives, educators of their children, and, increasingly, as active members of charitable organizations of various kinds. Michael Gross has recently posited that 'for German liberals the women's question and the "Catholic problem" were one and the same'.[117] For Caroline Ford, the onslaught on female religious orders in France grew out of a sense that the 'principle of paternal authority', as well as the 'integrity of the family', had been challenged as a result of women's heightened public profile.[118]

How far this turn against Catholic women drew inspiration from liberal norms and preoccupations is difficult to say. What is evident, however, is that Catholic men's efforts to restore their embattled status—the charge of being members of an effeminate religion may have weighed heavily on many Catholic men—could sometimes assume decidedly misogynist overtones. Could it be that the unease that many of Augsburg's male Catholics appear to have felt at the sight of women playing a prominent part in religious practice reflects the challenge they appeared to pose to a rhythm of life that, according to the scriptures, was sacred? A rhythm of life, furthermore, whose pillar, they insisted, was to be the male-dominated family? Could it be that the sight (and spectre) of the full-time nun, whose schedule was arguably incommensurate with the paternal family, disturbed many a pious Catholic man, just as it disturbed many liberal apostles of progress? If so, this would suggest that, in a crucial sphere of social life, conservative

Catholics and liberal nationalists were committed to a similar rhythm of life. Or, at the very least, that the socio-temporal patterns they held dear were in fact quite closely aligned, more closely, at any rate, than the rhetorical battles that accompanied the culture war might make us believe.[119]

Affinities

What accounts for the fact that liberal nationalists and ultramontane Catholics—in spite of their at times contrasting moralities, the mutual rhetorical broadsides they hurled at each other, and their readiness to step in when a procession threatened to expand beyond what were perceived its acceptable limitations—remained engaged, through a multitude of threads, in a dialogue? To put the question more starkly: why did they not repeatedly come to blows as they sought to demonstrate their respective causes in large public rituals? That they did not do so should not be taken for granted, for there are good reasons to accept Donald Horowitz's assertion that a procession (or a modern religious or nationalist parade) 'derives its power from its violent possibilities.'[120] In the early-modern period, Corpus Christi processions frequently erupted into murderous violence.[121] In view of the relatively high death toll characterizing early-modern religious conflict, the lack of violent confrontation between liberal nationalists and ultramontane Catholics requires explanation.[122]

Anti-Catholic intimidation was admittedly a stock item of the German *Kulturkampf*: meetings were prohibited, churches were closed, priests were sacked, homes were searched, and Catholics taking part in processions were frequently ridiculed. As the previous examinations have shown, moreover, liberal nationalists and ultramontane Catholics sometimes struggled to accept each others' use of public space. Most liberals were adamant that a Corpus Christi procession should not block off the public's access to the local train station, not even for half an hour. Just as various critics of Sedan Day sought to disrupt the nationalist rhythm embodied by the parades, furthermore, some opponents of the Corpus Christi processions attempted to restrict their spatial expansion. In spite of a multitude of interventions, however, there were no open calls to disturb, let alone prevent, the nineteenth-century urban processions through the use of violent means. Nor did Catholics who participated in the processions condone violence as a means to gain hegemony within the urban arena, not even where they constituted the majority confession.[123]

One way to explain the maintenance of a dialogue would be to insist that local life was different. That it had little, if anything, in common with the logic that shaped Germany's larger political culture at the time. Nineteenth-century towns and cities, one might say, evolved distinctive patterns of interaction and sociability. Not only did many towns become more diverse in terms of their religious and confessional composition in the wake of industrialization and mass migration. While existing reservations remained marked, with urbanization the frequency of different confessional groups interacting with each other increased. More and more, one might say, urban space began to be divided according to the functional criteria of a modern mass economy. This put pressure on the integrity of religious communities. In Ludwighshafen, for instance, thousands of young men of different confessions worked side by side in the large chemical factories (the chemical and machine industries employed few women); many of them inhabited the same company-owned housing estates.[124] Augsburg's textile and metalworking factories must have seen a similar degree of interaction between Protestant and Catholic men and women (female employment was relatively high in the textile sector).[125] Even in Ulm, the least industrialized of the three towns, the construction of railroads and the building of a large military fortress from the 1840s onward led to a steady increase in the Catholic population. Here too, then, interaction between different confessional and religious communities became exceedingly common.[126]

This trend seems to have affected the lives of ordinary people in several ways. One of these concerns marriage patterns. As has been previously noted, in each of the three towns the rate of intermarriage between Catholics and Protestants was considerably above the imperial average, particularly in Ulm (where it was around 25 per cent on average during the imperial period) and Ludwighshafen (where it was above 30 per cent during the same period). In Augsburg the average intermarriage rate in the last third of the nineteenth century was between 13 and 17 per cent. Another way in which interdenominational interaction was marked was via education. Admittedly, liberal nationalists' efforts to turn Germany into a land of non-confessional schools ended in failure, although, as we have seen, southern German liberals were slightly more successful in this respect.

That the annual Corpus Christi processions also created opportunities for interaction across the denominational divide has already been noted. If the public debate over the decoration of houses situated along the route of the processions is anything to go by, this sometimes benefited inter-confessional relations. It is striking, at any rate, how frequently both liberal and Catholic newspapers wrote of non-Catholics decorating their houses to mark their respect for the occasion. Conservative Catholic newspapers and associations sometimes explicitly referred to these signs of respect by non-Catholics in their fight against the local proponents of the *Kulturkampf*. At the 1872 procession in Augsburg, for instance, the Catholic *Neue Augsburger Zeitung* praised the 'non-Catholic fellow citizens' for decorating their houses, while expressing deep regret at well-known Catholics who had refused to do likewise.[127] Moreover, at the 1884 procession, the liberal *Augsburger Neueste Nachrichten* noted with admiration that the 'owners and inhabitants of the houses located along the route of the procession' had been 'competing with each other for the decoration of their houses.'[128] The Catholic *Ulmer Volksbote*, in its report on the 1907 procession, detected the same competitive spirit at work, prompting a comment that was cautiously affirmative of the trend: even 'people of different faith had decorated [their houses] reasonably nicely.'[129]

Even in Augsburg, where divisions between the ruling liberals and the conservative Catholics ran particularly deep, a closer look shows that rapprochement occurred alongside rhetorical dramatization. To begin with, there were Catholics who tried to make the processions more acceptable to non-Catholics. Thus, in 1868, in a letter to the *Neue Augsburger Zeitung*, 'several readers' questioned whether the Corpus Christi procession, in its present form, made a favourable impression on contemporary observers.[130] Interestingly, the criticism expressed in the letter referred not to the devotional, but to the aesthetic aspects of the procession. The joint authors of the letter singled out for special criticism 'the colossal and barely transportable flags' that some members of the recently abolished guilds had carried through the streets during the previous procession. To prevent this in future, they proposed that those members buy themselves smaller flags that would be more pleasing to the eye and hence more appropriate for the occasion. 'That which is large,' they noted with more than a hint of condescension, 'is not necessarily beautiful too.' The readers also expressed concern about the 'ugly and unaesthetic dress' of the flag carriers: 'One must not disregard the times in which we live, both as individuals and as members of a municipal town. Black robe and gown would be both more suitable and more tasteful.'[131]

These gestures of mutual accommodation were not confined to Catholic circles. Liberal editors condemned instances of disrespectful behaviour towards the processions and its supporters. Certainly as far as Augsburg's leading liberal daily was concerned, mockery and ridicule were incommensurate with the dignity of a religions occasion. Thus, in 1877 its editors censured the actions of a number of Protestant youth who had apparently mingled with the praying Catholic faithful during the procession while ostentatiously keeping their heads covered. By acting in this way, those concerned had only exposed 'the low level of their education' to everyone present. Whoever regarded the processions 'as a bone of contention' should 'simply abstain':'The truly educated person will never express his reservations through rude behaviour. Although we are anything but enthusiastic supporters of the so-called processions, we feel nevertheless obliged to protect the honour of those who happen not to share our views, and we therefore roundly condemn the actions of a number of uneducated youths.'[132] When, in 1871, Councillor Zimmermann (a liberal Catholic) suggested that the processions be banned, he was swiftly reminded by his colleagues that the law provided no basis for interfering in matters concerning the Catholic cult.[133]

But dialogue entailed more than the condemnation of mockery or radical proposals to curtail the right of Catholics to practice their religion in public. It also included expressions of open admiration for the organizers' ability to conduct an event of the magnitude of the Corpus Christi procession in an orderly fashion. When things did go wrong, however, liberals did not shy away from apportioning blame. In 1868, for example, the *Augsburger Neuste Nachrichten* noted wryly: 'The stewards have not earned themselves much praise, as on two occasions the processions came to a halt, forcing the clergy to stand still and wait for nearly a quarter of an hour.'[134] Neither did they hesitate to extend praise, however, when the processions went according to plan: 'Several gentlemen from amongst the public deserve praise for ensuring that the order of the long procession was maintained in exemplary fashion.'[135]

In Augsburg, where the main procession regularly attracted in excess of 10,000 people, the event also created opportunities for urban sociability and leisure activities. Here, Corpus Christi was also a day off work, and for many it was, above all, a day out in the countryside. While pious Catholics (and not a few non-Catholics) tended to attend the processions as either participants or onlookers, Protestants and Catholics of liberal persuasion used the feast day to undertake forays into the surrounding countryside. The local association of gymnasts, for instance (an organization that not only in Augsburg was dominated by Protestants of broadly liberal conviction) would spend the day exercising and holding various competitions. Entire families left town in search of some relaxation, such as playing hide-and-seek or having a picnic. A typical newspaper story in 1883 reported that 'the forays on Corpus Christi Day were so numerous…that it is impossible to mention all of them. From early in the day entire caravans left the town by foot, train, or tramway in order to enjoy this fresh and rosy May day.'[136] In 1885, too, the same daily described Corpus Christi Day as a day marked by multiple journeys—journeys whose rhythms were strangely and inexplicably in tune with one another:

> In the afternoon, induced by the glorious weather, the town's population, divided into procession-like contingents, flocked to the free countryside. Some made their journey on foot while others used the horse-drawn tramway or the railway.[137]

In quest of a shared rhythm

Yet urban sociability offers at best a limited explanation. What was just as decisive, it seems, was the degree to which both sides were locked in a struggle for mutual recognition. Its participants drew on competing yet not incompatible moralities. For many liberal proponents of *Reichsnationalismus*, few things were more troublesome than powerful demonstrations of confessional solidarity. From their perspective, such activity posed a threat to the integrity of the German nation-state. This was one of the reasons why from the 1860s onwards liberal nationalists supported demands for a redistribution of social status, honour, and prestige on the basis of a cultural morality that stressed educational and economic achievement in the service of a powerful nation-state, thereby challenging existing patterns of status and recognition. In so doing, they set in train a struggle over individual and collective self-worth rather than a mere jostling for position. In such a climate, many Catholics found their very existence called into question. This was the case even where liberals made no explicit use of anti-Catholic symbols and stereotypes. For, in a sense, the questioning of a Catholicism that was conservative in its piety and demonstrative in its manifestations was inscribed in the institutional fabric of the German *Kaiserreich*. Many Catholics got drawn into what some political theorists have described as a politics of mutual recognition.[138] Faced with the threat of long-term stigmatization, Catholics often took the first step in a process of mutual accommodation. In this sense, their efforts can be seen as an attempt at 'stigma management.'[139]

But this only explains why a dialogue was sought. It does not explain why it could be initiated in the first place, or why it favoured the synchronization of competing rhythms. What enabled it was the language and emotional style that liberal nationalists and ultramontane Catholics employed. The transcendental language of Christianity and the emotional and symbolic repertoire it furnished was not only familiar to both groups.[140] It was also highly valued by both communities. For most German liberals did not reject religion per se, let alone Christianity in either its Protestant or its Catholic variety. What they felt unable to accept was confessional religion, but only insofar as it was demonstrative and self-assertive, because they perceived it as undermining the strength of the imperial nation-state. In their positive embrace of Christian codes and symbols, however, German liberals were in contrast to, for example, French republicans, whose anticlericalism could at times border on atheism.[141] The legitimacy of Christianity in defining temporal maps was not seriously questioned. Sedan Day, for instance, drew significantly on Christian (rather than merely Protestant) symbolism and practices: the parades themselves were modelled on Christian religious processions; synchronized church services formed part of the festival's ritual practice; and the event itself entailed a clear proselytizing dimension, in that those who remained sceptical—above all Catholics loyal to the Pope, democrats, socialists, and others—were to be brought back into the (national) fold.

Let me draw on an intriguing example to show that Christianity went largely unchallenged. It concerns the consecration of the new flag of Augsburg's veterans association in 1873. Had things gone according to plan, the association's new flag would have been consecrated in a religious ceremony conducted by a clergyman from either of the two Christian confessions. But on 1 August, just a few days before the consecration was to take place, the veterans association's executive informed the city authorities that the planned ceremony would have to be cancelled; the association's flag would therefore be consecrated without priestly blessings.[142] What had prompted this decision was the Catholic bishop's dissatisfaction with the procedure that had been agreed on between the Catholic and Protestant parish clergy. Had it been followed, the Protestants would have held their church service at ten o'clock in the morning, with the Catholics conducting theirs an hour later. Yet the bishop insisted at virtually the last minute that Augsburg's Catholics, because they constituted the majority denomination, were entitled to hold their service first. The Protestants refused to accept the bishop's unexpected request, but in order to prevent the incident from turning into a major confessional row, it was decided to dispense with any religious ceremony.[143] In a speech he delivered during the secular consecration ceremony, Augsburg's mayor made skilful use of the incident, juxtaposing Christianity and the belief in one God with what he portrayed as the destructive insularity of clerical leaders engaged in status wars and preoccupied with clerical protocol. As Fischer stated in his public address:

> While the churches could not agree on a procedure for the religious part of the consecration ceremony, this flag will be blessed nevertheless, not least because the avowal, expressed today under the open sky, that 'We all believe in one God!' is a prayer that will not remain unheard. God in heaven will bless this flag in a more forceful way than anyone else could have done.[144]

This conception of a national religion uniting all Germans, which Augsburg's mayor promoted, appears to have provided pious Catholics with more scope for manoeuvre than some historians have been prepared to concede. Liberal Protestants sometimes endorsed Christianity as a concept to bolster their quest for a unified and powerful nation, while Catholics resorted to it to endow their efforts at mutual accommodation with both meaning and legitimacy.[145]

As the 1890 Württemberg *Katholikentag* in Ulm shows, Catholic references to a shared Christianity had become common. Organized by the *Katholischer Volksverein*, this event attracted close to ten thousand Catholics from various parts of the state.[146] Its main purpose was to achieve a repeal of the 1872 ban on the Jesuit order (the repeal itself would have to wait until 1917). The two themes that dominated the dozens of speeches that day were laboured in an attempt to make the appeal more palatable to the state's Protestant majority. One theme was antisocialism; the other was Christianity as the only bond capable of uniting Germans of different confessions (there was no reference to non-Christian Germans). Christianity, so various speakers insisted, was the most potent weapon in the 'fight against Social Democracy,' a fight that was portrayed as the 'duty of all Christians.'[147] Social Democracy, according to this narrative, was both cause and consequence of a society emptied of Christian faith and morality: Only in a society that 'turned its back on Christian faith' could the 'dangerous doctrines and ambitions of Social Democracy' succeed.[148] Only a 'general revival of Christian life' could fend off the threat that was facing Germany through Social Democrat agitation. One of the keynote speakers offered a shared Christianity as the bridge that would unite a divided nation:

We Catholics do not rejoice in quarrelling. We Catholics wish to be men of peace, proper and genuine citizens of a state based on parity. We shall extend our hand to our Evangelical compatriots in the interest of united action ... Is the split dividing our German fatherland to grow yet further until it becomes unbridgeable? Let us overcome the struggle between the confessions! For whatever difference may separate us, we have enough in common to achieve a rapprochement.[149]

In a similar vein, defending the Corpus Christi processions against those who saw in it merely a demonstration of confessional religion, the *Ulmer Volksbote* insisted that the processions' main purpose was to defend Christ against his deniers. 'Every Christian, including non-Catholics, can thus rejoice at the sight of a well attended Corpus Christi procession, as it offers visible proof not only of a lively faith in the Holy Sacrament, but also of a positive Christianity, which forms the backbone of all Christian confessions.'[150] Three decades before, while the official *Kulturkampf* was still in full swing, the *Augsburger Postzeitung* had offered a much more drastic version of this Christian theme. In an article entitled 'A word about the Jews,' it made the following plea:

There can be no doubt that the solution of the Jewish question represents an existential question for the Christian population, and now that the Christians have realised that the Jews, pursuing the strategy of *divide et impera*, have pro-voked them, they will approach the necessary solution of the Jewish question with a seriousness commensurate with the potential threat that it poses. And above all: 'Let there be peace among you Christians!' May this call for peace not remain unheaded![151]

To stress the merely occasional usefulness of such Christian talk would be less than persuasive. The theme of a shared Christianity would hardly have moved into the foreground, let alone been cultivated over several decades, had it been lacking in normative appeal. For German Catholics in particu-lar, the invocation of Christianity offered a possibility of moving towards liberal nationalists while stopping well short of a national-religious concep-tion in which the nation had assumed godlike properties.

Whatever differences remained between the two communities regard-ing their respective object of reverence, the way in which they demarcated the boundaries between sacred and profane, or the rhythmic structure underpinning their ways of life and core rituals—urban space became, in more and less conspicuous ways, changed in a Christian key. To those who worshipped them, both Christ and the German nation carried redemptive qualities. Their presence was simultaneously physical and transcendental, in and out of this world. The accentuation of Christian symbolic codes at various levels and in different spheres buttressed the search for a shared rhythm of life. Drawing on a morality that fused nationalist and religious narratives and images, it helped facilitate a silent revolution, one that brought liberal nationalists and ultramontane Catholics closer together. It was a revolution that occurred amid fierce lamentations about Germany's segregation into separate denominational communities.

Conclusion

But it is precisely from these dislocations that social life draws its rhythm, a rhythm that is nearly always punctuated by irregularities. Likewise, an individual's different souls, to use the pluralistic language of ancient psychology, rarely constitute an identical age: how many mature human beings still preserve the spaces of childhood!

Marc Bloch[1]

In the late 1870s Ulm experienced what some contemporaries came to describe as the 'needle and booklet war.'[2] For the better part of a year, Ulm's *Frauenarbeitsschule* was the focus of a public controversy. A former private institute that was subsequently incorporated into the municipality's secondary school system, the school offered advanced instruction in handicraft for girls from age 14.[3] What had outraged sections of Ulm's business community was the school's sale of paraphernalia to its pupils. For once, Ulm's trading and crafts community was united in its protest against what it regarded as the inappropriate commercial activity of a secondary girls' school.

According to the *Handelsverein*, the school had engaged in a 'formal trade' with a range of items stocked also by local shops. These included needles, silk, threads, cotton and linen cloth, buttons as well as other, more specialized goods that were required for the design and making of shirts and trousers and other garments and household textiles on the school's premises. The daughter of a local yarn merchant had reportedly been asked to purchase her thread at the school, on the grounds that it was more suitable for learning to practice the required skill.[4] Some female teachers were taken to task for having praised American over German sewing machines. In doing so, they had undermined the 'local patriotism' that was so needed to 'promote the national trades and crafts' in a difficult economic climate. Some teachers were further accused of having accepted orders from private customers. In the main, however, the school was rebuked for acting 'too much like a trading company.'[5]

No less severe in its criticisms was the *Gewerbeverein*. Its chairman, furniture manufacturer Foerstler, shared a sense of bewilderment at the teachers' purported commercial leanings. He further criticized the institute for its genteel character, which he identified as the main reason for the 'lack of appeal' it suffered among ordinary families. According to Foerstler, the school was out of touch with modern times. In offering its pupils an 'opportunity to hone their skills in female manual work,' it had failed to find what ought to be its real mission: to 'improve the female sex's ability to earn a living.' The *Frauenarbeitsschule* had to become a 'seedbed of industrial activity' within Ulm and the wider region. In functioning as a 'higher girls' school,' it was making no contribution to 'raising the national income.'[6]

The school's director, Dr Weitzel, responded swiftly to these charges. What had prompted the head mistresses to purchase the items in question—including, as he freely admitted, buttons, canvas, lambs wool, leather, lining, needles, pattern and drawing paper, silk, thread, as well as other things the girls needed almost daily as they practised their skills—had not been personal or commercial motives. Weitzel described his school's procurement procedures thus: 'The head mistress purchases the required goods on behalf and in the name of the school. She then sells them to the pupils at the exact same price as they are sold in the local shops, so as to avoid any competition. Any discount she is given by the suppliers is paid into the school's piggy bank. A precise account, which is open to inspection, is kept of all the individual purchases and sales.'[7] Next he offered a compilation detailing the volume of the transactions in question. It showed that, within a period of four-and-a-half months, material at a total cost of 592 marks and 89 pfennig had been sold to pupils. The remaining items had been used to carry out commissioned orders.[8] Nor could the school's character be described as genteel. Its pupils, Weitzel insisted, were 'recruited from all classes.' In fact, in seeking to impart in the young girls the value of 'self-reliance,' the school's agenda had to be described as progressive. At a meeting in July 1878, the city council endorsed Dr Weitzel's viewpoint, emphasizing in particular that the trade conducted at the school was 'too insignificant' to warrant any kind of official intervention.[9]

It is tempting to situate the above incident within the long-running debate concerning the modernity of German culture, politics, and society in the latter part of the nineteenth century.[10] Depending on one's standpoint, the controversy over Ulm's *Frauenarbeitsschule* may appear as a confirmation of the persistent weight of traditionalism in German society. In a spirit reminiscent of the former guilds, one might surmise, even the local trade association sought to circumscribe the freedom of a vocational school for girls, because they saw it as a threat to the German middle classes. In Württemberg and maybe even in the German South, one might conclude, these conservative 'hometownsmen' were fighting a rearguard battle against the movers and doers, in this case represented by the director and staff of a vocational girls' school. Conversely, one might read the reactions of the city's two leading economic associations as a progressive stance against a class-based bourgeois ethos, one which relegates middle-class women to the private sphere, instead of preparing them for future employment in local factories. Seen from this perspective, rather than reactionary and inward-looking, the critics of the *Frauenarbeitsschule* might appear as promoting a distinctly modern agenda. What we observe is thus not an urban middle-class lacking in entrepreneurial spirit, but confident exponents of the crafts and small-trade sectors challenging bourgeois predominance in the cultural and economic fields.

As I hope this book has demonstrated, there are more compelling ways of making sense of incidents such as the one just described. The choice historians face is not, in my view, between the 'framing of the German past as a narrative of national development ... or as a set of competing counter stories, stressing social diversity.'[11] The question, rather, is how these different levels might be connected with each other. This requires concepts that can mediate between different analytical scales (whether local, national, or global) and thematic perspectives (ranging from social and economic to cultural and political history). In employing and elaborating the concepts of journey, place and rhythm, this book represents an attempt to move in this direction. The light that this approach has shed on life in the nineteenth century can be discussed under three broad themes.

The first concerns 'modernization' and its place in the construction of communal life. This book has not argued that *any* notion of the modern is fit for the conceptual dustbin. What it has challenged are the rather uniform and totalizing assumptions that often still inform historical accounts investigating aspects of the long nineteenth century. The fact that such claims now tend to be less openly made than when the paradigm experienced its heyday in the 1970s and 1980s does not alter this fact. Implicitly, they continue to be carried through familiar concepts such as 'urbanization,' 'industrialization,' 'nation formation,' or—indeed—'modernity' and 'modernization.' Whether historians use these terms to tell a story of how contemporaries came to either endorse or resist processes commonly associated with modern development: the underlying premise tends to postulate the relative inevitability of a powerful current that affected individuals and communities from the outside—not as something that they constructed and then configured in line with their own perceived interests, ambitions, desires, and experiences. In this narrative, people face modern developments as a fait accompli that they could either accept or resist.

Instead, this book has tried to capture change as an unpredictable process whose protagonists are individuals and communities pursuing different ambitions and projects within the same urban space of reference. When it comes to grasping change through the interaction of various scales, both spatial and temporal, towns offer ideal laboratories. This is because, in focusing on urban communities, we do not lose sight of the regional, national or inter- and transnational dimensions, which undoubtedly influenced the concerns and preoccupations of many contemporaries during this period. Indeed, by opting for such an approach, we gain an additional level of analysis, rendering our contexts denser than they would otherwise have been. Towns thus enable historians to explore the operations of 'modernization' in what might be termed contexts of high institutional and interactive density. Under such conditions—and particularly if the perspective employed is comparative—notions of a shared, let alone an inevitable, modernity are hard to sustain. What such a perspective brings to the fore, to use Marc Bloch's formulation, is that social life is punctuated by irregularities and dislocations. Emerging from the interplay of past, present and future, as well as of local, regional, national, and global events and structures, local life in this period could not be a purely local affair.

At the same time, however, this perspective reveals that local life is no mere reflection of larger trends. This book has shown, for example, that national legislation on free movement and social relief could indeed pose constraints on the actions of local actors, but that it is the various practices of locally embedded actors who turned imperial laws from a formal set of rules into something we can call experience. By defining and constructing their communities in new ways—ways that involved a fair degree of exclusion—they were engaging in activities that had repercussions far beyond the local level. Seen in this way, the nation—its institutional and cultural fabric—was a local creation rather than merely a local metaphor.

More specifically, this perspective has demonstrated that the nineteenth century did not see the colonization of place through space. Neither the railway nor the freedom of movement or increased migration undermined the centrality in the lives of ordinary people of attachments to specific places. No doubt people's lives were defined by various kinds of dislocation during this period. But what this book has set into relief is that the main effect of such dislocation was to prompt men and women to foster novel strategies for relocation. They only reinforced the inventiveness with which they sought to rebuild their environments in accordance with their interest, tastes, and expectations. What many contemporaries habitually and stubbornly described as a defence of the status quo was in fact an inherently creative activity. Whether towns such as Ulm, Augsburg, and Ludwigshafen defended their relative autonomy vis-à-vis perceived encroachments from the state, or whether their residents took part in the founding and running of a crafts museum, a municipal theatre, a new warehouse, a school, or a national festival or religious procession—what we are seeing are people seeking to create new, meaningful environments.

What we are witnessing is thus not the reproduction of *Gemeinschaft* in a world increasingly shaped by the structural requirements of *Gesellschaft*. Nor are we confronted with a series of re-enchantments in an increasingly disenchanted world. Such juxtapositions are part of the teleological understandings of modernization this book has sought to challenge. The towns whose development this study has traced over the course of half a century were not closed to the outside world. As human communities they had thus little—or perhaps one should say, less and less—in common with the hometowns Mack Walker examined in his pioneering classic some four decades ago. Being inward-looking was not really an option for a middle-sized town in Germany during this period—not if our definition of inward-looking involves more than a series of rhetorical postures and symbolic gestures. Yet sustaining a sense of place, at various levels, remained crucial in a period in which people were given the tools to imagine new spatial horizons irrespective of where they happened to reside.

This book has also highlighted the challenge resulting from what some historians have called the acceleration of time.[12] Here, too, its analyses suggest that the notion of a transformation in the experience of time offers too blunt an instrument to capture the socio-temporal dislocations people undoubtedly faced during the latter half of the nineteenth century. For neither these dislocations, nor the ways in which human beings coped with them, were marked by uniformity. The age of 'high industrialization' and of the developed nation-state knew various speeds. Attempts at making particular rhythms hegemonic only succeeded superficially. The pulse set by the factory clock or the nationalist calendar never achieved an outright victory over alternative socio-temporal patterns. The image of a society underpinned by a hegemonic rhythm is the stuff of modernist dreams that have been with us ever since the Enlightenment.[13] What is of great significance, however—and perhaps here we are looking at a phenomenon that warrants inclusion among the defining features of a shared modern condition (at least in relation to the latter part of the nineteenth century)—is the moral charging of different socio-temporal ideals and practices: that influential groups now proclaimed, with increasing frequency, that their preferred rhythm of life was more conducive to the welfare of society than those to which others subscribed. What appears to have been novel, then, at least in the intensity of its manifestations, was the tendency to declare other rhythms as deviant or even destructive.

It was because of this moral charging that the question of the right pulse of life began to preoccupy the individuals and communities that populate this book, and why coming to terms with multiple rhythms absorbed a fair amount of their emotional energies. The example of Ulm's *Frauenarbeitsschule*, cited at the outset, proves again instructive here. Thus, in his defence of the school's procurement procedures, its director talked above all else about the timing of individual lessons, insisting that 'external purchases would result in a loss of time.'[14] By being taught to work according to a precise temporal routine, the girls would learn a generic skill, namely that of setting their own schedules and rhythms of life. The theme of time also figured prominently in the report produced by the two head teachers, Misses Hartmann and Keppler, in defence of the schools modus operandi. Yet whereas Weitzel placed the main weight of emphasis on the danger of losing time, the two frontline teachers stressed the inextricable connection between a regular work pattern and the quality of the products made on the school's premises. What the school sought to achieve was neither 'artistry, nor subtlety, nor elegance.' Rather, what it was trying to attain was 'uniformity of measures,' a 'sense of regularity,' as well as 'cleanness and analogy.'[15] They were thus taught, one might paraphrase the teachers' educational vision, to become their own independent little production units. This, it seems, was one of the things that upset some representatives of Ulm's incipient manufacturing industry: the school did not prepare the girls for the rhythm of the local factory.

★ ★ ★

A second theme this book has addressed concerns the role played by liberalism in the construction of civic communities in nineteenth-century Germany. Liberals were admittedly not the only ones to have contributed to the formation of such communities. Conservatives of various shades, as well as those further to the left of the political spectrum, played an important part as well. For Germany in the age of the nation-state, however, the impact of urban liberalism is hard to overestimate. Liberals often acted as catalysts, setting the ball rolling on various issues affecting the lives of urban communities and their residents. In part this was because liberals during this period showed a strong inclination to politicize everyday affairs as well various aspects of public life. They were also more likely than their opponents to couch their comments and judgements on local events in the moral languages of progress and nationhood.

Once again: the important question to address is not whether liberals behaved in modern, traditional, or even reactionary ways. That question is hard to answer, not least because, then as well as now, what is modern and what is traditional depends on one's standpoint. Whether historians consider German nationalism irreconcilable with liberalism is much less relevant from a historical point of view than the fact that most German liberals during this period declared the nation as one of the key vectors of progress in the economic, political, and cultural spheres. Many liberals saw it as their mission to change their immediate as well as the wider, state and national environments of which they were a part. It was this attachment to a particular vision of progress that they shared irrespective of the plurality of normative orientations that makes it so hard to speak of a liberal movement. Their critics, too, often named this attachment as the element that defined liberalism in practice. Many conservative Catholics, for instance, named the preoccupation with progress as the defining feature of what they saw as the liberals' misguided ideology. Some liberal movements, such as that of Bavaria, included the word *Fortschritt* in their party name. Others, like the liberals of Württemberg, congregated in the *Deutsche Partei*, with the word German serving as a synonym for progress and modernity.

Perhaps the main factor that rendered this morality so consequential was that it proved inherently intolerant towards alternative temporalities—that its champions put pressure on those who were either unwilling or unable to accept the pace of reform they demanded. For some neither could nor wanted to keep pace. As the then chairman of Augsburg's *Neuer Bürgerverein*, an association founded in opposition to the ruling liberals, and one that had many Catholics among its members, expressed these concerns:

> There will be few in Augsburg who deny that much has been created here over the last decade that is beautiful, great and good—in the Augsburg whose garb has been transformed more powerfully perhaps than in any other Bavarian town during such a short period. If one criticism is warranted, however, and it is a criticism that has been made even in parts of the city's administration, it is that, after hardly anything had happened for several decades, now everything is supposed to happen instantly; and all this at a time of economic crisis that demands that we consolidate the economic and moral constitution [of our city].[16]

The fact that the liberal vision of progress had little regard for civic inclusion hardly boosted its popularity among the broader urban public. Mainstream liberals had accepted universal manhood suffrage at the national level with gritted teeth when it came. Most were intent on preventing a similar trend in their own municipal backyards. Unlike many on the left, they had no difficulty in reconciling demands for cultural and socio-economic reform with the conviction that access to full citizenship ought to be restricted in the interest of the larger community. The acquisition of social rights as a result of imperial legislative reform only appears to have strengthened this exclusionary impulse. As the nation-state imposed constraints on municipalities wishing to shut out their residents from access to poor relief, Germany's urban liberals doubled their efforts at protecting the *Bürgergemeinde* from what they saw as the threat of socio-economic depletion. The partial decoupling of someone's financial status from their political rights—which was the premise that implicitly informed the introduction of universal manhood suffrage in Germany at the time—was anathema to most liberals.

Yet while everywhere liberals were preoccupied with progress and practised social exclusion, the precise focus of these tendencies, as well as their consequences, could differ profoundly. Here, too, comparing different towns allows us to qualify important insights of a more general nature, and hence to identify different scenarios behind the sheer complexity of urban life. Augsburg's liberals were mainly concerned with public culture (such as schools or the *Stadttheater*) and infrastructure (such as sewage pipes and water supplies), which they viewed as incommensurate with the status of a modern, ambitious city. In Ludwigshafen am Rhein the main emphasis was placed on non-denominational schools, while in Ulm many liberals worried about the relative lack of factory industry compared with up-and-coming towns such as Reutlingen or Heilbronn. Moreover, in Ludwigshafen and particularly in Augsburg, liberals defined *Fortschritt* in decidedly anti-clerical terms, which was much less the case in Ulm. In each instance, however, expectations of progress shaped the dynamics of urban life, and the publication of statistical information—on matters ranging from mortality rates to demographic and economic performance levels at municipal level—meant that these initially liberal preoccupations drew in wider sections of the population.

However, while liberals everywhere sought to defend the civic core through exclusion of the lower classes from the enjoyment of full civic rights, the urban comparisons show that the success of this intention depended to an important degree on local cultures and power constella-tions. Whereas in Augsburg and Ulm liberals succeeded in their aim of retaining the political *Bürgergemeinde* as a relatively exclusive core, in Ulm the civic community underwent an expansion that owed much to the oppo-sition liberals faced from democratic circles. This left the discrepancy between national and local levels of enfranchisement small by comparison. Ulm thus appears to confirm arguments concerning early liberalism's defence of the 'classless society,' a society in which most people participated in civic affairs, a conception that was, according to Lothar Gall, increasingly abandoned with the expansion of free-market capitalism in the second half of the century.[17]

What this example shows, however, is that this more inclusive con-ception of civic community did not necessarily end with the advance-ment of industrial capitalism and mass politics in the last third of the nineteenth century. More generally, it suggests that it may be unwise to place the main weight of emphasis upon class. Certainly for a substantial portion of Ulm's liberals, class differentials did not constitute the main irritant. The decisive issue, it seems, was the spectre of their town being turned into what felt like a community of strangers, with strangeness being defined in terms of civic status rather than social class. While these two aspects of communal self-understanding may be closely related, they nevertheless point to different conceptions of community. It seems that the urge to uphold class distinctions, and particularly their translation into differential civic status, could be less significant than the wish to minimize the degree to which a town—because it entailed a large sub-section of non-citizens—could be experienced as a place that felt increasingly unfamiliar.

★ ★ ★

The question of communal belonging leads onto a third theme of this book, which concerns the relationship between the local and the national, and more specifically the ways in which nationalism affected the reconstruction of urban life and institutions.

The first thing to note here is that local communities exist and prosper as long as there are people who believe they have a stake in them—something that was recognized by many contemporaries. The fact that towns evolved both hard (e.g. in the form of buildings and waterworks) and soft (e.g. in the shape of legislation and rules) infrastructures, or that inhabitants evoked certain traditions, does not alter this fact. Even in the nineteenth century, urban communities in particular tended to be internally diverse, and they were often deeply divided. Residents who took part in public life rarely agreed on very many things. Differences of opinion and social status translated into distinctive patterns of sociability, allegiance, or argumentative, and rhetorical style. People who adhered to different political or religious views may have encountered each other on a few occasions each year, but otherwise they belonged to separate associations and met up in different inns. This plurality of perspectives and practices makes it difficult to talk of local interests and concerns in relation to a particular town or municipality. That vocal contemporaries claimed to speak on behalf of an entire town often tells us more about the ambitions of these individuals and the groups they represented than about the urban communities in whose interests they claimed to act. Claims to promote the welfare of an entire community constituted a central rhetorical device in an era of German history that saw increased labour migration, declining rates of church attendance, or an increased emphasis on individual success and the value of self-determination in the economic field.

Viewing German history in this light calls into question any strict distinction between the local and the national. Indeed, the separation of these two spheres helps maintain a number of unrealistic assumptions about the social, political, and cultural life in Germany during this period. One concerns the invasion of the local by national developments; or, conversely, the resistance of such developments by local concerns and interests. Even the assumption of a permeation of local life by nationalist normative assumptions, albeit more plausible, needs to be qualified. What we are confronted with is not the imposition of a nationalist morality on local life, but rather the selective and creative appropriation of such a morality by locally embedded actors.

What this book suggests, therefore, is that historians might profit from looking at nationalism in novel ways. This admittedly elusive phenomenon is normally discussed in terms of its impact on the public at large. Working in this spirit, some historians have examined the creation of national institutions within the context of a state that claims to act on behalf of an entire nation. Others have studied the formation of national cultures or the creation of public rituals and symbols designed to promote national awareness. Most of the time, they have done this with the aid of an implicit or explicit model that differentiates between producers and consumers of nationalist ideologies, symbols, and practices. Increasingly conscious of the fact that concepts such as 'invented traditions' or 'imagined communities' may raise more questions than they can answer, historians have begun to resist the temptation of assuming a straightforward transfer of nationalist messages from its alleged elite producers to the wider populace. Some have con-ceded the complex methodological problems that the question of nation-alism's impact inevitably raises. In spite of these critical reflections, however, the relegation of the public to the role of mere recipient or mediator of nationalist constructs—as members of folk song or gymnastic associations, for instance, or as participants in various kinds of patriotic festivals—is still fairly common.

Rather than viewing nationalism in this way—as an ideological pro-gramme that some promoted and others either rejected or, with time, came to endorse—historians might benefit from imagining it more like some-thing resembling a complex dance, one that owed its existence less to generic rules than to the improvisation of its participants: as a form of social exchange and interaction, that is, which relied on the contributions of a diverse public. While some of the participants undoubtedly exerted greater influence on the shape the dance would assume at certain points, they never managed to gain control over its overall dynamics, let alone its performance. Certain dancers were at times innovating and leading the way, but at other times they were just dragged along, whether they were aware of it or not, by other participants whose moves they could neither comprehend nor have anticipated. As well as questioning the still common top-down per-spective of nationalist inculcation, the conceptual metaphor of the dance shifts our focus towards nationalism as a collective practice, one in which people from different walks of life took part with varying degrees of inten-tion and awareness.[18] It also opens up a space for seeing nationalism less as something that reached people in the form of pre-packaged ideological and cultural programmes, but rather as a process that was contentious and open-ended. The fact that nationalism came to exert a destructive influence on German society should not make us consign it exclusively to the murky waters of right-wing politics; nor should it prevent us from recognizing that people engaged with the phenomenon creatively.[19]

In line with this argument, this book's focus has been less on nationalism as sentiment and belief (aspects that remain of undoubted importance) than on its practical operations. This has revealed that, as a powerful moral narrative, nationalism could influence the dynamics of local life in significant ways. Urban liberals, many of whom had joined the movement in support of national unification in the 1850s and 1860s, were often the first to endorse it as they sought to stamp the local worlds they inhabited with their vision of progress. Whether they fought for the creation of interdenominational schools, asked for the improvement of sanitary infrastructures, or proposed measures designed to support economic and demographic growth—liberals often buttressed these demands by connecting them with a nationalist narrative in which the fate of town and nation appeared one and the same.

Other sections within the urban population fostered alternative national narratives as they responded to the liberals' provocations and challenges. The most interesting example in this respect is offered by conservative Catholicism. While Catholics opposing the liberal project for Germany were rarely genuine nationalists (as opposed to most liberals), their engagement with liberal expectations and accusations sometimes favoured the cultivation of an alternative nationalist narrative. Confronted with the liberals' association of progress with the hegemony of secular institutions in public life, some argued that what could bridge the divisions that ran through the nation was a common Christianity. Religion and German nationhood were thus by no means seen as a contradiction in terms. Taken as a whole, these and other examples demonstrate that the construction of the nation-state (both before and after 1871) derived, in a fundamental sense, from the reconstruction of local worlds.

What this book proposes, finally, is that nationalism was particularly pertinent where people got engaged in struggles over the rhythms of life, whose proliferation may well be seen as a hallmark of this period of German (and, quite possibly, European) history. Many of the most emotive debates in the three towns centred on questions of differential speeds (as did the discussions over demographic growth), on the regularity of temporal rhythms (manifested in the preoccupation with tramway timetables), or on the danger of disruptions or delays to normal patterns of work and circulation (caused, for example, by parades or processions). Public struggles over mundane urban affairs were underpinned by the conviction that some individuals and communities were out of sync with the wheel of progress, and that they deserved to be blemished for this. It is here that nationalist arguments could function as a moral justification for those who wished to delegitimize rhythms that appeared to be out of touch with the ones to which they themselves had come to regard as an existential necessity. Here, a sense of lagging behind, and a felt need to catch up with other communities and places, provided the decisive impetus.

This explains why, for some apostles of progress, their cities remained a source of irritation and concern. Of the three communities examined, Ludwigshafen conformed most closely to the liberal-nationalist vision. Indeed, progress and speed had become stock-in-trades in the town's self-description, not only for the liberal movers and doers that dominated its political and economic life. On both postcards and other icons of urban self-assertion, Ludwigshafen was portrayed as that unique fusion of outcast and hero—a community that owed its existence to the raw energy of its population, and one that was still evolving in ways that struck the bourgeois visitor as cha-otic and soulless. Many of Ludwigshafen's residents, well beyond its vocal middle-class core, saw their town as progress personified. In more than one way, the city thus stands for a reversal of the conventional story of causality that defined the nationalist narratives of most urban liberals. Seen from the 'German Chicago,' Germany appeared as a reflection of one's own achieve-ments, and less as the example to be emulated. In this telling of the story, Germany had to look to a place like Ludwigshafen for inspiration. The 'city of work' seemed well qualified to act as the nation's pace-maker. As an editorial in the national-liberal *Pfälzischer Kurier* reflected on why Ludwigshafen and its industrial landscape might make for just as interesting a visit as picturesque Heidelberg across the Rhine:'Those who don't eschew to seek life where it is pulsating most quickly...will not regret to leave the beaten tourist tracks for a few moments and follow us.'[20]

Where the pulse of life seemed in need of quickening, nationalism could assume a different role. This explains why in Ulm and Augsburg nationalist arguments were often deployed to undermine the legitimacy of alternative rhythms of life. In Augsburg this was the case until, in the first decade of the twentieth century, the introduction of proportional representation and the inevitable expansion of the local franchise spelled the end of a liberal regime that had lasted for nearly half a century. In Ulm, meanwhile, the elec-tion of a new mayor in 1890 marked a deliberate assault on the city's liberal nationalists. When his supporters asked the city's new mayor, Heinrich

Wagner, to declare that he would refrain from standing as a candidate for the German Reichstag, they were not expressing their advocacy for a slower pace. Nor were they making an anti-nationalist stance. Yet in their view, the hegemonic nationalism of the *Deutsche Partei* had hindered the city's progress. What they sought to revive, then, was a communal self-understanding in which different pulses could be tolerated as equally legitimate. Theirs was a plea for respecting different rhythms of life.

Endnotes

INTRODUCTION

1. Bruno Latour, *Reassembling the Social: An Introduction to Actor-Network Theory* (Oxford: Oxford University Press, 2005), 179.
2. USP, no. 243 (18 October 1885).
3. Cited in USP, no. 4 (6 January 1885). A Catholic journeymen's house was inaugurated three years later. *Beschreibung des Oberamts Ulm*. Herausgegeben von dem K. Statistischen Landesamt, vol. I (Stuttgart: Kommissionsverlag von W. Kohlhammer, 1897), 745–6.
4. On the political dimension of change during this period, see Geoff Eley, 'Is there a History of the *Kaiserreich?*' in Geoff Eley (ed.), *Society, Culture, and the State in Germany 1870–1930* (Michigan: University of Michigan Press, 1997), 6. On other aspects of this transformation, see various contributions in Helmut Walser Smith (ed.), *The Oxford Handbook of Modern German History* (Oxford: Oxford University Press, 2011).
5. J. E. Malpas, *Place and Experience. A Philosophical Topography* (Cambridge: Cambridge University Press, 1999), 191. As Celia Applegate has noted, it is 'the experience of strangeness and unknown places' that 'casts light on the mental operations of place-making.' Celia Applegate, 'Sense of Places', in Smith (ed.), *Oxford Handbook of Modern German History* 50. On this theme, see also David Blackbourn, *A Sense of Place: New Directions in German History. The 1998 Annual Lecture of the German Historical Institute London* (London: German Historical Institute, 1999) and by the same author, *The Conquest of Nature: Water, Landscape and the Making of Modern Germany* (New York: Norton, 2006).
6. On the dynamic and contested nature of routines, see Billy Ehn and Orvar Löfgren, *The Secret World of Doing Nothing* (Berkeley: University of California Press, 2010), 80–1. For an historical application of this insight, see Frank Trentmann, 'Disruption is Normal: Blackouts, Breakdowns and the Elasticity of Everyday Life', in Elizabeth Shove, Frank Trentmann and Richard Wilk (eds.), *Time, Consumption and Everyday Life: Practice, Materiality and Culture* (Oxford: Berg, 2009), 69.
7. On the illusion of the social, and on the problem of explaining human life on the basis of a hierarchy of social contexts, see Latour, *Reassembling the Social*, 97, 184–7, 238.

8. On Augsburg, see Ilse Fischer, *Industrialisierung, sozialer Konflikt und politische Willensbildung in der Stadtgemeinde: Ein Beitrag zur Sozialgeschichte Augsburgs 1840–1914* (Augsburg: Hieronymus Mühlberger, 1977); Frank Möller, *Bürgerliche Herrschaft in Augsburg 1790–1880* (Munich: Oldenbourg Verlag, 1998). On Ludwigshafen am Rhein, see Stefan Mörz und Klaus Jürgen Becker (eds.), *Geschichte der Stadt Ludwigshafen am Rhein, Band I: Von den Anfängen bis zum Ende des Ersten Weltkrieges* (Zwickau: Westermann Druck, 2003), particularly the excellent contribution by Wolfgang von Hippel. On Ulm, see various contributions in Hans Eugen Specker (ed.), *Ulm im 19. Jahrhundert. Aspekte aus dem Leben der Stadt* (Stuttgart: Kohlhammer, 1990).

9. Rainer Braun, Augsburg als Garnison und Festung in der ersten Hälfte des 19. Jahrhunderts, in: Rainer A. Müller (ed.), *Aufbruch ins Industriezeitalter, Bd. 2: Aufsätze zur Wirtschafts- und Sozialgeschichte Bayerns von 1750–1850* (Munich: Oldenbourg, 1985), 65–78; Ernst Erhart, *Eisenbahnknotenpunkt Augsburg: Drehscheibe des Eisenbahnverkehrs* (Munich: GeraNova, 2000).

10. *Ulm und die Eisenbahn. Eine Chronik der Ereignisse.* Arranged by Stefan J. Dietrich (Ulm: Stadtarchiv, 2000), 10–17.

11. Willi Breunig, 'Vom Handelsplatz zum Industriestandort', in Stefan Mörz & Klaus Jürgen Becker (eds.), *Geschichte der Stadt Ludwigshafen am Rhein*, vol. I, 275–6, 294–313.

12. Fischer, *Industrialisierung, sozialer Konflikt und politische Willensbildung*; Möller, *Bürgerliche Herrschaft*. Mörz and Becker, (eds.), *Geschichte der Stadt Ludwigshafen am Rhein, Band*; Hans Eugen Specker (ed.), *Ulm im 19. Jahrhundert*.

13. As is well known, beginning in the 1980s this controversy has generated a veritable stream of monographs and articles that are too numerous to be cited here. Its foundational statements can be found in Hans-Ulrich Wehler, *The German Empire, 1871–1918*, trans. Kim Traynor (Leamington Spa: Berg, 1985) and David Blackbourn and Geoff Eley, *The Peculiarities of German History: Bourgeois Society and Politics in Nineteenth-century Germany* (New York: Oxford University Press, 1984). For a showdown between two leading exponents of these positions, see Hans-Ulrich Wehler, 'A Guide to Future Research on the Kaiserreich?' *Central European History* 29 (1996), 541–72; Geoff Eley, 'Theory and the Kaiserreich. Problems with Culture: German History after the Linguistic Turn', *Central European History* 31 (1998) 197–227. See also: Glenn Penny, 'The Fate of the Nineteenth Century in German Historiography', *Journal of Modern History* 80 (March 2008), 81–108; 'Forum: The Long Nineteenth Century', *German History* 26,1 (2008), 72–91. In Germany, the debate has given rise to large-scale projects on the German *Bürgertum*, whose academic hubs were the universities of Bielefeld and Frankfurt, respectively. For typical examples, see Jürgen Kocka (ed.), *Bürgertum im 19. Jahrhundert*, 3 vols. (Munich: DTV, 1988); Ute Frevert (ed.), *Bürgerinnen und Bürger: Geschlechterverhältnisse im 19. Jahrhundert* (Göttingen: Vandenhoeck, 1988); Lothar

Gall, *Bürgertum in Deutschland* (Berlin: 1989), and by the same author (ed.), *Stadt und Bürgertum im Übergang von der traditionalen zur modernen Gesellschaft* (Munich: Oldenbourg, 1993), 1–16. See also Thomas Nipperdley, *Nachdenken über die deutsche Geschichte* (Munich: C. H. Beck, 1986).

14. Albeit less explicitly than in its heyday, the *Sonderweg* continues to be a key reference for much research in the field of modern German history, including some more recent works of cultural history, many of which carry the words 'modernity' or 'modernism' in their title. See, for example, Kevin Repp, *Reformers, Critics, and the Paths of German Modernity: Anti-Politics and the Search for Alternatives* (Cambridge, MA: Harvard University Press, 2000); Jennifer Jenkins, *Provincial Modernity: Local Culture & Liberal Politics in Fin-de-Siècle Hamburg* (Ithaca: Cornell University Press, 2003); Maiken Umbach, *German Cities and Bourgeois Modernism 1890–1924* (Oxford: Oxford University Press, 2009). For a recent intervention calling for a longer-term historical perspective (which, of course, was at the heart of early adherents of a *Sonderweg* view in the vein of intellectual history) that caused some controversy, see Helmut Walser Smith, 'When the *Sonderweg* Debate left us', *German Studies Review* 31(2) (May, 2008), 225–40; and by the same author, *The Continuities of German History: Nation, Religion, and Race across the Long Nineteenth Century* (Cambridge: Cambridge University Press, 2008). For useful reflections on the debate, see Konrad H. Jarausch and Michael Geyer, *Shattered Past: Reconstructing German Histories* (Princeton: Princeton University Press), 37–60, 85–110. For a measured critique of the anti-*Sonderweg* narrative, see James Retallack, 'Obrigkeitsstaat und politischer Massenmarkt', in Sven Oliver Müller and Cornelius Torp (eds.), *Das Deutsche Kaiserreich in der Kontroverse* (Göttingen: Vandenhoeck & Ruprecht, 2009), 121–35. For important works that posit the emergence of a German civil society before 1848, see Isabel V. Hull, *Sexuality, State, and Civil Society in Germany, 1700–1815* (Ithaca and London: Cornell University Press, 1996); Ian F. McNeely, *The Emancipation of Writing: Civil Society in the Making, 1790s–1820s* (Berkeley: University of California Press, 2003).

15. Recent pleas for integrating macro and micro, as well as social and cultural history include William H. Sewell, *The Logics of History: Social Theory and Social Transformation* (Chicago: Chicago University Press, 2005); Geoff Eley & Keith Nield, *The Future of Class in History* (Ann Arbor: University of Michigan Press, 2007).

16. Methodological reflections on the history of German cities can be found in Jürgen Reulecke (ed.), *Die deutsche Stadt im Industriezeitalter* (Wuppertal: Peter Hammer Verlag, 1978) and, especially, in Hans Jürgen Teuteberg, 'Historische Aspekte der Urbanisierung: Forschungsstand und Probleme', in Hans Jürgen Teuteberg (ed.), *Urbanisierung im 19. Und 20. Jahrhundert. Historische und Geographische Aspekte* (Köln: Böhlau Verlag, 1983), 2–34. See also David Blackbourn and James

Retallack (eds.), *Localism, Landscape, and the Ambiguities of Place. German-Speaking Central Europe, 1860–1930* (Toronto: University of Toronto Press, 2007), Introduction; Helmut W. Smith, 'The Boundaries of the Local in Modern German History', in James Retallack (ed.), *Saxony in German History: Culture, Society, and Politics, 1830–1933* (Michigan: University of Michigan Press, 2000), 63–76.

17. For a critique of experience as a 'thing out there', see Joan W. Scott, 'The Evidence of Experience', *Critical Inquiry* 17 (Summer, 1991), 773–97.

18. Giovanni Levi, 'On Microhistory', in Peter Burke (ed.), *New Perspectives on Historical Writing* (Cambridge: Polity, 1991), 102, 109. For a sympathetic critique of microhistory, see Sewell, *Logics of History*, 35, 75–6. For an impressive recent example of this genre, see Roger Chickering, *The Great War and Urban Life in Germany: Freiburg 1914–1918* (Cambridge: Cambridge University Press, 2007).

19. This applies even to allegedly ultra-centralized France. On this topic see, *inter alia*, the important work of Jean-François Chanet: *L'Ecole républicaine et les petites patries* (Paris: Aubier, 1996) and *Vers l'armée nouvelle. République conservatrice et réforme militaire, 1871–1879* (Rennes: Presses Universitaires de Rennes, 2006); Ted W. Margadant, *Urban Rivalries in the French Revolution* (Princeton: Princeton University Press, 1992). On the reality and myth of centralization in France, see also Jacques Revel, 'Régions, provinces, lieux: d'impensable diversité de la France', in Revel, *Un Parcours Critique. Douze Exercices d'Histoire Sociale* (Paris: Galaade Éditions, 2006), 336–70.

20. For pioneering accounts employing a regional perspective, see Celia Applegate, *A Nation of Provincials: The German Idea of Heimat* (Berkeley: University of California Press, 1990); Alon Confino, *The Nation as a Local Metaphor: Württemberg, Imperial Germany, and National Memory, 1871–1918* (Chapel Hill: University of North Carolina Press, 1997). See also James Retallack, '"Why can't a Saxon be more like a Prussian?" Regional identities and the birth of modern political culture in Germany, 1866–67', *Canadian Journal of History*, XXXII (April 1997), 26–55; Dieter Langewiesche & Georg Schmidt (eds.), *Föderative Nation: Deutschlandkonzepte von der Reformation bis zum Ersten Weltkrieg* (Munich: Oldenbourg, 2000). For a critique of the tendency to portray regions as virtuous counterweights to projects at hegemonic control, whether Prussian or nationalist in origin, see Celia Applegate, A Europe of Regions: Reflections on the Historiography of Sub-National Places in Modern Times', *American Historical Review*, vol. 104 (October 1999), 1158; Abigail Green, 'The Federalist Alternative? A New View of Modern German History', *Historical Journal*, 46 (2003), 187–202. For specific case studies, see Hans-Werner Hahn, *Altständisches Bürgertum zwischen Beharrung und Wandel. Wetzlar 1689–1870* (Munich: Oldenbourg, 1991); Karin Schambach, *Stadtbürgertum und industrieller Umbruch. Dortmund 1780–1870* (Munich: Oldenbourg Verlag, 1996).

21. Applegate, 'A Europe of Regions', 1164.

22. For a critique of a social history that restricts itself to the task of reconstructing the 'process of formation and dissolution of multiplicities of conventions

holding societies together at different points in time', see Gareth Stedman Jones, 'The New Social History in France', in Colin Jones and Dror Wahrman (eds.), *The Age of Cultural Revolutions: Britain and France, 1750–1820* (Berkeley: University of California Press, 2002), 94–105. A defence of a flexible notion of structure in the study of the past can be found in Sewell, *Logics of History*, esp. chapters 8 and 9.

23. A work that can still serve as an inspiration in this regard is Gert Zang (ed.), *Provinzialisierung einer Region. Zur Entstehung der bürgerlichen Gesellschaft in der Provinz* (Frankfurt: Syndikat, 1978). A deeply researched account by historians operating outside the guilded sector of Germany's historical profession, its contributors successfully integrated social, cultural, and political history.

24. The view of emotions as embodiments of self-referential norms (rather than as something that is separate from both language and thought) has been elaborated by Martha Nussbaum, *Upheavals of Thought: The Intelligence of Emotions* (Cambridge: Cambridge University Press, 2003). See also Barbara Rosenwein, *Emotional Communities in the Early Middle Ages* (Ithaca: Cornell University Press, 2007). According to Sewell (*Logics of History*, 249), 'the emotional tone of action can be an important sight of structural dislocation and rearticulation.'

25. Sewell, *Logics of History*, 363.

26. Tim Cresswell, *Place: A Short Introduction* (Oxford: Blackwell, 2004), 33.

27. Malpas, *Place and Experience*, 35.

28. Wolfgang Schivelbusch, *Geschichte der Eisenbahnreise. Zur Industrialisierung von Raum und Zeit im 19. Jahrhundert* (Frankfurt am Main: Fischer, 2000 [1977]).

29. Historical works written in this spirit include Wolfgang Kaschuba, *Die Überwindung der Distanz. Zeit und Raum in der europäischen Moderne* (Frankfurt: Fischer, 2004); Patrick Joyce, *The Rule of Freedom: Liberalism and the Modern City* (London: Verso, 2003). For an account that portrays Germany's development from the early-modern period to the nineteenth century as a journey from 'place' to 'space', see Yair Mintzker, *The Defortification of the German City, 1689–1866*. University of Stanford PhD, 2009.

30. Michel de Certeau, *The Practice of Everyday Life* (Berkeley: University of California Press, 1984), 111. Recent research has shown that even the early-twenty-first-century railway carriage tends to inspire not a perception of spatial uniformity but creative place-making activity. On this theme, see Tom O'Dell, 'My Soul for a Seat: Commuting and the Routines of Mobility', in E. Shove, F. Trentmann and R. Wilk (eds.), *Time, Consumption and Everyday Life*, 85–98.

31. Robert David Sack, *Place, Modernity, and the Consumer's world. A Relational Framework for Geographical Analysis* (Baltimore: Johns Hopkins University Press, 1992), 82. See also Robert David Sack, *Homo Geographicus: A Framework for Action, Awareness, and Moral Concern* (Baltimore: John Hopkins University Press, 1997); Marc Augé, *Non-Lieux. Introduction à une Anthropologie de la Surmodernité* (Paris: Éditions de Seuil, 1992).

32. The most powerful portrait of this *project* is still Eugene Weber, *Peasants into Frenchmen: The Modernisation of Rural France 1870–1914* (Stanford: Stanford University Press, 1978). For a similar take on Germany, see Siegfried Weichlein, *Nation und Region: Integrationsprozesse im Bismarckreich* (Düsseldorf: Droste, 2004). For works that challenge this narrative, see, *inter alia*, Chanet, *L'École républicaine*; Applegate, *Nation of Provincials*.

33. Most theorists of modern spaces—with the notable exceptions of Michel de Certeau and Robert D. Sack—have tended to portray the relationship between space and place as something of a zero-sum game. Some, such as Foucault or Augé, while recognizing the powerful appeal of place in the modern world, have conceived of it in terms of cognitive codes rather than the result of creative agency. See Michel Foucault, 'Space, Knowledge, and Power', in James D. Faubion, (ed.), *Michelle Foucault: Power. Essential Works of Foucault 1954–1984. Vol. III* (London: Penguin, 2001), 349–64. Marc Augé, *Non-Lieux*.

34. Cresswell, *Place*, 82.

35. De Certeau, *Practice*, ch. IX.

36. De Certeau, *Practice*, 117.

37. De Certeau, *Practice*, 120.

38. Henri Lefebvre, *The Production of Space*, translated by Donald Nicholson-Smith (Oxford: Blackwell, 1991), 205–7; Eviatar Zerubavel, *Hidden Rhythms: Schedules and Calendars in Social Life* (Berkeley: University of California Press, 1985). See also the discussions in E. Shove, F. Trentmann and R. Wilk (eds.), *Time, Consumption, and Everyday Life*, esp. Introduction.

39. Zerubavel, *Hidden Rhythms*, 10.

40. Ibid., 2.

41. Zerubavel, *Hidden Rhythms*, 11. See also the pioneering article by E. P. Thompson 'Time, Work-Discipline, and Industrial Capitalism', *Past & Present* 38 (1967), 56–97.

42. For illuminating reflections on the emotional energies ensconced in temporal and other kinds of routines, see Ehn and Löfgren, *The Secret World of Doing Nothing*, ch. 2.

43. As Ehn and Löfgren have argued in *The Secret World of Doing Nothing*, 121: 'There is nothing routine about the making of routines.'

44. On the provincialism of the global, see Latour, *Reassembling the Social*, 190.

45. 'The important condition for reading or writing about the home towns collectively is always to remember that they lived individually. When they ceased to do so they stopped being home towns.' Mack Walker, *German Home Towns. Community, Society, and General Estate, 1648–1817* (Ithaca: Cornell University Press, 1971), 6.

PART I. PROLOGUE

1. Latour, *Reassembling the Social*, 204.
2. USP, no. 217 (17 September 1889).
3. See, for example, Lenger, 'Economy and society', in Jonathan Sperber (ed.), *Germany 1800–1870* (Oxford: Oxford University Press, 2004), 111–13.
4. For recent surveys of Germany's economic development in the nineteenth century, see James Brophy, 'The End of the Economic Old Order: The Great Transition, 1750–1860', in Smith (ed.), *Oxford Handbook of Modern German History*, 169–94, as well as the contributions by Frank B. Tipton and John Breuilly in Sheilagh Ogilvie and Richard Overy (eds.), *Germany: A New Social and Economic History since 1800* (London: Arnold, 2003).
5. Stephen Broadberry, Rainer Fremdling, and Peter Solar, 'Industry', in Stephen Broadberry and Keven H. O'Rourke (eds.), *The Cambridge Economic History of Modern Europe. Volume 1: 1700–1870* (Cambridge: Cambridge University Press, 2010), 172; Stephen Broadberry, Giovanni Federico, and Alexander Klein, 'Sectoral developments, 1870–1914', in S. Broadberry and K. H. O'Rourke (eds.), *The Cambridge Economic History of Modern Europe. Volume 2: 1870 to the Present* (Cambridge: Cambridge University Press, 2010), 70.
6. Broadberry, Fremdling, and Solar, 'Industry', 169.
7. Carreras and Josephson, 'Aggregate growth, 1870–1914', in Broadberry and O'Rourke (eds.), *Cambridge Economic History of Modern Europe*, vol. II, 69.
8. John Maynard Keynes, *The Economic Consequences of the Peace* (Los Angeles: Indo European Publishing, 2010 [1920]), 5.
9. Jean Quataert, 'Demographic and Social Change', in Roger Chickering (ed.), *Imperial Germany: A Historiographical Companion* (Westport CT: Greenwood Press, 1996), 105. Timothy W. Guinnane, 'Population and the economy in Germany, 1800–1990', in S. Ogilvie & R. Overy (eds.), *Germany since 1800*, 46–52.
10. See Quaetaert, 'Demographic and Social Change', 107.
11. While Mack Walker's 'home town' had mostly (although not universally) disappeared as an institutional reality, people's sense of place, often underpinned by some kind of communal bond, had not. See Walker, *German Home Towns*, ch. XII. More recently, see James Brophy, 'The End of the Economic Old Order', 169–94. The persistence of corporatist institutions and patterns of thought in the nineteenth century was of course not a German peculiarity. Their continued pertinence, as well as their capacity to adapt to changing circumstances, has been highlighted in a number of important works. On France, see William H. Sewell, *Structure and Mobility: The Men and Women of Marseille, 1820–1870* (Cambridge: Cambridge University Press, 1985).
12. Tipton, 'Technology and Industrial Growth', in Chickering (ed.), *Imperial Germany*, 89.
13. On the crafts see Friedrich Lenger, *Sozialgeschichte des deutschen Handwerks* (Frankfurt am Main: Suhrkamp, 1988), 104, 118–21, 131, 136–8; Thomas Nipperdey, *Deutsche Geschichte 1800–1866. Bürgerwelt und Starker Staat* (Munich: C. H. Beck, 1983), 260.

14. John C. Brown, Timothy W. Guinnane, 'The Fertility Transition in a rural, Catholic Population: Bavaria, 1880–1910', *Population Studies* 56 (2002), 35–50.

15. Jürgen Reulecke, *Geschichte der Urbanisierung in Deutschland* (Frankfurt am Main: Suhrkamp, 1985), 201. On Bavaria, see Werner von der Ohe, 'Bayern im 19. Jahrhundert—ein Entwicklungsland?', in Claus Grimm (ed.), *Aufbruch ins Industriezeitalter. Band I: Linien der Entwicklungsgeschichte* (Munich: Oldenbourg Verlag, 1985), 186.

16. Wolfgang von Hippel, 'Wirtschafts- und Sozialgeschichte 1800 bis 1918', in Hansmartin Schwarzmaier, Hans Fenske, Bernhard Kirchgaessner, Paul Sauer, Meinrad Schaab (eds.), *Handbuch der Baden-Württembergischen Geschichte, vol. III: Vom Ende des Alten Reiches bis zum Ende der Monarchien* (Stuttgart: Klett-Cotta, 1992), 663, 705–11.

17. Von Hippel, 'Wirtschafts- und Sozialgeschichte 1800–1918', 668–72, 680–8.

18. Karl-Heinz Preisser, *Die industrielle Entwicklung Bayerns in den ersten drei Jahrzehnten des Deutschen Zollvereins* (Weiden: Eurotrans-Verlag, 1993), 31.

19. Peter Marschalck, *Bevölkerungsgeschichte Deutschlands im 19. Und 20. Jahrhundert* (Frankfurt: Suhrkamp, 1984).

20. Wolfgang Zorn, 'Bayerns Gewerbe, Handel, und Verkehr (1806–1970)' in Max Spindler (ed.), *Handbuch der Bayerischen Geschichte*, vol. 4/2 (Munich: C. H. Beck, 1978), 782–845. See also Hans-Peter Schäfer, 'Bayerns Verkehrswesen im frühen 19. Jahrhundert', in Rainer A. Müller (ed.), *Aufbruch ins Industriezeitalter. Band 2: Aufsätze zur Wirtschaftsgeschichte Bayerns 1750–1850* (Munich: R. Oldenbourg Verlag, 1985), 308–22.

21. Gary Herrigel, *Industrial Constructions. The sources of German industrial power* (Cambridge: Cambridge University Press, 1996), esp. Introduction and chs 2 and 4. For an overview, see Frank Tipton, 'The regional dimension: economic geography, economic development, and national integration in the nineteenth and twentieth centuries', in Ogilvie and Overy (eds.), *Germany: A new Social History*, 1–34. Richard Sylla and Gianni Toniolo (eds.), *Patterns of European Industrialization. The Nineteenth Century* (London: Routledge, 1991), Introduction. In the historiography of modern Germany, the modern-backward dichotomy plays a prominent part. See, for example, Jürgen Kocka, *Industrial Culture & Bourgeois Society: Business, Labour, and Bureaucracy in Modern Germany* (Oxford: Berghahn, 1999), esp. chs 4, 7–9.

22. Herrigel, *Industrial Constructions*, 112–23.

23. Examples include: *Württembergische Jahrbücher für Statistik und Landeskunde*, Hrsg. königliches statistisch-topographisches Bureau (später königliches statistisches Landesamt), Stuttgart 1863ff.; Friedrich Wilhelm von Reden, *Deutschland und das übrige Europa. Handbuch der Bodens-, Bevölkerungs-, Erwerbs- und Verkehrs-Statistik. Des Staatshaushaltes und der Streitmacht in vergleichender Darstellung*, Wiesbaden 1854. *Vierteljahrshefte zur Statistik des Deutschen Reichs*, Hrsg. Kaiserliches Statistisches Amt, Berlin 1874ff.

24. For two recent accounts on this theme, see McNeely, *The Emancipation of Writing*; Jenkins, *Provincial Modernity*.

CHAPTER I

1. UT, no. 222 (23 September 1887).

2. The postcard is reproduced in chapter 5, p. 188.

3. Wilhelm H. Riehl, *Culturstudien aus drei Jahrhunderten*, vierter unveränderter Abdruck (Stuttgart: Cottasche Buchhandlung, 1873), 317.

4. *Beschreibung des Oberamts Ulm*, 189.

5. As Thomas Nipperdey has reminded historians, its interventionist and anti-liberal economic tendencies notwithstanding, the Kaiserreich's economic underpinnings were those of a liberal market economy. The tariffs that Germany imposed on average on imported goods (13 per cent) were undoubtedly higher than those of Britain, the Netherlands, or Switzerland, but still lower than those of France, the USA, or Russia. See Nipperdey, *Deutsche Geschichte 1866–1918*, Vol. I Arbeitswelt und Bürgergeist (Munich: C. H. Beck, 1998), 281.

6. For a rather schematic perspective on the impact of economic liberalism on urban development, see Peter Marschalck, 'Zur Rolle der Stadt für den Industrialisierungsprozess in Deutschland in der 2. Hälfte des 19. Jahrhunderts', in Reulecke (ed.), *Die deutsche Stadt im Industriezeitalter*, 63.

7. Peter Schaller, *Die Industrialisierung der Stadt Ulm zwischen 1828/34 und 1875. Eine wirtschafts- und sozialgeschichtliche Studie über die 'zweite Stadt' in Württemberg* (Stuttgart: Kohlhammer, 1999), 175.

8. Peter Schaller, 'Zur Wirtschaftsgeschichte Ulms' in Specker (ed.), *Ulm im 19. Jahrhundert*, 151.

9. UT, no. 8 (12 January 1887).

10. SAL E 179 II 3330, Ergebnis der Visitation des Oberamts Ulm. Verhandelt am 14 Oktober 1875 in Gegenwart des Oberamtsvisitations-Commissärs, Regierungsraths Renschler in Ulm, und des Oberamtmannes Regierungsrath Rampacher in Ulm.

11. UT, no. 169 (23 July 1879).

12. *Beschreibung Oberamt Ulm*, 519.

13. Schaller, *Industrialisierung*, 191.

14. Schaller, 'Zur Wirtschaftsgeschichte Ulms', 147.

15. Schaller, *Industrialisierung*, 221.

16. Schaller, *Industrialisierung*, 183–4, 211, 225.

17. Schaller, 'Zur Wirtschaftsgeschichte Ulms', 150.

18. Ulrich Wagner, *Die wirtschaftlichen Verhältnisse in Ulm im 19. Jahrhundert* (Ulm, 1895), 70.

19. The figures can be found in USP, no. 273 (23 November 1881); USP, no. 256 (3 November 1885). If Ulm's total revenue from direct municipal tax was low

by comparison with other Württemberg municipalities such as Heilbronn, this owed much to the extraordinary wealth of its private charities or *Stiftungen*. As late as 1889, Ulm covered less than twenty per cent of its annual expenses through direct taxation, at a time when the respective figure for Stuttgart and Heilbronn was close to thirty per cent. USP, no. 217 (17 September 1889). On the role of Ulm's charities, see Michael Wettengel, 'Zur Geschichte der Stiftungen in Ulm', in Ulmer Bürger Stiftung (ed.), *Handbuch Ulmer Stiftungen* (Ulm: Stadtarchiv, 2004), 10–46.

20. By the early 1880s, the merchants and industrialists contributed more than eighty per cent to the town's tax revenue. At a meeting of the *Handelsverein* in January 1881, the following figures were presented: 199 merchants and traders ('Kaufleute'), plus 69 industrialists ('Grossindustrielle') paid 2207.49 marks in tax, while 76 craftsmen ('Handwerker') paid 102.05 marks. Despite their moderate contribution to the town's revenue from direct taxation, however, the crafts had three to four representatives on the district's chamber of trade and commerce, which was higher than in either Stuttgart, Heilbronn, Reutlingen, Heidenheim or Ravensburg. UT, no. 6 (9 January 1881).

21. SAL E 179 II, Oberbürgermeister v. Heim an Visitationskommmissaer Herrn Regierungsrat Rentschler, 12 October 1875.

22. The position was formulated unmistakably during several of its meetings. See, for instance, UT, no. 285 (4 December 1878). According to its intellectual leader, the merchant Gustav Maier, Ulm's *Handelsverein* was one of the few German associations of its kind. In 1878 it openly criticized Bismarck's protectionist turn. Stadtarchiv Zürich Na 4263: Gustav Maier, *Siebzig Jahre politischer Erinnerungen und Gedanken* (typescript, 1918), 14–15.

23. Compared with these declining crafts, the over 80 bakeries, seventy butchers, and close to 300 hotels and inns may have enjoyed a more stable existence. For statistical information on this topic, see USP, no. 37 (14 February 1886). See also UT, no. 169 (23 July 1879).

24. Most commentators in Ulm saw the success of the *Wanderlager* as a sign that the consuming public was lacking in taste and education; only a minority took it as proof that *Gewerbefreiheit* was not working, although there was broad support for voluntary *Innungen*. See, for example, UT, no. 29 (5 February 1876): 'Das Hausieren, die Wanderlager und die Schwindel-Auktionen'; UT, no. 172 (28 July 1877): 'Wanderlager, Waarenauctionen und Jahrmarktstroedel.' However, in Ulm the number of Wanderlager decreased from seventy to four between 1876 and 1878, and the controversy died down as a result. See UT, no. 90 (19 April 1879).

25. On the economic implications of the fortress during its period of construction, see Schaller, *Die Industrialisierung der Stadt*, 105–14.

26. On the federal fortresses, see Mintzker, *Defortification*, 245.

27. *Beschreibung des Oberamts Ulm*, 192.

28. StadtAU 774/13, no. 43.

29. StadtAU B060/23, no. 1, Beschwerde von Seiten des Johannes Schwenk zum Kupferhammer, die Expropriation eines Teils seines Anwesens für die Bundesfestung Ulm betreffend, 5 June 1845. See also StadtAU 060/25 Nr. 9, Einquartierung und Durchmärsche von Bundes- und fremden Truppen 1848–66.

30. See Schaller, *Die Industrialisierung der Stadt Ulm*, 174–9; Bernd Lemke, 'Die Ulmer Garnison und ihre Bedeutung fuer das städtische Leben, 586–641, in Specker (ed.), *Ulm im 19. Jh.*; Walter Güssmann, 'Stadtentwicklung', in Specker, (ed.), *Ulm im 19. Jahrhundert*, 568–85.

31. Wagner, *Wirtschaftliche Verhältnisse in Ulm*, 69–70.

32. A concise recent history of Ulm's garrison has been provided by Simon Palaoro, *Stadt und Festung. Eine kleine Geschichte der Bundesfestung Ulm* (Ulm: Klemm & Oelschläger, 2009).

33. Julius Schuster, *Antrag des Stadtschultheissen Schuster betreffend das Armenwesen der Stadt Ulm, gestellt an den Stiftungsrath und Bürgerausschuss am Tage der Feier des 71sten Geburtstagsfestes Sr Majestät des Königs Wilhelm von Württemberg* (1852), 8–13.

34. UT, no. 290 (12 December 1885).

35. UT, no. 245 (20 October 1886).

36. UT, no. 143 (23 June 1885); no. 188 (14 August 1885).

37. UT, no. 249 (25 October 1885).

38. UT, no. 303 (30 December 1885).

39. Ibid.

40. USP, no. 222 (23 September 1887).

41. UT, no. 189 (16 August 1890). USP, no. 202 (30 August 1889).

42. On this debate, see, for example, UT, no. 162 (15 July 1875); USP, no. 160 (13 July 1875); USP, no. 178 (3 August 1875).

43. Gustav Maier, *Denkschrift über die Handelsbedeutung der Stadt Ulm und ihrer Umgebung. Im Auftrage und unter Mitwirkung des Comité's für Erstrebung einer Reichsbank-Stelle* (Ulm: Druck der J. Ebnerschen Buchdruckerei, 1875).

44. Ibid., 40.

45. Maier, *Denkschrift*, 3, 41.

46. Ibid., 3–4.

47. Maier, *Denkschrift*, 39.

48. UT, no. 138 (17 June 1875).

49. USP, no. 160 (13 July 1875).

50. USP, no. 162 (15 July 1875). The same reader's letter appeared in the *Ulmer Tagblatt*, which at that point was still the forum for Ulm's *Kleingewerbe*. See UT, no. 162 (15 July 1875).

51. USP, no. 169, (23 July 1875).

52. Ibid. 'Achte dich selbst und es werden dich auch andere achten—Haeltst du Dich selbst gering, so wirst du gewiss bald ueberall Geringschaetzung ernten.' (Ibid.).

53. USP, no. 178 (3 August 1875).

54. USP, no. 177 (1 August 1875).

55. UT, no. 210 (10 September 1875); no. 211 (11 September 1875).

56. StadtAU 724/22, no. 1, Schreiben des Handelsvereins an den Gemeinderath Ulm, 2 Februar 1874: 'Die ausnahmsweise günstige Lage Ulms als Eisenbahn-knotenpunkt an der Kreuzung von sechs Linien,—den Verkehrsardern zwischen Sued und Nord, West und Ost,—muss die Aufmerksamkeit des Kaufmanns unwillkuerlich auf den hiesigen Platz lenken; in der Mitte zwischen den Hauptproductions- und Konsumtions-Ländern, nämlich Österreich-Ungarn und Galizien einerseits und Frankreich, Italien, der Schweiz andererseits, eignet sich Ulm vorzugsweise [und mehr als Thalkirchen (München)] zur Vermittlung der bedeutenden Exportgeschäfte, welche zwischen diesen Ländern und Deutschland jährlich gemacht werden.' See also USP, no. 240 (15 October 1874).

57. SAL E 179 II, Antwort OB v. Heim an Visitationskommmissaer Herrn Regierungsrath Rentschler, 12 October 1875.

58. USP, no. 294 (17 December 1875); no. 32 (9 February 1876).

59. USP, no. 166 (20 July 1877).

60. USP, no. 198 (26 August 1877).

61. USP, no. 222 (23 September 1877).

62. USP, no. 241 (26 September 1877).

63. UT, no. 206 (6 September 1877).

64. UT, no. 206 (6 September 1877).

65. UT, no. 167 (22 July 1877).

66. Ibid.

67. USP, no. 18 (23 January 1880). UT, no. 18 (23 January 1880).

68. USP, no. 40 (18 February 1880).

69. USP, no. 38 (15 February 1880).

70. USP, no. 42 (20 February 1880).

71. UT, no. 110 (12 May 1888), no. 183 (7 August 1888).

72. After having demonstrated, over several years, his ability as head of Ulm's Reichsbanknebenstelle, Frankfurt offered Maier the job. See his memoirs in Stadtarchiv Zürich Na 4263: Maier, *Siebzig Jahre politischer Erinnerungen und Gedanken.*

73. USP, no. 291 (11 December 1878); UT, no. 291 (11 December 1878).

74. USP, no. 191 (15 August 1878).

75. UT, no. 291 (11 December 1878).

76. UT, no. 211 (11 September 1879).

77. USP, no. 205 (4 September 1879).

78. UT, no. 59 (11 March 1880).

79. UT, no. 210 (10 September 1879).

80. UT, no. 272 (18 November 1884); USP, no. 265 (13 November 1885).

81. UT, no. 176 (31 July 1887); no. 189 (16 August 1887).

82. UT, no. 183 (9 August 1887).

83. UT, no. 186 (12 August 1887).

84. UT, no. 217, (17 September 1887).

85. UT, no. 193 (20 August 1887).

86. UT, (7 August 1887) no. 182.

87. Ibid.

88. UT, no. 73, (28 March 1890).

89. Breunig, *Kommunalpolitik*, 43.

90. *Landes- und Volkskunde der Bayerischen Rheinpfalz. Bearbeitet von einem Kreise heimischer Gelehrter* (Munich, 1867), 215.

91. Just a few weeks before the Bavarian state acquired the *Rheinschanze* (as Ludwigshafen was called until Bavaria bought the trading area across the Rhine from Mannheim) in March 1843, the Bavarian war ministry (on an order of Ludwig I) released it from its status as a fortification area. The act underscores that the strategic importance assigned to Ludwigshafen was not as a military but as a trading town. See Breunig, 'Vom Handelsplatz zum Industriestandort', 275. See also von Hippel, 'Zwischen kleindeutscher Reichsgründung und Weltkriegskatastrophe', in Mörz and Becker (eds.), *Geschichte der Stadt Ludwigshafen*, 372–3.

92. Denkschrift des Regierungsrates Lamotte vom 31 Dezember 1853 über die Verhältnisse von Ludwigshafen am Rhein. Reprinted in Oskar Poller, (ed.), *Zur Geschichte der Stadt Ludwigshafen am Rhein. Ludwigshafen 1853 und 1873. Die Denkschriften von Lamotte und Matthäus* (Ludwigshafen a. Rh.: Verlag der Arbeitsgemeinschaft Pfälzisch-Rheinische Familienkunde e.V., 1974), 11.

93. Breunig, 'Vom Handelsplatz zum Industriestandort', 339.

94. Von Hippel, 'Zwischen kleindeutscher Reichsgründung und Weltkriegskatastrophe', 372.

95. Ibid., 418.

96. *Geschichte der Stadt Ludwigshafen am Rhein. Entstehung und Entwicklung einer Industrie- und Handelsstadt in fuenfzig Jahren, 1853–1903. Mit einem geschichtlichen Rückblick. Aus Anlass des 50jährigen Bestehens der Stadt Ludwigshafen am Rhein. Herausgegeben vom Bürgermeisteramt* (Ludwigshafen am Rhein: Julius Waldkirch & Cie., 1903), 124; *Geschichte der Stadt Ludwigshafen am Rhein, vol. I* (2003).

97. Wolfgang von Hippel, 'Stadtentwicklung und Stadtteilbildung in einer Industrieansiedlung des 19. Jahrhunderts: Ludwigshafen am Rhein 1853–1914', in Teuteberg, (ed.), *Urbanisierung im 19. und 20. Jahrhundert*, 367.

98. Von Hippel, 'Zwischen Kleindeutscher Reichsgründung und Weltkriegs-Katastrophe', 385, 436–8.

99. Willi Breunig, *Kommunalpolitik und Wirtschaftsentfaltung in Ludwigshafen am Rhein 1843–1871* (Weinheim: Druckhaus Diesbach, 1995), 20–3, 26.

100. Von Hippel, 'Zwischen kleindeutscher Reichsgründung und Weltkriegs-Katastrophe', 374.

101. Ibid., 430–2.

102. Von Hippel, 'Zwischen kleindeutscher Reichsgründung und Weltkriegskatastrophe', 434–5.

103. Ibid., 428.

104. *Geschichte der Stadt Ludwigshafen am Rhein 1853–1903*, 532.

105. Von Hippel, 'Zwischen kleindeutscher Reichsgründung und Weltkriegs-Katastrophe', 377, 388.

106. Ibid., 387–408, 414–17.

107. Von Hippel, 'Zwischen Kleindeutscher Reichsgründung und Weltkriegs-Katastrophe', 455.

108. *Geschichte der Stadt Ludwigshafen 1853–1903*, 210.

109. Willi Breunig, *Soziale Verhältnisse der Arbeiterschaft und sozialistische Arbeiterbewegung in Ludwigshafen am Rhein 1869–1919* (Darmstadt.: Dissertationsdruck Darmstadt, 1990), 48.

110. Von Hippel, 'Zwischen Reichsgründung und Weltkriegs-Katastrophe', 456, 458–9.

111. Von Hippel, 'Stadtentwicklung und Stadtteilbildung', 352.

112. Von Hippel, 'Zwischen kleindeutscher Reichsgründung und Weltkriegs-Katastrophe', 380–3.

113. Adam Ritzhaupt, *In Sonne und Rauch. Erzählungen aus dem Kinderleben* (Karlsruhe: Verlag C. F. Müller, ohne Datum), 6.

114. StadtAL Pa I, no. 8, p. 471–2. 7 October 1885.

115. 'Der Hemshof, die Farbenstadt Deutschlands', *Pfälzischer Kurier* (28/29 March 1889). 'Der Hemshof, diese Fabrikstadt par eminence, ist der Sitz der Ludwigshafener Grossindustrie, ein Stück Amerika, wie es kaum ein anderer Fleck deutschen Bodens wieder zeigt, ein Hauptort der modernen Farbenindustrie, er ist die Farbenstadt, das Chromopolis Deutschlands.'

116. Ibid.

117. StadtAL M 286: Georg Kuhn, *Aus der Geschichte des Handwerker- und Gewerbeverbandes Ludwigshafen am Rhein* (typescript, February 1944).

118. Kuhn, *Geschichte*, 2–3.

119. Ibid.

120. StadtAL M 380, 'Der Hemshof, die Farbenstadt Deutschlands', *Pfälzischer Kurier*, 28/29 March 1889.

121. Von Hippel, 'Zwischen kleindeutscher Reichsgründung und Weltkriegs-Katastrophe', 378–9.

122. The reformed *Reichsgewerbeordnung* of 1879, § 33, section II, entitled state governments to make the issuing of licences for inns dependent on a means test. Based on this imperial law, the Bavarian government in August 1879 decreed that licence restrictions would indeed apply for towns under 15,000 inhabitants.

123. StadtAL Lua 60.

124. StadtAL Lua 60, Bezirksamt Speyer an Bürgermeisteramt, 29 August 1885.

125. StadtAL Lua 60, Gastwirteverein an Bürgermeisteramt, 3 October 1885.

126. StadtAL Lua 60, Bürgermeisteramt an Bezirksamt, 19 October 1885.
127. StadtAL Lua 60, Bürgermeister Kutterer an Bezirksamt, 25 October 1885.
128. Ibid.
129. StadtAL Lua 60, K. Bezirksamt an Bürgermeisteramt, 13 November 1885.
130. StadtAL Lua 60, Sitzung Stadtrat (Entwurf zhd. Regierung der Pfalz), 26 November 1885.
131. StadtAL Lua 60, Bezirksamt Speyer and Bürgermeisteramt, 15 February 1886.
132. StadtAL Lua 60, Gesuch des Gastwirtevereins Ludwigshafen an den Gemeinderat Ludwigshafen, 9 July 1896.
133. LAS H3 7221, Gewerbeverein Ludwigshafen an die Stadtverwaltung Ludwigshafen. Betreff. Errichtung einer Gewerbeschule dahier, 17 July 1884.
134. Ibid.
135. LAS H3 7221, Gewerbeverein Ludwigshafen an Stadtverwaltung Ludwigshafen. Betreff: Gesuch des Gewerbevereins um Errichtung einer Gewerbe-Schule, 20 December 1884.
136. Ibid., Auszug aus dem Protokoll des Gemeinderates Ludwigshafen, 28 January 1885.
137. Nipperdey, *Deutsche Geschichte 1866–1918, vol. I*, 253–60; Lenger, *Sozialgeschichte des deutschen Handwerks*, 104, 118–21, 131, 136–8.
138. StadtAL ZR 4060/5. See also *Statut der Bäcker-Innung zu Ludwigshafen a. Rh.* (Ludwigshafen am Rhein: Buchdruckerei von Julius Waldkirch, 1885).
139. StadtAL ZR 4060/5, Vorstand der Bäcker-Innung Ludwigshafen an das Bezirksamt, 12 December 1887.
140. StadtAL ZR 4060/5, Bürgermeisteramt Ludwigshafen an K. Bezirksamt. 18 January 1888.
141. StadtAL ZR 4060/5, Bezirksamt an K. Regierung der Pfalz, 7 February 1888.
142. StadtAL ZR 4060/5, Bayrische Regierung an Bezirksamt, 15 April 1888.
143. StadtAL ZR 4060/5, Verzeichnis der in Ludwigshafen beschäftigten Bäckerlehrlinge. Aufgestellt vom Bürgermeisteramt am 6 April 1888.
144. StadtAL ZR 4060/5, Bayrische Regierung der Pfalz an Bezirksamt Ludwighafen, 1 May 1888.
145. Fischer, *Industrialisierung*, 114–16.
146. Urban geography was important here. While working-class districts of the Wertach tended to attract unskilled migrants from rural Bavaria, Augsburg's northern working-class district (whose inhabitants tended to work for the machine works) displayed a higher proportion of skilled, long-distance migrants. See Fischer, *Industrialisierung*, 114.
147. Fischer, *Industrialisierung*, 78–9, 83.
148. Ibid., 85–6.
149. Ibid. 97–83, 95.
150. These figures are drawn from Fischer, *Industrialisierung*, 33–4.
151. Ibid., 61–2, 90–3.

152. Fischer, *Industrialisierung*, 25.

153. Ibid., 29.

154. Ibid.

155. Peter Fassl 'Wirtschaftsgeschichte 1800–1914', in G. Gottlieb *et al.* (eds.), *Geschichte der Stadt Augsburg. 2000 Jahre von der Römerzeit bis zur Gegenwart* (Stuttgart: Konrad Theiss Verlag, 1984), 598.

156. Fischer, *Industrialisierung*, 31–2.

157. Ibid., 98.

158. Fischer, *Industrialisierung*, 53–4.

159. Statistisches Jahrbuch für das Königreich Bayern (1894), 9.

160. Augsburg's extremely high mortality rates, particularly among toddlers, did not help either. Fischer, *Industrialisierung*, 48, 66–8. For an overview, see also the essay by Mark Häberlein, 'Wirtschaftsgeschichte vom Mittelalter bis zur Gegenwart', in: *Augsburger Stadtlexikon*, 2nd edn., Günther Grünsteudel *et al.* (3ds) (Augsburg: Perlach Verlag 1998), 146–61.

161. Riehl, *Culturstudien*, 317.

162. Fischer, *Industrialisierung*, 104, 107–10, 112.

163. StadtAA 10/403, Mitgliederversammlung, 2 July 1890.

164. StadtAA 5/559, Mitgliederversammlung, 5 October 1883.

165. StadtAA 5/559, Mitgliederversammlung, 5 October 1882.

166. StadtAA 5/559, Mitgliederversammlung, 9 March 1882.

167. StadtAA 3/707, Bekanntmachung die Handwerksgesellen betreffend. Augsburg, 28 June 1862.

168. Augsburger Anzeigeblatt, 12 February 1860.

169. Augsburger Anzeigeblatt, 26 January 1860.

170. Frank Möller, *Bürgerliche Herrschaft in Augsburg 1790–1880* (Munich: Oldenbourg Verlag, 1998), 405.

171. StadtAA 5/267, Stadtmagistrat Augsburg an Stadtmagistrat Kissingen, 17 March 1880.

172. On the reception of List's ideas by German liberals of different shades, see Matthew P. Fitzpatrick, *Liberal Imperialism in Germany: Expansionism and Nationalism 1848–1884* (Oxford: Berghahn, 2008), 55–61.

173. Möller, *Bürgerliche Herrschaft*, 391.

174. Ibid., 403–5.

175. Bismarck's undoubted influence on German economy and society notwithstanding, at least in relation to economic orientations among leading entrepreneurs, talk of a 'Bismarckian turn' appears questionable. The position remains influential. On this issue see, for example, Helmut Walser Smith, 'Authoritarian State, Dynamic Society, Failed Imperialist Power, 1878–1914', in H. W. Smith (ed.), *Oxford Handbook of Modern Germany*, 308–11; Thomas Nipperdey, *Deutsche Geschichte 1866–1918, vol. II: Machtstaat vor der Demokratie* (Munich: C. H. Beck, 1998), 389–91.

176. Fischer, *Industrialisierung*, 25–8.

177. Nipperdey, *Deutsche Geschichte 1866–1918, vol. I*, 235.

178. StadtAA 5/422, Mitgliederversammlung, 28 November 1876.

179. StadtAA 5/422, Mitgliederversammlung, 10 December 1878.

180. StadtAA 5/422, Mitgliederversammlung, 21 April 1880.

181. StadtAA 5/422, Mitgliederversammlungen, 10 June 1879, 25 June 1879.

182. StadtAA 5/37, 12 February 1883.

183. Ibid.

184. StadtAA 5/37, Mitgliederversammlung 6 March 1883.

185. Ritzhaupt, *In Sonne und Rauch*, 5.

CHAPTER 2

1. NAZ, Nr. 141 (23 May 1865).

2. StadtAL ZR 5002/2, Bürgermeister, Adjunkt und Gemeinderat an K. Staatsministerium d. Innern für Kirchen- und Schulangelegenheiten, 8 August 1872.

3. SAL E 179 II/3329, Bürgermeister von Heim an Regierungsrat Renschler, 12 October 1875.

4. StadtAA: 1/1294. *Verwaltungsbericht des Stadtmagistrats 1871*, 6–7.

5. Ibid.

6. ANN, no. 8 (9 January 1872).

7. SAL E 179 II/3329, Bürgermeister von Heim an Regierungsrat Renschler, 12 October, 1875.

8. UT, no. 5 (8 January 1875); UT, no. 35 (10 February 1878).

9. USP, no. 62 (15 March 1874).

10. U 9764. Gedruckte Schulprogrammschriften des Königl. Gymnasiums Ulm. UT, no. 226 (26 September 1878).

11. Ibid. UT, no. 244 (17 October 1878); UT, no. 245 (18 October 1878).

12. Von Hippel, 'Zwischen kleindeutscher Reichsgründung und Weltkriegs-Katastrophe', 616, 624.

13. StadtAL ZR 5000/20, Erläuterungsbericht des königlichen Lokal-schulinspektors Dr Geistbeck zum Schulorganisationsplan für die kon-fessionell gemischten Volksschulen zu Ludwigshafen am Rhein pro 1888/89.

14. StadtAL ZR 5000/20, Sitzung Ortschulkommission, 10 December 1897.

15. Various historians have pointed out that the link between educational reform and economic growth (let alone social mobility) was tenuous at best. For an argument linking nineteenth-century educational reform to status reproduction rather than social mobility, see Detlef K. Müller, Fritz Ringer and Brian Simon (eds.), *The rise of the Modern Education System: Structural Change and Social Reproduction* (Cambridge: Cambridge University Press, 1987), especially Introduction by Ringer.

16. On the German *Volksschule* in general, see Nipperdey, *Deutsche Geschichte 1866–1918*, vol. I, 532–42; James Albisetti, 'Education', in Chickering (ed.), *Imperial Germany: A Historical Companion*, 244–71.

17. I owe this observation to Jim Brophy.

18. StadtAL ZR 5000/19, K. Regierung der Pfalz an Bezirksamt Speyer. 28 December 1869; Lehrer Mai an Bürgermeisteramt Ludwigshafen, 13 January 1870.

19. StadtAL ZR 5530–1, Bürgermeister Ludwigshafen an Synagogen-Ausschuss, 10 August 1863.

20. StadtAA 10/300, Schreiben der Israelitischen Cultusverwaltung an den Magistrat der Stadt Augsburg, 25 July 1864.

21. Bischöfliches Ordinariat an Pfarrklerus. Betreff: Abhaltung von Gottesdiensten während der Unterrichtszeit in der Volksschule, 19 June 1878. In: *Oberhirtliche Generalien der Diözese Augsburg vom 11. Oktober 1876 bis 23 September 1886* (Augsburg: Druck der F.C. Kremerschen Buchdruckerei, 1887).

22. On the role of schools in the standardization of time, see Thompson, 'Time, Work-Discipline, and Industrial Capitalism', 84–5.

23. Nipperdey, *Deutsche Geschichte 1866–1918*, vol. I, 539.

24. By the 1870s the so-called one-class elementary school had become virtually unknown in Germany, except in very small, rural communities. The typical elementary school now entailed at least three, and often four or more, age-specific grades. On this, see Nipperdey, *Deutsche Geschichte 1866–1914, vol. I*, 534. In the 1880s, for example, Frankfurt's *Volksschule* ran four grades, with each pupil being stuck in the same age cohort for two years. See Jan Palmowski, *Urban Liberalism in Imperial Germany: Frankfurt am Main 1866–1914* (Oxford: Oxford University Press, 1999), 184–5.

25. StadtAA 10/389, Mitgliederversammlung Augsburg Casino, 17 January 1895.

26. See Marjorie Lamberti, *State, Society, & the Elementary School in Imperial Germany* (New York: Oxford University Press, 1989), chs 2–3.

27. Nipperdey, *Deutsche Geschichte 1866–1914*, vol. I, 534.

28. The proportion was only marginally higher in the Prussian countryside. See Klewitz, 'Preussische Volksschule', 554; Lamberti, *Elementary School*, ch. 3.

29. Lamberti, *Elementary School*, 96.

30. Lamberti, *Elementary School*, 96.

31. Karl A. Schleunes, *Schooling and Society: The Politics of Education in Prussia and Bavaria 1750–1900* (Oxford: Berg, 1989), 186.

32. Alfred Dehlinger, *Württembergs Staatswesen in seiner geschichtlichen Entwicklung bis heute*. 2 vols. (Stuttgart: W. Kohlhammer Verlag, 1951), 463–79. See also Bernhard Mann, 'Württemberg 1800–1866', in H. Schwarzmaier, H. Fenske, B. Kirchgässner, M. Schaab (eds.), *Handbuch der Baden-Württembergischen Geschichte, vol. III: Vom Ende des Alten Reiches bis zum Ende der Monarchien* (Stuttgart: Klett-Cotta, 1992), 366.

33. Nippedey, *1866–1918*, vol. I, 536–37.

34. StadtAL 5000/19, Bürgerkomittee an Bürgermeister Hoffmann, 17 June 1869.

35. StadtAL ZR 5000/19.

36. StadtAL ZR 5000/19, Flugschrift 'An die Bewohner Ludwigshafens', 1869.

37. Ibid.

38. Ibid.

39. StadtAL ZR 5000/19.

40. PfK, no. 146 (25 June 1869).

41. StadtAL ZR 5000/19, Bekanntmachung des Bürgermeisteramts, 21 June 1869.

42. StadtAL ZR 5000/19, Einführung der Kommunalschulen zu Ludwigshafen, hier die Abstimmung betreffend. Geschehen zu Ludwigshafen den 24 Juni 1869.

43. StadtAL ZR 5000/19, Polizeikommissar an königliches Bezirksamt, 26 June 1869.

44. StadtAL ZR 5000/19, Polizeikommissar an königliches Bezirksamt, 26 June 1869.

45. Verwaltungs-Bericht des Bürgermeisteramts Ludwigshafen am Rhein für das Jahr 1905: Situation an den Volksschulen der Stadt im Jahre 1904/5.

46. StadtAL ZR 5000/19, Stadtratskommission betreffend Einrichtung der Kommunalschule, 9 August 1869.

47. StadtAL ZR 5000/19, Sitzung der Schulkommission der Stadt Ludwigshafen, 9 August 1869.

48. StadtAL ZR 5007/7. See also *Verwaltungsbericht des Bürgermeisteramts Ludwigshafen am Rhein für das Jahr 1905*, 85. On the Prussian situation, see Nipperdey, *Deutsche Geschichte 1866–1918*, vol. I, 539.

49. StadtAL ZR 5000/20, Königliche Regierung d. Pfalz an Landeskommissariat, 18 August 1856.

50. StadtAL ZR 5000/20, Königliche Regierung d. Pfalz an Landeskommissariat. 28 March 1856; Königliches Landeskommissariat an Bürgermeisteramt Ludwigshafen, 26 June 1856.

51. StadtAL ZR 5000/20, Königlich Bayrische Regierung d. Pfalz an Landeskommissariat, 18 November 1859.

52. *Stadtgeschichte Ludwigshafen*, 290.

53. An urban history of 1903 concluded that the progress of Ludwigshafen's *Volksschule* since its existence could only have been achieved through the *Communalschule*. *Stadtgeschichte Ludwigshafen*, 291.

54. StadtAL ZR 5000/19, Sitzung Ortsschulkommission vom 9 September 1869; Bedenken der geistlichen Mitglieder der Ortsschulkommission sowie der beiden Distriktschulinspektionen, 29 September 1869.

55. Ibid.

56. StadtAL, Sitzung Ortsschulkommission, 9 September 1869.

57. Ibid.

58. StadtAL ZR 5000/19, L. Gelbert, P. Tuehrer, C. Ludovici an Bürgermeisteramt. 19 April 1870.

59. StadtAL ZR 5002/2, Bürgermeister und Gemeinderat an Bayrisches Staatsministerium des Innern für Kirchen- und Schulangelegenheiten, 8 August 1872.

60. Ibid.

61. StadtAL ZR 5000/16, Versammlung Lokalschulkommission, 7 June 1872.

62. StadtAL ZR 5000/20. The evidence does indeed suggest that confessional parity was strictly observed.

63. Hofherr refers to the last population census, which revealed that Ludwigshafen's population comprised 3854 Catholics and 3744 Protestants. StadtAL ZR 5000/16, Antrag der Königlich Katholischen Lokalschulinspektion betr. Einrichtung neuer Schulstellen a.d. Communalschule zu Ludwigshafen, 7 July 1872.

64. StadtAL ZR 5000/16, Königliches Bezirksamt Speyer an Katholische Lokal-Schulinspektion, 17 July 1872; Königlich Bayrische Regierung der Pfalz an Bezirksamt Speyer, 7 September 1872.

65. StadtAL, ZR 5002/2, Bürgermeister, Adjunkt und Gemeinderat an Bezirksamt Speyer, 23 May 1872.

66. StadtAL ZR 5002/2, Gemeinderat an Bürgermeisteramt, 31 May 1872.

67. StadtAL ZR 5002/2, Bürgermeister, Adjunkt und Gemeinderat an Königliches Staatsministerium des Innern für Kirchen- und Schulangelegenheiten, 8 August 1872.

68. StadtAL ZR 5002/2, 26 April 1876.

69. StadtAL ZR 5007/7, Königlich Bayrische Regierung der Pfalz an Königliches Bezirksamt Speyer, 15 July 1879.

70. StadtAL ZR 5007/7, Königlich Bayrische Regierung der Pfalz an Königliches Bezirksamt Speyer, 16 September 1879.

71. StadtAL ZR 5007/5, Klassenbildung für den katholischen Religionsunterricht, Schuljahr 1886/87. Gefertigt nach dem Schülerstande vom 5. May 1886.

72. For an example of complaints of this kind, see StadtAL ZR 5002/2, Königliches Bezirksamt Speyer an Regierung der Pfalz, 26 April 1876; Bürgermeisteramt Ludwigshafen an Bezirksamt Speyer, 7 October 1881.

73. In 1876 some teachers made their support contingent on the appointment of teacher Dörr, the town's longest-serving primary school teacher. StadtAL ZR 5002/2, Volksschullehrer an Bürgermeisteramt, 3 July 1876.

74. StadtAL ZR 5002/2, Bayrische Regierung der Pfalz an Königliches Bezirksamt Speyer, 19 March 1884.

75. StadtAL ZR 5002/2, Sitzung Ortsschul-Kommission, 7 April 1884.

76. StadtAL ZR 5002/2, Gemeinderatssitzung vom 11. September 1885; Bürgermeister an Königliches Bezirksamt Speyer, 12 September 1885.

77. StadtAL ZR 5002/2, Beeidigung des Lokalschulinspektors Dr Alois Geistbeck.

78. On the opening of the Hemshof school, see Gemeinderatssitzung, 12 December 1878: StadtAL ZR 5000/20.

79. StadtAL ZR 5010/6, Sitzung Ortsschulkommission betreffend das Vorrücken der Lehrer vom Hemshof in die Stadt, 12 April 1887; Verschiedene Lehrer des Hemshof an das Königliche Bezirksamt, 12 August 1887.

80. Ibid.

81. Ibid.

82. StadtAL ZR 5010/9, Beschwerde der Lehrer an das Königliche Bezirksamt Speyer, 10 December 1890.

83. StadtAL ZR 5010/9, Bürgermeisteramt an Königliches Bezirksamt Speyer, 5 January 1891.

84. ANN, no. 249 (22 October 1886); ANN, no. 264 (12 November 1897).

85. StadtAA 2/4074, Stadtmagistrat an Regierung von Schwaben und Neuburg, Übersicht Schuljahr 1865/66; ANN, no. 230 (30 September 1886).

86. StadtAA 2/1186, Bericht des Bezirks-Schulkommissärs Ludwig Bauer über den Stand der hiesigen Volksschulen im Schuljahr 1892/93 betreffend, 18 January 1894.

87. StadtAA 5/548, Versammlung Christlicher Arbeiterverein, 8 June 1879.

88. StadtAA 10/389, Versammlung Katholisches Casino, 2 February 1889.

89. StadtAA 3/225, Stadtmagistrat an Gemeindebevollmächtigte, 5 June 1858.

90. StadtAA 2/1211, Priorin des Klosters St. Ursula an die K. Lokal-Schulkommission, 8 November 1865.

91. StadtAA 2/1211, Katholische Schulkommission an Stadtmagistrat, 23 November 1865.

92. StadtAA 3/225, Stadtmagistratssitzung, 23 March 1854.

93. StadtAA 2/1213, Protestantischer Schulinspektor, Pfarrer Dr Göringer, an die K. Lokalschulkommission, 10 June 1867.

94. StadtAA 3/225, Stadtmagistrat an Gemeindebevollmächtigte, 18 October 1862.

95. See, for example, ANN, no. 230 (30 September 1886); ANN, no. 264 (12 November 1897).

96. StadtAA 2/1225, Verhandlungen der k. Lokalschulkommission, 12 September 1866. StadtAA 2/1213, Antrag der k. protestestantischen Bezirksschulinspektion an die k. Lokalschulkommission, 10 May 1867. StadtAA 2/4074, Schulgesetz für die deutschen Volksschulen betreffend 1867.

97. See Gerd Hohorst, Jürgen Kocka und Gerhard A. Ritter (eds.), *Sozialgeschichtliches Arbeitsbuch: Materialien zur Statistik des Kaiserreichs 1870–1914* (Munich: Beck, 1975).

98. StadtAA 2/4062, Bericht Städtischer Schulrat Ludwig Bauer an Stadtmagistrat, November 1875.

99. ANN, no. 247 (17 October 1872).

100. ANN, no. 83 (6 April 1873).

101. AP, no. 141 (17 June 1873).

102. See Martin Niesseler, *Die Augsburger Schulen im Wandel der Zeit* (Augsburg: Verlag Hieronymus Mühlberger, 1984).

103. NAZ, Nr. 141, (23 May 1865).

104. AP, no. 141 (17 June 1873).

105. StadtAA 2/1186, Regierung v. Schwaben und Neuburg an die K. Lokalschulkommission Augsburg, die Schulvisitations-Protokolle pro 1855/56 und 1856/57 betreffend, 5 April 1859; Regierung v. Schwaben & Neuburg an die Lokalschulkommission Augsburg, die Schulvisitationen in den protestantischen Schulen der Stadt Augsburg pro 1859/60 betreffend, 22 January 1861.

106. Ibid.

107. StadtAA 2/1186, Regierung v. Schwaben & Neuburg an Lokalschulkommission Augsburg die Schulvisitationen in den protestantischen Schulen der Stadt Augsburg pro 1859/60 betreffend, 22 January 1861. Regierung v. Schwaben und Neuburg an die Lokalschulkommission Augsburg, 15 May 1875.

108. Ibid.

109. Ibid.

110. StadtAA 2/1186, Regierung v. Schwaben & Neuburg an die k. Lokalschulkommission in Augsburg, 3 February 1875/15 May 1875.

111. Ibid.

112. StadtAA 2/1186, Bericht des k. Bezirks-Schulkommissärs Ludwig Bauer über den Stand der hiesigen Volksschulen im Schuljahr 1892/93 betr., 18 January 1894.

113. Speech by Ludwig Fischer: ANN, no. 6 (7 January 1872).

114. ANN, no. 8 (9 January 1872).

115. StadtAA 5/555, Versammlung Neuer Bürgerverein, 9 November 1878.

116. StadtAA 5/424, Versammlung Katholisches Casino, 14 November 1879.

117. StadtAA 5/548, Versammlung Christlicher Arbeiterverein, 8 June 1879.

118. ANN, no. 124 (20 June 1889).

119. ANN, no. 205 (3 September 1894).

120. StadtAA 2/1187, Visitationsprotokolle der hiesigen Volksschulen 1897/98.

121. StadtAA 2/1188, Visitationsbericht für die Simultanschulen in der Wertach-Vorstadt, 20 November 1899.

122. StadtAA 2/1186, Regierung von Schwaben und Neuburg an Stadtmagistrat, 21 April 1891; Lokalschulkommkission an Stadtmagistrat, 25 June 1891. These problems prompted the district government to set the maximum of pupils allowed to repeat a class at 12.5 per cent: StadtAA 2/1186, Lokalschulkommission an Lehrer an den Augsburger Volksschulen, 9 September 1891.

123. StadtAA 5/559, Mitgliederversammlung, 12 November 1888.

124. StadtAA 10/389, Versammlung Katholisches Casino, 14 February 1889.

125. StadtAA 10/389, Vortrag Lehrer Wörle von Pfersee, 17 January 1895.

126. Manfred Kindl, 'Die öffentlichen Schulen in Ulm', in Specker (ed.), *Ulm im 19. Jahrhundert*, 452.

127. Kindl, 'Öffentliche Schulen', 453.

128. Kindl, 'Öffentlichen Schulen', 454. See also USP, no. 226 (27 September 1872).

129. USP, no. 296 (18 December 1872).

130. USP, no. 252 (29 October 1874).

131. USP, no. 234 (7 October 1880).

132. USP, no. 247 (22 October 1870).

133. USP, no. 242 (16 October 1886); no. 215 (15 September 1886).

134. UT, no. 250 (27 October 1886).

135. USP, no. 243 (17 October 1886).

136. Even though it did not promote the *Kulturkampf* along lines that are familiar from Baden or Prussia, Württemberg was not the oasis of peace as that it has sometimes been described. In Ulm, too, tensions between reformers and religious conservatives surfaced from the 1870s or even before. Instead of erupting into a full-blown conflict, however, they were often diffused, at least in part, by persistent dialogue. Dehlinger, *Württembergs Staatswesen*, 463–79; Mann, 'Württemberg 1800–1866', 366.

137. See the correspondence in StadtAU B211/00, Nr. 1.

138. As the Catholic authorities were keen to point out: StadtAU B211/00, no. 1, Gemeinderatssitzung, 30 January 1900.

139. StadtAU B211/00, no. 1, Katholisches Stadtschulamt an Stadtrat Ulm, 26 September 1870.

140. StadtAU B211/00, no. 1, Sitzung Gemeinderat, 11 October 1870.

141. Ibid., Sitzung Gemeinderat, 9 March 1871.

142. StadtAU B211/00, no. 1, Sitzung Gemeinderat, 29 April 1872.

143. Wagner, *Die wirtschaftlichen Verhaeltnisse der Stadt Ulm im 19. Jahrhundert*, 56.

144. StadtAU B211/00, no. 1, Sitzung Gemeinderat, 19 April 1900.

145. In this respect, Ulm was indeed the exception that other Württemberg towns, including Stuttgart, tried to emulate. See *Vorschlaege zur Verbesserung des Stuttgarter Schulwesens. Im Auftrage des Buergerausschusses zusammengestellt von J. Loechner, Lehrer und Buergerausschussobmann* (Stuttgart: Th. Spöttle, 1905).

146. StadtAU B211/00, no. 1, Sitzung Gemeinderat, 19 April 1900.

147. Ibid., Sitzung Gemeinderat, 26 July 1900.

148. StadtAU B211/00, no. 1, Katholischer Kirchenrat an Oberamt Ulm, 4 September 1900.

149. Ibid., Sitzung Gemeinderat, 18 September 1900.

150. StadtAU B211/20, no. 3, Sitzung Gemeinderat, 12 October 1905. Meeting municipal council, 12 October 1905.

151. StadtAU B 211/20, no. 6, Katholischer Kirchenrat Stuttgart an K. Oberamt in Schulsachen Ulm, 11 October 1904.

152. UT, no. 5 (8 January 1875); UT, no. 35 (10 February 1878).

153. SAL E 179II, no. 3329. Oberbürgermeister von Heim an Regierungsrat Renschler, 12 October 1875.

154. *Beschreibung des Oberamts Ulm*, 710–15.

155. UT, no. 205 (31 August 1878).

156. See the table in Kindl, 'Öffeutliche Schulen', 455.

157. UT, no. 6 (8 January 1878).

158. USP, no. 252 (28 October 1883).

159. USP, no. 79 (3 April 1878).

160. UT, no. 15 (20 January 1892).

161. *Stadtgeschichte Ludwigshafen*, 299–300.

PART II. PROLOGUE

1. Georg Simmel, *On Individuality and Social Forms: Selected Writings*, edited and with an Introduction by Donald N. Levine (Chicago: University of Chicago Press, 1971), 143.

2. See Friedrich Lenger and Dieter Langewiesche, 'Internal Migration: Persistence and Mobility', in Klaus J. Bade (ed.), *Population, Labour and Migration in 19th and 20th Century Germany* (Leamington Spa: Berg, 1987), 87–100.

3. Ernest Benz, 'Escaping Malthus: population explosion and human movement, 1760–1884', in Smith (ed.), *The Oxford Handbook of Modern German History*, 195–210.

4. Andreas Fahrmeier, *Citizens and Aliens: Foreigners and the Law in Britain and the German States, 1789–1870* (New York: Berghahn, 2000), 65. Larry Frohman, *Poor Relief and Welfare in Germany from the Reformation to World War I* (Cambridge: Cambridge University Press, 2008), 83–4.

5. On this new legislation, see, *inter alia*, Weichlein, *Nation und Region*, esp. 202–3; Dieter Gosewinkel, *Einbürgern und Ausschliessen: Die Nationalisierung der Staatsangehörigkeit vom Deutschen Bund bis zur Bundesrepublik Deutschland* (Göttingen: Vandenhoeck & Ruprecht, 2001); Frohman, *Poor Relief*, chs 4–5.

6. Württembergische Verfassungsurkunde vom 25. September 1819, §62, in: Württembergisches Staats- und Regierungsblatt 1819. On the introduction of the *Unterstützungswohnsitz* in Württemberg, see Dehlinger, *Württembergs Staatswesen*, 359–60.

7. Frohman, *Poor Relief*, ch. 5; George Steinmetz, *Regulating the Social: The Welfare State and Local Politics in Imperial Germany* (Princeton: Princeton University Press, 1993), ch. 6.

8. See Walker, *German Home Towns*, 288, 303, 417; Fahrmeier, *Citizens and Aliens*, 64; Gosewinkel, *Einbürgern und Ausschliessen*, 53, 57. More generally on the staying power of corporatist structures in nineteenth-century Germany, see John Breuilly, 'Modernisation as Social Evolution: The German Case, *c.* 1800–1880', *Transactions of the Royal Historical Society* 15 (2005), 117–47.

9. Gosewinkel, *Einbürgern und Ausschliessen*, 123.

10. Gosewinkel, *Einbürgern und Ausschliessen*, 126–7.

11. Fahrmeier, *Citizens and Aliens*, 67.

12. As Dieter Langewiesche put it bluntly: 'The state imposed a set of new rules but left the business of settling the bill with the municipalities.' Dieter Langewiesche, '"Staat" und "Kommune". Zum Wandel der Staatsaufgaben in Deutschland im 19. Jahrhundert', *Historische Zeitschrift* 248 (1989), 628.

13. Douglas Ashford, 'The Structural Comparison of Social Policy and Intergovernmental Politics', *Policy and Politics* 12 (1984), 376; Suphan Andic and Jindrich Veverka, 'The Growth of Government Expenditure in Germany since the Unification', Finanzarchiv, n.s., 23:2 (1963), 270.

14. Hans-Ulrich Wehler, *Deutsche Gesellschaftsgeschichte. Vol. III: 1849–1914* (Munich: C.H. Beck, 1995), 130–7.

Drawing on legal records, Dieter Gosewinkel (*Einbürgern und Ausschliessen*, 149) has argued that the municipalities proved powerless to stop the state-induced 'decommunalization of state membership', while Harry Frohman (*Poor Relief*, 83) associates the move from *Heimat* to *Wohnsitz* with a transformation from 'self-governing bodies endowed with corporate privileges to administrative units of the sovereign state.' Employing a Foucaultian framework, George Steinmetz, in his *Regulating the Social* (esp. ch. 6) also depicts localities as executioners of state initiatives.

15. At no point in their history had German communes really enjoyed autonomy if by that we mean complete independence from outside interference. Germany's *freie Reichsstädte* had not been free to do as they pleased, either. See, for example, Klaus Schreiner, '"Kommunenbewegung" und "Zunftrevolution". Zur Gegenwart der mittelalterlichen Stadt im historisch-politischen Denken des 19.Jahrhunderts', in Franz Quartal und Wilfried Setzler (eds.), *Stadtverfassung, Verfassungsstaat, Pressepolitik. Festschrift fuer Eberhard Naujoks zum 65. Geburstag* (Sigmarien: Jan Thorbecke, 1980), 139–68.

16. According to Fahrmeier (*Citizens and Aliens*, 67), between 1815 and 1848 it was 'close to prohibitive for all but the upper middle classes' to acquire citizenship in states such as Baden and Bavaria.

17. Fahrmeier, *Citizens and Aliens*, 30.

18. Max von Seydel, 'Die Reform des bayerischen Heimatrechtes', *Blätter für administrative Praxis* XLVI, no. 4 (1896), 121–2.

19. Paul Hirsch und Hugo Lindemann, *Das kommunale Wahlrecht* (Berlin: Buchhandlung Vorwaerts, 1905), 4.

20. On such formal and informal, 'thick' and 'thin', types of citizenship, see the contributions in Geoff Eley and Jan Palmowski (eds.), *Citizenship and National Identity in Twentieth-Century Germany* (Stanford: Stanford University Press, 2009).

CHAPTER 3

1. UT, no. 27 (1 February 1878).

2. StadtAA 10/2697. Reply to a request form the *Deutsche Gemeindezeitung*, 5 November 1877.

3. F. J. Ehrhart, *Das bayerische Heimatgesetz mit Erläuterungen nebst Anhang über den Erwerb der Staatsangehörigkeit, der Naturalisation und des Armengesetzes* (Ludwigshafen: Josef Huber, 1901), VIII.

4. Schuster, *Antrag des Stadtschultheissen Schuster betreffend das Armenwesen der Stadt Ulm.*

5. Schuster, *Antrag*, 15–23.

6. Ibid.

7. StadtAU B400/0, no. 2, Skizze eines Gesetzes über die Armenunterstützung von 1862.

8. StadtAU B400/0, no. 2, Antwort des Ulmer Stadtrats (Adam) an das K. Oberamt, 6 May 1863.

9. StadtAU B122/51, no. 60, Sitzung Gemeinderat, 29 October 1863.

10. Ibid., Sitzung Gemeinderat, 15 April 1865.

11. StadtAU B122/51, no. 60, Sitzung Gemeinderat, 23 April 1864.

12. Ibid., Sitzung Gemeinderat, 23 November 1869.

13. See, for instance, UT, no. 27 (1 February 1878).

14. On Ulm's charitable foundations, see Michael Wettengel, 'Zur Geschichte der Stiftungen in Ulm', 10–46.

15. SAL E179II/3329, Oberbürgermeister von Heim an Oberamt Ulm, 12 October 1875. StadtAU B008/00, no. 2, Stadtgemeinde Ulm an Regierungsrat Renschler (Bericht der Ortsarmenbehörde betreffend Armenversorgung in Ulm), 26 October 1875).

16. USP, no. 5 (8 January 1885). These complaints confirm Dieter Langewiesche's argument that it was Germany's municipalities that prepared the ground for the modern welfare state. See Langewiesche, '"Staat" und "Kommune"', 623. See also Hans-Peter Jans, *Sozialpolitik und Wohlfahrtspflege in Ulm 1870–1930* (Stuttgart: W. Kohlhammer, 1994), 14.

17. USP, no. 30 (6 February 1885).

18. For details, see the Reichsgesetz über die Freizügigkeit, 1 November 1867, §4, 5. On the social responsibilities of the communes in the context of *Freizügigkeit*, see in particular Frohman, *Poor Relief*, chs 4–5.

19. StadtAU B401/2, no. 3, Stadtpolizeiamt an Armenpfleger, 4 May 1874.

20. Ibid., Stadtpolizeiamt an Armenpfleger, 16 June 1874.

21. SAL E 179 II: 8000.

22. SAL E 179 II: 7987.

23. SAL E 179 II: 7979.

24. SAL E 179 II/7979, An die Königliche Regierung für den Donaukreis in Ulm. Klageschrift des Rechtsanwalts R. Ebner in Ulm namens der Ortsarmenbehörde Ulm in deren Rechtssache als Klägerin, gegen den Ortsarmenverband Langenau, Beklagten, Erstatz für einer Wittwe Ursula Liebert von Langenau gereichten Unterstützung betreffend, 19 June 1882.

25. SAL E 179 II/7979, K. Regierung des Donaukreises als Verwaltungsgericht. Urtheil. Beschlossen Ulm in der Sitzung vom 28. Dezember 1882.

26. StadtAU B400/0, no. 1, Armenordnung vom 22. Januar 1861.

27. StadtAU B400/0, no. 1, Armenordnung vom 22. Januar 1861. See also Frohman, *Poor Relief*, chs 5, 6. On Ulm, see Jans, *Sozialpolitik und Wohlfahrtspflege*, 32–40.

28. UT, no. 8 (11 January 1874). See also Statut der Verwaltung der öffentlichen Armenpflege in Ulm. The statute was approved by the K. Ministerium des Innern on 17 April 1876.

29. USP, no. 131 (8 June 1880).

30. Langewiesche, '"Staat" und "Kommune"'.

31. See StadtAU B 026/5, B 401/1, no. 2. The gamut of social relief institutions and other mechanisms that were invented in Ulm in the 1870s and 1880s (and which included a nursery, a workhouse, a municipal *Fremdenbureau* for travelling journeymen, as well as various organizations on a charitable basis) is described in Jans, *Sozialpolitik und Wohlfahrtspflege*, 58–100.

32. StadtAU B 401/2, no. 2, Verzeichnis der nach dem Statut über die Verwaltung der öffentlichen Armenpflege aufgestellten Armenräte.

33. StadtAU 400/0, no. 3, Verzeichnis der nach dem Statut über die Verwaltung der öffentlichen Armenpflege aufgestellten Armenräte. Den 1. August 1876. StadtAU 401/2, no. 2, Verzeichnis der nach dem Statut über die Verwaltung der öffentlichen Armenpflege aufgestellten Armenräte. Den 1. April 1889. See also Jans, *Sozialpolitik und Wohlfahrtspflege*, 58–63.

34. StadtAU 401/2, no. 1, Armechnungen presented by Armenpfleger Wolfenter: jährlicher Aufwand von 1875–1886, Ulm, 18 August 1886.

35. StadtAU 401/2, no. 1, Armenpfleger an das Stadtschultheissenamt Ulm. 8 August 1886.

36. Throughout the 1880s, Ulm featured Württemberg's highest rate of criminal convictions relating to begging. See Jans, *Sozialpolitik und Wohlfahrtspflege*, 87–90, 210–11, 304–10.

37. 'Denkschrift des Regierungsrates Lamotte vom 31 Dezember 1853 ueber die Verhaeltnisse von Ludwigshafen am Rhein', 11.

38. Peter Marschalck, 'Zur Rolle der Stadt für den Industrialisierungsprozeß, 57–66.

39. StadtAL Lua, no. 650, Bürgermeisteramt an Landescommissariat, 20 April 1858.

40. Ibid.

41. StadtAL Lua, no. 650, Bürgermeisteramt an Landescommissariat, 20 April 1858.

42. StadtAL ZR 1025/11, Gutachten der Stadtverwaltung Ludwigshafen am Rhein zur bevorstehenden Reform der bayrischen Heimat- und Armengesetzgebung, April 1911.

43. Ibid., 34–6.

44. Ibid., 28–9.

45. See Hirsch & Lindemann, *Das kommunale Wahrecht*, 26–7.

46. For an illuminating discussion of these developments, see F. J. Ehrhart, *Das bayerische Heimatgesetz mit Erläuterungen nebst Anhang über den Erwerb der Staatsangehörigkeit, der Naturalisation und des Armengesetzes* (Ludwigshafen: Josef Huber, 1904), VIII.

47. Ibid.

48. F. J. Ehrhart, *Das bayerische Heimatgesetz und seine Anwendung in der Pfalz nebst Anleitung zur Erwerbung des bayerischen Staatsbürgerrechts* (Ludwigshafen a. Rh.: Verlag der 'Pfälzischen Post', ohne Datum), 9.

49. StadtAL Lua 650, Bürgermeisteramt an Landescommissariat, 20 April 1858.

50. Ibid.

51. StadtAL Lua 650, Landeskommissariat an Bürgermeisteramt, 26 April 1858.

52. StadtAL Pa I, no. 4, 116, Sitzung Stadtrat, 16 February 1866.
53. StadtAL, Pa I, no. 4, 215, Sitzung Stadtrat, 22 February 1867.
54. StadtAL, Pa I, no. 4, 154, Sitzung Stadtrat, 12 September 1867; Pa I, no. 4, 187, Sitzung Stadtrat, 11 November 1867.
55. See the example of the factory worker Stephan Satter from Niersheim in Hesse: StadtAL Pa I, no. 4, 394, Sitzung Stadtrat, 22 October 1869.
56. *Geschichte der Stadt Ludwigshafen am Rhein*, 233.
57. StadtAL Lua 650, Landrat an K. Regierung der Pfalz, 27 June 1853, K. Bayrische Regierung der Pfalz an K. Landeskommissariat, 21 July 1853.
58. For the successive reduction of citizenship fees, see: StadtAL Pa I, no. 5, 293–5, Sitzung Stadtrat, 12 July 1872. See also StadtAL Lua 650, Heimat-Gebühren-Tarif der Stadt Ludwigshafen vom 29. April 1897; Heimat-Gebühren-Tarif der Stadtgemeinde Ludwigshafen am Rhein, aufgestellt auf Grund des Stadtratsbeschlusses vom 9. Oktober 1903.
59. StadtAL Lua 595, Bürgermeisteramt an Jakob Werner Zimmermann, 6 December 1886.
60. StadtAL Lua 595, Sitzung Stadtrat, 17 September 1886. StadtAL Pa I, no. 9, 203, Sitzung Stadtrat, 17 September 1886.
61. StadtAL, Lua 595, Entscheid Stadtrat, 20 November 1886; Bezirksamt an Bürgermeisteramt, 6 November 1886.
62. The council debate is summarized in *Pfälzischer Kurier*, no. 260 (19 September 1886).
63. StadtAL Pa I, no. 9, 279, Sitzung Stadtrat, 10 December 1886.
64. StadtAL PaI, no. 9, 38–40, Sitzung Stadtrat, 16 March 1886.
65. StadtAL ZR 1025/2, Bürgermeisteramt Ludwigshafen an Bürgermeisterämter Kaiserslautern, Speyer, Landau, Neustadt, Zweibrücken, Pirmasens, 27 September 1883.
66. Ibid.
67. StadtAL Pa I, no. 13: 133, 153–4, Sitzung Stadtrat, 21 September 1894; 12 October 1894.
68. ANN, no. 142 (24 May 1863).
69. StadtAA 10/3659, Sitzung Stadtmagistrat, 1 August 1868.
70. *Intelligenz-Blatt der königlich Bayerischen Stadt Augsburg*, no. 56 (30 August 1868).
71. StadtAA 10/3659, Magistrat Augsburg an Magistrat Erlangen, 23 December 1884.
72. StadtAA 1/1294, Verwaltungs-Berichte des Stadtmagistrats Augsburg. StadtAA 10/2697, Jahresberichte über das Armenwesen.
73. *Intelligenz-Blatt der k. Bayerischen Stadt Augsburg*, no. 56 (30 August 1868).
74. StadtAA 10/3659, Stadtmagistrat Regensburg an Stadtmagistrat Augsburg, 19 October 1883.
75. StadtAA 10/3659, Stadtmagistrat Augsburg an Stadtmagistrat Regensburg, 29 October 1883.

76. StadtAA 10/3659, Stadtmagistrat Augsburg an Stadtmagistrat Neu-Ulm, 3 December 1896.

77. StadtAA 10/3659, Stadtmagistrat Augsburg an Stadtmagistrat Hof, 20 April 1899.

78. StadtAA 10/3659, Stadtmagistrat München an Stadtmagistrat Augsburg, 22 January 1902.

79. StadtAA 10/3659, Stadtmagistrat Augsburg an Stadtmagistrat München, 28 January 1902.

80. StadtAA 10/3659, Direktion der Augsburger elektrischen Strassenbahn an Stadtmagistrat Augsburg, 6 February 1902.

81. StadtAA 10/3659, Beschluss Stadtmagistrat Augsburg, 15 February 1902.

82. StadtAA 10/3659, Petition des Stadtmagistrat Augsburg an die Kammer der Abgeordneten in München, March 1896.

83. Ibid. See also StadtAA 10/3677, Augsburger Petition an die Kammer der Abgeordneten und die Kammer der Reichsräte in München, 7 March 1896.

84. Ibid.

85. StadtAA 10/3659, Beschluss Stadtmagistrat, 23 February 1891.

86. Ibid.

87. StadtAA 10/3659, Beschluss Stadtmagistrat, 22 April 1897.

88. StadtAA 10/3659, Verzeichnis derjenigen Städte, welche der hiesigen Stadtgemeinde gegenüber von der Befugnis des Art. 7a des Heimatgesetzes Gebrauch gemacht haben. Dem Stadtmagistrat vorgelegt duch den Polizei-Offizianten, den 24 April 1897.

89. StadtAA 10/3659, Beschluss Stadtmagistrat, 3 May 1897.

90. Applicants whose *Heimatgemeinde* was outside Augsburg had hitherto been the responsibility of Augsburg's magistrate office. See StadtAA 27/1, Rechtsrat Dr Grassmann an Stadtmagistrat Augsburg. Betreff: Vollzug der Novelle zum Armengesetz vom 17. Juni 1896, 2 July 1896.

91. StadtAA 27/1, Armenpflegschaftsrat der Stadt Augsburg an Stadtmagistrat. Betreff: Der Vollzug der Novelle zum Armengesetz vom 17. Juni 1896, 23 July 1896.

92. StadtAA 27/1, Armenpflegschaftskassier Frey a.d. Stadmagistrat, 7 July 1896. See also StadtAA 27/1, Beschluss Stadtmagistrat, 22 September 1896; Schreiben des Armenpflegschaftsrats der Stadt Augsburg an den Stadtmagistrat, 1 October 1896.

93. StadtAA 27/1, Armenpflegschafts-Kassier Frey an Stadtmagistrat, 6 January 1902.

94. Max von Seydel, 'Die Reform des bayerischen Heimatrechtes', *Blätter für administrative Praxis* XLVI, no. 4 (1896), 116–17.

95. StadtAA 10/2697, Stadtmagistrat an Redaktion der dt. Gemeinde-Zeitung in Berlin, 5 November 1877.

96. StadtAA 10/3677, Stadtmagistrat an Regierung von Schwaben u. Neuburg, 1894.

97. StadtAA 10/3659, Petition des Stadtmagistrat Augsburg an die Kammer der Abgeordneten, March 1896.
98. Hirsch & Lindemann, *Das kommunale Wahlrecht*, 4.
99. StadtAA 10/3677, Bericht des städtischen Armenverwalters Heuberger zhd. Stadtmagistrat, 11 April 1911.
100. StadtAA 10/3677, Bericht von Stadtkämmerer Frei zhd. Stadtmagistrat, 14 April 1911.
101. Ibid.

CHAPTER 4

1. StadtAA 10/3760, Sitzung Stadtmagistrat, 4 February 1906; Bericht des Polizei-Offizianten, 5 February 1906.
2. StadtAL, Pa I, no. 9, 457, Sitzung Stadtrat, 16 August 1887.
3. USP, no. 285 (6 December 1885).
4. Brett Fairbairn, 'Political Mobilization', in Chickering (ed.), *Imperial Germany*, 303–402; Margaret L. Anderson, *Practicing Democracy: Elections and Political Culture in Imperial Germany* (Princeton: Princeton University Press, 2000), 5.
5. James Sheehan, 'Liberalism and the City in Nineteenth-Century Germany', *Past & Present* 51 (1971), 136. In the same vein argues Nipperdey, *Deutsche Geschichte 1866–1918*, vol. 2, 535.
6. Nipperdey, *Deutsche Geschichte 1866–1918*, vol. 2, 521. Alan S. Kahan, *Liberalism in Nineteenth-Century Europe: The Political Culture of Limited Suffrage* (New York: Palgrave, 2003).
7. See in particular Karl Heinrich Pohl, 'Kommunen, Liberalismus und Wahlrechtsfragen: Zur Bedeutung des Wahlrechts fuer die "moderne" Kommunalpolitik in Deutschland am Ende des 19. Jahrhunderts', *Jahrbuch zur Liberalismus-Forschung* 13 (2001): 113–30; and by the same author, 'Kommunalpolitik in Dresden und München vor 1914', in James Retallack (ed.), *Sachsen in Deutschland Politik, Kultur und Gesellschaft 1830–1918* (Bielefeld: Verlag für Regionalgeschichte, 2000), 171–88. Pohl's argument on municipal liberalism echoes a position that Dieter Langewiesche formulated in the middle of the 1990s (for a summary, see his *Liberalism in Germany*, 218–27). See also John Breuilly, 'Urbanization and social transformation, 1800–1914', in Ogilvie and Overy (eds.), *Germany: A New Social and Economic History since 1800* 210–18.
8. Jenkins, *Provincial Modernity*. See also Umbach, *German Cities*.
9. *Beschreibung des Oberamts Ulm*, 193.
10. Hirsch & Lindemann, *Das kommunale Wahlrecht*, 35.
11. UT, no. 27 (1 February 1878).
12. UT, no. 27 (1 February 1878).
13. UT, no. 28 (2 February 1878).
14. USP, no. 255 (1 November 1879).

15. USP, no. 72 (27 March 1881). See also Weichlein, *Region und Nation*, 221–2.
16. UT, no. 6 (8 January 1884).
17. UT, no. 6 (8 January 1884).
18. UT, no. 5 (8 January 1886). USP, no. 273 (23 November 1881).
19. For details see the citizenship files in StadtAU, B 122/51.
20. Hirsch & Lindemann, *Das kommunale Wahlrecht*, 34.
21. UT, no. 270 (19 November 1885); USP, no. 285 (6. December 1885). Of the 2122 residents who in 1884 possessed the local franchise without being Ulm citizens, 212 were military personnel, 171 civil servants, 854 traders and artisans, and 885 workers, assistants and journeymen. See UT, no. 10, (14 January 1886).
22. UT, no. 10 (14 January 1886).
23. UT, no. 4, (6 January 1886).
24. UT, no. 10 (14 January 1886).
25. Ibid.
26. USP, no. 285 (6 December 1885).
27. UT, no. 3 (4 January 1889).
28. In 1890, by which time close to 4000 Ulmers were citizens, 5935 of Ulm's residents were entitled to take part in elections to the Reichstag. See UT, no. 42 (20 February 1890). For a broadly comparative examination of political inclusion and exclusion as part of liberal thought and practice, see Kahan, *Liberalism*.
29. UT, no. 8 (12 January 1886); USP, no. 277 (27 November 1885).
30. UT, no. 8 (12 January 1886); USP, no. 277 (27 November 1885). The figures are based on Jans, *Sozialpolitik und Wohlfahrtspflege*, 108.
31. UT, no. 8 (12 January 1886); USP, no. 277 (27 November 1885). The figures are based on Jans, *Sozialpolitik und Wohlfahrtspflege*, 108.
32. StadtAL Lua 650, Sattlermeister Brubacher und Fotter an Landeskommissariat Speyer, 4 June 1857.
33. StadtAL Lua 650, K. Landeskommisariat an Petenten Brubacher und Fotter, 6 June 1857.
34. StadtAL Lua 595, C. Bähr an K. Regierung der Pfalz, Kammer des Innern, 28 January 1858; Staatsministerium des Innern an K. Regierung d. Pfalz, 9 November 1858.
35. On the so-called *Zwangsbürger*, see also Hirsch and Lindemann, *Das kommunale Wahlrecht*, 27.
36. StadtAL Lua 650, Sitzung Stadtrat, 11 April 1867.
37. StadtAL Lua 650, K. Bezirksamt Speyer an Bürgermeisteramt Augsburg, 26 April 1867.
38. StadtAL Pa I, no. 4, 224–7, Sitzung Stadtrat, 11 April 1867.
39. StadtAL Pa I, no. 4, 247–9, Sitzung Stadtrat, 19 September 1867. StaLu: Pa I, no. 4, 247–9.
40. StadtAL Lua 650, Sitzung Stadtrat, 13 July 1871.
41. StadtAL Lua 650, Tobias Beyer to Bürgermeisteramt, 21 September 1871.
42. StadtAL Lua 650, Peter Hähn to Bürgermeisteramt, 4 August 1871.

43. StadtAL Lua 650, Thomas Pfeiffer to Bürgermeisteramt, 27 July 1871; Max Rapp to Bürgermeisteramt, 31 August 1871.
44. StadtAL Lua 650, Bezirksamt Speyer an Bürgermeisteramt Ludwigshafen, 12 September 1871. StadtAL Pa I, no. 5, 182–4, Sitzung Stadtrat, 12 October 1871.
45. StadtAL Pa I, no. 5, 172, Sitzung Stadtrat, 13 July 1871.
46. StadtAL Pa I, no. 5, 182–4, Sitzung Stadtrat, 12 October 1871.
47. StadtAL ZR 1025/26, Bericht über die Verhandlungen des 5. pfälzischen Städtetages, den 23. Dezember 1901. It was the Bavarian government that had instituted this accelerated pathway to local citizenship, for one simple reason: If a *heimatloser Bayer* fell into poverty, the state, not the municipality, had to pick up the bill. The 1896 law minimized the state's risk in this area. See the communications in StadtAL ZR 1025/6.
48. StadtAL ZR 1025/26, Bürgermeisteramt an Stadträte Ries and Ehrhart, 9 November 1900.
49. Von Hippel, 'Zwischen kleindeutscher Reichsgründung und Weltkriegs-Katastrophe', 709–13.
50. Willi Breunig, *Soziale Verhältnisse der Arbeiterschaft*, 207, 248, 341.
51. Von Hippel, 'Zwischen kleindeutscher Reichsgründung und Weltkriegs-Katastrophe', 516–17.
52. Willi Breunig, Vom Handelsplatz zum Industriestandort', 298.
53. Ibid., 311.
54. StadtAL Pa I, no. 1, 175–6, Sitzung Stadtrat, 13 August 1886.
55. StadtAL Pa I, no. 9, 198–9, Sitzung Stadtrat, 17 September 1886. Council meeting, 17 September 1886.
56. StadtAL Pa I, no. 9, 267–77, Sitzung Stadtrat, 10 December 1886. See also StadtAL Pa I, no. 9, 324.
57. StadtAL Pa I, no. 9, 40–1, Sitzung Stadtrat, 3 March 1886.
58. StadtAL Pa I, no. 9, 318–19, Sitzung Stadtrat, 2 February 1887.
59. StadtAL ZR 1025/3, Gesuch Heinrich Klag an Bürgermeisteramt, 28 April 1888.
60. Ibid., Direction der Pfälzischen Eisenbahnen an Bezirksamt, 14 July 1889; K. Bayrische Regierung der Pfalz an Bürgermeisteramt, 7 July 1889.
61. Breunig *Soziale Verhältnisse der Arbeiterschaft*, 209.
62. F. J. Ehrhart, *Das bayerische Heimatgesetz mit Erläuterungen nebst Anhang über den Erwerb der Staatsangehörigkeit, der Naturalisation und des Armengesetzes*, VIII.
63. StadtAL 1025/26, Bericht über die Verhandlungen des 5. pfälzischen Städtetages, 23 December 1901. The circle of critics of the Bavarian *Heimatrecht* extended beyond the political left and included liberals like the jurist and statistician Max von Seydel: 'Die Reform des bayerischen Heimatrechtes', 113–27.
64. The figure of 3,500 for 1885 reflects an estimate by the Catholic Casino association. See StadtA 5/424; StadtA 10/3659. However, as early as 1874 13,711 inhabitants of Augsburg were entitled to vote in national elections. The figure is reported in Hauptstaatsarchiv München, Minn (Innenministerium) 44381.
65. StadtAA 10, no. 3659.

66. StadtAA 10/3659, Stadtmagistrat Nürnberg and Stadtmagistrat Augsburg, 4 January 1878.

67. StadtAA 10/3659, Magistrat Augsburg and Magistrat Erlangen, 23 December 1884.

68. StadtAA 10/3677, Stadtmagistrat Augsburg an Regierung v. Schwaben und Neuburg, 17 February 1894.

69. StadtAA 10/3677, Magistrat an Polizeioffiziant Sänger, 29 August 1896.

70. StadtAA 10/3659, Gesuch einiger Kriegsveteranen an den Stadtmagistrat Augsburg, 4 August 1895.

71. StadtAA 10/3659, Antwort des Stadtmagistrats auf das Gesuch der Veteranen, 17 August 1895.

72. StadtAA 10/3677, Gesuch eines Veteranen an Stadtmagistrat, August 1899.

73. StadtAA 10/3677, Beschluss des Stadtmagistrats, 14 August 1900.

74. Ibid.

75. StadtAA 10/3659, Anfrage des Stadtmagistrats Augsburg an die Stadtmagistraten von München, Nürnberg, Fürth, Würzburg, Bamberg, Bayreuth, Regensburg, Landshut, Kempten und Erlangen. 4 November 1902.

76. StadtAA 10/3659, Stadtmagistrat Kempten an Stadtmagistrat Augsburg, 10 November 1902; Stadtmagistrat München an Stadtmagistrat Augsburg, 11 November 1902.

77. StadtAA 10/3659, Stadtmagistrat Nürnberg an Stadtmagistrat Augsburg, 10 November 1902.

78. StadtAA 10/3659, Stadtmagistrat Fürth an Stadtmagistrat Augsburg, 15 November 1902.

79. StadtAA 10/3659, Stadtratsbeschluss, 21 November 1903; Amts-Blatt der K. Bayerischen Stadt Augsburg, no. 79, 28 September 1905.

80. StadtAA 10/3659, Stadtratsbeschluss, 21 November 1903.

81. StadtAA 10/3659, Vorsitzende der Lehrerinnengruppe Augsburg an Stadtmagistrat, 8 December 1903.

82. StadtAA 10/3677, Bericht von Stadtkämmerer Frei zhd. Stadtmagistrat, 14 April 1911.

83. StadtAA 10/3670, Gründung eines Vereins zur Erwerbung des Heimat- und Bürgerrechtes zu Augsburg, 8 July 1896.

84. StadtAA 10/3670, Versammlung Verein zur Erwerbung des Heimat- und Bürgerrechtes zu Augsburg, 1 August 1896.

85. Ibid.

86. StadtAA 10/3670, Versammlung Verein zur Erwerbung des Heimat- und Bürgerrechts zu Augsburg, 1 August 1896.

87. StadtAA 10/3671, Gründungsversammlung Kath. Heimat- und Bürgerrechts-Erwerbs-Verein für die Stadt Augsburg, 2 March 1899.

88. NAZ, no. 34 (11 February 1914).

89. Geoff Eley, 'Some General Thoughts on Citizenship in Germany', in Eley and Palmowski (eds.), Citizenship, 242.

90. The consumer cooperatives were part of a much wider movement raising the banner of consumption and of the consumer. For recent work on this topic, see Mark Bevir and Frank Trentmann (eds.), *Governance, Consumers and Citizens: Agency and Resistance in Contemporary Politics* (Basingstoke: Palgrave, 2007). For a particularly inventive account, see Vanessa Taylor and Frank Trentmann, 'Liquid Politics: Water and the Politics of Everyday Life in the Modern City', *Past & Present* 211 (May 2011), 199–241.

91. Fairbairn, 'Rise and Fall', 268. On the consumer cooperatives in Germany, see in particular the work by Brett Fairbairn: 'the Rise and Fall of Consumer Cooperation in Germany', in Ellen Furlourh and Carl Strickwerda (eds.), *Consumers against Capitalism? Consumer Cooperation in Europe, North America, and Japan, 1840–1990* (Lanham/Oxford: Rowman & Littlefield, 1999), 267–302; 'History from the Ecological Perspective: Gaia Theory and the Problem of Cooperatives in Turn-of-the-Century Germany', *American Historical Review* 99, 4 (October 1994), 1203–39. 'Membership, Organization, and Wilhelmine Modernism', in G. Eley and J. Retallack (eds.), *Wilhelminism and its Legacies. German Modernities, Imperialism, and the Meaning of Reform, 1890–1930* (Oxford: Berghahn, 2003), 34–50. See also Uwe Spiekermann, *Basis der Konsumgesellschaft. Entstehung und Entwicklung des modernen Kleinhandels in Deutschland 1850–1914* (Munich: C. H. Beck, 1999); Michael Prinz, *Brot und Dividende. Konsumvereine in Deutschland und England vor 1914* (Göttingen: Vandenhoeck & Ruprecht, 1996).

92. Prinz, *Brot und Dividende*, 166. Fairbairn, 'Rise and Fall', 269, 275–6.

93. Spiekermann, *Basis der Konsumgesellschaft*, 257–9; Prinz, *Brot und Dividende*, 191.

94. Rudolf Schmidt, 'Die Konsumvereine vor dem Reichstage', *Blätter für Genossenschaftswesen*, vol. 11 (1895).

95. Cited in Fairbairn, 'Rise and Fall', 271.

96. Spiekermann, *Basis der Konsumgesellschaft*, 239.

97. Prinz, *Brot und Dividende*, 182–3, 191.

98. For a general overview of its activities from its foundation to the First World War, see Wolf D. Hepach, 125 Jahre Konsum-coop Ulm. Die Geschichte einer Verbrauchergemeinschaft (Ulm: Helmuth Abt, 1991), 10–33. The founding meeting is described in UT, no. 66 (20 March 1866).

99. StadtAU Protokoll band Konsumverein Ulm. Aufsichtsratssitzung, 6 June 1872. Hepach, *125 Jahre Konsum*, 16–18, 29–31.

100. StadtAU 774/07, no. 1, Antrag des Gewerbevereins Ulm an den Gemeinderat Ulm, 3 August 1869.

101. Ibid.

102. Ibid.

103. Ibid.

104. StadtAU 774/07, no. 1, Oberbürgermeister von Heim an Gewerbeverein, 3 August 1869.

105. StadtAU 774/07, no. 1, Oberbürgermeister von Heim an die hohen Beamten der Stadt und der Stiftungen, 30 October 1869.

106. StadtAU, Protokollband Konsumverein Ulm. Aufsichtsratssitzung, 29 July 1892.

107. StadtAU, Protokollband Konsumverein Ulm. Sitzung, 22 September 1869.

108. StadtAU, Protokollband Konsumverein Ulm, Ausschusssitzung, 9 September 1872.

109. StadtAU, Protokollband Konsumverein Ulm, Generalversammlung, 30 September 1892.

110. Ibid.

111. StadtAU, Protokollband Konsumverein Ulm, Aufsichtsratssitzung, 20 June 1899. See also *50 Jahre Konsumverein Ulm a. D. 1866–1916* (no place or publisher, 1916). Hepbach, *125 Jahre Konsumverein*, 31–2.

112. StadtAU, Protokollband Konsumverein Ulm, Aufsichtsratssitzung, 20 June 1899.

113. StadtAU, Protokollband Konsumverein Ulm, Aufsichtsratssitzung, 21 December 1899.

114. *50 Jahre Consumverein Ulm.*

115. StadtAU, Protokollband Konsumverein Ulm, Aufsichtsratssitzung, 3 October 1902.

116. The cooperative's statutes of the 1850s can be consulted in StadtAA 4/C64.

117. According to the statutes submitted to the city magistrate on 10 January 1860: StadtAA 4/C64.

118. ANN, no. 55 (27 May 1862).

119 StadtAA 4/C64, Bewerbung, 20 April 1863.

120. StadtAA 4/C64, Magistrat an Vorstand, 2 May 1863.

121. ANN, no. 23 (27 January 1876).

122. ANN, no. 66 (17 March 1876).

123. ANN, no. 78 (31 March 1876).

124. StadtAA 34/250.

125. StadtAA 34/250. Jahresbericht 1901/1902.

126. StadtAA 34/250.

127. StadtAA 34/250, Jahresbericht 1899/1900.

128. StadtAA 34/250, Geschäfts-Bericht Allgemeiner Consum-Verein Augsburg für das 10. Geschäftsjahr vom 1. Oktober 1899 bis 30. September 1900.

129. In a report on its founding meeting, the *Ludwigshafener Anzeiger* no. 221 (22 September 1873) noted that 'several directors and civil servants' had been elected to the cooperative's governing body.

130. PfK, no. 407 (31 August 1889).

131. *Geschichte der Stadt Ludwigshafen*, 200; *Beschreibung des Oberamts Ulm*, 476–7.

132. Rudolf Schmidt, 'Die Konsumvereine vor dem Reichstage'.

133. J. Keller, H. Koob namens des Konsum-Vereins Ludwigshafen, 'Der Zwischenhandel und die Konsumvereine', *Blätter für Genossenschaftswesen*

(Innung der Zukunft). Organ des Allgemeinen Verbandes deutscher Erwerbs- und Wirtschafts-Genossenschaften begründet von Dr. Schulze-Delitzsch,, no. 15 (11. April 1896).

134. Ibid.

135. StadtAL M 153, Nachtrag zum Gedächtnisprotokoll des Oberbürgermeisters a. D. v. Bauer. Ludwigshafen, Ebertstr. 10: Zur Geschichte d. Konsumvereins Ludwigshafen.

136. Walker, *German Home Towns*, 29.

PART III. PROLOGUE

1. Friedrich List, *Das Nationale System der politischen Oekonomie*, sechste Auflage (Jena: Verlag von Gustav Fischer, 1950 [1841]), 294.

2. AAZ, no. 254 (16 September 1871).

3. Sheehan, 'Liberalism and the City'; Jürgen Kocka, (ed.), *Bürgertum im 19. Jahrhundert*. 11–78; Wehler, *Deutsche Gesellschaftsgeschichte*, vol. 3, 539; Nipperdey, *Deutsche Geschichte (vol. 2)*, 157–8; Retallack, 'Why Can't a Saxon be more like a Prussian?', 32–5.

4. Whether this amalgamation of nationalism with liberal status concerns was more accentuated in Germany than elsewhere is a question this book cannot answer. Information on this topic can be found in Andreas Biefang, *Politisches Bürgertum in Deutschland 1857–1868. Nationale Organisationen und Eliten* (Düsseldorf: Droste, 1994), especially ch. 11 & conclusion; Dieter Langewiesche, *Liberalism in Germany* (Princeton: Princeton University Press, 2000). On nationalism in the 1848 Revolution, see Brian Vick, *Defining Germany: The 1848 Frankfurt Parliamentarians and the National Question* (Cambridge MA: Harvard University Press, 2002). See also Matthew Levinger, *Enlightened Nationalism: The Transformation of Prussian Political Culture, 1806–1848* (Oxford: Oxford University Press, 2000). On the early nineteenth-century roots of imperialist nationalism in the liberal imagination, see Fitzpatrick, *Liberal Imperialism in Germany*.

5. On the self-referential qualities of many powerful ideologies, see Nussbaum, *Upheavals of Thought*, 52. The self-referential dimension of German nationalism remains unacknowledged in the otherwise highly subtle contributions in Zang, *Provinzialisierung einer Region*. The authors who most directly engage with the phenomenon reduce nationalism to an instrument liberals employed in order to shore up their local power. According to Bellmann (249), for instance, nationalism only assumed prominence once Konstanz' liberals lost hope in their ability to shape economic development independently out of their local context, whereas Zang, in his own contribution, regards the turn towards *Reichnationalismus* as a response to the state's unwillingness to devolve power to the localities (277–8, 297).

6. *Stadtgeschichte Ludwigshafen am Rhein*, 402.

7. The most prominent voice to have argued that Germany's National Liberals were 'bereft of serious self-doubt' is that of Wehler. See Wehler, *Deutsche*

Gesellschaftsgeschichte, vol. 3 866. Admittedly, as late as 1911 approximately sixty per cent of German municipalities with more than 10,000 inhabitants in the Rhineland and Westphalia were still ruled by liberals; in Catholic Bavaria in 1911 liberals gained on average 35 per cent of the vote in towns with more than 4,000 inhabitants, while in Munich it was close to 50 per cent. Nipperdey, *Deutsche Geschichte 1866–1918, vol. II*, 535. These figures can be misleading, however. If liberals continued to be influential locally long after their national power had declined, this owed much to highly exclusive urban suffrages. Once the local franchise widened, from the turn of the century, this almost invariably weakened their position. The same trend strengthened the democrats (especially in Ulm), political Catholicism (in both Ulm and Augsburg), and Social Democracy (in Augsburg and particularly in Ludwigshafen). For classical statements on urban liberalism, see Sheehan, 'Liberalism and the City', 116–37; Lothar Gall, 'Liberalismus und "Bürgerliche Gesellschaft". Zu Charakter und Entwicklung der liberalen Bewegung in Deutschland', *Historische Zeitschrift* 220 (1975), 324–56. See also W. J. Mommsen, 'Der deutsche Liberalismus zwischen "klassenloser Bürgergesellschaft" und "organisiertem Kapitalismus". Zu einigen neueren Liberalismusinterpretationen', *Geschichte und Gesellschaft* 4 (1978), 77–90. Langewiesche, *Liberalism in Germany*; Nolte, *Gemeindebürgertum und Liberalismus in Baden*. Wehler, *Deutsche Gesellschaftsgeschichte*, vol. 3, 539.

8. David Blackbourn, *Populists and Patricians: Essays in Modern German History* (London: Unwin Hyman, 1987), 160.

9. German elites were not alone in perceiving the nation-state as a vulnerable, even precarious, entity. But the relative lateness of *kleindeutsch* unification, combined with Germany's cultural significance and economic weight, may have heightened this awareness. In a lucid examination, Aviel Roshwald has argued that the dominant sentiment when it comes to political nationhood among its advocates had been one not of strength but of fragility. See his essay, 'The Post-1989 Era as Heyday of the Nation-State', *International Journal of Politics, Culture and Society*, 24 (2011), 11–19.

10. This awareness of 'lagging behind' and of the need to 'catch up' manifested itself in different spheres. It was particularly marked in the economic field, as the extremely influential work of Friedrich List attests. On this see Fitzpatrick, *Liberal Imperialism*. In relation to furniture and other kinds of design, see Maiken Umbach, *German Cities and Bourgeois Modernism*, ch. 5.

11. Geoff Eley, 'State Formation, Nationalism, and Political Culture: Some Thoughts on the Unification of Germany', in Raphael Samuel and Gareth Stedman Jones (eds.), *Culture, Ideology and Politics* (London: Routledge & Kegan Paul, 1982), 75. Important work on the vast theme of the *Kulturkampf* includes Margaret Lavinia Anderson, "Die Grenzen der Säkularisierung: Zur Frage des katholischen Aufschwungs im Deutschland des 19. Jahrhunderts," in Hartmut Lehmann (ed.), *Säkularisierung, Dechristianisierung, Rechristianisierung im neuzeitlichen Europa*, (Göttingen, 1997), 220–1, and by the same author:

Practicing Democracy, chs 4 and 5; David Blackbourn, 'The Catholic Church in Europe since the French Revolution', *Comparative Studies in Society and History*, 33 (1991), 778–90; David Blackbourn, *Marpingen: Apparitions of the Virgin Mary in Nineteenth-Century Germany* (New York: Alfred A. Knopf, 1994); Michael Gross, *The War against Catholicism: Liberalism and the Anti-Catholic Imagination in Nineteenth-Century Germany* (Ann Arbor, MI, University of Michigan Press, University of Michigan Press, 2004), 10, 26.; Helmut W. Smith, *German Nationalism and Religious Conflict: Culture, Ideology, Politics, 1870–1914* (Princeton: Princeton University Press, 1995); Thomas Nipperdey, *Religion im Umbruch* (Munich: C. H. Beck, 1988), 24–31.

12. On ultramontanism, see Anderson, 'Grenzen der Säkularisierung', 219–20; Nipperdey, *Religion im Umbruch*, 18–20; Christopher Clark and Wolfram Kaiser (eds.), *Culture Wars: Secular-Catholic Conflicts in Nineteenth Century Europe* (Cambridge: Cambridge University Press, 2004) 18–19, 24–6.

13. Smith, *German Nationalism*, 48. See also Margaret Lavinia Anderson and Kenneth Barkin, 'The Myth of the Puttkamer Purge and the Reality of the Kulturkampf: Some Reflections on the Historiography of Imperial Germany', *Journal of Modern History* 54 (December 1982), 647–86; Manuel Borutta, *Antikatholizismus. Deutschland und Italien im Zeitalter der europäischen Kulturkämpfe* (Göttingen: Vandenhoeck & Ruprecht, 2010). The association of German nationalism with Protestantism (rather than Christianity) still dominates the historiography on Germany in the nineteenth century. One of its strongest proponents, Wolfgang Altgeld, has argued that the nationalist solution to the reality of the confessional division was the fostering of a *Nationalreligion* built on Protestant foundations. Wolfgang Altgeld, 'Religion, Denomination, and Nationalism in Nineteenth-Century Germany', in Helmut W. Smith (ed.), *Protestants, Catholics, and Jews in Germany, 1800–1914*, (Oxford: Berg, 2001), 56.

14. The centrality of bodily rhythm in religious practice is evident. Yet, so is the fluidity of the boundary separating allegedly profane and religious kinds of rhythmical experience. As Richard Sennet (*The Craftsman*, 177–8) has observed in relation to the craftsman: 'As theologians have long pointed out, religious rituals need to be repeated to become persuasive, day after day, month after month, year upon year…But equally, the person able to perform a duty again and again has acquired a technical skill, the rhythmic skill of a craftsman, whatever the god or gods to which he or she subscribes.'

15. Historians studying Sedan Day have usually done so from a mostly regional perspective, and without relating them to specifically Catholic forms of public worship like the Corpus Christi processions. The focus has tended to be on symbolic representation. See Confino, *Local Metaphor*, 39, 84; Weichlein, *Nation und Region*. Although these issues are relevant to my own concerns, the focus

of this chapter lies elsewhere, namely, on the often contradictory motivations that went into the making of these public parades and processions.

CHAPTER 5

1. ANN, no. 261 (6. November 1878).
2. UT, no. 301 (25 December 1890).
3. The postcard is reproduced on page 188.
4. For general accounts taking this line of argument, see Heinrich-August Winkler (ed.), *Nationalismus* (Bodenheim: Athenaeum, 1978), introduction by Winkler. For a short account written almost entirely in the spirit of moral condemnation, see Hans-Ulrich Wehler, *Nationalismus. Geschichte—Formen—Folgen* (Munich: C.H. Beck, 2001). For balanced views, see Dieter Langewiesche, *Nation, Nationalismus, Nationalstaat in Deutschland und Europa* (Munich: C. H. Beck, 2000); James Retallack, *The German Right 1860–1920: Political Limits of the Authoritarian Imagination* (Toronto: University of Toronto Press, 2006). For an interesting recent take on liberalism in practice, see the collection by Angelika Schaser and Stefanie Schüler-Springorum (ed.), *Liberalismus und Emanzipation. In- und Exklusionsprozesse im Kaiserreich und in der Weimarer Republik* (Stuttgart: Franz Steiner Verlag, 2010). On nationalism and antisemitism, see Karsten Krieger (ed.), *Der 'Berliner Antisemitismusstreit' 1879–1881. Eine Kontroverse um die Zugehörigkeit der deuschen Juden zur Nation*, 2 vols. (Munich: K. G. Saur, 2003).
5. David Blackbourn, *Marpingen: Apparitions of the Virgin Mary in Nineteenth-Century Germany* (New York: Alfred Knopf, 1994), xxxiv. See also Blackbourn and Eley, *Peculiarities of German History*.
6. Jenkins, *Provincial Modernities*; Palmowski, *Liberalism in Frankfurt*; Nipperdey, *Deutsche Geschichte 1866–1918* vol. 2, 155–6. See also Pohl, 'Kommunalpolitik in Dresden und München vor 1914', 171–88, and by the same author, 'Kommunen, Liberalismus und Wahlrechtsfragen', 113–30.
7. This is not to deny that Catholics were more likely to oppose the Imperial Constitution of March 1849. When the members of Augsburg's council (*Gemeindebevollmächtigte*) and magistrate were asked to express their views on the matter, the six delegates who voted against the constitution were all Catholics; of the twelve who requested moderations, all except one belonged to the Catholic confession; and of the 26 who endorsed the constitution without qualification, sixteen were Protestants and ten were Catholics. Möller, *Bürgerliche Herrschaft*, 320.
8. Like in much of Bavaria, the left liberals were an insignificant minority in Augsburg. On left liberalism in Germany, see Alastair Thompson, *Left Liberals, the State, and Popular Politics in Wilhelmine Germany* (Oxford: Oxford University Press, 2000).

9. Volker Dotterweich, 'Die bayerische Ära 1806–1870', in G. Gottlieb (ed.), *Geschichte der Stadt Augsburg. 2000 Jahre von der Römerzeit bis zur Gegenwart* (Stuttgart: Konrad Theiss Verlag, 1984), 551–68.

10. The extensive communication between the district governor and the government in Munich over Fischer's respective appointments to deputy and principal mayor can be found in SAA: Regierung, no. 8689.

11. For a character portrait see his obituary in the *Neue Augsburger Zeitung*, 12 January 1900. See also the entry on Ludwig Fischer in the *Augsburger Stadtlexikon*, 2. Auflage, edited by Günther Grünsteudel, Günter Hägele und Rudolf Frankenberger (Augsburg: Perlach Verlag, 1998).

12. Möller, *Bürgerliche Herrschaft*, 369–70.

13. Cited in AAZ, no. 8 (9 January 1900). The article was published the day after Fischer's death.

14. Ibid.

15. On political radicalization from within liberal movements, see Carl E. Schorske, 'Politics in a New Key: An Austrian Triptych', *The Journal of Modern History* 39 (December 1967), 343–86.

16. See Gerhard Hetzer, 'Presse und Politik 1890–1945. Beobachtungen eines lokalen Kraftfeldes', in Helmut Gier and Johannes Janota (eds.), *Augsburger Buchdruck und Verlagswesen von den Anfängen bis zur Gegenwart* (Wiesbaden: Harrassowitz Verlag, 1997), 1135–7; Fassl, *Konfession, Wirtschaft und Politik. Von der Reichsstadt zur Industriestadt 1750–1850* (Sigmaringen: Thorbecke, 1988), 425.

17. Riel, *Culturstudien*, 317–18.

18. On the role of confessional parity in Augsburg, see Étienne François, 'Das System der Parität', in G. Gottlieb (ed.), *Geschichte der Stadt Augsburg. 2000 Jahre von der Römerzeit bis zur Gegenwart* (Stuttgart: Konrad Theiss Verlag, 1984), 514–19.

19. Clearly, the conflicts between ultramontane Catholicism and liberal nationalists that Augsburg witnessed in the latter half of the nineteenth century had lost the purely ritualized character that Étienne François identified as the main feature of Augsburg's confessional culture during the seventeenth and eighteenth centuries. Étienne François, *Die unsichtbare Grenze: Protestanten und Katholiken in Augsburg 1648–1806* (Sigmaringen: Thorbecke Verlag, 1991). On this shift, see also Fassl, *Konfession, Wirtschaft und Politik*, 321, 347; and Möller, *Bürgerliche Herrschaft*.

20. ANN, no. 252 (28 October 1884). Emphasis in the original.

21. ANN, no. 279 (28 November 1884).

22. Bernhard Mann, 'Württemberg 1800–1866', 327–9; Dieter Langewiesche, *Liberalismus und Demokratie in Württemberg zwischen Revolution und Reichsgründung* (Düsseldorf: Droste Verlage, 1974). The view of Württemberg's most important national-liberal politician are discussed in Dieter Langewiesche, *Das Tagebuch Julius Hölders 1877–1880* (Stuttgart: W. Kohlhammer, 1977), 1–40.

23. Eckhard Trox, 'Bürger in Ulm:Vereine, Parteien, Gesellingkeit', in Specker (ed.), *Ulm im 19. Jahrhundert*, 219–21.
24. UT, no. 300 (24 December 1871).
25. USP, no. 297 (21 December 1879).
26. See StadtAU B 123/131, no. 1; DAR G. 1.1, C 14.2 b.
27. This was demonstrated, for example, during the inauguration of the Catholic Gesellenhaus in 1888. See UT, no. 279 (27 November 1888).
28. UT, no. 7 (10 January 1874).
29. UT, no. 304 (28 December 1877).
30. USP, no. 20 (25 January 1881).
31. UT, no. 304 (28 December 1877).
32. UT, no. 298 (21 December 1879).
33. UT, no. 284 (5 December 1885).
34. See, for example, USP, no. 285, (5 December 1883); UT, no. 282 (2 December 1883); UT, no. 284 (5 December 1885); USP, no. 283 (6 December 1885).
35. UT, no. 283–284 (3 & 4 December 1887).
36. USP, no. 15 (20 January 1891).
37. UT, no. 13 (17 January 1891); USP, no. 13 (17 January 1891).
38. Ibid.
39. UT, no. 16 (21 January 1891).
40. Ibid.
41. Thus during the period from 1834 to 1890, for example, Ulm's population had only risen by 134 per cent, which placed it behind Heilbronn (179 per cent), Stuttgart (267 per cent) and Cannstatt (301 per cent). Wagner, *Die wirtschaftlichen Verhältnisse in Ulm*, 68.
42. UT, no. 301 (25 December 1890).
43. UT, no. 6 (8 January 1893).
44. The following outline of the situation in Ludwigshafen draws on Rolf Weidner, *Wahlen und soziale Strukturen in Ludwigshafen am Rhein 1871–1914* (Ludwigshafen: Veröffentlichungen des Stadtarchivs Ludwigshafen am Rhein, 1984), 257–69.
45. *Geschichte der Stadt Ludwigshafen am Rhein* (1903), 236–40.
46. On this, see Weidner, *Wahlen*, 165–97.
47. Weidner, *Wahlen*, 259.
48. Weidner, *Wahlen*, 260.
49. Ibid., 261.
50. Weidner, *Wahlen*, 263; According to Breunig, the council election of 1899 marked the end of the *Honoratiorenregime* in Ludwigshafen. See Willi Breunig, *Soziale Verhältnisse*, 251, 335.
51. Weidner, *Wahlen*, 264.
52. Weidner, *Wahlen*, 265.
53. See Jakob Knauber, *Albert von Jäger. Direktor der Pfälzischen Eisenbahnen 1814– 1887. Ein Lebensbild unter Berücksichtigung der Pfalzbahnen und der Katholischen Pfarrei St. Ludwig* (Ludwigshafen:Verlag der kath. Pfarrämter, 1925), 37–9.

54. StadtAL M 605.

55. StadtAL M 604.

56. StadtAL M 605.

57. See the discussion in Weidner, *Wahlen*, 625–30. For the more decidedly middle-class Catholicism of the Rhineland, see Thomas Mergel, *Zwischen Klasse und Konfession. Katholisches Bürgertum im Rheinland 1794–1914* (Göttingen: Vandenhoeck & Ruprecht, 1994).

58. SAA: 9608, Wochenbericht des Magistrats-Vorstandes Augsburg, 16 February 1873.

59. Möller, *Bürgerliche Herrschaft*, 188.

60. Cited in Möller, *Bürgerliche Herrschaft*, 193.

61. Ibid.

62. AA (28 December 1859). Cited in Möller, *Bürgerliche Herrschaft*, 353.

63. ANN, no. 249 (19. October 1872).

64. ANN, no. 2 (2 April 1862).

65. ANN, no. 221 (17 January 1872).

66. ANN, no. 221 (17 January 1872).

67. ANN, no. 26 (30 January 1873). The editors name the increase of the town's Jewish population as one of the reasons for this development.

68. ANN, no. 228 (25 September 1872).

69. ANN, no. 228 (25 September 1872).

70. ANN, no. 29 (2 February 1873).

71. ANN, no. 37 (12 February 1873).

71. ANN, no. 37 (12 February 1873).

72. ANN, no. 40 (15 February 1873).

73. ANN, no. 42 (17 February 1873).

74. Peter Stoll, 'Stadttheater', in http://www.stadtlexikon-augsburg.de.

75. Loges, 'Das Ulmer Theater', in Specker (ed.), *Ulm im 19. Jahrhundert*, 480–1.

76. Loges, 'Das Ulmer Theater', 478, 484.

77. Loges, 'Das Ulmer Theater', 493.

78. USP, no. 10 (12 January 1878).

79. USP, no. 88 (17 April 1879).

80. UT, no. 238 (13 October 1877).

81. UT, no. 15 (18 January 1878); no. 17 (20 January 1878).

82. USP, no. 237 (11 October 1877).

83. USP, no. 283 (1 December 1878).

84. USP, no. 12 (16 January 1886).

85. Friedrich Burschell, *Erinnerungen 1889–1919* (Ludwigshafen: Stadtarchiv LU, 1997), 41–2.

86. *Pfälzer Zeitung*, 12 June 1853.

87. Von Hippel, 'Zwischen kleindeutscher Reichsgründung und Weltkriegs-Katastrophe', 636–7.

88. LUA, no. 208 (6 September 1882).

89. LUA, no. 110 (10 May 1884).

90. On this theme, see Margaret Kraul, 'Bildung und Bürgerlichkeit', in Jürgen Kocka, (ed.), *Bürgertum im 19. Jahrhundert. Deutschland im europäischen Vergleich* (Munich: DTV, 1988), 45–73.

91. Burschell, *Erinnerungen 1889–1919*, 41–2.

92. 'Der Hemshof, die Farbenstadt Deutschlands' (erschienen im *Pfälzischen Kurier*, 28./29. März 1889).

93. Ritzhaupt, *In Sonne und Rauch*, 5–6.

94. Burschell, *Erinnerungen 1889–1919*, 32.

95. On this theme, see, for example, Allan Mitchell, 'Bourgeois Liberalism and Public Health: A Franco-German Comparison', in Jürgen Kocka and Allan Mitchell (eds.), *Bourgeois Society in Nineteenth-Century Europe* (Oxford: Berg, 1993), 346–64; Richard Evans, *Death in Hamburg. Society and Politics in the Cholera Years* (Penguin: London, 1990). On public intellectuals and health during the Wilhelmine period, see Repp, *Reformers*. See also Taylor and Trentmann, 'Liquid Politics', (May 2011), 199–241.

96. For a report on the 1854 epidemic, see Max Pettenkofer, *Untersuchungen und Beobachtungen über die Verbreitung der Cholera nebst Betrachtungen über Massregeln, derselben Einhalt zu gebieten* (Munich, 1855), 97–9.

97. See ANN, no. 200 (24 August 1873). On the cholera epidemics in Augsburg, see Möller, *Bürgerliche Herrschaft*, 356; Fischer, *Industrialisierung*, 62–70.

98. StadtAA 10/403, Monatsversammlung Liberaler Bürgerverein der Wertachvorstädte, 14 September 1992. On Hamburg, see Evans, *Death in Hamburg*.

99. StadtAA 5/422, Versammlung Bürger-Verein Augsburg, 18 January 1875.

100. ANN, no. 111 (13 May 1877).

101. ANN, no. 111 (13 May 1877).

102. ANN, no. 78 (2 April 1878).

103. Ibid. ANN, no. 78 (2 April 1878).

104. Another factor that most likely contributed to Augsburg's high death toll among toddlers, and the one which the town magistrate regarded as the main cause, was that the town's factory industry relied on a high level of female employment. See, for example, *Verwaltungsberichte des Stadtmagistrats* 1894, 184. According to Luise Fischer (*Industrialisierung*, 66) only very few of Augsburg's factories had set up their own nurseries before the 1890s. For the high mortality rate among working-class women in Augsburg, see Fischer, *Industrialisierung*, 141.

105. Fischer, *Industrialisierung*, 65.

106. StadtAA 5/542, Versammlung Bürgerverein Augsburg, 11 July 1882; 18 July 1882.

107. StadtAA 11/56, Versammlung Bürgerverein Augsburg, 25 February 1896. See also the report in ANN, no. 49 (27 February 1896).

108. Ibid.

109. ANN, no. 49 (27 February 1896).

110. Wagner, *Die wirtschaftlichen Verhältnisse in Ulm*, 16–20.
111. Ibid., 19.
112. Wagner, *Die wirtschaftlichen Verhältnisse in Ulm*, 59.
113. Ibid.
114. As does the fact that he was cited in the mayor's 1896 report on the city's economic status quo. See Wagner, *Die wirtschaftlichen Verhältnisse in Ulm*, 60.
115. Ibid., 41–2.
116. For an early argument along those lines, see USP, no. 302 (24 December 1876).
117. The committee consisted of members of Ulm's (Protestant) economic and political elite, and included the wife of Oberbürgermeister v. Heim and other local notables. The original initiative seems to have derived from Ulm's deacon, who had observed the effects of nurseries in Stuttgart as well as in the more industrialized Cannstatt and Heilbronn. See USP, no. 6 (9 January 1877); USP, no. 18 (23 January 1877).
118. USP, no. 190 (14 August 1878).
119. USP, no. 88 (13 April 1889).
120. UT, no. 27 (2 February 1890).
121. UT, no. 9, (12 January 1893).
122. Von Hippel, 'Zwischen kleindeutscher Reichsgründung und Weltkriegs-Katastrophe', 464–5.
123. Ibid., 559.
124. Cited in Von Hippel, 'Zwischen kleindeutscher Reichsgründung und Weltkriegs-Katastrophe', 498.
125. Ibid., 560.
126. Ibid., 498–500.
127. A comparison with Hamburg proves instructive here. As Richard Evans has shown, when the great cholera epidemic of 1892 threatened to bring the city to its knees, causing a death toll that attracted world-wide attention and brought its trading activities to a temporary halt, this failed to undermine the confidence of Hamburg's ruling notables. Thus, in 1893, Hamburg's Burgomaster Johannes Versmann noted grumpily that during the cholera epidemic of the previous year, it had been 'the Imperial Health Office and Prof. Koch who ran things here.' As far as Hamburg's notables were concerned, being a Hamburg burgher was being a member of the most civilized and advanced community in the whole of Germany. There was therefore no need to take advice from the nation's leading experts on questions of public health. This is not to say that Hamburg's liberals were incapable of nationalist sentiment. What it does mean, however, is that insofar as Hamburg's established elite initiated sanitation and other health reforms in their city, their inspiration was for the most part local patriotism rather than nationalism. See Evans, *Death in Hamburg*, 491, 508–9.

CHAPTER 6

1. UT, no. 206 (4 September 1887).
2. LUA, no. 206 (2 September 1876).
3. ANN, no. 204 (2 September 1894).
4. On Bodelschwingh and his efforts on behalf of Sedan Day, see Hartmut Lehmann, *Religion und Religiosität in der Neuzeit Historische Beiträge*, edited by Von M. Jakubowski-Tiessen und O. Ulbricht (Göttingen: Vandenhoeck & Ruprecht, 1996), 205–32.
5. Ibid.
6. Confino, *Local Metaphor*, 39.
7. For example, see Jens Flemming, Klaus Saul, Peter-Christian Witt (eds.), *Quellen zur Alltagsgeschichte der Deutschen 1871–1914* (Darmstadt: Wissenschaftliche Buchgesellschaft, 1997), 61–4.
8. Confino, *Local Metaphor*, ch. 2.
9. On the often intimate relationship between ritual and routine—between the conscious and emotionally charged and the unconscious, seemingly reflexlike rhythms of life—see Ehn and Löfgren, *The Secret of Doing Nothing*, 120–1.
10. Alan Confino has argued that 'a common tradition of national festivals' that had emerged in the wars against Napoleon explains why, formally speaking, Sedan Day appeared self-evident to most people. What my own evidence suggests, however, is that few of the residents of Augsburg, Ulm and Ludwigshafen (not even those who noisily championed the event) perceived Sedan Day as familiar in either form or rhythm. See Confino, *Local Metaphor*, 42.
11. SAA: 9710, Reports of 25 January and 25 February 1859. On 23 May 1859 the commissioner informs his superior that the most recent issue of the *Augsburger Anzeiger* had been confiscated.
12. SAA: 9602, 11 September 1866.
13. SAA: 9602, Commissioner to district government, 8 August 1866.
14. For the communication surrounding the festival, see StadtAA 3/380.
15. AAZ, no. 263 (25 September 1863). Nuremburg and Landshut cited financial reasons to justify their negative response, pointing out that expenses for festivals of this kind required permission from the Bavarian government, which would not be given unless the organizing committee was able to offer definitive figures.

     Meanwhile, the magistrate of Würzburg described the 'delirious craving for festivals' as an 'illness and an obstacle to true patriotism', while in Nuremberg a committee of thirty men expressed their wish to attend the commemoration in Leipzig in an 'unofficial capacity.' The attitudes of several Bavarian towns are reported in AAZ, no. 272 (4 October 1863); no. 277 (9 October 1863).
16. The magistrate's decision was signed by both of Augsburg's mayors (*Erster Bürgermeister* Geog von Forndran, and his deputy, *Zweiter Bürgermeister* Ludwig Fischer).

17. AAZ, no. 274 (6 October 1863).

18. AAZ, no. 286 (18 October 1863).

19. AAZ, no. 287 (19 October 1863).

20. The Catholic *Augsburger Postzeitung*, whose editors bitterly lamented the one-sided character of the festival in Leipzig (describing it as a 'party-political festival' and an 'act of self-worship by the *Nationalverein*'), did not apply the same negative judgement to the festival in Augsburg. See APZ, no. 247 (19 and 20 October 1863). Many members of the organizing committee for the Leipzig event were indeed members of the *Nationalverein* which, incidentally, held its annual general meeting on the eve of the celebrations. But nor did the *Postzeitung* refrain from criticizing (the majority) of South-German councils that had decided against attending the celebrations in Leipzig. In doing so, they had left the national stage to the National Liberals. See AP, no. 245 (17 October 1863).

21. SAA: 9602, Bericht des Commissairs der Stadt Augsburg, K. Regierungsrath v. Burchtorff, ex officio, betreffend das III. bayerische Turnfest zu Augsburg, 19 July 1865.

22. AAZ, no. 208 (31 July 1867).

23. AAZ, no. 211 (3 August 1867).

24. AAZ, no. 215 (7 August 1867).

25. AAZ, no. 219 (12 August 1867).

26. AAZ, no. 226 (19 August 1867).

27. Speech by Dr Voelk at a meeting of the *Bürgerverein Augsburg* Cited in AAZ, no. 217 (10 August 1867). See also Möller, *Bürgerliche Herrschaft*, 397–8.

28. Möller, *Bürgerliche Herrschaft*, 398.

29. After having held a secret meeting on the question, on 8 May 1868 the magistrate justified its attitude towards the municipal council. As well as stressing the fact that Nuremberg, Würzburg and Landshut had also decided against staging a festival, the magistrate insisted that 'no sober and rational-thinking human being' would perceive the decision as an 'expression of indifference' towards the 50th-year anniversary of the Bavarian constitution. Augsburg's loyalty to the Bavarian king was described as beyond questioning. See StadtAA 3/97, Stadtmagistrat an Kollegium der Gemeindebevollmächtigten. Betreff: Das fünfzigjährige Jubiläum der bayrischen Verfassung, 8 May 1868.

30. SAA 9604, Weekly Report, 19 May 1868.

31. SAA 9604, Weekly Reports, 25 May 1868/2 June 1868. The reports noted that Augsburg's example had been emulated in some parts of Swabia, while in rural parts the anniversary had been celebrated with enthusiasm.

32. StAA 9604, Weekly Report, 30 August 1870.

33. See above all, Simon Palaoro, *Stadt und Festung*. Lemke, 'Die Ulmer Garnison.' Another element of the urban built environment that throughout the nineteenth century fostered links between local and national imagination was the *Ulmer Münster*, which in 1890, after a series of renovations and extensions, at 161

metres became the highest church building in the world. See StadtAU B 372/50, no. 7; B 372/8, nos 3 & 4.

34. StadtAU B060/23, no. 1, Eingabe an die deutsche National-Versammlung das deutsche Festungswesen betreffend, 24 June 1848.

35. Ibid.

36. Ibid. The petitioners also argued that a truly national defence ring would necessitate an extension of the existing network of fortresses.

37. StadtAU 060/25, no. 9. On several occasions citizens approached the municipal council with complaints and suggestions. See, for example, the letters of 22 and 29 April 1848.

38. StadtAU 060/25, no. 9. See, for example, Ministerium des Innern in Stuttgart an Oberamt Ulm, 6 December 1848.

39. StadtAU 060/25, no. 10. Stadtrat Ulm an Königlich Württembergisches Gouvernement der Bundesfestung Ulm, 21 April 1859. These concerns were anything but unfounded. In May 1859, the fortress government tried to bully the local authorities into relinquishing a large public building (Zehntstadel) at a rent that was clearly below current market levels. See StadtAU 060/25, no. 10, Letters of the fortress government to the government official (Oberamt) of 23 May and 6 June 1859.

40. StadtAU 060/25, no. 9, Sitzung Stadtrat, 23 October 1860.

41. See Abigail Green, 'How did German Federalism Shape Unification?', in Ronald Speirs and John Breuilly (ed.), *Germany's two unifications. Anticipations, Experiences, Responses* (Basingstoke: Palgrave Macmillan, 2005), 122–38; John Breuilly, 'Nationalism and the First Unification', in Speirs and Breuilly (ed.), *Germany's two unifications,* 101–21.

42. UT, no. 295 (14 December 1869).

43. UT, no. 28 (4 February 1870).

44. UT, no. 53 (5 March 1870).

45. USP, no. 159 (12 July 1870).

46. USP, no. 246 (21 October 1870).

47. Mann, 'Württemberg 1800–1866', 348–53.

48. UT, no. 235 (7 October 1870).

49. UT, no. 117 (21 May 1871).

50. USP, no. 173 (28 July 1870).

51. USP, no. 232 (5 October 1870).

52. On this theme see Applegate, *Nation of Provincials.*

53. Breunig, *Kommunalpolitik*; Weidner, *Wahlen.*

54. StadtAL: M380.

55. StadtAL PaI, no. 4, 132–3, Sitzung Stadtrat, 3 May 1866.

56. See Stefan Mörz, *Vom Westboten zur Rheinpfalz. Zur Geschichte der Presse im Raum Ludwigshafen von den Anfängen bis zur Gegenwart* (Ludwigshafen: Veröffentlichungen des Stadtarchivs Ludwigshafen, 1994).

57. *Geschichte der Stadt Ludwigshafen,* 421–40.

58. Ludwig Allmann, *Die Wahlbewegung zum I. deutschen Zollparlament in der Rheinpfalz* (Borna-Leipzig: Buchdruckerei Robert Noske, 1913), 58–9.
59. Breunig, 'Vom Handelsplatz zum Industriestandort', 341.
60. LUA, no. 205 (2 September 1871).
61. LUA, no. 206 (4 September 1871).
62. StadtAL Pa I, no. 5, 409.
63. StadtAL Pa I, no. 5, 444–5.
64. Ibid.
65. Ibid.
66. StadtAL Pa I, no. 5, 444–5, Sitzung Stadtrat, 24 August 1873. See also the report on the meeting in LUA, no. 198 (25 August 1873).
67. LUA, no. 200 (27 August 1873).
68. LUA, no. 206 (4 September 1873).
69. *Geschichte der Stadt Ludwigshafen*, 421–40.
70. StastAL Pa I, no. 6, 365–6.
71. StadtAL ZR 1000/6a.
72. NPfK. (4 September 1893).
73. NPfK, no. 242 (4 September 1897).
74. StadtAL 060/05, no. 1, Oberbürgermeister von Heim an den Stadtrat, 3 September 1870.
75. StadtAL 060/05, no. 1, Rektor des Gymnasiums an den Stadtrat, 3 September 1870.
76. StadtAU 060/05, no. 1, Sitzung Gemeinderat, 25 August 1873.
77. Ibid.
78. Ibid.
79. Ibid. Of those present, six voted against and three in favour of the proposal, with one abstention.
80. StadtAU 060/05, no. 1, Sitzung Gemeinderat, 29 August 1873. See also the report in USP, 31 August (no. 203) 1873.
81. The announcement was published in the national-liberal *Ulmer Schnellpost*, no. 203 (31 August 1873).
82. StadtAU 060/05, no. 1, Sitzung Gemeinderat, 29 August 1873.
83. Ibid.
84. In 1873 the permission was granted, with three democratic deputies abstaining. StadtAU 060/05, no. 1, Fest-Programm zur Nationalfeier am 2. September d. J. Festgestellt durch eine Anzahl hiesiger Bürger in einer Versammlung im *Deutschen Kaiser* am 29 August 1873; Grössere Anzahl hiesiger Bürger (25) and Stiftungsrath & Gemeinderat, 30 August 1873.
85. StadtAU 060/05, no. 1, Versammlung Gemeinderat, 25 August 1874. During that meeting von Heim explicitly used the inauguration of the *Gymnasium* on 2 September to gain legitimacy for a separate committee charged with the festival's organization.

86. See, for example, StadtAU 060/05, no. 1. Oberbürgermeister von Heim an Gouvernement der Reichsfestung Ulm, 27 August 1875.

87. UT, no. 205 (2 September 1876).

88. StadtAU 060/05, no. 1, Sitzung Gemeinderat, 26 August 1880.

89. StadtAU 060/05, no. 2, Sitzung Gemeinderat, 18 July 1895/22 August 1895.

90. SAA 9605, Commissair der Stadt Augsburg an Regierung von Schwaben u. Neuburg, 6 September 1870.

91. NAZ, no. 209 (3 September 1872).

92 ANN, no. 247 (17 October 1872).

93. Ibid.

94. ANN, no. 247 (17 October 1872).

95. StadtAA 19/554, Anfrage des Civilconservierungsbureaus, 13 December 1872.

96. StadtAA 19/554, Stadtmagistrat an Gemeindebevollmächtigte, 16 January 1872.

97. StadtAA 19/554, Stadtmagistrat an Städtischen Baurat, 7 December 1872; Magistrate to municipal building commission, 7 December 1872; See also Protokoll der Besichtigung und Begutachtung im Rathaus am 9 Mai 1874.

98. One councillor declared that it was the 'duty of monumental art…to raise the people's belief in their own power and strength.' This position was represented in a report which the magistrate received from the local artist Wagner, dated 22 Juni 1873: StadtAA 19/554.

99. AAZ, no. 244 (3 September 1876).

100. AAZ, no. 244 (3 September 1876).

101. ANN, no 204 (4 September 1883).

102. See also ANN, no. 207 (3 September 1886).

103. See, for example, ANN, no. 204 (2 September 1892), no. 205 (3 September 1892), no. 203 (1 September 1893), no. 206 (5 September 1893).

104. ANN, no. 203 (1 September 1894).

105. ANN, no. 204 (2 September 1894).

106. USP, no. 203 (31 August 1873).

107. USP, no. 203 (31 August 1873).

108. USP, no. 198 (26 August 1881).

109. StadtAU 060/05, no. 1, Veteranen-Verein Ulm (Prinz-Hermann zu Sachsen-Weimar) an das Stadtschultheissenamt, 3 August 1891; Sitzung der städtischen Collegien, 6 August 1891.

110. UZ, no. 245 (6 September 1900).

111. LUA, no. 193 (19 August 1873).

112. LUA, No. 202 (29 August 1873).

113. USP, no. 204 (2 September 1873).

114. USP, no. 192 (19 August 1874).

115. USP, no. 198 (25 August 1876).

116. StadtAU 060/05, no. 2, Sitzung Gemeinderat, 18 July 1895; Sitzung Gemeinderat, 22 August 1895.

117. StadtAU 060/05, no. 2, Schreiben des Ausschusses des Arbeitersängerbunds Ulm an Stadtschultheiss Wagner, 30 August 1895.
118. USP, no. 207 (7 September 1875).
119. USP, no. 204 (2 September 1877).
120. See, for example, the editorial in USP, no. 204 (2 September 1881). In the very same year, the democrat *Ulmer Tagblatt* criticized general Moltke for his advocacy of war as a veritable school for life, adding acerbically that the 'crime statistics following great wars contradict the general's claim in the most drastic of fashions.' UT, no. 32 (9 February 1881).
121. USP, no. 206 (2 September 1884).
122. ANN, no. 247 (17 October 1872).
123. For an early expression of this opposition, see, for example, AP, no. 201 (28 August 1873).
124. AP, no. 212 (6 September 1872).
125. AP, no. 201 (28 August 1873).
126. AP, no. 208 (5 September 1873).
127. ANN, no. 197 (25 August 1895).
128. ANN, no. 205 (4 September 1895).
129. NAA, no. 201 (30 August 1895).
130. ANN, no. 203 (1 September 1895).
131. StadtAL ZR 1000/6a, The mayor's explanation must have settled the matter, as his letter prompted no further reply from the district government.
132. AP, no. 146 (20 June 1872).
133. AP, no. 203 (30 August 1873).
134. ANN, no. 208 (4 September 1874).
135. StadtAA: 19/544, Bischof an Stadtmagistrat, 26 August 1876. AAZ, no. 244 (3 September 1876).
136. StadtAL ZR 1000/6a, K. Bayrische Regierung der Pfalz an K. Bezirksamt Speyer, 31 August 1875.
137. StadtAL ZR 1000/6a.
138. StadtAL ZR 1000/6a.
139. It is very likely that the reference here was to Ulm's Catholic school. USP, no. 207 (5 September 1882).
140. USP, no. 206 (5 September 1873).
141. See, for example, USP, no. 205 (4 September 1874). The only exception to this rule occurred when the day of the Sedan Day celebrations coincided with a Catholic holiday. This was the case in 1879, when the Catholic Church celebrated the Feast of the Guardian Angel. See StadtAU 060/05, no. 1. Oberbürgermeister von Heim an Katholisches Stadtpfarramt, 28 August 1879; and the Catholic parish's reply of 29 August 1879.
142. See, for example, USP, no. 204 (2 September 1887) and no. 205 (3 September 1886).

143. StadtAU 060/05, Festkommission an katholisches Stadtpfarramt, 27 August 1878; and the Catholic parish's reply of 29 August 1878.

144. UT, no. 205 (3 September 1889).

145. A glance at the newspaper reports leaves no doubt that the liberal preoccupation with the decoration of private buildings on Sedan Day was effectively restricted to this particular political group. In Augsburg, Catholic newspapers did sometimes point out that the decorations had been sparse in order to undermine liberal claims that Sedan Day was popular. In Ulm, where at least until the early 1880s the *Ulmer Tagblatt* represented a democratic viewpoint that was opposed to the *Deutsche Partei*, its editors showed little interest in decorations and flags.

146. ANN, no. 208 (4 September 1874).

147. ANN, no. 205 (4 September 1877).

148. ANN, no. 205 (4 September 1895).

149. LUA, no. 207 (4 September 1876).

150 PfK, no. 409 (3 September 1890).

151. USP, no. 214 (12 September 1878).

152. UT, no. 205 (4 September 1879).

153. UT, no. 205 (3 September 1886). Such references became very common. See also no. 205 (3 September 1887) and no. 208 (6 September 1892).

154. UT, no. 205 (3 September 1887).

CHAPTER 7

1. NAZ, no. 131 (2 June 1872).

2. NAZ, no. 125 (30 May 1888).

3. UVB, no. 134 (15 June 1900).

4. ANN, no. 139 (18 June 1897); ANN, no. 139 (19 June 1897).

5. ANN, no. 151 (3 July 1897); NAZ, no. 151 (3 July 1897).

6. NAZ, no. 152 (4 July 1897).

7. Verlautbarungen des bischöflichen Ordinariats Augsburg bezüglich der pfarramtlichen Behandlung gemischter Ehen, in Oberhirtliche Generalien der der Diözese Augsburg vom 28 November 1858 bis 21 Dezember 1864 (Augsburg: F. E. Kremerschen Buchdruckerei, 1864), 5–6.

8. StadtAA 10/280. See also the case of the Württemberg major and Ulm citizen Eduard Heinzmann: StadtAA 10/281.

9. See Oberhirtliche Generalien der Diözese Augsburg vom 4 Januar 1865 bis 23 August 1876 (Augsburg: F. E. Kremerschen Buchdruckerei, 1876), 232; and Oberhirtliche Generalien der der Diözese Augsburg vom 19 Januar 1887 bis 15 Oktober 1894 (Augsburg: F. E. Kremerschen Buchdruckerei, 1895), 509.

10. For an early critique of the milieu thesis, see Wilfried Loth, *Katholiken im Kaiserreich: Der politische Katholizismus in der Krise des wilhelminischen Deutschland* (Düsseldorf: Droste, 1984), and by the same author, 'Soziale Bewegungen im

Katholizismus des Kaiserreichs', *Geschichte und Gesellschaft*, 17 (1991), 279–310. The relative fluidity of the Catholic milieu is also highighted in Mergel, *Zwischen Klasse und Konfession*; Oliver Zimmer, 'Nation und Religion. Von der Imagination des Nationalen zur Verarbeitung von Nationalisierungsprozesen', *Historische Zeitschrift*, 283 (2006), 617–56. For a powerful challenge by a historian to viewing corporate identities as realities rather than as strategic resources, see Jacques Revel, 'Institution et le social', in Revel, *Un Parcours Critique*, 85–139.

11. Gangolf Hübinger, 'Confessionalism', in Chickering (ed.), *Imperial Germany*, 160.

12. In Ulm, the figures on mixed Protestant-Catholic marriages were published at the beginning of each year in the two local newspapers, the *Ulmer Schnellpost* and the *Ulmer Tagblatt*. For Ludwigshafen, see von Hippel, 'Zwischen klein-deutscher Reichsgründung und Weltkriegs-Katastrophe', 657. My calculations on Augsburg—where the average rate was 13.9 per cent in the working-class parish of St. Georg (between 1864 and 1889), and 17.6 per cent in the middle-class parish of St. Moritz (between 1870 and 1895)—are based on Archiv des Bistums Augsburg (ABA): Pfarrmatrikeln Augsburg St. Moritz, Band 11, 20; Pfarrmatrikeln Augsburg St. Georg, Band 17, 36.

13. Miri Rubin, *Corpus Christi: The Eucharist in Late Medieval Culture* (Cambridge: Cambridge University Press 1991), 181.

14. Ibid., 137.

15. According to Peter Hersche, its demonstrative quality is one of the main characteristics of Baroque religion. See Peter Hersche, *Musse und Verschwendung. Europäische Gesellschaft und Kultur im Barockzeitalter* (Freiburg: Herder, 2006), 944.

16. Ibid., 259.

17. Hersche, *Musse und Verschwendung*, 353. See also Christopher Elwood, *The Body Broken: The Calvinist Doctrine of the Eucharist and the Symbolization of Power in Sixteenth-Century France* (New York: Oxford University Press, 1999). On Corpus Christi processions as sites of violence, see Natalie Zemon Davis, 'The Rites of Violence: Religious Riot in Sixteenth-Century France', *Past & Present*, 59 (1975), 51–91.

18. Hersche, *Musse und Verschwendung*, 419.

19. Austen Ivereigh, (ed.), *The Politics of Religion in an Age of Revival: Studies in Nineteenth-Century Europe and Latin America* (London: Institute of Latin American Studies, 2000), 1.

20. There exists no single study of Corpus Christi processions in Germany in the modern period. But, as a phenomenon, they appear to be reflective of the 'new Catholicism' that Christopher Clark has identified as a Europe-wide phenomenon. See Clark and Kaiser (eds.), *Culture Wars*, introduction by Clark.

21. Generallandesarchiv Karlsruhe 357/21887. The inquiry was sent out on 7 June 1904, and the replies arrived just a few days later.

22. According to Peter Hersche, the Catholic church offered a far greater 'repertoire of opportunities for status manifestation' than does its Protestant counterpart. Hersche, *Musse und Verschwendung*, 225, 423.

23. StadtAL Pa I, no. 13, 367–8, 27 September 1895.

24. ANN, Nr. 136 (12 June 1884).

25. UT, no. 129 (6 June 1885).

26. There were 261 Jews living in Ulm in 1858 (amounting to 0.119 per cent of the total population), rising by 1895 to 643 (1.64 per cent of the population). On Ulm's confessional demography, see *Beschreibung des Oberamts Ulm*, 487–8.

27. UVB, no. 125 (3 June 1899).

28. Von Hippel, 'Zwischen kleindeutscher Reichsgründung und Weltkriegs-Katastrophe', 452–74, 653–66.

29. StadtAL ZR 5504/9, Alleruntertänigste Bitte der Einwohnerschaft zu Ludwigshafen um allergnädigste Errichtung einer Pfarrei sowohl für die katholische als auch für die protestantische Confession allda betreffend, 24 December 1855.

30. LAS, H3, no. 5446. There were 180 Jews living in Ludwigshafen in 1871 (representing 2.3 per cent of its inhabitants), rising to 747 by 1910 (which, at that point, amounted to less than 1 per cent of the town's population). See von Hippel, 'Zwischen kleindeutscher Reichsgründung und Weltkriegs-Katastrophe', 656, 665.

31. The historical background is outlined in Knauber, *Albert Jäger: Direktor der Pfälzischen Eisenbahnen 1814–1887*.

32. François, *Die unsichtbare Grenze*.

33. On the processions in Bavaria, see Stefan Laube, *Fest, Religion und Erinnerung. Konfessionelles Gedächtnis in Bayern von 1804 bis 1917* (Munich: C.H. Beck, 1999).

34. ABSP ÄA Nr. P 630, Bistum Speyer an Expositus Stock in Ludwigshafen, 19 March 1857.

35. Ibid., Domkapitel Speyer an Herrn Pfarrer Hofherr, 19 June 1876.

36. ABSP ÄA Nr. P 630, Pfarrer Hofherr and Hcohwürdiges Capitular-Vicariat, 24 June 1876.

37. Ibid., Capitular-Vikariat an Pfarrer Hofherr, 26 June 1876.

38. ABSP ÄA Nr. P 630, Pfarrer Hofherr an Capitular-Vicariat, 30 June 1876.

39. Ibid.

40. ABSP ÄA Nr. P 630, Capitular-Vicariat an Pfarrer Hofherr, 3 July 1876.

41. Ibid.

42. On 12 February 1882, Johannes von Lutz, Bavaria's minister of culture and education, endorsed the district government's point of view, which settled the matter for good. See ABSP ÄA Nr. P 630, Staatsministerium des Innern für Kirchen- und Schulangelegenheiten (Dr von Lutz) an katholischen Fabrikrat Ludwigahfen, 12 February 1882.

43. PfK, no. 277 (16 June 1892).

44. SAL E 211 VI, no. 994, Kath. Dekanat an Kreisregierung Ulm, Oberamt und Dekanatsamt Ulm, 2 May 1822.

45. Ibid. In 1874 Ulm was one of only four towns in Württemberg where a public Corpus Christi procession had established itself. The others were Geislingen, Göppingen and Aalen. In Stuttgart, Canstadt, Horb, Reutlingen, Freudenstadt, Crailsheim, and Tuttlingen the procession was conducted inside the church, while the procession in Ludwigsburg was confined to the church surroundings. See SAL E 211, no. 994, Bericht kath. Kirchenrath an das Ministerium des Kirchen- und Schulwesens in Stuttgart, 24 September 1874.

46. SAL E 211, no. 994, Ulmer Stadtpfarramt an kath. Kirchenrat in Stuttgart, 28 July 1874.

47. UVB, no. 130 (12 June 1903).

48. UVB, no. 123 (3 June 1904). 'Dem Allerheiligsten folgte eine Anzahl von Beamten und die Mitglieder des Kirchenstiftungsrates; das Offizierskorps war dieses Mal, soviel wir beobachten konnten, nicht vertreten. Die kath. Vereine waren vollzählig erschienen der kath. Arbeiterverein zum ersten Male mit seiner prächtigen neuen Fahne.'

49. UVB, no. 141 (23 June 1905).

50. UVB, no. 141 (23 June 1905).

51. UVB, no. 120 (29 May 1907).

52. StadtAA 4/F185, Einladung des Regierungspräsidiums an sämtliche königlichen und Lokalbehörden dahier, 13 June 1835.

53. StadtAA 4/F185, Einladung des Regierungspräsidiums an Stadtmagistrat Augsburg, 2 June 1860.

54. StadtAA 3/98.

55. StadtAA 4/F 185.

56. StadtAA 4/F185, Antwort des I. Bürgermeisters an das Regierungspräsidium betreffend Feier des Frohnleichnamsfestes, 11 June 1870. See also NAZ, no. 165 (18 Juni 1870).

57. As the President of the district government wrote to the magistrate on 13 June 1870: 'In reference to your report of the 11th of this month, we herewith return the scraps of paper that arrived here today.' StadtAA 4/F185.

58. StadtAA 4/F185, I. Bürgermeister Fischer an Präsidium der k. Regierung von Schwaben und Neuburg, die Feier des Frohnleichnamsfestes betreffend, 6 June 1871/13 June 1871. 6 Juni 1871, 13 June 1871. Emphases in the original.

59. StadtAA 4/F185, K. Präsidium der Regierung von Schwaben u. Neuburg an alle Vorstände der Distriktspolizeibehörden des Regierungsbezirks, 11 June 1873.

60. At a meeting of the Catholic Casino on 6 June 1898, one member argued that the King's 1875 decision largely explained the general decline in participation on the side of Bavarian officialdom. See StadtAA 10/389.

61. SAA 9607, Stadtmagistrat an Regierungspräsidium, 4 July 1872.

62. NAZ, no. 130 (1 June 1872).

63. AP, no. 140 (13 June 1871). In Augsburg, too, the extent—and nature—of decorations during the processions was a stock-in-trade of Catholic reporting.

64. AP, no. 133 (8 June 1874).

65. AP, no. 128 (4 June 1877).

66. NAZ, no. 136, (14 June 1879); AP, no. 133 (8 June 1874).

67. See, for example, the meetings of the *Katholischer Männerverein links und rechts der Wertach:* StadtAA 5/546.

68. See the meetings of the *Christlicher Arbeiterverein:* StadtAA 5/549.

69. StadtAA 5/548–49, Versammlung Christlicher Arbeiterverein, 19 June 1881.

70. NAZ, no. 138 (12 June 1873).

71. ANN, no. 140 (18 June 1892).

72. ANN, no. 132 (11 June 1898).

73. NAZ, no. 139 (19 June 1897).

74. NAZ, no. 133 (12 June 1909).

75. StadtAU B374/10, no. 1.

76. LUA, no. 132, (9 June 1881).

77. Ibid.

78. For a summary of the incident and the subsequent history of Corpus Christi in Ludwigshafen, see Knauber, *Albert von Jäger*, 37–9.

79. LUA, no. 132 (9 June 1881).

80. The article appeared in the *Pfälzische Kurier* on 1 June 1881; cited in Knauber, *Albert von Jäger*, 38.

81. StadtAL PaI, no. 7, 283–4.

82. PfK, no. 129 (4 June 1881).

83. ABSP ÄA Nr. P 630, Pfarrer Hofherr an Hochwürdigen Bischof, 4 June 1881.

84. Ibid., Pfarrer Hofherr an Hochwürdigen Bischof, 5 June 1881.

85. ABSP ÄA Nr. P 630, Bischöfliches Ordinariat Speyer an Stadtpfarrer Hofherr in Ludwigshafen, 6 June 1881. Consisting of senior Catholic employees of the Pfälzische Bahn, the *Fabrikrat* acted as organizer of the procession.

86. LUA, no. 138 (17 June 1881); *Pfälzischer Kurier*, quoted in Knauber, *Albert von Jäger*, 38. The council's appeal was unsuccessful.

87. LUA, no. 136 (13 June 1884).

88. StadtAA 4/F185, Schreiben des Bischöflichen Stadtdekanats Augsburg an den Magistrat, 29 May 1881; Weisung des Bürgermeisters an den Polizeioffizier, 8 June 1887.

89. Such parish-based processions had been known in many of the larger late-medieval towns. See Rubin, *Corpus Christi*, 261.

90. For a relatively extensive correspondence relating to the processions at St. Georg, see StadtAA: 5/253. The continuation of tramway traffic during the processions prompted much irritation, even anger, among those who took part. On the tensions over tramway traffic in Karlsruhe in the period from 1902 and 1913, see Generallandesarchiv Karlsruhe 357/21887.

91. StadtAA 5/253.

92. StadtAA 4/F185, Anfrage der Haupt- und Residenzstadt Karlsruhe an den Magistrat der Stadt Augsburg, 5 February 1896.

93. StadtAA 5/253, Stadtpfarramt St. Georg an Stadtmagistrat, 22 May 1883. See also the response by the city magistrate of 26 May 1883.

94. StadtAA 5/253, Gesuch des kath. Stadtpfarramts St. Georg (Dr Koch) an den Magistraten der Stadt Augsburg, 30 May 1889. Emphasis in the original.

95. Von Hippel, 'Zwischen kleindeutscher Reichsgründung und Weltkriegs-Katastrophe', 505–8.

96. StadtAL Pa I, no. 11, 506–7, Sitzung Stadtrat, 6 May 1891.

97. The debate was summarized at a meeting of the council on 30 May 1892: StadtAL Pa I, no. 12, 175–6.

98. Ibid.

99. ANN, no. 129 (5 June 1909); NAZ, no. 128 (5 June 1909).

100. NAZ, no. 129 (5 June 1909).

101. NAZ, no. 128, 5 June 1909.

102. The advertisement was reprinted in UZ, no. 136 (13 June 1895).

103. Ibid.

104. StadtAU E 152/1. This was not the first time the organization had become active in Ulm. In November 1890, around 12,000 Catholics converged on Ulm to attend the Württembergischer Katholikentag, at which leading representatives of political Catholicism called (in vain) for a repeal of the anti-Jesuit law. This prompted the Bund (in alliance with the *Deutsche Partei*) to organize a counter-meeting, which was attended by 1500 people. It culminated in the launching of a petition, which within the space of a month would be signed by 2854 people in Ulm alone (in the much larger Stuttgart, the same petition received 'only' 4700 signatures). See UT, no. 300 (24 December 1890).

105. StadtAU E 152/1, Versammlung Evangelischer Bund Ulm, 14 June 1895.

106. Ibid.

107. StadtAU B 374/10, no. 1, Sitzung Gemeinderat, 27 June 1895.

108. Ibid.

109. StadtAU B 374/10, no. 1, Stadtpolizeiamt an Oberamt Ulm, 21 June 1901.

110. Ibid., Stadtpolizeiamt an Oberamt, 28 June 1901; Kreisregierung an K. Oberamt, 10 June 1901.

111. StadtAU B 374/10, no. 1, Sitzung Gemeinderat, 27 August 1901. The lack of further debate on the matter suggests that Wagner's solution alleviated the problem.

112. NAZ, no. 131 (2 June 1872).

113. AP, no. 133 (8 June 1874).

114. StadtAA 5/548, Versammlung Christlicher Arbeiterverein, 18 April 1880.

115. 'Früher habe man gesagt: "Weiber-Geschlecht, frommes Geschlecht!", jetzt dürfe man fast sagen: "Männer-Geschlecht, frommes Geschlecht; Weiber-Geschlecht, schlechtes Geschlecht!" (Bravo-Rufe!).' StadtAA 5/546.

116. See above all Gross, *War against Catholicism*, 215–17; and Norbert Busch, 'Die Feminisierung der Frömmigkeit', in *Wunderbare Erscheinungen: Frauen und katholische Frömmigkeit im 19. Und 20. Jahrhundert*, (ed.) Irmtraud Götz von Olenhusen (Paderborn, 1995), 203–19. On France, see Claude Langlois, *Le catholicisme au feminine: Les congregations françaises à supérieure générale au XIXe siècle* (Paris, 1984); Ruth Harris, *Lourdes: Body and Spirit in the Secular Age* (London: Penguin, 1999); Caroline Ford, *Divided Houses: Religion and Gender in Modern France* (Ithaca: Cornell University Press, 2005). For a comparative perspective, see Hugh McLeod, 'Weibliche Frömmigkeit—männlicher Unglaube? Religion und Kirchen im bürgerlichen 19. Jahrhundert', in Ute Frevert (ed.), *Bürgerinnen und Bürger*, 134–56; and Caroline Ford, 'Religion and Popular Culture in Modern Europe', *Journal of Modern History* 65 (March 1993), 166.

117. Gross, *The War against Catholicism*, 197, 186–7. For an elaboration of Gross' thesis through comparative analysis, see Geoff Eley, '"an embarrassment to the family, to the public, and to the state": Liberalism and the Rights of Women, 1860–1914', in Dominik Geppert and Robert Gerwarth (eds.), *Wilhelmine Germany and Edwardian Britain: Essays on Cultural Affinity* (Oxford: Oxford University Press, 2008), 143–71.

118. C. Ford, *Divided Houses*, 7.

119. The stance taken by Ulm's influential democrat politician Robert Ebner (a Protestant), on the question of female teachers' role in primary education, is instructive here. Like the majority in Württemberg's lower house of which he was a member, Ebner opposed the state government's 1878 proposal in favour of appointing women to permanent teaching positions. What had led him to this view were not only doubts as to whether women's 'physical and mental' ability qualified them to anything other than a partial and subsidiary role in the teaching profession. He also expressed concern about the 'competition' that would thus arise for men, particularly over 'the better posts.' He further warned of the 'extreme religious orientations' that might gain weight if the profile of female teachers was further enhanced. See UT, no. 255 (30 October 1878). As research by Amanda Vickery, among others, has shown, such anti-women rhetoric was by no means an invention of the nineteenth century. What might render the German nineteenth-century examples interesting is perhaps less its fusion with anti-Catholicism, but the role it played in the construction of a Christian-centric, class-transcendent nationalism. See Amanda Vickery, *The Gentleman's Daughter: Women's Lives in Georgian England* (Yale: Yale University Press, 1998), Introduction.

120. Donald Horowitz, *The Deadly Ethnic Riot* (Berkeley: University of California Press, 2001), 275.

121. On Corpus Christi processions as sites of violence, see Davis, 'The Rites of Violence. The only exception that comes to mind is the Moabit *Klostersturm* of 1869, a riot-like wave of physical and verbal intimidation, directed against a Dominican order, in which Berlin Protestants of different social backgrounds took part and which had to be dissolved through extensive police deploy-

ment. See Manuel Borutta, 'Enemies at the Gate: The Moabit *Klostersturm* and the *Kulturkampf* in Germany', in Clark and Kaiser, *Culture Wars*, 227–54. On anti-Jesuit rhetoric and legislation, see Anderson, *Practising Democracy*, 94–1-1; Róisín Healy, 'Anti-Jesuitism in Imperial Germany: The Jesuit as Androgyne', in Smith, *Protestants, Catholics, and Jews*, 153–81. On the popular dimension of confessional conflict in the Prussian Rhineland, see James M. Brophy, *Popular Culture and the Public Sphere in the Rhineland 1800–1850* (Cambridge: Cambridge University Press, 2007), ch. 6.

122. Not least when it comes to violence, the notion of a *zweites konfessionelles Zeitalter* is overwrought. Nineteenth-century Germans were not prepared to die over religion in the same manner as sixteenth-century Europeans. See Olaf Blaschke, *Konfessionen im Konflikt: Deutschland zwischen 1800 und 1970: ein zweites konfessionelles Zeitalter* (Göttingen: Vandenhoeck, 2001).

123. To attribute the absence of sustained physical violence to the strength of local and national authorities in post-unification Germany is tempting but hardly convincing. Thus, when large-scale anti-Jewish riots broke out in Pomerania in 1881, in Xanten (Rhineland) in 1890, and in Konitz (West Prussia) in 1900, the violence could be contained only trough massive (and frequently bloody) military intervention. An entire battalion was sent to Konitz in June 1900 on the order of Wilhelm II, where it stayed until January of the following year. On this theme, see Christhard Hoffmann, 'Political Culture and Violence against Minorities: The Antisemitic Riots in Pomerania and West Prussia', 67–92; and Helmut Walser Smith, 'Konitz, 1900: Ritual Murder and Antisemitic Violence', 93–122, both in Christhard Hoffmann, Werner Bergmann, and Helmut Walser Smith (eds.), *Exclusionary Violence: Antisemitic Riots in Modern German History* (Ann Arbor, MI, 2002).

124. Von Hippel, 'Zwischen kleindeutscher Reichsgründung und Weltkriegs-Katastrophe', 583–91.

125. Fischer, *Industrialisierung*, 80–95.

126. *Beschreibung des Oberamtes Ulm*, 189; Koenig, 'Kirchliches Leben in Ulm', 355–441.

127. NAZ, no. 131 (2 June 1872).

128. ANN, no. 137 (14 June 1884).

129. UV, no. 121 (31 May 1907).

130. NAZ, no. 161 (13 June 1868).

131. Ibid.

132. ANN, no. 128 (5 June 1877).

133. NAZ, no. 155 (7 June 1871), no. 162 (15 June 1871).

134. ANN, no. 161 (13 June 1868).

135. ANN, no. 123 (30 May 1891).

136. ANN, no. 119 (26 May 1883).

137. ANN, no. 129 (6 June 1885).

138. On this important theme, see Axel Honneth, 'Redistribution as Recognition: A Response to Nancy Fraser', in Nancy Fraser and Axel Honneth, *Redistribution or Recognition* (London: Verso, 2003), 173.

139. A concept first elaborated by Erving Goffman, *Stigma Management: Notes on the Management of Spoiled Identity* (New York: Prentice-Hall, 1963).
140. On Christianity as a common language in the nineteenth century, see Hugh McLeod and Werner Ustorf (eds.), *The Decline of Christendom in Western Europe, 1750–2000* (Cambridge: Cambridge University Press, 2003), 11.
141. On France, see James McMillan, '"Priest hits girl": On the Front Line in the "War of the two Frances"', in Clark and Kaiser (eds.), *Culture Wars*, 77–101.
142. StadtAA 5/421.
143. AAZ, no. 212 (4 August 1873).
144. Ibid. The *Augsburger Postzeitung* condemned Fischer's speech as liberal propaganda (AP, no. 182, 5 August 1873).
145. See Till van Rahden's work on Breslau, where both liberals and Catholics came to endorse Christianity in the contest over urban school reform, implicitly or explicitly excluding Jews in the process: Van Rahden, Till, 'Unity, Diversity, and Difference: Jews, Protestants, and Catholics in Breslau Schools during the Kulturkampf', in Smith (ed.), *Protestants, Catholics, and Jews*, 223–33.
146. USP, no. 274 (22 November 1890).
147. Cited in UT, no. 269 (18 November 1890).
148. Cited in ibid., no. 275 (25 November 1890).
149. Ibid.
150. UV, no. 133 (13 June 1906).
151. AP, no. 139 (14 Juni 1876) 'So viel ist unzweifelhaft, dass die *Lösung der jüdischen Frage* für die christliche Bevölkerung eine Lebensfrage ist, und nachdem die Christen eingesehen haben werden, dass sie von den Juden nach dem Motto: "divide et impera" aufgestachelt worden sind, wird man an die Lösung der jüdischen Frage mit dem Ernst herantreten, welchen die drohende Gefahr erheischt. Darum vor allem: "Friede unter euch Christen!" Möge die Friedensmahnung nicht ungehört verklingen!'

CONCLUSION

1. Marc Bloch, *Apologies pour L'Histoire or le Métier l'Historien* (Paris: Librairie Armand Colin, 1949), 88.
2. USP, no. 66 (20 March 1879).
3. The municipality would henceforth support it with an annual amount of around 5000 marks. The school fee per pupil was approximately 65 marks per year. See UT, no. 35 (10 February 1878). The conflict was termed 'needle *and* booklet war' because some teachers at elementary schools also drew fire for allegedly having sold booklets to their pupils. However, the activities of the *Frauenarbeitsschule* created far greater waves than those of the teachers who had sold booklets to their pupils.
4. StadtAU B121/005, no. 4, Handelsverein (Magirus) an den Gemeinderat der Stadt Ulm, 7 May 1878.

5. Ibid.
6. StadtAU B 257/9, no. 3, Gewerbeverein (Foerstler) an Stiftungsrat, 7 September 1878. See also the petition of 24 February 1879. Its 48 signatories (which described themselves as 'members of the business and crafts community') identified the sale of teaching material (including writing paper, note pads, pencils and books at the elementary schools) as a pervasive tendency, one that went far beyond the Frauenarbeitsschule, which they saw as the main culprit: StadtAU B 257/9, no. 3.
7. StadtAU B 257/9, no. 3, Rektor der Frauenarbeitsschule (Dr Weitzel) an den Stiftungsrat, 5 May 1878.
8. Ibid.
9. USP, no. 167 (18 July 1878).
10. For a recent summary of the debate, see Umbach, *German Cities*, 1–6.
11. Jarausch and Geyer, *Shattered Past*, 37.
12. See in particular Reinhard Koselleck, *Zeitschichten. Studien zur Historik* (Frankfurt am Main: Suhrkamp, 2003), esp. 150–76.
13. Even some of the most brilliant historical research on nineteenth-century society and culture, such as Alain Corbin's work on the role of time and rhythms in the lives of ordinary people, tends to conclude that this period saw a homogenisation of rhythms and habits, a view which follows in the footsteps of Norbert Elias and Michel Foucault (both of whom Corbin cites in support of his views). See Alain Corbin, *Les Cloches de la Terre: Paysage Sonore et Culture Sensible dans les Campagnes au XIX Siècle* (Paris: Flammarion, 1994) and *Historien du Sensible* (Paris: La Découverte—Cahiers libres, 2000). For a pioneering essay that cautions against assumptions concerning a homogenisation of socio-temporal patterns in the modern period, see Thompson', 'Time, Work-Discipline, and Industrial Capitalism'.
14. StadtAU B 257/9, no. 3, Rektor der Frauenarbeitsschule (Dr Weitzel) an den Stiftungsrat, 5 May 1878.
15. StadtAU B 257/9, no. 3, Oberlehrer Hartmann und Keppler an das K. Schulinspektorat, 30 June 1878.
16. StadtAA 5/556, Versammlung Neuer Bürgerverein, 25 October 1879.
17. Lothar Gall, 'Liberalismus und "bürgerliche Gesellschaft"', 324–56. For an assessment of these various approaches to urban liberalism, see in particular John Breuilly, 'The German Bourgeoisie from Radicalism to Nationalism', *German History*, 14, no. 2 (1996), 223–31).
18. A number of objections have been raised against viewing nationalism in such participatory terms. The most common states that people did not attend, for example, national celebrations and festivals out of conviction but because they enjoyed the spectacle and entertainment that such events provided. Festivals of this kind, some historians have argued, offered a few hours of distraction, a day out with one's friends or family. Most people who took part in these events did therefore not do so out of patriotic (let alone nationalist) conviction, but for

reasons of sociability and gaiety. In my view, such arguments rely on a very restrictive view of how nationalism operates, reducing it to an explicit ideological commitment, one that remains disjointed from their everyday lives. Yet why should public enjoyment and (conscious or unconscious) identification with a patriotic or national cause be mutually exclusive? For interesting theoretical reflections on this theme, see, for example, Michael Billig, *Banal Nationalism* (London: Sage, 1995).

19. As Christopher Bayly has summed up the problem: 'Historians have often tried to have their cake and eat it. They like to argue that the peasant, the tribesman, the woman, or the working-class man have "autonomy". Yet, when it comes to emotions like patriotism or nationalism, of which they disapprove, that agency is denied to ordinary people who are deemed to be dupes of the elites or automata easily stamped with the mark of state power.' Christopher Bayly, *The Birth of the Modern World*, 1780–1914 Global Connections and Comparisons (Oxford: Blackwell, 2004), 280. For an impressive recent example of how a public fostered patriotic narratives out of its critical engagement with a series of popular nationalist songs and pamphlets, see James M. Brophy, 'The Rhine Crisis of 1840 and German Nationalism: Chauvinism, Skepticism, and Regional Reception', *Journal of Modern History* 85/1 (forthcoming 2013).

20. 'Der Hemshof, die Farbenstadt Deutschlands', *Pfälzischer Kurier* (28/29 March 1889).

Bibliography

ARCHIVAL SOURCES

Stadtarchiv Augsburg (StadtAA).

1: 1294.

2: 1186; 1188; 1211; 1213; 4062; 4074.

3: 97; 98; 225; 380; 707.

4: F185.

5: 37; 253; 267; 421; 422; 424; 542; 546; 548; 549; 555; 559.

10: 280–81; 300; 389; 403; 2697; 3659; 3670; 3671; 3677.

11: 56.

19: 554.

27: 1.

Stadtarchiv Ludwigshafen am Rhein (StadtAL).

LU: 595.

Lua: 60; 650.

M: 153; 286; 380; 604; 605.

Pa I: 4; 5; 6; 7; 8; 9; 13.

ZR: 1000/6a; 1025/2/3/6/11; 4060/5; 5000/16/19/20; 5002/2; 5007/5/7; 5010/6/9;
    5504/9; ZR 5530–1, 2.

Stadtarchiv Ulm (StadtAU).

060: 05/23/25.

724/22, no. 1.

774/13, no. 43.

B 008/00, no. 2.

B 026/5.

B121/005, no. 4.

B 123/131 no. 1.

B 211/20, no. 3.

B 211/20, no. 6.

B 257/9, no. 3.

B 372/8, nos 3 and 4.

B 372/50, no. 7.

B 374/10, no. 1.

B 377/40, nos 1, 2.

B 400/0, nos 1–2.
B 401/1, no. 2.
B 401/2, nos, 1, 3.
B 122/51 nos 60–62.
E 152, no. 1.

Staatsarchiv Augsburg (SAA).
Regierung: 8689; 9602; 9604; 9605; 9607; 9608; 9710.

Staatsarchiv Ludwigsburg (SAL).
E 179 II: 3329–3330; 7979; 7987; 8000.
E 211 VI: 994.

Landesarchiv Speyer (LAS).
H3: 141; 5446; 7221.

Archiv Des Bistums Augsburg (ABA).
Pfarrmatrikeln Augsburg St. Moritz, Band 11, 20.
Pfarrmatrikeln Augsburg St. Georg, Band 17, 36.

Archiv Des Bistums Speyer (ABSP).
ÄA Nr. P 630.

Diözesanarchiv Rottenburg-Stuttgart (DAR)
G. 1.1, C 14.2 b.

NEWSPAPERS

Augsburger Abendzeitung (AAZ).
Augsburger Allgemeine Zeitung (AZ).
Augsburger Anzeigeblatt (AA).
Augsburger Neueste Nachrichten (ANN).
Augsburger Postzeitung (AP).
Neue Augsburger Zeitung (NAZ).
Ludwigshafener Anzeiger (LUA).
General Anzeiger Ludwigshafen am Rhein (GAL).
Neuer Pfälzischer Kurier (NpfK).
Ulmer Tagblatt | (UT).
Ulmer Schnellpost (USP).
Ulmer Zeitung (UZ).
Ulmer Volksbote (UV).

PRINTED SOURCES

Beschreibung des Oberamts Ulm. Herausgegeben von dem K. Statistischen Landesamt, vol. I (Stuttgart: Kommissionsverlag von W. Kohlhammer, 1897).

Burschell, Friedrich, *Erinnerungen 1889–1919* (Ludwigshafen: Stadtarchiv LU, 1997).

Denkschrift des Regierungsrates Lamotte vom 31. Dezember 1853 über die Verhältnisse von Ludwigshafen am Rhein. Reprinted in *Zur Geschichte der Stadt Ludwigshafen am Rhein. Ludwigshafen 1853 und 1873. Die Denkschriften von Lamotte und Matthaeus. Hg. Und mit einem genealogischen Teil versehen von Oskar Poller* (Ludwigshafen a. Rh: Verlag der Arbeitsgemeinschaft Pfaelzisch-Rheinische Familienkunde e.V., 1974).

'Der Hemshof, die Farbenstadt Deutschlands,' *Pfälzischer Kurier*, 28/29 March 1889.

Ehrhart, Franz Josef, *Das bayerische Heimatgesetz mit Erläuterungen nebst Anhang über den Erwerb der Staatsangehörigkeit, der Naturalisation und des Armengesetzes* (Ludwigshafen: Josef Huber, 1904).

Ehrhart, Franz Josef, *Bayerisches Heimatgesetz und seine Anwendung nebst Anleitung zur Erwerbung des Bayerischen Staatsbürgerrechts* (Ludwigshafen: Verlaf Pfälzische Post, without date).

Geschichte der Stadt Ludwigshafen am Rhein. Entstehung und Entwicklung einer Industrie- und Handelsstadt in fünfzig Jahren, 1853–1903. Mit einem geschichtlichen Rückblick. Aus Anlass des 50jährigen Bestehens der Stadt Ludwigshafen am Rhein. Herausgegeben vom Bürgermeisteramt (Ludwigshafen am Rhein: Julius Waldkirch & Cie., 1903).

Hirsch, Paul and Hugo Lindemann, *Das kommunale Wahlrecht* (Berlin: Buchhandlung Vorwärts, 1905).

Keller, J. & H. Koob namens des Konsum-Vereins Ludwigshafen, 'Der Zwischenhandel und die Konsumvereine,' *Blätter für Genossenschaftswesen (Innung der Zukunft). Organ des Allgemeinen Verbandes deutscher Erwerbs- und Wirtschafts-Genossenschaften begründet von Dr. Schulze-Delitzsch*, no. 15 (11 April 1896).

Knauber, Jakob & Albert von Jäger. Direktor der Pfälzischen Eisenbahnen 1814–1887. *Ein Lebensbild unter Berücksichtigung der Pfalzbahnen und der Katholischen Pfarrei St. Ludwig* (Ludwigshafen: Verlag der kath. Pfarrämter, 1925).

50 Jahre Konsumverein Ulm a. D. 1866–1916 (no place or publisher, 1916).

Landes- und Volkskunde der Bayerischen Rheinpfalz. Bearbeitet von einem Kreise heimischer Gelehrter (Munich, 1867).

List, Friedrich, *Das Nationale System der politischen Oekonomie* sechste Auflage (Jena: Verlag von Gustav Fischer, 1950 [1841]).

Maier, Gustav, Denkschrift über die Handelsbedeutung der Stadt Ulm und ihrer Umgebung. Im Auftrage und unter Mitwirkung des Comité's für Erstrebung einer Reichsbank-Stelle (Ulm: Druck der J. Ebnerschen Buchdruckerei, 1875).

Oberhirtliche Generalien der Diözese Augsburg vom 28. November 1858 bis 21 Dezember 1864 (Augsburg: F. E. Kremerschen Buchdruckerei, 1864).

Oberhirtliche Generalien der Diözese Augsburg vom 4. Januar 1865 bis 23. August 1876 (Augsburg: F. E. Kremerschen Buchdruckerei, 1876).

Oberhirtliche Generalien der Diözese Augsburg vom 19. Januar 1887 bis 15. Oktober 1894 (Augsburg: F. E. Kremerschen Buchdruckerei, 1895).

Pettenkofer, Max, *Untersuchungen und Beobachtungen über die Verbreitung der Cholera nebst Betrachtungen über Massregeln, derselben Einhalt zu gebieten* (München, 1855).

Poller, Oskar (ed.), *Zur Geschichte der Stadt Ludwigshafen am Rhein. Ludwigshafen 1853 und 1873. Die Denkschriften von Lamotte und Matthäus* (Ludwigshafen a. Rh.: Verlag der Arbeitsgemeinschaft Pfälzisch-Rheinische Familienkunde e.V., 1974).

Riehl, Wilhelm H., *Culturstudien aus drei Jahrhunderten*, vierter unveränderter Abdruck (Stuttgart: Cottasche Buchhandlung, 1873).

Riehl, Wilhelm H., *Die Pfälzer. Ein rheinisches Volksbild*. (Kaiserslautern, 1964 [1857]).

Ritzhaupt, Adam, *In Sonne und Rauch. Erzählungen aus dem Kinderleben* (Karlsruhe: Verlag C. F. Müller, without date).

Schmidt, Rudolf, 'Die Konsumvereine vor dem Reichstage,' *Blätter für Genossenschaftswesen*, vol. 11 (1895).

Schuster, Julius, *Antrag des Stadtschultheissen Schuster betreffend das Armenwesen der Stadt Ulm, gestellt an den Stiftungsrath und Bürgerausschuss am Tage der Feier des 71sten Geburtstagsfestes Sr. Majestät des Königs Wilhelm von Württemberg* (1852).

Statut der Bäcker-Innung zu Ludwigshafen a. Rh. (Ludwigshafen am Rhein: Buchdruckerei von Julius Waldkirch, 1885).

Verlautbarungen des bischöflichen Ordinariats Augsburg bezüglich der 'pfarramtlichen Behandlung gemischter Ehen,' in *Oberhirtliche Generalien der der Diözese Augsburg vom 28. November 1858 bis 21 Dezember 1864*.

Von Seydel, Max, 'Die Reform des bayerischen Heimatrechtes,' *Blätter für administrative Praxis* XLVI, no. 4 (1896), 113–27.

Vorschläge zur Verbesserung des Stuttgarter Schulwesens. Im Auftrage des Bürgerausschusses zusammengestellt von J. Loechner, Lehrer und Bürgerausschussobmann (Stuttgart: Th. Spoettle, 1905).

Wagner, Ulrich, *Die wirtschaftlichen Verhältnisse in Ulm im 19. Jahrhundert* (Ulm, 1895).

SECONDARY WORKS

Alain Corbin, Les Cloches de la Terre: Paysage Sonore et Culture Sensible dans les Campagnes au XIX Siècle (Paris: Flammarion, 1994).

Alain Corbin, *Historien du Sensible* (Paris: La Découverte—Cahiers libres, 2000).

Albisetti, James, 'Education,' in Chickering (ed.), *Imperial Germany: A Historiographical Companion*, 244–71.

Allmann, Ludwig, *Die Wahlbewegung zum I. deutschen Zollparlament in der Rheinpfalz* (Borna-Leipzig: Buchdruckerei Robert Noske, 1913).

Altgeld, Wolfgang, 'Religion, Denomination, and Nationalism in Nineteenth-Century Germany,' in Helmut W. Smith (ed.), *Protestants, Catholics, and Jews in Germany, 1800–1914* (Oxford: Berg, 2001), 49–66.

Anderson, Benedict, *Imagined Communities: Reflections on the Origin and Spread of Nationalism*, 2nd edn. (London: Verso, 1991).

Anderson, Margaret Lavinia, 'Die Grenzen der Säkularisierung: Zur Frage des katholischen Aufschwungs im Deutschland des 19. Jahrhunderts,' in Hartmut Lehmann (ed.), *Säkularisierung, Dechristianisierung, Rechristianisierung im neuzeitlichen Europa* (Göttingen: Vandenhoeck & Ruprecht 1997), 194–222.

Anderson, Margaret Lavinia, *Practicing Democracy: Elections and Political Culture in Imperial Germany* (Princeton: Princeton University Press, 2000).

Anderson, Margaret L. and Kenneth Barkin, 'The Myth of the Puttkammer Purge and the Reality of the *Kulturkampf:* Some Reflections on the Historiography of Imperial Germany,' *Journal of Modern History* 63 (December 1991), 681–716.

Andic, Suphan and Jindrich Veverka, 'The Growth of Government Expenditure in Germany since the Unification,' *Finanzarchiv*, n.s., 23:2 (1963), 169–273.

Applegate, Celia, *A Nation of Provincials: The German Idea of Heimat* (Berkeley: University of California Press, 1990).

Applegate Celia, 'A Europe of regions: reflections on the historiography of sub-national places in modern times,' *American Historical Review* 104 (October 1999), 1157–82.

Applegate, Celia, 'Sense of Places,' in Helmut W. Smith (ed.), *Oxford Handbook of Modern German History*, 49–70.

Ashford, Douglas, 'The Structural Comparison of Social Policy and Integrovernmental Politics,' *Policy and Politics* 12 (1984), 369–90.

Augé, Marc, *Non-Lieux. Introduction à une Anthropoligie de la Surmodernité* (Paris: Éditions de Seuil, 1992).

Augsburger Stadtlexikon, 2. Auflage, edited by Günther Grünsteudel, Günter Hägele und Rudolf Frankenberger (Augsburg: Perlach Verlag, 1998).

Bayly, Christopher, *The Birth of the Modern World, 1780–1914: Global Connections and Comparisons* (Oxford: Blackwell, 2004).

Benz, Ernest, 'Escaping Malthus: population explosion and human movement, 1760–1884,' in Smith (ed.), *The Oxford Handbook of Modern German History*, 195–210.

Bevir, Mark and Frank Trentmann (eds.), *Governance, Consumers and Citizens: Agency and Resistance in Contemporary Politics* (Basingstoke: Palgrave, 2007).

Biefang, Andreas, *Politisches Bürgertum in Deutschland 1857–1868: Nationale Organisationen und Eliten* (Düsseldorf: Droste Verlag, 1994).

Blackbourn, David, *Populists and Patricians: Essays in Modern German History* (London: Unwin Hyman 1987).

Blackbourn, David, *Class, Religion and Local Politics in Wilhelmine Germany: The Centre Party in Württemberg before 1914* (Wiesbaden: Franz Steiner Verlag, 1980).

Blackbourn, David, 'The Catholic Church in Europe since the French Revolution,' *CSSH* 33 (1991): 778–90.

Blackbourn, David, *Marpingen: Apparitions of the Virgin Mary in Nineteenth-Century Germany* (New York: Alfred A. Knopf, 1994).

Blackbourn, David, *A Sense of Place: New Directions in German History. The 1998 Annual Lecture of the German Historical Institute London* (London: GHIL, 1999).

Blackbourn, David, *The Conquest of Nature: Water, Landscape and the Making of Modern Germany* (New York: Norton, 2006).

Blackbourn, David & Geoff Eley (eds.), *The Peculiarities of German History: Bourgeois Society and Politics in Nineteenth-Century Germany* (Oxford: Oxford University Press, 1984).

Blackbourn, David and James Retallack (eds.), *Localism, Landscape and the Ambiguities of Place: German-Speaking Central Europe, 1860–1930* (Toronto: University of Toronto Press, 2007).

Olaf Blaschke, *Konfessionen im Konflikt: Deutschland zwischen 1800 und 1970: ein zweites konfessionelles Zeitalter* (Göttingen: Vandenhoeck, 2001).

Blaschke, Olaf and Frank-Michael Kuhlemann (eds.), *Religion im Kaiserreich: Milieus—Mentalitäten—Krisen* (Göttingen: Vandenhoeck & Ruprecht, 1996).

Borutta, Manuel, *Antikatholizismus. Deutschland und Italien im Zeitalter der europäischen Kulturkämpfe* (Göttingen: Vandenhoeck & Ruprecht, 2010).

Borutta, Manuel, 'Enemies at the Gate: The Moabit *Klostersturm* and the *Kulturkampf* in Germany,' in Clark and Kaiser (eds.), *Culture Wars*, 227–54.

Braun, Rainer, 'Augsburg als Garnison und Festung in der ersten Hälfte des 19. Jahrhunderts' in: Rainer A. Müller (ed.): *Aufbruch ins Industriezeitalter, Bd. 2: Aufsätze zur Wirtschafts- und Sozialgeschichte Bayerns von 1750–1850* (Munich: Oldenbourg, 1985), 65–78.

Breuilly, John, *Nationalism and the State*, 2nd edn (Manchester: Manchester University Press, 1993).

Breuilly, John, 'Urbanization and social transformation, 1800–1914,' in Ogilvie and Overy (eds.), *Germany: A New Social and Economic History*, 192–226.

Breuilly, John, 'Modernisation as Social Evolution: The German Case, c. 1800–1880,' *Transactions of the Royal Historical Society* 15 (2005), 117–47.

Breuilly, John, 'Nationalism and the First Unification,' in Ronald Speirs and John Breuilly (eds.), *Germany's two unifications. Anticipations, Experiences, Responses* (Basingstoke: Palgrave Macmillan, 2005), 101–21.

Breunig, Willi, *Soziale Verhältnisse der Arbeiterschaft und sozialistische Arbeiterbewegung in Ludwigshafen am Rhein 1869–1919* (Darmstadt: Dissertationsdruck Darmstadt, 1990).

Breunig, Willi, *Kommunalpolitik und Wirtschaftsentfaltung in Ludwigshafen am Rhein 1843–1871* (Weinheim: Druckhaus Diesbach, 1995).

Breunig, Willi, 'Vom Handelsplatz zum Industriestandort,' in Mörz and Becker (eds.), *Geschichte der Stadt Ludwigshafen am Rhein*, vol. I, 266–363.

Broadberry, Stephen and Kevin H. O'Rourke (eds.), *The Cambridge Economic History of Modern Europe, vols. 1 & 2* (Cambridge: Cambridge University Press, 2010).

Broadberry, Stephen, Giovanni Federico and Alexander Klein, 'Sectoral developments, 1870–1914,' in Broadberry and O'Rourke (eds.), *The Cambridge Economic History of Modern Europe, vol. 2*, 59–83.

Broadberry, Stephen, Rainer Fremdling, and Peter Solar, 'Industry,' in Broadberry and o'Rourke (eds.), *The Cambridge Economic History of Modern Europe. Volume 1*, 164–86.

Brophy, James M., *Popular Culture and the Public Sphere in the Rhineland 1800–1850* (Cambridge: Cambridge University Press, 2007).

Brophy, James M., 'The End of the Economic Old Order: The Great Transition, 1750–1860,' in Smith (ed.), *Oxford Handbook of Modern German History*, 169–94.

Brophy, James M., 'The Rhine Crisis of 1840 and German Nationalism: Chauvinism, Skepticism, and Regional Indifference,' *Journal of Modern History* 85/1 (forthcoming 2013).

Brown, John C., Timothy W. Guinnane, 'The Fertility Transition in a rural, Catholic Population: Bavaria, 1880–1910,' *Population Studies* 56 (2002), 35–50.

Busch, Norbert, 'Die Feminisierung der Frömmigkeit,' in Irmtraud Götz von Olenhusen (ed.), *Wunderbare Erscheinungen: Frauen und katholische Frömmigkeit im 19. Und 20. Jahrhundert* (Paderborn: Ferdinand Schöningh, 1995), 203–19.

Carreras, Albert and Camilla Josephson, 'Aggregate growth, 1870–1914: growing at the production frontier,' in Broadberry and O'Rourke (eds.), *The Cambridge Economic History of Europe, Vol. II: 1870–1914*, 30–58.

Chanet, Jean-François, *L'école républicaine et les petites patries* (Paris: Aubier, 1996).

Chanet, Jean-François, *Vers l'armée nouvelle. République conservatrice et réforme militaire, 1871–1879* (Rennes: Presses Universitaires de Rennes, 2006).

Chickering, Roger (ed.), *Imperial Germany: A Historiographical Companion* (London/Westport: Greenwood Press, 1996).

Chickering, Roger, *The Great War and Urban Life in Germany: Freiburg, 1914–1914* (Cambridge: Cambridge University Press, 2007).

Clark, Christopher and Wolfram Kaiser (eds.), *Culture Wars: Secular-Catholic Conflicts in Nineteenth-Century Europe* (Cambridge: Cambridge University Press 2004).

Confino, Alon, *The Nation as a Local Metaphor: Württemberg, Imperial Germany, and National Memory, 1871–1914* (Chapel Hill/London: University of North Carolina Press, 1997).

Conrad, Sebastian and Jürgen Osterhammel (eds.), *Das Kaiserreich transnational. Deutschland in der Welt 1871–1914* (Göttingen: Vandenhoeck & Ruprecht, 2004).

Cooper, Frederick, *Colonialism in Question: Theory, Knowledge, History* (Berkeley: University of California Press, 2005).

Cresswell, Tim, *Place: A short Introduction* (Oxford: Blackwell, 2004).

De Certeau, Michel, *The Practice of Everyday Life* (Berkeley: University of California Press, 1984).

Dehlinger, Alfred, *Württembergs Staatswesen in seiner geschichtlichen Entwicklung bis heute*, zwei Bände (Stuttgart: W. Kohlhammer Verlag, 1951).

Dietrich, Rosemarie, *Die Integration Augsburgs in den bayerischen Staat, 1806–21* (Sigmaringen: Jan Thorbecke, 1993).

Dipper, Christoph, 'Wirtschaftspolitische Grundsatzentscheidungen in Süddeutschland,' in Hans-Peter Ullmann and Clemens Zimmermann (eds.), *Restaurationssystem und Reformpolitik: Süddeutschland und Preussen im Vergleich* (Munich: Oldenbourg Verlag, 1994), 139–62.

Dotterweich, Volker, 'Die bayerische Ära 1806–1870,' in G. Gottlieb *et al.* (eds.), *Geschichte der Stadt Augsburg. 2000 Jahre von der Römerzeit bis zur Gegenwart* (Stuttgart: Konrad Theiss Verlag, 1984), 551–68.

Ehn, Billy and Orvar Löfgren, *The Secret World of Doing Nothing* (Berkeley: University of California Press, 2010).

Eley, Geoff, 'Is there a History of the *Kaiserreich?*' in Geoff Eley (ed.), *Society, Culture, and the State in Germany 1870–1930* (Michigan: University of Michigan Press, 1997), 1–42.

Eley, Geoff, 'Theory and the Kaiserreich. Problems with Culture: German History after the Linguistic Turn,' *Central European History* 31 (1998) 197–227.

Eley, Geoff, '"an embarrassment to the family, to the public, and to the state": Liberalism and the Rights of Women, 1860–1914,' in Dominik Geppert and Robert Gerwarth (eds.) *Wilhelmine Germany and Edwardian Britain: Essays on Cultural Affinity* (Oxford, Oxford University Press, 2008), 143–71.

Eley, Geoff, 'State Formation, Nationalism, and Political Culture: Some Thoughts on the Unification of Germany,' in Raphal Samuel and Gareth Stedman Jones (eds.), *Culture, Ideology and Politics* (London: Routledge & Kegan Paul, 1982), 277–301.

Eley, Geoff and Keith Nield, *The Future of Class in History* (Michigan: Michigan University Press, 2007).

Eley, Geoff and Jan Palmowski (eds.), *Citizenship and National Identity in Twentieth-Century Germany* (Stanford: Stanford University Press, 2009).

Elwood, Christopher, *The Body Broken: The Calvinist Doctrine of the Eucharist and the Symbolization of Power in Sixteenth-Century France* (New York: Oxford University Press 1999).

Evans, Richard, *Death in Hamburg. Society and Politics in the Cholera Years* (Penguin: London, 1990).

Fahrmeier, Andreas, *Citizens and Aliens. Foreigners and the Law in Britain and the German States 1789–1870* (New York: Berghahn, 2000).

Fairbairn, Brett, 'History from the Ecological Perspective: Gaia Theory and the Problem of Cooperatives in Turn-of-the-Century Germany,' *American Historical Review* 99, 4 (October 1994), 1203–39.

Fairbairn, Brett, 'Political Mobilization,' in Chickering (ed.), *Imperial Germany: A Historical Companion*, 303–42.

Fairbairn, Brett, 'the Rise and Fall of Consumer Cooperation in Germany,' in Ellen Furlourh and Carl Strickwerda (eds.), *Consumers against Capitalism? Consumer Cooperation in Europe, North America, and Japan, 1840–1990* (Lanham/Oxford: Rowman & Littlefield, 1999), 267–302.

Fairbairn, Brett, 'Membership, Organization, and Wilhelmine Modernism,' in G. Eley and J. Retallack (eds.), *Wilhelminism and its Legacies. German Modernities, Imperialism, and the Meaning of Reform, 1890–1930* (Oxford: Berghahn, 2003), 34–50.

Fassl, Peter, 'Wirtschaftsgeschichte 1800–1914,' in G. Gottlieb *et al.* (eds.), *Geschichte der Stadt Augsburg. 2000 Jahre von der Römerzeit bis zur Gegenwart* (Stuttgart: Konrad Theiss Verlag, 1984), 592–607.

Fassl, Peter, *Konfession, Wirtschaft und Politik. Von der Reichsstadt zur Industriestadt, Augsburg 1750–1850* (Sigmaringen: Jan Thorbecke Verlag, 1988).

Fischer, Ilse, *Industrialisierung, sozialer Konflikt und politische Willensbildung in der Stadtgemeinde: Ein Beitrag zur Sozialgeschichte Augsburgs 1840–1914* (Augsburg: Hieronymus Mühlberger, 1977).

Fitzpatrick, Matthew P., *Liberal Imperialism in Germany: Expansionism and Nationalism 1848–1884* (New York/Oxford: Berghahn, 2007).

Flemming, Jens, Klaus Saul, Peter-Christian Witt (eds.), *Quellen zur Alltagsgeschichte der Deutschen 1871–1914* (Darmstadt: Wissenschaftliche Buchgesellschaft, 1997).

Ford, Caroline, 'Religion and Popular Culture in Modern Europe,' *History* 65 (March 1993), 152–75.

Ford, Caroline, *Divided Houses: Religion and Gender in Modern France* (Ithaca: Cornell University Press, 2005).

Foucault, Michel, 'Space, Knowledge, and Power,' in James D. Faubion (ed.), *Michelle Foucault: Power. Essential Works of Foucault 1954–1984. Vol. III* (London: Penguin, 2001), 349–64.

François, Étienne, 'Das System der Parität,' in G. Gottlieb et al. (eds.), *Geschichte der Stadt Augsburg. 2000 Jahre von der Römerzeit bis zur Gegenwart* (Stuttgart: Konrad Theiss Verlag, 1984), 514–19.

François, Étienne, *Die unsichtbare Grenze: Protestanten und Katholiken in Augsburg 1648–1806* (Sigmaringen: Thorbecke Verlag, 1991).

'Forum: The Long Nineteenth Century,' *German History* 26,1 (2008), 72–91.

Fraser, Nancy and Axel Honneth, *Redistribution or Recognition* (London: Verso, 2003).

Frevert, Ute (ed.), *Bürgerinnen und Bürger: Geschlechterverhältnisse im 19. Jahrhundert* (Göttingen: Vandenhoeck, 1988).

Frohman, Larry, *Poor Relief and Welfare in Germany from the Reformation to World War I* (Cambridge: Cambridge University Press, 2008).

Gall, Lothar, 'Liberalismus und "Bürgerliche Gesellschaft". Zu Charakter und Entwicklung der liberalen Bewegung in Deutschland,' *Historische Zeitschrift* 220 (1975), 324–56.

Gall, Lothar, *Bürgertum in Deutschland* (Berlin: Taylor & Francis, 1989).

Gall, Lothar (ed.), *Stadt und Bürgertum im Übergang von der traditionalen zur modernen Gesellschaft* (Munich: Oldenbourg, 1993).

Goffman, Erving, *Stigma Management: Notes on the Management of Spoiled Identity* (New York: Prentice-Hall, 1963).

Gosewinkel, Dieter, *Einbürgern und Ausschliessen: Die Nationalisierung der Staatsangehörigkeit vom Deutschen Bund bis zur Bundesrepublik Deutschland* (Göttingen: Vandenhoeck & Ruprecht, 2001).

Green, Abigail, *Fatherlands: State-Building and Nationhood in Nineteenth-Century Germany* (Cambridge: Cambridge University Press, 2001).

Green, Abigail, 'The Federalist Alternative? A New View of Modern German History,' *Historical Journal* 46 (2003), 187–202.

Gross, Michael, *The War against Catholicism: Liberalism and the Anti-Catholic Imagination in Nineteenth-Century Germany* (Ann Arbor: University of Michigan Press, 2004).

Guinnane, Timothy W., 'Population and the economy in Germany, 1800–1990,' in Ogilvie and Overy (eds.), *Germany since 1800*, 35–70.

Güssmann, Walter, 'Stadtentwicklung,' in Specker (ed.), *Ulm im 19. Jahrhundert*, 568–85.

Häberlein, Mark, 'Wirtschaftsgeschichte vom Mittelalter bis zur Gegenwart,' in: Günther Grünsteudel et al. (eds.), *Augsburger Stadtlexikon*, 2nd edn. (Augsburg: Perlach Verlag, 1998), 146–61.

Hahn, Hans-Werner, *Altständisches Bürgertum zwischen Beharrung und Wandel. Wetzlar 1689–1870* (Munich: Oldenbourg, 1991.

Harrington, Joel F. and Helmut W. Smith, 'Confessionalization, Community, and State Building in Germany, 1555–1870,' *Journal of Modern History* 69 (March 1997), 77–101.

Harris, Ruth, *Lourdes: Body and Spirit in the Secular Age* (London: Penguin, 1999).

Healy, Róisín, 'Anti-Jesuitism in Imperial Germany: The Jesuit as Androgyne,' in Smith (ed.), *Protestants, Catholics, and Jews*, 153–81.

Heilbronner, Oded, *'Freiheit, Gleichheit, Brüderlichkeit und Dynamit'. Populäre Kultur, populärer Liberalismus und Bürgertum im ländlichen Süddeutschland von den 1860ern bis zu den 1930ern* (Munich: Martin Meidenbauer, 2007).

Hepach, Wolf, *125 Jahre Konsum—Coop Ulm. Die Geschichte einer Verbrauchergemeinschaft* (Ulm: Helmuth Abt, 1991).

Herrigel, Gary, *Industrial Constructions. The sources of German industrial power* (Cambridge: Cambridge University Press, 1996).

Hersche, Peter, *Musse und Verschwendung. Europäische Gesellschaft und Kultur im Barockzeitalter* (Freiburg: Herder, 2006).

Hetzer, Gerhard, 'Presse und Politik 1890–1945. Beobachtungen eines lokalen Kraftfeldes,' in Helmut Gier and Johannes Janota (eds.), *Augsburger Buchdruck und Verlagswesen von den Anfängen bis zur Gegenwart* (Wiesbaden: Harrassowitz Verlag, 1997), 1135–7.

Hippel, Wolfgang von, 'Wirtschafts- und Sozialgeschichte 1800 bis 1918,' in Hansmartin Schwarzmaier, Hans Fenske, Bernhard Kirchgaessner, Paul Sauer, Meinrad Schaab (eds.), *Handbuch der Baden-Wüerttembergischen Geschichte, vol. III: Vom Ende des Alten Reiches bis zum Ende der Monarchien* (Stuttgart: Klett-Cotta, 1992), 477–766.

Hippel, Wolfgang von, 'Stadtentwicklung und Stadtteilbildung in einer Industrieansiedlung des 19. Jahrhunderts: Ludwigshafen am Rhein 1853–1914,' in Teuteberg (ed.), *Urbanisierung im 19. Und 20. Jahrhundert*, 339–71.

Hippel, Wolfgang von, 'Zwischen kleindeutscher Reichsgründung und Weltkriegs-Katastrophe. Ludwigshafen zur Zeit des zweiten Deutschen Kaiserreichs 1870/71–1914,' in Mörz und Becker (eds.), *Geschichte der Stadt Ludwigshafen am Rhein, Band I: Von den Anfängen bis zum Ende des Ersten Weltkrieges* (Zwickau: Westermann Druck, 2003), 366–774.

Hoffmann, Christhard, Werner Bergmann and Helmut Walser Smith (eds.), *Exclusionary Violence: Antisemitic Riots in Modern German History* (Ann Arbor, University of Michigan Press, 2002).

Hohorst, Gerd, Jürgen Kocka und Gerhard A. Ritter (eds.), *Sozialgeschichtliches Arbeitsbuch: Materialien zur Statistik des Kaiserreichs 1870–1914* (Munich: Beck, 1975).

Horowitz, Donald, *The Deadly Ethnic Riot* (Berkeley: University of California Press, 2001).

Hübinger, Gangolf, 'Sozialmoralisches Milieu. Ein Grundbegriff der deutschen Geschichte,' in Steffen Sigmund, Gert Albert, Agathe Bienfait and Mateusz Stachura (eds.), *Soziale Konstellation und historische Perspektive. Festschrift für M. Rainer Lepsius* (Wiesbaden:Verlag für Sozialwissenschaften, 2008), 207–27.

Hübinger, Gangolf, 'Confessionalism,' in Chickering (ed.), *Imperial Germany: A Historical Companion*, 156–84.

Isabel V. Hull, *Sexuality , State , and Civil Society in Germany*, 1700–1815 (Ithaca and London: Cornell University Press, 1996).

Ivereigh,Austen (ed.), *The Politics of Religion in an Age of Revival: Studies in Nineteenth-Century Europe and Latin America* (London: Institute of Latin American Studies, 2000).

Jans, Hans-Peter, *Sozialpolitik und Wohlfahrtspflege in Ulm 1870–1930* (Stuttgart: W. Kohlhammer, 1994).

Jarausch, Konrad H. and Michael Geyer, *Shattered Past: Reconstructing German Histories* (Princeton: Princeton University Press, 2003).

Jenkins, Jennifer, *Provincial Modernity: Local Culture & Liberal Politics in Fin-de-Siècle Hamburg* (Ithaca: Cornell University Press, 2003).

Jensen, Uffa, 'Integrationalismus, Konversion und jüdische Differenz. Das Problem des Antisemitismus in der liberalen Öffentlichkeit des 19.Jahrhunderts,' in Schaser & Schüler-Springorum (eds.), *Liberalismus und Emanzipation*, 2010, 55–72.

John Breuilly, 'The German Bourgeoisie from Radicalism to Nationalism', *German History*, 14, no. 2 (1996), 223–31.

Joyce, Patrick, *The Rule of Freedom: Liberalism and the Modern City* (London:Verso, 2003).

Kahan, Alan S., *Liberalism in Nineteenth-Century Europe:The Political Culture of Limited Suffrage* (New York: Palgrave, 2003).

Kaschuba,Wolfgang, *Die Überwindung der Distanz. Zeit und Raum in der europäischen Moderne* (Frankfurt: Fischer, 2004).

Keynes, John Maynard, *The Economic Consequences of the Peace* (Los Angeles: Indo European Publishing, 2010 [1920]).

Kindl, Manfred, 'Die öffentlichen Schulen in Ulm,' in Specker (ed.), *Ulm im 19. Jahrhundert*, 442–63.

Klewitz, Marion,'Preussische Volksschule vor 1914. Zur regionalen Auswertung der Schulstatistik,' *Zeitschrift für Pädagogik*, vol. 27, no. 4 (August 1981), 551–74.

Kocka, Jürgen (ed.), *Bürgertum im 19.Jahrhundert. Deutschland im europäischen Vergleich*, 3 vols. (Munich: DTV, 1988).

Kocka, Jürgen, *Industrial Culture & Bourgeois Society: Business, Labour, and Bureaucracy in Modern Germany* (Oxford: Berghahn, 1999).

Koselleck, Reinhart, *Zeitschichten* (Frankfurt am Main: Suhrkamp, 2000).

Kraul, Margaret, 'Bildung und Bürgerlichkeit,' in Kocka (ed.), *Bürgertum im 19. Jahrhundert*, 45–73.

Krieger, Karsten (ed.), *Der 'Berliner Antisemitismusstreit' 1879–1881. Eine Kontroverse um die Zugehörigkeit der deutschen Juden zur Nation*, 2 vols. (Munich: K.G. Saur, 2003).

Lamberti, Marjorie, *State, Society, & the Elementary School in Imperial Germany* (New York: Oxford University Press, 1989).

Langewiesche, Dieter, *Liberalismus und Demokratie in Württemberg zwischen Revolution und Reichsgründung* (Düsseldorf: Droste, 1974).

Langewiesche, Dieter, *Das Tagebuch Julius Hölders 1877–1880* (Stuttgart: W. Kohlhammer, 1977).

Langewiesche, Dieter, '"Staat" und "Kommune". Zum Wandel der Staatsaufgaben im Deutschland im 19. Jahrhundert,' *Historische Zeitschrift* 248 (1989), 621–35.

Langewiesche, Dieter, *Liberalism in Germany* (Princeton: Princeton University Press, 2000).

Langewiesche, Dieter, *Nation, Nationalismus, Nationalstaat in Deutschland und Europa* (Munich: Beck, 2000).

Langewiesche, Dieter & Georg Schmidt (eds.), *Föderative Nation: Deutschlandkonzepte von der Reformation bis zum Ersten Weltkrieg* (Munich: Oldenbourg, 2000).

Langlois, Claude, *Le catholicisme au feminine: Les congregations françaises à supérieure générale au XIXe siècle* (Paris: Les Éditions du Cerf, 1984).

Latour, Bruno, *Reassembling the Social: An Introduction to Actor-Network Theory* (Oxford: Oxford University Press, 2005).

Laube, Stefan, *Fest, Religion und Erinnerung. Konfessionelles Gedächtnis in Bayern von 1804 bis 1917* (Munich: C.H. Beck, 1999).

Lefebvre, Henri, *The Production of Space*, translated by Donald Nicholson-Smith (Oxford: Blackwell, 1991).

Lehmann, Hartmut, *Religion und Religiosität in der Neuzeit. Historische Beiträge*, edited by M. Jakubowski-Tiessen und O. Ulbricht (Göttingen: Vandenhoeck & Ruprecht, 1996), 205–32.

Lemke, Bernd, 'Die Ulmer Garnison und ihre Bedeutung für das städtische Leben, in Specker (ed.), *Ulm im 19. Jh.*, 586–641.

Lenger, Friedrich, *Sozialgeschichte des deutschen Handwerks* (Frankfurt a. M.: Suhrkamp, 1988).

Lenger, Friedrich, 'Economy and Society,' in Sperber (ed.), *Germany 1800–1870*, 91–114.

Lenger, Friedrich and Dieter Langewiesche, 'Internal Migration: Persistence and Mobility,' in Klaus J. Bade (ed.), *Population, Labour and Migration in 19th and 20th Century Germany* (Leamington Spa: Berg, 1987), 87–100.

Levi, Giovanni, 'On Microhistory,' in Peter Burke (ed.), *New Perspectives on Historical Writing* (Cambridge: Polity, 1991), 97–119.

Levinger, Matthew, *Enlightened Nationalism: The Transformation of Prussian Political Culture, 1806–1848* (Oxford: Oxford University Press, 2000).

Liedhegener, Antonius, *Christentum und Urbanisierung: Katholiken und Protestanten in Münster und Bochum 1830–1933* (Paderborn: Ferdinand Schöningh, 1997).

Loges, Georg, 'Das Ulmer Theater,' in Specker (ed.), *Ulm im 19. Jahrhundert*. 478–501.

Loth, Wilfried, *Katholiken im Kaiserreich: Der politische Katholizismus in der Krise des wilhelminischen Deutschland* (Düsseldorf: Droste, 1984).

Loth, Wilfried, 'Soziale Bewegungen im Katholizismus des Kaiserreichs,' *Geschichte und Gesellschaft* 17 (1991), 279–310.

Malpas, J.E., *Place and Experience. A Philosophical Topography* (Cambridge: Cambridge University Press, 1999).

Mann, Bernhard, 'Württemberg 1800–1866,' in Hansmartin Schwarzmaier, Hans Fenske, Bernhard Kirchgaessner, Paul Sauer, Meinrad Schaab (eds.), *Handbuch der Baden-Wuerttembergischen Geschichte, vol. III: Vom Ende des Alten Reiches bis zum Ende der Monarchien* (Stuttgart: Klett-Cotta, 1992), 235–332.

Marc Bloch, *Apologies pour L'Histoire or le Métier l'Historien* (Paris: Librairie Armand Colin, 1949), 88.

Margadant, Ted W., *Urban Rivalries in the French Revolution* (Princeton: Princeton University Press, 1992).

Marschalck, Peter, 'Zur Rolle der Stadt für den Industrialisierungsprozess in Deutschland in der 2. Hälfte des 19. Jahrhunderts,' in: Jürgen Reulecke (ed.), *Die Stadt im Industriezeitalter*, 57–66.

Marschalck, Peter, *Bevölkerungsgeschichte Deutschlands im 19. Und 20. Jahrhundert* (Frankfurt: Suhrkamp, 1984).

McLeod, Hugh, 'Weibliche Frömmigkeit—männlicher Unglaube? Religion und Kirchen im bürgerlichen 19. Jahrhundert,' in Frevert (ed.), *Bürgerinnen und Bürger: Geschlechterverhältnisse im 19. Jahrhundert*, 134–56.

McLeod, Hugh and Werner Ustorf (eds.), *The Decline of Christendom in Western Europe, 1750–2000* (Cambridge: Cambridge University Press, 2003).

McMillan, James, "'Priest hits girl": On the Front Line in the "War of the two Frances",' in Clark and Kaiser (eds.), *Culture Wars*, 77–101.

McNeely, Ian F., *The Emancipation of Writing: German Civil Society in the Making, 1790s–1820s* (Berkeley: University of California Press, 2003).

Mergel, Thomas, *Zwischen Klasse und Konfession. Katholisches Bürgertum im Rheinland 1794–1914* (Göttingen: Vandenhoeck & Ruprecht, 1994).

Mergel, Thomas, "Mapping Milieus Regionally. On the Spatial Rootedness of Collective Identities in the Nineteenth Century,' in Retallack (ed.), *Saxony in German History*, 77–95.

Michael Billig, *Banal Nationalism* (London: Sage, 1995).

Mintzker, Yair, *The Defortification of the German City, 1689–1866.* (University of Stanford PhD, 2009).

Mitchell, Allan, 'Bourgeois Liberalism and Public Health: A Franco-German Comparison,' in Kocka and Mitchell (eds.), *Bourgeois Society in Nineteenth-Century Europe*, 346–64.

Möckl, Karl, *Die Prinzregentenzeit. Gesellschaft und Politik während der Ära des Prinzregenten Luitpold in Bayern* (Wien: Oldenbourg Verlag, 1972).

Möller, Frank, *Bürgerliche Herrschaft in Augsburg 1790–1880* (Munich: Oldenbourg Verlag, 1998).

Mommsen, W. J., 'Der deutsche Liberalismus zwischen "klassenloser Bürgergesellschaft" und "organisiertem Kapitalismus". Zu einigen neueren Liberalismusinterpretationen,' *Geschichte und Gesellschaft* 4 (1978), 77–90.

Mörz, Stefan, *Vom Westboten zur Rheinpfalz. Zur Geschichte der Presse im Raum Ludwigshafen von den Anfängen bis zur Gegenwart* (Ludwigshafen: Veröffentlichung en des Stadtarchivs Ludwigshafen, 1994).

Mörz Stefan and Klaus Jürgen Becker (eds.), *Geschichte der Stadt Ludwigshafen am Rhein, Band I: Von den Anfängen bis zum Ende des Ersten Weltkrieges*, (Zwickau, Westermann Druck, 2003).

Müller, Detlef K., Fritz Ringer and Brian Simon (eds.), *The rise of the Modern Education System: Structural Change and Social Reproduction* (Cambridge: Cambridge University Press, 1987).

Niesseler, Martin, *Die Augsburger Schulen im Wandel der Zeit* (Augsburg: Verlag Hieronymus Mühlberger, 1984).

Nipperdey, Thomas, *Deutsche Geschichte 1800–1866. Bürgerwelt und starker Staat* (Munich: C. H. Beck, 1983).

Nipperdey, Thomas, *Religion im Umbruch* (Munich: Beck, 1988).

Nipperdey, Thomas, *Nachdenken über die deutsche Geschichte* (Munich: C. H. Beck, 1986).

Nipperdey, Thomas, *Deutsche Geschichte 1866–1918. Band I: Arbeitswelt und Bürgergeist* (Munich: C. H. Beck, 1998).

Nipperdey, Thomas, *Deutsche Geschichte 1866–1918. Band II: Machtstaat vor der Demokratie* (Munich: C. H. Beck, 1998).

Nolte, Paul, *Gemeindebürgertum und Liberalismus in Baden, 1800–1850* (Göttingen: Vandenhoeck & Ruprecht, 1994).

Nussbaum, Martha, *Upheavals of Thought: The Intelligence of Emotions* (Cambridge: Cambridge University Press, 2003).

O'Dell, Tom, 'My Soul for a Seat: Commuting and the Routines of Mobility,' in Shove, Trentmann and Wilk (eds.), *Time, Consumption and Everyday Life*, 85–98.

Ogilvie, Sheilagh and Richard Overy (eds.), *Germany: A New Social and Economic History, vol. III: Since 1800* (London: Arnold, 2003), 1–34.

Ohe, Werner von der, 'Bayern im 19. Jahrhundert—ein Entwicklungsland?,' in Claus Grimm (ed.), *Aufbruch ins Industriezeitalter. Band I: Linien der Entwicklungsgeschichte* (Munich: Oldenbourg Verlag, 1985), 169–202.

Palaoro, Simon, *Stadt und Festung. Eine kleine Geschichte der Bundesfestung Ulm* (Ulm: Klemm & Oelschläger, 2009).

Palmowski, Jan, *Urban Liberalism in Imperial Germany: Frankfurt am Main 1866–1914* (Oxford: Oxford University Press, 1999).

Palmowski, Jan, 'Mediating the Nation: Liberalism and the Polity in Nineteenth-Century Germany,' *German History* 18 (2001), 573–98.

Penny, Glen, 'The Fate of the Nineteenth Century in German Historiography,' *Journal of Modern History* 80 (March 2008), 81–108.

Planert, Ute, 'Vater Staat und Mutter Germania: Zur Politisierung des weiblichen Geschlechts im 19. und 20. Jahrhundert,' in Ute Planert (ed.), *Nation, Politik und Geschlecht. Frauenbewegungen und Nationalismus in der Moderne* (Frankfurt am Main: Campus, 2000), 15–65.

Pohl, Karl Heinrich, 'Kommunen, Liberalismus und Wahlrechtsfragen: Zur Bedeutung des Wahlrechts für die "moderne" Kommunalpolitik in Deutschland am Ende des 19. Jahrhunderts,' *Jahrbuch zur Liberalismus-Forschung* 13 (2001), 113–30.

Pohl, Karl Heinrich, 'Nationalliberalismus und Kommunalpolitik in Dresden und München vor 1914,' in Retallack (ed.), *Sachsen in Deutschland*, 171–88.

Preisser, Karl-Heinz, *Die industrielle Entwicklung Bayerns in den ersten drei Jahrzehnten des Deutschen Zollvereins* (Weiden: Eurotrans-Verlag, 1993).

Prinz, Michael, *Brot und Dividende. Konsumvereine in Deutschland und England vor 1914* (Göttingen: Vandenhoeck & Ruprecht, 1996).

Quataert, Jean, 'Demographic and Social Change,' in Chickering (ed.), *Imperial Germany. A Historiographical Companion*, 97–130.

Repp, Kevin, *Reformers, Critics, and the Paths of German Modernity: Anti-Politics and the Search for Alternatives, 1890–1914* (Cambridge MA: Harvard University Press, 2000).

Retallack, James, '"Why Can't a Saxon be more like a Prussian?" Regional Identities and the Birth of Modern Political Culture in Germany, 1866–67,' *Canadian Journal of History* XXXII (April 1997), 26–55.

Retallack, James (ed.), *Saxony in German History: Culture, Society, Politics, 1830–1933* (Ann Arbor: University of Michigan Press, 2000).

Retallack, James, *The German Right 1860–1920: Political Limits of the Authoritarian Imagination* (Toronto: University of Toronto Press, 2007).

Retallack, James, 'Obrigkeitsstaat und politischer Massenmarkt,' in Sven Oliver Müller and Cornelius Torp (eds.), *Das Deutsche Kaiserreich in der Kontroverse* (Göttingen: Vandenhoeck & Ruprecht, 2009), 121–35.

Reulecke, Jürgen (ed.), *Die deutsche Stadt im Industriezeitalter* (Wuppertal: Peter Hammer Verlag, 1978).

Reulecke, Jürgen, *Geschichte der Urbanisierung in Deutschland* (Frankfurt am Main: Suhrkamp, 1985).

Revel, Jacques, *Un Parcours Critique. Douze Exercices d'Histoire Sociale* (Paris: Galaade Éditions, 2006).

Rosenwein, Barbara, *Emotional Communities in the Early Middle Ages* (Ithaca: Cornell University Press, 2007).

Roshwald, Aviel, 'The Post-1989 Era as Heyday of the Nation-State,' *International Journal of Politics, Culture and Society* 24 (2011): 11–19.

Rubin, Miri, *Corpus Christi: The Eucharist in Late Medieval Culture* (Cambridge: Cambridge University Press, 1991).

Sack, Robert David, *Place, Modernity, and the Consumer's World: A Relational Framework for Geographical Analysis* (Baltimore: Johns Hopkins University Press, 1992).

Sack, Robert David, *Homo Geographicus: A Framework for Action, Awareness, and Moral Concern* (Baltimore: John Hopkins University Press, 1997).

Scales, Leonard and Oliver Zimmer (eds.), *Power and the Nation in European History* (Cambridge: Cambridge University Press, 2005).

Schäfer, Hans-Peter, 'Bayerns Verkehrswesen im frühen 19. Jahrhundert,' in Rainer A. Müller (ed.), *Aufbruch ins Industriezeitalter. Band 2: Aufsätze zur Wirtschaftsgeschichte Bayerns 1750–1850* (Munich: Oldenbourg Verlag, 1985), 308–22.

Schaller, Peter, *Die Industrialisierung der Stadt Ulm zwischen 1828/34 und 1875. Eine wirt-schafts- und sozialgeschichtliche Studie über die 'zweite Stadt' in Württemberg* (Stuttgart: Kohlhammer, 1999).

Schaller, Peter, 'Zur Wirtschaftsgesichte Ulms,' in Specker (ed.), *Ulm im 19. Jahrhundert*, 105–68.

Schambach, Karin, *Stadtbürgertum und industrieller Umbruch. Dortmund 1780–1870* (Munich: Oldenbourg Verlag, 1996).

Schaser, Angelika and Stefanie Schüler-Springorum (eds.), *Liberalismus und Emanzipation. In- und Exklusionsprozesse im Kaiserreich und in der Weimarer Republik* (Stuttgart: Franz Steiner Verlag, 2010).

Schieder, Wolfgang, 'Kirche und Revolution: Sozialgeschichteliche Aspekte der Trierer Wallfahrt von 1844,' *Archiv für Sozialgeschichte* 14 (1974): 419–54.

Schivelbusch, Wolfgang, *Geschichte der Eisenbahnreise. Zur Industrialisierung von Raum und Zeit im 19. Jahrhundert* (Frankfurt am Main: Fischer, 2000 [1977]).

Schleunes, Karl A., *Schooling and Society: The Politics of Education in Prussia and Bavaria 1750–1900* (Oxford: Berg, 1989).

Schorske, Carl E., 'Politics in a New Key: An Austrian Triptych,' *Journal of Modern History*, 39 (December 1967), 343–86.

Schreiner, Klaus, '"Kommunenbewegung" und "Zunftrevolution". Zur Gegenwart der mittelalterlichen Stadt im historisch-politischen Denken des 19. Jahrhunderts,' in Franz Quartal und Wilfried Setzler (eds.), *Stadtverfassung, Verfassungsstaat, Pressepolitik. Festschrift fuer Eberhard Naujoks zum 65. Geburstag* (Sigmarien: Jan Thorbecke, 1980), 139–68.

Scott, Joan W., 'The Evidence of Experience,' *Critical Inquiry* 17 (Summer, 1991), 773–97.

Sennett, Richard, *The Craftsman* (London: Penguin, 2009).

Sewell, William H. Jr, *Structure and Mobility: The Men and Women of Marseille, 1820–1870* (Cambridge: Cambridge University Press, 1985).

Sewell, William H. jr, *The Logics of History: Social Theory and Social Transformation* (Chicago: Chicago University Press, 2005).

Sheehan, James, 'Liberalism and the City in Nineteenth-Century Germany,' *Past & Present* 51 (1971), 116–37.

Sheehan, James, *German Liberalism in the Nineteenth Century* (Chicago: University of Chicago Press, 1978).

Shove, Elizabeth, Frank Trentmann, and Richard Wilk (eds.), *Time, Consumption and Everyday Life: Practice, Materiality and Culture* (Berg: Oxford, 2009).

Simmel, Georg, *On Individuality: Selected Writings*, edited and with an Introduction by Donald N. Levine (Chicago: University of Chigago Press, 1971).

Smith, Helmut W., *German Nationalism and Religious Conflict: Culture, Ideology, Politics, 1870–1914* (Princeton: Princeton University Press, 1995).

Smith, Helmut W. 'The Boundaries of the Local in Modern German History,' in Retallack (ed.), *Saxony in German History*, 63–76.

Smith, Helmut W. (ed.), Protestants, Catholics, and Jews in Germany, 1800–1914 (Oxford: Berg, 2001).

Smith, Helmut W., *The Continuities of German History: Nation, Religion, and Race across the Long Nineteenth Century* (Cambridge: Cambridge University Press, 2008).

Smith, Helmut W., 'When the *Sonderweg* Debate left us,' *German Studies Review* 31 (May, 2008), 225–40.

Smith, Helmut W. (ed.), *The Oxford Handbook of Modern German History* (Oxford: Oxford University Press, 2012).

Smith, Helmut Walser, 'Authoritarian State, Dynamic Society, Failed Imperialist Power, 1878–1914,' in Smith (ed.), *Oxford Handbook of Modern Germany*, 307–35.

Specker, Hans Eugen (ed.), *Ulm im 19. Jahrhundert. Aspekte aus dem Leben der Stadt* (Stuttgart: Kohlhammer, 1990).

Sperber, Jonathan, *Popular Catholicism in Nineteenth-Century Germany* (Princeton: Princeton University Press, 1984).

Sperber, Jonathan, *The Kaiser's Voters: Electors and elections in Imperial Germany* (Cambridge: Cambridge University Press, 1997).

Sperber, Jonathan (ed.), *Germany 1800–1870* (Oxford: Oxford University Press, 2004).

Spiekermann, Uwe, *Basis der Konsumgesellschaft. Entstehung und Entwicklung des modernen Kleinhandels in Deutschland 1850–1914* (Munich: C. H. Beck, 1999).

Stachura, Peter D., 'Social policy and social welfare in Germany from the mid-nineteenth century to the present,' in Ogilvie and Overy (eds.), *Germany: A New Social and Economic History*, 227–50.

Stedman Jones, Gareth, 'The New Social History in France,' in Colin Jones and Dror Wahrman (eds.), *The Age of Cultural Revolutions: Britain and France, 1750–1820* (Berkeley: University of California Press, 2002), 94–105.

Steinhoff, Anthony J., 'Christianity and the Creation of Germany,' in Sheridan Giley and Brian Stanley (eds.), *The Cambridge History of Christianity*, vol. 8, *World Christianities, c. 1814–1914* (Cambridge: Cambridge University Press, 2006), 282–300.

Steinmetz, George, *Regulating the Social: The Welfare State and Local Politics in Imperial Germany* (Princeton: Princeton University Press, 1993).

Stoll, Peter, 'Stadttheater,' available at: http://www.stadtlexikon-augsburg.de.

Sylla, Richard and Gianni Toniolo (eds.), *Patterns of European Industrialization. The Nineteenth Century* (London: Routledge, 1991), Introduction.

Taylor, Vanessa and Frank Trentmann, 'Liquid Politics: Water and the Politics of Everyday Life in the Modern City,' *Past & Present* 211 (May 2011), 199–241.

Teuteberg, Hans Jürgen (ed.), *Urbanisierung im 19. Und 20. Jahrhundert. Historische und Geographische Aspekte* (Köln: Böhlau Verlag, 1983).

Thompson, Alastair, *Left Liberals, the State, and Popular Politics in Wilhelmine Germany* (Oxford: Oxford University Press, 2000).

Thompson, E. P., 'Time, Work-Discipline, and Industrial Capitalism,' *Past & Present* 38 (1967), 56–97.

Tipton, Frank, 'Technology and Industrial Growth,' in Chickering (ed.), *Imperial Germany. A Historiographical Companion*, 62–96.

Tipton, Frank B., 'The regional dimension: economic geography, economic development, and national integration in the nineteenth and twentieth centuries,' in Ogilvie and Overy (eds.), *Germany: A New Social and Economic History*, 1–34.

Trentmann, Frank, 'Disruption is Normal: Blackouts, Breakdowns and the Elasticity of Everyday Life,' in Shove, Trentmann and Wilk (eds.), *Time, Consumption and Everyday Life*, 67–84.

Trox, Eckhard, 'Bürger in Ulm: Vereine, Parteien, Geselligkeit,' in Eugen Specker (ed.), *Ulm im 19. Jahrhundert*, 169–238.

Umbach, Maiken, *German Cities and Bourgeois Modernism 1890–1924* (Oxford: Oxford University Press, 2009).

Van Rahden, Till, *Juden und andere Breslauer. Die Beziehungen zwischen Juden, Protestanten und Katholiken in einer deutschen Großstadt von 1860 bis 1925* (Göttingen: Vandenhoeck & Ruprecht, 2000).

Van Rahden, Till, 'Unity, Diversity, and Difference: Jews, Protestants, and Catholics in Breslau Schools during the Kulturkampf,' in Smith (ed.), *Protestants, Catholics, and Jews*, 217–42.

Vick, Brian, *Defining Germany: The 1848 Frankfurt Parliamentarians and the National Question* (Cambridge MA: Harvard University Press, 2002).

Vickery, Amanda, *The Gentleman's Daughter: Women's Lives in Georgian England* (Yale: Yale University Press, 1998).

Waibel, Raimund, 'Ein Jahrhundert wachsender Einflussmoeglichkeiten und Partizipationsforderungen der Bevoelkerung, 1810–1918,' in Hans Eugen Specker (ed.), *Die Ulmer Bürgerschaft auf dem Weg zur Demokratie* (Stuttgart: W. Kohlhammer, 1997), 276–332.

Walker, Mack. *German Home Towns: Community, State, and General Estate, 1648–1817* (Ithaca: Cornell University Press, 1971).

Weber, Eugene, *Peasants into Frenchmen: The Modernisation of Rural France 1870–1914* (Stanford: Stanford University Press, 1978).

Wehler, Hans-Ulrich, *The German Empire, 1871–1918*, trans. Kim Traynor (Leamington Spa: Berg, 1985).

Wehler, Hans-Ulrich, *Deutsche Gesellschaftsgeschichte. Vol. III: 1849–1914* (Munich: C.H. Beck, 1995).

Wehler, Hans-Ulrich, 'A Guide to Future Research on the Kaiserreich?,' *Central European History* 29 (1996), 541–72.

Wehler, Hans-Ulrich, *Nationalismus. Geschichte—Formen—Folgen* (Munich: C.H. Beck, 2001).

Weichlein, Siegfried, *Nation und Region: Integrationsprozesse im Bismarckreich* (Düsseldorf: Droste, 2004).

Weidner, Rolf, *Wahlen und soziale Strukturen in Ludwigshafen am Rhein 1871–1914* (Ludwigshafen: Veröffentlichungen des Stadtarchivs Ludwigshafen am Rhein, 1984).

Wettengel, Michael, 'Zur Geschichte der Stiftungen in Ulm,' in: Ulmer Bürger Stiftung (ed.), *Handbuch Ulmer Stiftungen* (Ulm: Stadtarchiv, 2004), 10–46.

Whyte, William and Oliver Zimmer (eds.), *Nationalism and the Reshaping of Urban Communities 1848–1914* (Basingstoke: Palgrave, 2011).

Winkler, Heinrich-August (ed.), *Nationalismus* (Bodenheim: Athenaeum, 1978).

Zang, Gert (ed.), *Provinzialisierung einer Region. Zur Entstehung der bürgerlichen Gesellschaft in der Provinz* (Frankfurt: Syndikat, 1978).

Zemon Davis, Natalie, 'The Rites of Violence: Religious Riot in Sixteenth-Century France,' *Past & Present* 59 (1975), 51–91.

Zerubavel, Eviatar, *Hidden Rhythms: Schedules and Calendars in Social Life* (Berkeley: University of California Press, 1985).

Zimmer, Oliver, *A Contested Nation: History, Memory and Nationalism in Switzerland, 1761–1891* (Cambridge: Cambridge University Press, 2003).

Zimmer, Oliver, 'Circumscribing Community in Construction of Swiss Nationhood,' in Timothy Baycroft and Mark Hewitson (eds.), *What is a Nation? Europe 1789–1914* (Oxford: Oxford University Press, 2006), 100–19.

Zimmer, Oliver, 'Nation und Religion. Von der Imagination des Nationalen zur Verarbeitung von Nationalisierungsprozesen,' *Historische Zeitschrift*, 283 (2006), 617–56.

Zorn, Wolfgang, 'Bayerns Gewerbe, Handel, und Verkehr (1806–1970)' in Max Spindler (ed.), *Handbuch der Bayerischen Geschichte*, vol. 4/2 (Munich: C. H. Beck Verlag, 1978), 782–845.

Index

Printed and bound by CPI Group (UK) Ltd, Croydon, CR0 4YY